UNITED NATIONS CONFERENCE ON TRADE AND DEVELOPMENT
GENEVA

TRADE AND DEVELOPMENT REPORT, 2014

Report by the secretariat of the
United Nations Conference on Trade and Development

UNITED NATIONS
New York and Geneva, 2014

Note

- Symbols of United Nations documents are composed of capital letters combined with figures. Mention of such a symbol indicates a reference to a United Nations document.

- The designations employed and the presentation of the material in this publication do not imply the expression of any opinion whatsoever on the part of the Secretariat of the United Nations concerning the legal status of any country, territory, city or area, or of its authorities, or concerning the delimitation of its frontiers or boundaries.

- Material in this publication may be freely quoted or reprinted, but acknowledgement is requested, together with a reference to the document number. A copy of the publication containing the quotation or reprint should be sent to the UNCTAD secretariat.

UNCTAD/TDR/2014

UNITED NATIONS PUBLICATION
Sales No. E.14.II.D.4
ISBN 978-92-1-112877-2 eISBN 978-92-1-056846-3 ISSN 0255-4607

Contents

Chapter VI

INTERNATIONAL FINANCE AND POLICY SPACE *121*

Annex to chapter VI

Chapter VII

FISCAL SPACE FOR STABILITY AND DEVELOPMENT: CONTEMPORARY CHALLENGES *161*

List of tables and boxes

List of charts

Classification by country or commodity group

The classification of countries in this *Report* has been adopted solely for the purposes of statistical or analytical convenience and does not necessarily imply any judgement concerning the stage of development of a particular country or area.

The major country groupings used in this *Report* follow the classification by the United Nations Statistical Office (UNSO). They are distinguished as:

» Developed or industrial(ized) countries: the countries members of the OECD (other than Mexico, the Republic of Korea and Turkey) plus the new EU member countries and Israel.

» Transition economies refers to South-East Europe and the Commonwealth of Independent States (CIS).

» Developing countries: all countries, territories or areas not specified above.

The terms "country" / "economy" refer, as appropriate, also to territories or areas.

References to "Latin America" in the text or tables include the Caribbean countries unless otherwise indicated.

References to "sub-Saharan Africa" in the text or tables include South Africa unless otherwise indicated.

For statistical purposes, regional groupings and classifications by commodity group used in this *Report* follow generally those employed in the *UNCTAD Handbook of Statistics 2013* (United Nations publication, sales no. B.13.II.D.4) unless otherwise stated. The data for China do not include those for Hong Kong Special Administrative Region (Hong Kong SAR), Macao Special Administrative Region (Macao SAR) and Taiwan Province of China.

Other notes

References in the text to *TDR* are to the *Trade and Development Report* (of a particular year). For example, *TDR 2013* refers to *Trade and Development Report, 2013* (United Nations publication, sales no. E.13.II.D.3).

The term "dollar" ($) refers to United States dollars, unless otherwise stated.

The term "billion" signifies 1,000 million.

The term "tons" refers to metric tons.

Annual rates of growth and change refer to compound rates.

Exports are valued FOB and imports CIF, unless otherwise specified.

Use of a dash (–) between dates representing years, e.g. 1988–1990, signifies the full period involved, including the initial and final years.

An oblique stroke (/) between two years, e.g. 2000/01, signifies a fiscal or crop year.

A dot (.) indicates that the item is not applicable.

Two dots (..) indicate that the data are not available, or are not separately reported.

A dash (-) or a zero (0) indicates that the amount is nil or negligible.

Decimals and percentages do not necessarily add up to totals because of rounding.

Abbreviations

AfDB	African Development Bank
AGP	Agreement on Government Procurement
BEPS	base erosion and profit shifting
BIS	Bank for International Settlements
BIT	bilateral investment treaty
CIS	Commonwealth of Independent States
CPI	consumer price index
DSM	dispute settlement mechanism
ECLAC	Economic Commission for Latin America and the Caribbean
EITI	Extractive Industries Transparency Initiative
EU	European Union
FATCA	Foreign Account Tax Compliance Act (of the United States)
FDI	foreign direct investment
FET	fair and equitable treatment
FTA	free trade agreement
GATS	General Agreement on Trade in Services
GATT	General Agreement on Tariffs and Trade
GDP	gross domestic product
GPM	Global Policy Model (of the United Nations)
GSP	Generalized System of Preferences
GTA	Global Trade Alert
IBRD	International Bank for Reconstruction and Development
ICSID	International Centre for Settlement of Investment Disputes
IFF	illicit financial flows
IIA	international investment agreement
ILO	International Labour Organization
IMF	International Monetary Fund
IP	intellectual property
IPR	intellectual property right

ISDS	investor-State dispute settlement
ITO	International Trade Organization
LDC	least developed country
MDG	Millennium Development Goal
MERCOSUR	Common Market of the South (Mercado Común del Sur)
MFN	most favoured nation
NAFTA	North American Free Trade Association (or Agreement)
NAMA	non-agricultural market access
ODA	official development assistance
OECD	Organisation for Economic Co-operation and Development
OFC	offshore financial centre
PPP	purchasing power parity
PWYP	Publish What You Pay
R&D	research and development
RTA	regional trade agreement
SCM	subsidies and countervailing measures
SDT	special and differential treatment
TARP	Troubled Assets Relief Program
TDR	Trade and Development Report
TJN	Tax Justice Network
TNC	transnational corporation
TRIMs	trade-related investment measures
TRIPS	trade-related aspects of intellectual property rights
UNCITRAL	United Nations Commission on International Trade Law
UNCTAD	United Nations Conference on Trade and Development
UN-DESA	United Nations Department of Economic and Social Affairs
URA	Uruguay Round Agreement
VAT	value added tax
WTO	World Trade Organization

OVERVIEW

Fifty years ago this year, and twenty years after a new multilateral framework for governing the post-war global economy was agreed at Bretton Woods, a confident South gathered in Geneva to advance its demands for a more inclusive world economic order. The first United Nations Conference on Trade and Development (UNCTAD) added a permanent institutional fixture to the multilateral landscape, with the responsibility "to formulate principles and policies on international trade and related problems of economic development". Moreover, and moving beyond the principles that framed the Bretton Woods institutions (and later the General Agreement on Tariffs and Trade (GATT)), it was agreed that "Economic development and social progress should be the common concern of the whole international community, and should, by increasing economic prosperity and well-being, help strengthen peaceful relations and cooperation among nations"

UNCTAD's 50th anniversary falls at a time when, once again, there are calls for changes in the way the global economy is ordered and managed. Few would doubt that, during the five intervening decades, new technologies have broken down traditional borders between nations and opened up new areas of economic opportunity, and that a less polarized political landscape has provided new possibilities for constructive international engagement. In addition, economic power has become more dispersed, mostly due to industrialization and rapid growth in East Asia, with corresponding changes in the workings of the international trading system. However the links between these technological, political and economic shifts and a more prosperous, peaceful and sustainable world are not automatic.

Indeed, growing global economic imbalances, heightened social and environmental fragilities and persistent financial instability, turning at times to outright crisis, should give pause for thought and further policy discussion. Hunger still remains a daily reality for hundreds of millions of people, particularly in rural communities, with children being the most vulnerable. At the same time, rapid urbanization in many parts of the developing world has coincided with premature deindustrialization and a degraded public sector, giving rise to poor working conditions and a growing sense of insecurity. Where these trends have collided with the ambitions of a youthful population, economic frustrations have spilled over into political unrest.

Back in 1964, the international community recognized that "If privilege, extremes of wealth and poverty, and social injustice persist, then the goal of development is lost". Yet, almost everywhere in recent years, the spread of market liberalism has coincided with highly unequal patterns of income and wealth distribution. A world where its 85 wealthiest citizens own more than its bottom three and a half billion was not the one envisaged 50 years ago.

There is no fast or ready-paved road to sustainable and inclusive development; but the past three decades have demonstrated that delivery is unlikely with a one-size-fits-all approach to economic policy that cedes more and more space to the profitable ambitions of global firms and market forces. Countries should ultimately rely on their own efforts to mobilize productive resources and, especially, to raise their levels of domestic investment (both public and private), human capital and technological know-how. However, for this, they need to have the widest possible room for manoeuvre to discover which policies work in their particular conditions, and not be subject to a constant shrinking of their policy space by the very international institutions originally established to support more balanced and inclusive outcomes.

Insisting on the importance of domestic institutions and policies does not mean adopting a closed or insular attitude to the many development challenges. On the contrary, access to external financial resources and technological know-how is still critical to unlocking the development potential of many poorer and vulnerable countries. Moreover, long-standing development issues – from sovereign debt problems to improved market access in a fairer international trading system, and from commodity price stabilization to financial markets that serve the real economy – can only be addressed through effective multilateral institutions supported by (and this is no small proviso) sufficient political will on the part of the leading economies. Added to these persistent challenges, today's interdependent world has thrown up a variety of new ones, such as health pandemics, food insecurity, and global warming, which require even bolder multilateral leadership and collective action.

Pursuing bold international collective action to correct the deep inequities of the world, along with determined and innovative domestic policy initiatives, was what motivated the participants at Bretton Woods 70 years ago and in Geneva 50 years ago. Henry Morgenthau, the United States Secretary of the Treasury, was on the mark when he insisted at Bretton Woods that "Prosperity like peace is indivisible. We cannot afford to have it scattered here or there among the fortunate or to enjoy it at the expense of others. Poverty, wherever it exists, is menacing to us all and undermines the well-being of each of us". As the international community frames an ambitious development agenda beyond 2015, the moment is right to propose another international "New Deal" that can realize the promise of "prosperity for all".

The world economy in 2014 still in the doldrums

The world economy has not yet escaped the growth doldrums in which it has been marooned for the past four years, and there is a growing danger that this state of affairs is becoming accepted as the "new normal". Policymakers everywhere, but particularly in the systemically important economies, need to assess current approaches and pay closer attention to signs of inclement economic weather ahead.

Growth in the world economy has been experiencing a modest improvement in 2014, although it is set to remain significantly below its pre-crisis highs. Its growth rate of 2.3 per cent in 2012 and 2013 is projected to increase moderately to between 2.5 and 3 per cent in 2014. This improvement is essentially due to growth in developed countries accelerating from 1.3 per cent in 2013 to around 1.8 per cent in 2014. Developing countries as a whole are likely to repeat their performance of the previous years, growing at between 4.5 and 5 per cent, while in the transition economies growth is forecast to further decelerate to around 1 per cent, from an already weak performance in 2013.

The moderate growth acceleration expected in developed countries should result from a slight pick-up in the European Union (EU), where a tentative easing of fiscal austerity and a more accommodating monetary policy stance, notably by the European Central Bank (ECB), has helped pull demand growth back to positive territory. In some countries (e.g. the United Kingdom), household demand is being supported by asset appreciation and the recovery of consumer and mortgage credit, and in others by some improvement in real wages (e.g. Germany). However, in a number of other large euro-zone economies (e.g. France, Italy and Spain) high levels of unemployment, stagnant or sluggish real wage growth, and persistent weakness in the banking sector continue to hinder the expansion of domestic credit and demand. In the United States, the economy is continuing its tentative recovery through a reliance on domestic private demand. The negative impact of fiscal austerity eased slightly in 2014, the unemployment rate has continued to fall, and asset price appreciations are encouraging the recovery of domestic borrowing and consumption. However, average real wages remain stagnant. Growth in Japan has also been relying on domestic demand, as private consumption and investment benefited from the expansionary monetary and fiscal policies of Abenomics. The effects of public spending for reconstruction following the 2011 earthquake, which helped propel the Japanese economy to higher growth in 2012–2013 have dissipated, while recent tax increases could hurt consumer spending, so that further stimulus packages may be needed to maintain positive growth and price targets.

The main developing regions are likely to more or less replicate their growth performance of 2012–2013. Asia is projected to remain the most dynamic region, growing at around 5.5 per cent. Among the major countries in this region, China continues to lead with an estimated growth rate of close to 7.5 per cent in 2014, based on domestic demand, with some tentative signs of an increasing role for private and public consumption. Growth in India is accelerating to an estimated 5.5 per cent as a result of higher private consumption and net exports; investment, on the other hand, remains flat. Most countries in South-East Asia should keep growing at around or above 5 per cent, driven by private consumption and fixed investment, with little or no contribution from net exports. Economic performance is more varied in West Asia, where several countries have been directly or indirectly affected by armed conflicts. Turkey has been exposed to financial instability and may not be able to sustain a growth rate that is heavily dependent on domestic credit expansion.

Growth in Africa also shows wide contrasts. It remains weak in North Africa due to ongoing political uncertainty and disruptions in oil production. It has also remained subdued in South Africa, at around 2 per cent, owing to a weakening of domestic demand and to strikes in the mining sector. By contrast, several large sub-Saharan economies have posted high growth rates, leading to projected growth for the subregion of almost 6 per cent in 2014. In several cases, historically high commodity prices have been supporting this growth that has persisted for more than a decade.

After a strong rebound in 2010, economic growth in Latin America and the Caribbean has slowed down to an estimated 2 per cent in 2014. This weak performance mainly reflects slow growth in the three main economies, Argentina, Brazil and Mexico, where domestic demand (their main driver of growth after the global crisis) has lost momentum. External financial shocks in mid-2013 and early 2014 also affected those economies, leading to macroeconomic policy tightening. Further financial instability might result from legal obstacles to the normal servicing of Argentina's sovereign debt. However, Argentina's solvency and sound macroeconomic fundamentals in most countries in the region should prevent this shock from developing into a regional financial crisis. Several countries exporting hydrocarbons or minerals have experienced significantly higher growth rates, pushed by strong domestic demand.

The European transition economies are likely to experience a further slowdown of growth this year, with stagnant consumption and investment demand in the Russian Federation exacerbated by financial instability and renewed capital outflows. On the other hand, the Central Asian transition economies, most of which are oil or mineral exporters, seem set to maintain fairly robust growth rates as a result of historically high terms of trade.

Trade winds not picking up

Six years after the onset of the global financial crisis, international trade remains lacklustre. Merchandise trade grew at close to 2 per cent in volume in 2012–2013 and the first few months of 2014, which is below the growth of global output. Trade in services increased somewhat faster, at around 5 per cent in 2013, without significantly changing the overall picture. This lack of dynamism contrasts sharply with the two decades preceding the crisis, when global trade in goods and services expanded more than twice as fast as global output (at annual averages of 6.8 per cent and 3 per cent respectively). During that period, the share of exports and imports of goods and services in GDP (at constant prices) virtually doubled, from around 13 per cent to 27 per cent in developed countries, and from 20 per cent to close to 40 per cent in developing countries.

Given the insufficiency of global demand, it is highly unlikely that international trade alone will be able to kick-start economic growth. Facilitating trade flows by modernizing customs procedures will be helpful in making the trading system more efficient over the longer term, but it will not address the main constraints on trade today. International trade has not slowed down or remained quasi-stagnant because of higher trade barriers or supply-side difficulties; its slow growth is the result of weak global demand. In this context, a lopsided emphasis on the cost of trade, prompting efforts to spur exports through wage reductions and an "internal devaluation", would be self-defeating and counterproductive, especially if such a strategy is pursued by several trade partners simultaneously. The way to expand trade at a global level is through a robust domestic-demand-led output recovery at the national level.

Although there is an overall lack of dynamism in trade at present, in some countries and regions imports have been growing (in volume) at relatively high rates: between 8 and 9 per cent in 2013. This has been the case in sub-Saharan Africa and West Asia that continue to benefit from high commodity prices by historical standards, and in China, which remains a strong market for several primary commodities.

That said, with a few but important exceptions, most commodity prices have been declining persistently since their peaks in 2011, although their downward trend seems to have been slowing down in 2013–2014. The main exceptions to this trend are oil, the price of which has remained remarkably stable at high levels since 2011, and tropical beverages (coffee and cocoa) and some minerals (most notably nickel), which experienced sharp price increases in 2014 due to supply shortages. Despite an overall declining trend, commodity prices in the first half of 2014 remained, on average, close to 50 per cent higher than during the period 2003–2008.

While recent developments in commodity prices have differed by commodity group and for particular commodities, a common feature in the physical markets is that supply-side factors have played a major role. This is reflected, for instance, in the lower prices of minerals, as investments made during the period of rapidly rising prices eventually translated into increased supplies. By contrast, changes in physical demand had only a minor impact on the evolution of commodity prices in 2013 and early 2014. In general, demand for commodities has continued to grow in line with the moderate economic growth of the world economy.

Short-term developments in commodity prices continued to be influenced by the substantial financialization of commodity markets during 2013 and the first half of 2014. However, regulatory changes in commodity futures trading have encouraged a shuffling of participants from banks towards other financial operators such as commodity trading companies, which often operate in a less transparent and less regulated environment than more traditional financial institutions.

From a longer term perspective, the conclusion of the analysis of *TDR 2013* that commodity prices are set to remain at relatively high levels in historical terms in the coming years, with some short-term corrections, remains valid. This does not suggest that producing countries should be complacent; rather they should try as far as possible to use the rents generated in these markets to finance structural transformation, particularly with a view to production and export diversification.

A "new normal"?

The apparent stabilization of relatively low growth rates across different groups of countries in the world economy may give the impression that it has reached a "new normal". However, to assess the sustainability of the present situation, it is necessary to examine not only the rates of GDP growth, but also its drivers.

After a brief experiment in 2009 and the first half of 2010 with expansionary fiscal measures in response to the immediate threat of a global financial meltdown, the policy mix used in the developed economies comprised, to varying degrees, a combination of fiscal austerity, wage containment and monetary expansion in the hope that increased investor confidence, labour market flexibility, greater competitiveness and the expected rehabilitation of banks' balance sheets would orchestrate a rapid and sustained recovery. However, with fiscal and labour market policies dampening domestic demand, liquidity expansion by monetary authorities was channelled mostly to financial, rather than productive, investments. This in turn led to significant increases in asset prices, despite anaemic economic growth, and to large capital outflows, much of them to emerging markets. Consequently, this policy mix only indirectly (and with a significant delay) supported a demand recovery in those countries where asset appreciation generated a sufficiently strong wealth effect and encouraged renewed consumer borrowing. As such, the new normal has some obvious parallels with the conditions that led to the global financial crisis.

In the case of emerging economies, the extent to which the expansion of domestic demand was being supported by genuine income expansion or by unsustainable asset bubbles and excessive consumer borrowing (with likely significant variations across countries) is still unclear. However, the potential vulnerability of developing and emerging economies in the new normal is heightened by persistent weaknesses in the international financial architecture. Under these circumstances, capital flows can have significant, and not always welcome, effects on the real economy and on the ability of policymakers to respond to unforeseen shocks.

Some developing countries also remain exposed to negative shocks originating from international trade, particularly in countries that rely mainly on exports of only a few primary commodities or on low-skill, labour-intensive manufactures. Diversification of their productive and export activities is a pending task for many transition and developing economies. The UNCTAD Merchandise Trade Specialization Index confirms that, despite the rapid rate of growth of trade in many developing economies over the period 1995–2012, the degree of specialization in their export structures has not varied significantly.

There is, in fact, nothing particularly "new" about the current financial cycle affecting developing and transition economies. These economies are now experiencing their fourth such cycle since the mid-1970s; and, much as before, because the present cycle is mainly driven by developed countries' economic conditions and monetary policy decisions, the resulting international capital movements do not necessarily coincide with the needs of developing countries. On the contrary, if recent history is any guide, they could have serious disruptive macroeconomic and financial effects. In order to create and maintain domestic macroeconomic and financial conditions that support growth and structural transformation, governments should have at their disposal suitable policy instruments for managing capital flows, and for preventing or coping with the recurrent shocks these can provoke. Multilateral rules in the IMF's Articles of Agreement and in the General Agreement on Trade in Services (GATS) of the World Trade Organization (WTO) do allow governments to manage their capital accounts, including a resort to capital controls. However, the emphasis has been on their use only for prudential reasons or crisis management. Instead, capital management measures should be seen as a normal instrument in policymakers' toolkit, rather than as an exceptional and temporary device to be employed only in critical times.

Some new bilateral and plurilateral trade and investment agreements that have been signed, or are being negotiated, introduce even more stringent commitments with respect to financial liberalization than those contained in multilateral agreements, which might further reduce policy space in this context. Therefore, governments that aim to maintain macroeconomic stability and wish to re-regulate their financial systems should carefully consider the risks in taking on such commitments.

The case for coordinated expansion

UNCTAD, using its Global Policy Model, has assessed an alternative, "balanced-growth" scenario, which could offer a way of escaping from the current global economic doldrums. The two scenarios used in the model have the value not of forecasting, but of demonstrating the direction of change that could be expected from a general shift in policy orientation. The balanced-growth scenario introduces the following elements: incomes policies to support growth of demand on a sustainable basis; growth-enhancing fiscal policies; industrial policies to promote private investment and structural transformation; regulation of systemically important financial institutions and capital controls to stabilize global financial markets; and development-oriented trade agreements. This is contrasted with a "baseline" scenario, which broadly continues with business-as-usual policies.

The simulations for the baseline scenario show that structural imbalances will keep on growing, even with continued moderate growth, with countries becoming increasingly vulnerable to shocks and financial instability. The longer such imbalances remain unresolved, the harsher the consequences will be, in the face of another serious crisis. The balanced-growth scenario, on the other hand, shows considerable improvements in growth rates, and, most importantly, a gradual resolution of global imbalances. The average growth of the world economy is significantly faster than it is under the baseline scenario. The faster growth rates for all regions are the result not only of individual stimuli, but also of strong synergic effects from the coordination of pro-growth policy stances among the countries. Finally, the results confirm greater growth convergence in the balanced-growth scenario, as well as improved financial stability.

While the results of such exercises need to be viewed with a familiar degree of caution and care, their underlying message is that, in an increasingly interconnected global economy, policies have to be consistent for the world as a whole. Taking into account real and financial feedbacks, it should be clear that a sustained and stable demand-led growth path has to start domestically, rather than having each country individually pushing for competitive reductions of costs and imports in order to generate a net-export-led recovery – a process to which, admittedly, surplus countries have much more to contribute.

The absence of effective institutions and mechanisms for international policy coordination can push policymakers into adopting strategies that may appear to be expedient in the short term, but which are effectively self-defeating in the medium term. It is therefore essential to continue with efforts to devise a more effective set of globally inclusive institutions to regulate markets, help correct unsustainable imbalances when they emerge, and better pursue the aims of global development and convergence.

Challenges towards a new development agenda

If macroeconomic policy is tacking uncomfortably close to the "business-as-usual" strategy of the pre-crisis years, the discussions now under way on a post-2015 development agenda are tending to break with the past. The push for a more universal, transformative and sustainable approach to development will play a key role in the setting of new goals and targets for policymakers, at both the national and international levels. The 17 goals and sundry targets agreed to at the United Nations Open Working Group on Sustainable Development already signal a level of ambition well beyond the Millennium Development Goals.

The international community faces three principle challenges in fashioning this new approach. The first is aligning any new goals and targets to a policy paradigm that can help raise productivity and per capita incomes everywhere, generate enough decent jobs on a scale to meet a rapidly growing and urbanizing global labour force, establish a stable international financial system that boosts productive investment, and deliver reliable public services that leave no one behind, particularly in the most vulnerable communities. The dominant economic paradigm of market liberalism has disappointed in most of these respects. In this context, as Pope Francis has recently suggested, we can no longer simply put our trust in "the sacralized workings of the prevailing system". Undoubtedly, fresh thinking is needed.

The second challenge to consider in formulating a new development agenda is the massive rise in inequality, which has accompanied the spread of market liberalism. This is important because, in addition to its moral implications, growing inequality can seriously damage social well-being, threaten economic progress and stability, and undermine political cohesion. Previous *Trade and Development Reports* (*TDR*s) have insisted on the need to look beyond some of the headline-grabbing numbers surrounding the top one per cent, and examine what has been happening to functional income dynamics, in particular, the divergence between wage and productivity growth and the growth of rentier incomes. Heightened capital mobility has not only reduced the bargaining power of labour, further amplifying the adverse distributive impact of unregulated financial activity; it has also made it harder to tax some incomes directly, thus increasing the State's reliance on more regressive taxes and on bond markets. This can, in turn, have a very corrosive impact on the legitimacy and effectiveness of the political process.

The third challenge is ensuring that effective policy instruments are available to countries to enable them to achieve the agreed goals and advance the development agenda. Restoring a development model that favours the real economy over financial interests, puts sustainability ahead of short-term gains and truly seeks to achieve prosperity for all will almost certainly require adding more instruments to the policy toolkit than is currently contemplated by economic orthodoxy.

The enduring case for policy space

Any widening and strengthening of the ambition of national development strategies will need to be accompanied by institutional changes. Markets require a framework of rules, restraints and norms to operate effectively. As such, the market economy is always embedded in a legal, social and cultural setting, and is sustained by political forces. How and to what extent the framework of rules and regulations is loosened or tightened is part of a complex political process specific to each society, but it cannot be dispensed with without threatening a breakdown of the wider economic and social order.

International markets and firms, no less than their domestic counterparts, also require a framework of rules, restraints and norms. And, as at the domestic level, the loosening and tightening of that framework is a persistent feature of governance of the global economy. States must decide on whether and how much of their own independence they are willing to trade for the advantages of having international rules, disciplines and supports. Inevitably, in a world of unequal States, the space required to pursue national economic and social development aspirations varies, as does the likely impact of an individual country's policy decisions on others. The challenges of managing these trade-offs are particularly pronounced at the multilateral level, where the differences among States are significant. While the extent to which an adopted growth and development path responds to national needs and priorities can obviously be limited or circumscribed by multilateral regimes and international rules, it can equally be affected by economic and political pressures emanating from the workings of global markets, depending on the degree and nature of economic integration of the country concerned.

The interdependence among States and markets provides the main rationale for a well-structured system of global economic governance comprising multilateral rules and disciplines. The guiding principle of these arrangements should be their ability to generate fair and inclusive outcomes by providing global public goods and minimizing adverse international spillovers and other negative externalities, regardless of whether these are created by national economic policies or the profit-making decisions of private actors.

These various tensions between national policy autonomy, policy effectiveness and international economic integration are captured, in part, by the idea of "policy space"; this refers to the freedom and ability of governments to identify and pursue the most appropriate mix of economic and social policies to achieve equitable and sustainable development in their own national contexts, but as constituent parts of an interdependent global economy. It can be defined as the combination of de jure policy sovereignty, which is the formal authority of policymakers over their national policy goals and instruments, and de facto national policy control, which involves the ability of national policymakers to set priorities, influence specific targets and weigh possible trade-offs.

For some countries, signing on to multilateral disciplines can spur them to redouble their efforts to use their remaining policy space more effectively than when they had greater policy space; this seems to be true, in particular, for countries emerging from conflict, as well as for many former socialist economies. Moreover, these disciplines can operate to reduce the inherent bias of international economic relations in favour of countries that have greater economic or political power. Thus, such disciplines can simultaneously restrict (particularly de jure) and ease (particularly de facto) policy space, since constraints on one country's behaviour also apply to other countries, thereby affecting the external context as a whole.

But there are also valid concerns that the various legal obligations emerging from multilateral, regional and bilateral agreements have reduced national policy autonomy by affecting both the available range and the efficacy of particular policy instruments. In addition, the effectiveness of national policies tends to be weakened − in some instances very significantly − by forces of globalization (especially financial globalization) and by the internalization of markets, which affect national economic processes.

Inclusive multilateralism: Back to the future

History has a tendency to repeat itself, though not necessarily as tragedy or farce. Consequently, there are always positive lessons to be learned from examining how earlier generations of policymakers dealt with big challenges. The need for reconciling the requirements of policy sovereignty at the national level with the imperatives of an interdependent world economy may seem today to be relatively new. In fact, it is a long-standing challenge that has been discussed extensively, and from many different angles, for almost two centuries, though none as compelling or significant as those arising from the crises of the inter-war era.

The principal objective of the architects of Bretton Woods was to design a post-war international economic structure that would prevent a recurrence of the opportunistic actions and damaging contagion that had led to the breakdown of international trade and payments in the 1930s. Accordingly, such a structure would need to support the new policy goals of rising incomes, full employment and social security in the developed economies. But a prominent group of Roosevelt's New Dealers also struggled to place development issues firmly on the multilateral agenda in the 1930s and 1940s. This included measures that sought to expand the policy space for State-led industrialization and to increase the level and reliability of the multilateral financial support necessary to meet the needs of developing countries − efforts that eventually met with considerable resistance.

Those results set the stage for the North-South conflicts of the post-war period. In that context, the construction of a more development-friendly international economic order was a much slower and more uneven process after the war than the Bretton Woods architects had anticipated. It took the growing voices of newly independent developing countries in the late 1950s and early 1960s to shift multilateralism on to a more inclusive footing. This led to the creation of UNCTAD in 1964, and to a subsequent broadening of the development agenda around a new international economic order. The often forgotten Bretton Woods development vision and the details of its various proposals can still provide some inspiration for those seeking to advance an inclusive development agenda today.

Managing creative destruction

None of today's developed countries depended on market forces for their structural transformation and its attendant higher levels of employment, productivity and per capita incomes. Rather, they adopted country-specific measures to manage those forces, harnessing their creative side to build productive capacities and provide opportunities for dynamic firms and entrepreneurs, while guiding them in a more socially desired direction. They also used different forms of government action to mitigate the destructive tendencies of those same market forces. This approach of managing the market, not idolizing it, was repeated by the most rapidly growing emerging market economies − from the small social democratic economies of Northern Europe to the giant economies of East Asia − in the decades following the end of the Second World War.

Weak initial economic conditions and low administrative and institutional capabilities, as well as policy errors and external shocks explain, to varying degrees, why other developing countries have been less successful in replicating these earlier experiences. However, international economic governance has also increasingly posed greater constraints on the options for individual countries to pursue economic policies to achieve their development objectives.

The post-war multilateral trade regime was essentially designed not to compromise the policy space of the developed countries to achieve an appropriate level of economic security through the pursuit of full employment and extended social protection. But it also sought to limit mercantilist practices among its members and provide predictability in international trading conditions. What emerged was a regime of negotiated, binding and enforceable rules and commitments with built-in flexibilities and derogations.

Subsequent multilateral trade negotiations under the auspices of the GATT culminated in the Uruguay Round Agreements (URAs), which entered into force in 1995. The scope of those negotiations was considerably widened, both in terms of the countries participating and the tariff lines involved. They also extended into trade-related areas beyond trade in goods, with the most-favoured-nation and national-treatment principles being applied not only to trade in goods, but also to trade in a wide range of services, such as finance, tourism, education and health provision. As a result, all WTO member States accepted restrictions on their conduct of a wider set of policies, including some designed to promote and direct the structural transformation of their economies. Yet some of the policy space they gave up had played an important role in successful development processes in the past. The following are some examples.

- The use of subsidies, circumscribed by the Agreement on Subsidies and Countervailing Measures (SCM), had been a preferred instrument to support structural transformation, particularly in East Asian countries.

- Performance requirements on foreign investors with respect to exports, domestic content and technology transfer, restricted under the Agreement of Trade-related Investment Measures (TRIMs), had been frequently used to enhance the creation of linkages between foreign investors and local manufacturers.

- Reverse engineering and imitation through access to technology, curtailed under the Agreement on Trade-related Aspects of Intellectual Property Rights (TRIPS), had previously been used by many countries, including the now developed ones.

Despite greater restrictions on the use of certain policy instruments, WTO members retain some flexibility to support structural transformation, including in tariff policy where some lines are still unbound, and where the difference between bound and applied tariffs provides room for modulating them in support of development goals. WTO members can also continue to use certain kinds of subsidies and standards to promote research and development and innovation activities, as well as exploit flexibilities in the use of export credits. Under the TRIMs Agreement, policymakers may continue to impose sector-specific entry conditions on foreign investors, including industry-specific limitations. The agreement also allows some flexibility through the mechanism of compulsory licensing (whereby authorities can allow companies other than the patent owner to use the rights to a patent) and parallel imports (i.e. imports of branded goods into a market which can be sold there without the consent of the owner of the trademark in that market).

Weighing the loss of policy space in specific areas against the potential gains of a more predictable open multilateral trading system is no easy task. In any event, the more immediate question is how best to use the space that remains to support more sustainable and inclusive outcomes than have been achieved by most developing countries over the past three decades. In this respect, practices and capacities linked to the institutional construct of a developmental State are still key, as UNCTAD has long insisted. But it is also important to recognize that inconsistencies and gaps across the multilateral architecture, particularly at the interface of trade and financial flows, continue to make it difficult for developing countries to make the most of the space that remains. Moreover, many of them need much better support from the international community to use the current arrangements in a way that will help their transformation efforts. In many respects that support has been given reluctantly, or has not been forthcoming at all. UNCTAD's proposal for an independent commission to undertake a development audit of the multilateral trading system to examine these and other tensions that disturb the smooth workings of this system could offer a way forward.

The steady erosion of policy space

Since the early 1990s, there has been a wave of bilateral and regional trade agreements (RTAs) and international investment agreements (IIAs), some of which contain provisions that are more stringent than those covered by the multilateral trade regime, or they include additional provisions that go beyond those of the current multilateral trade agreements.

Provisions in RTAs have become ever more comprehensive, and many of them include rules that limit the options available in the design and implementation of comprehensive national development strategies. Even though these agreements remain the product of (often protracted) negotiations and bargaining between sovereign States, there is a growing sense that, due to the larger number of economic and social issues they cover, the discussions often lack the transparency and the coordination − including among all potentially interested government ministries − needed to strike a balanced outcome.

Regardless of the countries involved, by signing those agreements developing-country governments relinquish some of the policy space they have been endeavouring so hard to preserve at the multilateral level. This may seem puzzling, but it could be mainly because some governments fear exclusion when other countries signing up to such agreements gain preferential market access and become potentially more attractive as destinations for FDI. They may also see participation in a free trade agreement as a means to facilitate the entry of their domestic firms into international production networks.

However, as discussed in previous *TDR*s, participation in international production networks runs the risk of generating adverse terms-of-trade effects on countries, particularly those at the lower ends of production chains, and it creates few domestic linkages and technology spillovers. Moreover, developing countries at an early stage of industrialization may become locked into low-value-added activities due to stiff competition from other suppliers to keep labour costs low, and because the tight control over intellectual property and expensive branding strategies of the lead firm block them from moving up the value chain. Even relatively successful middle-income countries do not face a level playing field in many of these networks. China is an interesting case in point. Considerable attention has been given to its rise as a dominant exporter of electronics goods, to the extent that it now accounts for as much as one-third of total trade in this sector. But there are, in fact, very few Chinese firms that control the different parts of the electronics chain. More telling still, Chinese firms, on one recent estimate, account for just 3 per cent of total profits in this sector. Thus, developing countries need to carefully weigh both the costs and benefits when considering an industrialization strategy that places considerable emphasis on participation in international production networks if this pushes them to a race to conclude ever more and increasingly stringent agreements without a full and proper understanding of their development potential.

Policy space is not only reduced by free trade agreements, but also when countries sign up to IIAs. When most such agreements were being concluded in the 1990s, any loss of policy space was seen as a small price to pay for an expected increase in FDI inflows. This perception began to change in the early 2000s, as it became apparent that investment rules could obstruct a wide range of public policies, including those aimed at improving the impact of FDI on the economy. Besides, empirical evidence on the effectiveness of bilateral investment treaties and investment chapters in RTAs in stimulating FDI is ambiguous. Moreover, the lack of transparency and coherence characterizing the tribunals established to adjudicate on disputes arising from these agreements, and their perceived pro-investor bias, added to concerns about their effectiveness. A range of possibilities is currently under consideration to rebalance the system and recover the needed space for development policies. These include: (i) progressive and piecemeal reforms through the creation of new agreements based on investment principles that foster sustainable development; (ii) the creation of a centralized, permanent investment tribunal; and (iii) a retreat from investment treaties and reverting to national law.

Along with the proliferation of trade agreements and their expansion into trade-related areas, there has been a global revival of interest in industrial policy. Reconciling these two trends is a huge challenge. Many developed countries, especially since the recent financial crisis, have begun to explicitly acknowledge the important role that industrial policy can play in maintaining a robust manufacturing sector. The United States, while often portrayed as a country that takes a hands-off approach to industrial policy, has been, and remains, an avid user of such a policy. Its Government has acted as a leading risk taker and market shaper in the development and commercialization of new technologies, adopting a wide range of policies to support a network of domestic manufacturing firms that have the potential for innovation, exports and the creation of well-paid jobs. By contrast, the experience of the EU illustrates how intergovernmental agreements can constrain the policy choices of national policymakers, and how industrial policies that are limited to the adoption of only horizontal measures may hamper the achievement of stated objectives.

As some developing countries have reassessed the merits of industrial policy in recent years, they have also used some of their policy space to induce greater investment and innovation by domestic firms so as to enhance their international competitiveness. Some of the measures adopted include, sector-specific modulation of applied tariffs, using the difference between bound and applied tariff rates; applying preferential import duties; offering tax incentives; providing long-term investment financing through national development banks or subsidizing commercial loans; and using government procurement to support local suppliers. Various policy measures continue to be used in countries at different levels of development – from Viet Nam to Brazil – in an effort to create a virtuous circle between trade and capital accumulation.

Safeguarding policy space while strengthening multilateral mechanisms

UNCTAD has been arguing for some time that if developing countries are to maintain and improve their recent growth trajectories, they should widen and deepen the structural transformation of their economies. The resulting policy challenge is a familiar one in commodity exporters, where a lack of diversification makes their economies vulnerable to exogenous shocks and policy shifts. But also, stronger growth does not automatically translate into improved living standards for the majority of the population. While structural transformation is imperative for all developing countries for similar reasons, in the coming years they are likely to find a much less favourable global economic environment than existed in the opening decade of this century. Consequently, structural transformation will be extremely difficult without greater flexibilities in policymaking.

Thus, strengthening the governance of global trade in support of development goals will need to be part of a more comprehensive and integrated package to help preserve the policy space for proactive trade and industrial policies. Such reform should complement macroeconomic and financial reforms. It will need to include various elements, foremost among them being the strengthening of multilateral mechanisms. The new momentum from the WTO's Bali Ministerial Conference in December 2013 should be taken forward to achieve an outcome of the Doha Round negotiations that justifies its description as a "development round". Any renewal of such a commitment could include an emphasis on implementation issues and maintaining the principle of a single undertaking, rather than moving towards a variable geometry whereby a range of mandatory core commitments is supplemented by plurilateral agreements. The greatest benefit from this may well be simply maintaining the public good character of multilateral rules.

A refocusing of trade negotiations on multilateral agreements would imply reconsidering provisions that go beyond existing WTO agreements; but it should also look into greater flexibility in the application of the IIRAs by responding constructively to a number of recent developments. For example, the flexibilities introduced into the system of intellectual property rights protection with respect to public health could be extended to support technology adoption and innovation at all stages of structural transformation. Further negotiations on industrial tariff reductions could also provide greater flexibility for sector-specific public support policies. The latter would imply changing the sector-specific level and structure of tariffs over time, while maintaining considerable dispersion of tariffs across economic sectors.

Fiscal space in the global context

Fiscal space goes hand in hand with policy space. Even if governments are allowed to design and implement the development policies of their choice within the existing international framework of negotiated rules and accepted norms, they will still need to finance the investment and other general and targeted expenditures required for implementing those policies. Thus, strengthening government revenues is key.

Fiscal space is both a cause and an effect of economic growth and structural change. Higher average levels of income, expansion of the modern sectors of the economy and a shrinking of the informal economy broaden the tax base and strengthen the governments' capacities to mobilize fiscal revenues. This, in turn, allows for higher growth-enhancing public spending, both on the supply side (e.g. investment in infrastructure, research and development, and education) and on the demand side (e.g. social transfers). Conversely, limited, or even a diminished, fiscal space is often part of a vicious circle of underdevelopment. The need for reclaiming and expanding fiscal space faces particular challenges in an increasingly globalizing economy. Official development assistance (ODA) can support the expansion of fiscal space, particularly in the least developed countries (LDCs), as can foreign borrowing, and on a more sustainable basis if it is used for expanding productive capacities. However, the unpredictability of ODA can make it difficult for long-term policy planning, and it can also delay the establishment of political mechanisms that support the developmental State. Moreover, in most cases, relying on others' savings to fund basic State activities raises questions about voice and legitimacy. Also, excessive reliance on foreign sources has led to overindebtedness and chronic deficits in countries' fiscal and external balances, thereby reducing fiscal space in the long run. Therefore, expanding fiscal space should rely, as far as possible, on domestic revenue sources if it is to sustain a national development strategy. Foreign finance can complement, but not replace, such revenues.

A major problem is that globalization has affected the ability of governments to mobilize domestic revenues. Their lowering of tariffs has resulted in reduced revenues in many developing countries, often significantly so, while the increased mobility of capital and its greater use of fiscal havens have considerably altered the conditions for taxing income – both personal and corporate – and wealth. The dominant agenda of market liberalism has led to a globalized economy that encourages tax competition among countries, at times pushing them to a "race to the bottom" in offering incentives in the form of reduced direct taxation. Corporate tax rates have been on a declining trend in developed and developing countries alike, often accompanied by subsidies or exemptions to attract or retain foreign investment. In addition, finance-led globalization has led to the proliferation of off-shore financial centres, tax havens and secrecy jurisdictions that provide various means of tax avoidance or evasion on a scale that is measured in billions, if not trillions, of dollars.

Taxation problems for the international community

Trade mispricing, including through transfer pricing (i.e. the valuation of intra-firm cross-border transactions by international company groups), has become the evasion mechanism of choice for many companies. If the intracompany or intragroup price does not reflect the price that would be paid in a market where each participant acts independently in its own interest, profits within a company group can be effectively shifted to low-tax or no-tax jurisdictions, while losses and deductions are shifted to high-tax jurisdictions. Another way of shifting profits and losses among jurisdictions is through "thin capitalization", which occurs when a company has a high proportion of debt in relation to its equity capital, and mixes and matches intragroup debts and interest payments across its subsidiaries to minimize tax payments and generate higher overall profits.

The international tax architecture has failed, so far, to properly adapt to this reality, thereby allowing a massive haemorrhaging of public revenues. The opacity surrounding tax havens may partly explain the difficulties faced by policymakers in collecting public revenues, but the main obstacle is political: the major providers of financial secrecy are to be found in some of the world's biggest and wealthiest countries, or in specific areas within these countries. Indeed, offshore financial centres and the secrecy jurisdictions that host them are fully integrated into the global financial system, channelling large shares of trade and capital movements, including FDI.

Recently, a number of developments aimed at improving transparency and exchange of information for tax purposes have taken place. They include a declaration by G20 leaders to promote information sharing with respect to all kinds of abuses and fraudulent activities, an OECD Action Plan on Base Erosion and Profit Shifting (BEPS), increased monitoring by several national tax authorities of tax abuses by rich individuals and TNCs, and numerous bilateral tax treaties (BTTs) and tax information exchange agreements (TIEAs).

While these initiatives are steps in the right direction, their implementation and enforcement have generally been very slow. This is particularly so with regard to transfer pricing abuses, which are extremely harmful for developing countries. Because these initiatives are mostly led by the developed economies – the main homes to TNCs and to some secrecy jurisdictions – there are risks that the debate will not fully take into account the needs and views of developing and transition economies. It will therefore be important to give a more prominent role to institutions like the United Nations Committee of Experts on International Cooperation in Tax Matters, and to consider the adoption of an international convention against tax avoidance and evasion.

Although the very nature of the problem suggests the need for a multilateral approach, governments can also apply measures at the national level. They can, for instance, legislate for the adoption of a general anti-avoidance rule (GAAR) so that "aggressive" tax schemes can be declared illegal when challenged in courts. They can also be more effective in combating transfer mispricing in their international trade by using reference pricing for a number of homogeneous traded goods.

Natural resources for public revenue

In many developing countries, collecting higher public revenues through rents from natural resources – and particularly from the extractive industries – is of particular importance for the financing of development. The main contribution of these activities to development is what they pay in government revenues, as they often generate enclave economies with weak or no linkages with the rest of the economy. However, as the rise of commodity prices during the past decade or so led to a tenfold increase in the profits of the world's largest mining companies, it became obvious that the public gains from resource rents were lagging far behind. Corruption may be partly to blame, but the main reason has been overly generous taxation regimes established at a time of low prices, and often on the recommendation of the Bretton Woods institutions, with the aim of attracting international firms and investors to the sector.

As a result, many governments – both from developed and developing countries – have begun to revise their policies relating to the extractive industries. This has included renegotiation or cancellation of existing contracts, increases in tax or royalty rates, introduction of new taxes and changes in the degree of State ownership of the extractive projects. Host governments can also benefit from a strengthening of their bargaining positions in contract negotiations with TNCs involved in the extractive industries due to the emergence of new major players, such as companies from emerging economies. However, these changing market conditions should not obscure the wider policy challenges faced by producing countries in making the most of extractive industries for development.

A comprehensive policy aimed at improving revenues from natural resources needs to incorporate several elements. First, governments should retain their right to review the tax regimes and ownership structures whenever deemed necessary for the economic and development interests of the country. A minimum level of taxation could also be negotiated at the regional or international levels to avoid a race to the bottom. Second, they should have the means to enforce the rules and obtain the due revenues by being able to control TNCs' transfer pricing manoeuvres and underreporting of export volumes. Third, they should be allowed to do so without the threat of legal retribution through the existing investment dispute mechanisms.

Most of the needed measures can be taken at the national level, but multilateral cooperation is still of the utmost importance. Transparency initiatives such as the Extractive Industries Transparency Initiative (EITI) should be made mandatory and extended: they should not focus only on governments, but also on producing firms and commodity trading companies. There should also be a greater focus on monitoring, auditing and accountability, as well as enforcement of the fiscal conditions and regulations under which extractive industries operate. Institutional development and capacity-building are crucial, in particular to improve the capacity to negotiate contracts, but also to ameliorate the monitoring of production costs, import and export prices, volumes, qualities and time of delivery of the natural resources extracted, as well as for data collection and processing. Given its expertise in the area of commodities, transport, customs and trade, UNCTAD could provide support in this domain. Regional cooperation in capacity-building can also prove very useful. The international donor community has an important role to play in supporting such initiatives.

Preventing the resource drain caused by illicit financial flows and tax avoidance can help provide the necessary revenues to finance the attainment of new development goals. Thus, given their relevance for many developing countries and transition economies, fiscal space and related governance issues should be prominent components of the post-2015 development agenda.

Mukhisa Kituyi
Secretary-General of UNCTAD

RECENT TRENDS IN THE WORLD ECONOMY

A. Global growth

The world economy has seen a modest improvement in growth in 2014, although it will remain significantly below its pre-crisis highs. Its growth rate of around 2.3 per cent in 2012 and 2013 is projected to rise to 2.5–3 per cent in 2014. This mild increase is essentially due to growth in developed countries accelerating from 1.3 per cent in 2013 to around 1.8 per cent in 2014. Developing countries as a whole are likely to repeat their performance of the previous years, growing at between 4.5 and 5 per cent, while in the transition economies growth is forecast to further decelerate to around 1 per cent, from an already weak performance in 2013 (table 1.1).

1. Developed countries

A moderate acceleration of growth is expected in developed countries as a result of a slight pick-up in the European Union (EU), since the performance of Japan and the United States is not expected to improve in 2014. In Europe, tentative easing of fiscal austerity and a more accommodating monetary policy stance, including by the European Central Bank (ECB), has shifted the direction of domestic demand from negative to positive territory. In some countries (e.g. the United Kingdom), household demand is being supported by asset appreciation and the recovery of consumer and mortgage credit, and in others by some improvement in real wages (e.g. Germany). However, in a number of other large euro-zone economies (e.g. France, Italy and Spain) high levels of unemployment, stagnant or sluggish real wage growth, and persistent weakness in the banking sector continue to dampen the expansion of domestic credit conditions and restrain demand growth. Net exports should make a positive, though very small, contribution to Europe's overall growth performance in 2014.

The United States economy is continuing its moderate recovery from the Great Recession through a reliance on domestic private demand. Fiscal austerity has been a drag on economic growth since 2011, albeit with a slight easing of the negative impact in 2014. Unemployment is continuing to fall thanks to job creation in the corporate sector. However, average real wages remain stagnant. Continued liquidity expansion, although much less aggressive than in previous years, along with asset price appreciations, has helped to support the recovery of domestic borrowing and consumption.

Growth in Japan has also been relying on domestic demand. Private consumption and investment have benefited from the expansionary monetary and fiscal policies of the "Abenomics" plan. There was an increase in public spending, mainly for

Table 1.1

WORLD OUTPUT GROWTH, 2006–2014

(Annual percentage change)

Region/country	2006	2007	2008	2009	2010	2011	2012	2013	2014[a]
World	**4.1**	**4.0**	**1.5**	**-2.1**	**4.1**	**2.8**	**2.3**	**2.3**	**2.7**
Developed countries	**2.8**	**2.5**	**0.0**	**-3.7**	**2.6**	**1.4**	**1.1**	**1.3**	**1.8**
of which:									
Japan	1.7	2.2	-1.0	-5.5	4.7	-0.6	1.4	1.6	1.4
United States	2.7	1.8	-0.3	-2.8	2.5	1.6	2.3	2.2	2.1
European Union (EU-28)	3.4	3.2	0.3	-4.6	2.1	1.7	-0.3	0.1	1.6
of which:									
Euro area[b]	3.2	2.9	0.3	-4.5	2.0	1.6	-0.6	-0.4	1.1
France	2.5	2.3	-0.1	-3.1	1.7	2.0	0.0	0.2	0.7
Germany	3.7	3.3	1.1	-5.1	4.0	3.3	0.7	0.4	1.9
Italy	2.2	1.7	-1.2	-5.5	1.7	0.4	-2.4	-1.9	0.1
United Kingdom	2.8	3.4	-0.8	-5.2	1.7	1.1	0.3	1.7	3.1
New EU member States after 2004	6.4	6.0	4.0	-3.8	2.1	3.0	0.6	1.1	2.7
South-East Europe and CIS	**8.5**	**8.7**	**5.3**	**-6.6**	**4.8**	**4.7**	**3.3**	**2.0**	**1.3**
South-East Europe[c]	4.6	5.9	5.0	-2.1	1.7	1.9	-0.8	2.0	2.0
CIS, incl. Georgia	8.7	8.9	5.3	-6.8	4.9	4.8	3.5	2.0	1.2
of which:									
Russian Federation	8.2	8.5	5.2	-7.8	4.5	4.3	3.4	1.3	0.5
Developing countries	**7.7**	**8.0**	**5.4**	**2.6**	**7.8**	**6.0**	**4.7**	**4.6**	**4.7**
Africa	5.8	6.1	5.5	2.5	4.9	0.9	5.3	3.5	3.9
North Africa, excl. Sudan	5.3	4.8	6.1	2.9	4.2	-6.8	8.7	2.0	2.4
Sub-Saharan Africa, excl. South Africa	6.4	7.5	6.2	4.5	6.4	5.1	4.6	5.3	5.9
South Africa	5.6	5.5	3.6	-1.5	3.1	3.6	2.5	1.9	1.8
Latin America and the Caribbean	5.5	5.5	3.7	-1.6	5.7	4.3	3.0	2.6	1.9
Caribbean	9.4	5.8	3.1	-0.2	2.6	2.4	2.5	2.6	2.8
Central America, excl. Mexico	6.4	7.0	4.1	-0.3	4.1	5.3	5.1	4.3	4.3
Mexico	5.0	3.1	1.4	-4.7	5.1	4.0	4.0	1.1	2.0
South America	5.5	6.7	4.9	-0.3	6.4	4.5	2.4	3.1	1.7
of which:									
Brazil	4.0	6.1	5.2	-0.3	7.5	2.7	1.0	2.5	1.3
Asia	8.7	9.1	6.0	4.0	8.9	7.2	5.2	5.3	5.6
East Asia	9.9	11.1	7.0	6.0	9.6	7.7	6.0	6.3	6.4
of which:									
China	12.7	14.2	9.6	9.2	10.4	9.3	7.7	7.7	7.5
South Asia	8.3	8.9	5.3	4.6	9.1	6.9	3.6	3.8	5.0
of which:									
India	9.4	10.1	6.2	5.0	11.0	7.9	4.9	4.7	5.6
South-East Asia	6.1	6.6	4.3	1.2	8.1	4.7	5.6	4.9	4.4
West Asia	7.5	5.5	4.7	-1.0	6.9	7.4	3.8	3.8	4.0
Oceania	2.8	3.4	2.7	2.4	3.7	4.9	4.3	2.9	3.2

Source: UNCTAD secretariat calculations, based on United Nations, Department of Economic and Social Affairs (UN-DESA), *National Accounts Main Aggregates* database, and *World Economic Situation and Prospects (WESP): Update as of mid-2014;* ECLAC, 2014; OECD, 2014; IMF, *World Economic Outlook,* April 2014; Economist Intelligence Unit, *EIU CountryData* database; JP Morgan, *Global Data Watch*; and national sources.

Note: Calculations for country aggregates are based on GDP at constant 2005 dollars.

a Forecasts.

b Excluding Latvia.

c Albania, Bosnia and Herzegovina, Montenegro, Serbia and the former Yugoslav Republic of Macedonia.

reconstruction, following natural catastrophes in 2011, and a stimulus package propelled the Japanese economy to higher growth in 2012–2013. As the effects of those measures dissipate and the rise in the consumer tax rate in April 2014 begins to discourage household spending in the medium term, a new stimulus package may be needed to help maintain growth targets for gross domestic product (GDP) and domestic prices. Indeed, sustained growth of nominal GDP would be the only viable way to progressively bring down the very high ratio of public debt to GDP.

Despite some differences in their policy stances, all developed regions are expected to grow at a similar rate of around 1.5–2 per cent in 2014. GDP in the EU is likely to return to its pre-crisis level of 2007, albeit one year after Japan and three years after the United States. The international trade of these countries remains weak, but has recovered somewhat since the last quarter of 2013. A progressive relaxation of fiscal austerity in the EU and the United States, and the tapering off of very expansionary monetary policies in the latter country, have led some observers to believe that these economies are reaching a "new normal", and that they have managed to avert most systemic risks. However, in the new situation, growth is likely to be slower than before the crisis, since investment rates remain relatively low and several countries still have a long way to go before unemployment rates fall and overindebtedness, in both the public and private sectors, is addressed. Chapter II of this *Report* discusses some of the policies behind this modest growth regime, and warns of its potential fragility.

2. Developing and transition economies

The main developing regions look set to repeat much the same growth performance as in 2012–2013. Asia is set to remain the most dynamic region, with an estimated growth rate of around 5.5 per cent. Among the largest economies, China should maintain its lead with a growth rate of close to 7.5 per cent in 2014, based on domestic demand, including an increasing role of private and public consumption. Growth in India has recovered slightly from the significant deceleration of the two previous years, led by higher consumption and net exports, but at around 5.5 per cent it is substantially lower than before the crisis. Most countries in South-East Asia, including

Indonesia, Malaysia, the Philippines and Viet Nam, are expected to continue to grow at around or above 5 per cent, driven by private consumption and fixed investment, but with little or no contribution from net exports. The main exception is Thailand, where political crisis has caused the economy to stagnate. Economic performance is more contrasted in West Asia: several countries have been directly or indirectly affected by war, the Gulf countries are expected to maintain growth rates of 4–5 per cent, and Turkey, which has been exposed to financial instability, may not be able to sustain a fairly rapid growth trajectory that is driven by domestic credit expansion.

Growth in Africa also shows wide contrasts: it remains weak in North Africa, with marginal improvements in Egypt and Tunisia, but a continued fall in Libya, due to armed conflict and disruptions in oil production. Growth has also remained subdued in South Africa, at around 2 per cent, owing to a weakening of domestic demand and strikes in the mining sector. By contrast, several large sub-Saharan economies (including Angola, Côte d'Ivoire, the Democratic Republic of the Congo, Ethiopia, Mozambique, Nigeria and the United Republic of Tanzania) posted high growth rates, which is likely to result in 6 per cent growth in the subregion in 2014. In several countries, historically high levels of commodity prices have been supporting this growth for more than a decade, but other factors, such as improvements in agriculture and recovery from civil conflicts, have also played an important role. However, there are downside risks as demonstrated by the recent return of both Ghana and Zambia to the IMF, in the face of sharp declines in their currency.

The transition economies are set for a continued economic slowdown in 2014. Slow growth in the European transition economies is mainly attributable to stagnating consumption and investment in the Russian Federation since mid-2013, as financial instability has led to increased capital outflows. On the other hand, Central Asian transition economies, most of which are oil or mineral exporters, were able to maintain fairly high growth rates, as a result of historically high terms of trade.

Following a strong rebound in 2010, economic growth in Latin America and the Caribbean has experienced a continuous slowdown, and is projected to be about 2 per cent in 2014. This weak performance mainly reflects slow growth in the three main economies, Argentina, Brazil and Mexico, where domestic demand (their main driver of growth after the global crisis) has lost momentum. External financial shocks in mid-2013 and early 2014 also affected those economies, leading to a tightening of macroeconomic policy. However, well-capitalized banking systems, low external and fiscal deficits, external debts at historical lows and sufficient levels of international reserves have prevented these shocks from developing into financial crises. Several countries exporting hydrocarbons or minerals (e.g. the Plurinational State of Bolivia, Colombia and Ecuador) are showing significantly higher growth rates, pushed by high levels of domestic demand, in terms of both consumption and investment.

Generally speaking, developing countries have managed to recover from the Great Recession faster than developed countries. Many of them have benefited from high commodity prices, especially those whose governments were able to capture a significant share of natural resources rents and use the additional revenues for supporting domestic spending. Other countries, despite being exposed to the vagaries of international finance, were able to tackle the consequences of the global financial crisis by supporting domestic demand with countercyclical policies. However, there are limits to what can be achieved by both countercyclical policies and gains from the

terms of trade, and new sources of dynamism will need to be found. In addition to demand side policies that may include redistribution policies, several countries need to improve their domestic investment and conduct industrial policies aimed at an expansion of their productive capacity and competitiveness so as to respond to rising demand without excessive pressure on domestic prices or trade balances.

Developing countries will also have to face the challenge of persistent instability of the international financial system. This should involve prudential macroeconomic and regulatory policies, mainly applied at the domestic level, but also better regulation at the global level. In this respect, it is evident that, despite the generally favourable trends in recent years, the present framework for sovereign debt restructuring is inappropriate. This is well illustrated by the legal obstacles currently faced by Argentina in the normal servicing of its restructured sovereign debt.[1] Argentina's experience shows that this framework not only discourages new debt restructuring, but that it may even jeopardize successful past restructurings. Establishing a multilateral structure for dealing with sovereign debt restructuring that would take into consideration general interests, and not just the private ones – a proposal made by UNCTAD two decades ago – appears more pertinent and urgent than ever.

B. International trade

Six years after the onset of the global financial crisis, international trade remains lacklustre. Merchandise trade grew slightly above 2 per cent in volume in 2012–2013 (and was even slower if measured in current dollars), which is below the growth of global output. Trade in services increased somewhat faster, at around 5.5 per cent in 2013 at current prices. This lack of dynamism contrasts sharply with its rapid expansion in the two decades preceding the crisis, when global trade in goods and services expanded more than twice as fast as global output, at annual averages of 6.8 per cent and 3 per cent respectively. During that period, the share of

exports and imports of goods and services in GDP virtually doubled, from around 13 per cent to 27 per cent in developed countries, and from 20 per cent to close to 40 per cent in developing countries.

1. Trade in goods

International trade in goods has remained subdued. Following its post-crisis rebound in 2010, it slowed down to around 2 per cent in 2012 and 2013 (table 1.2). This trend is expected to continue into

Table 1.2

EXPORT AND IMPORT VOLUMES OF GOODS, SELECTED REGIONS AND COUNTRIES, 2010–2013

(Annual percentage change)

Region/country	Volume of exports				Volume of imports			
	2010	2011	2012	2013	2010	2011	2012	2013
World	**13.9**	**5.5**	**2.3**	**2.2**	**13.8**	**5.4**	**2.1**	**2.1**
Developed countries	**12.9**	**4.9**	**0.5**	**1.3**	**10.8**	**3.4**	**-0.4**	**-0.4**
of which:								
Japan	27.5	-0.6	-1.0	-1.8	10.1	4.2	3.8	0.5
United States	15.4	7.2	4.0	2.6	14.8	3.8	2.8	0.9
European Union	11.6	5.5	-0.1	1.4	9.4	2.8	-2.5	-1.2
Transition economies	**11.4**	**4.1**	**1.3**	**1.0**	**17.6**	**16.8**	**5.0**	**2.7**
of which:								
CIS, incl. Georgia	11.3	3.9	1.5	0.3	19.9	17.7	5.8	2.4
Developing countries	**16.0**	**6.7**	**4.6**	**3.4**	**18.5**	**7.7**	**5.3**	**5.5**
Africa	10.3	-6.8	7.8	-1.8	6.5	3.9	11.8	5.6
Sub-Saharan Africa	11.9	0.9	1.2	2.3	6.7	9.3	7.1	8.0
Latin America and the Caribbean	8.1	5.1	3.1	1.5	22.3	11.3	3.1	2.4
East Asia	24.3	10.7	5.3	5.2	22.5	7.7	4.4	7.8
of which:								
China	29.5	13.4	7.4	4.8	25.0	10.7	6.1	8.8
South Asia	11.0	9.4	-7.1	1.9	14.5	5.6	2.9	-0.6
of which:								
India	14.0	15.0	-1.8	7.6	13.8	9.7	5.5	0.1
South-East Asia	10.0	4.7	2.2	4.9	22.0	7.0	6.1	3.8
West Asia	4.2	9.1	9.8	2.2	8.6	8.2	8.7	8.6

Source: UNCTAD secretariat calculations, based on *UNCTADstat*.

2014: UNCTAD-WTO (*UNCTADstat*) estimated that international trade grew at 2 per cent (seasonally-adjusted and annualized rate) in the first quarter of 2014. All regions have experienced a deceleration in their volume of trade in varying degrees, the greatest slowdown being in the developed countries, the transition economies and Latin America.

In 2013, developed countries' imports shrank by 0.4 per cent for the second consecutive year, owing to a contraction of 1.2 per cent in the EU. This is primarily the result of weak intra-EU trade. Japan and the United States also experienced significant slowdowns. EU exports picked up to 1.4 per cent in 2013 due to growth of EU exports to countries outside the region, while those from the United States slowed down to 2.6 per cent. By contrast, Japan's exports contracted further to 1.8 per cent, despite the depreciation of the yen.[2] During the first quarter of 2014, estimated trade volumes for developed economies grew 2.4 per cent, year on year, albeit from a rather low base.

Trade in developing and transition economies also decelerated. The slowdown was particularly acute in the transition economies, owing to weak European demand for their exports, while the growth rate of their imports halved, to 2.7 per cent, as a result of a slowdown in their own GDP growth. In developing countries, the growth of exports weakened further, to 3.4 per cent in 2013, also reflecting weak external demand, in particular from developed economies. A notable exception was developing countries' imports, which have remained resilient, growing at close to 5.5 per cent, due to robust demand in some of their largest economies. In addition, persistently high (although in some cases declining) export prices of commodities allowed some of them (particularly in Africa and West Asia) to increase their imports (by volume) even though the volume of their exports grew at a slower rate. Their higher imports provided some impetus for export growth in other countries.

Within the general trend of a slower growth of trade in developing regions, there is considerable variation. Exports remained weak in Africa in 2013 and the first months of 2014, partly due to the shutting down of two important oil-exporting ports in Libya since July 2013 and to falling exports in South Africa. But during this period, export growth improved in several other sub-Saharan countries whose exports have tended to shift direction towards the faster growing Asian developing countries. Imports remained strong, particularly in the sub-Saharan African countries, where they expanded by 8 per cent in volume, in line with rapid GDP growth in the subregion.

Trade in East Asia decelerated dramatically, from annual growth rates of 20 per cent or more (in volume) during the pre-crisis years to 5–6 per cent in 2012 and 2013. Trade in the Republic of Korea was virtually stagnant in these latter years, as exports were affected by a recession in developed-country markets and by its own currency appreciation. However, much of the slowdown of trade in this subregion reflects the steep fall in the growth rate of Chinese exports to developed countries, from an average of 25 per cent before the Great Recession to a mere 2.5 per cent in 2012 and 2013. As China's trade with developing countries still grows at double-digit rates, at present these account for as much as 53 per cent of China's exports, compared with 42 per cent in 2004. Concomitantly, growth of Chinese imports have also slowed down, although more moderately, to 8.8 per cent in volume in 2013. Nevertheless, China remains a very important market for many developing countries, especially because of the rapidly increasing share of commodities in Chinese imports, which climbed from 18 per cent in 2004 to 31 per cent in 2011–2013.

In South Asia, the rebound in India's exports supported the economic recovery in the region. In particular, the country registered double-digit growth of its exports to some of its largest developing-country partners, such as China and the United Arab Emirates. Exports in the subregion as a whole grew much less, owing to restrictions on trade with the Islamic Republic of Iran.

In South-East Asia, growth in trade remained well below pre-crisis trends, mainly due to virtual stagnation in Thailand and Indonesia, though strong domestic demand, including investment in export-oriented sectors, stimulated trade growth in the Philippines and Viet Nam. In West Asia, internal instabilities and stable oil output significantly slowed export growth.

In Latin America and the Caribbean, the trade volume slowed down significantly to a growth rate of around 2 per cent. Slow GDP growth in its major markets (including the United States and the main intraregional partners) and real exchange rate appreciation affected the region's exports: Brazil's exports stagnated in 2013, and in the rest of South America, the modest growth in the volume of exports was more than offset by the fall in export unit prices, leading to an overall reduction in the total value of exports. A moderate increase in Mexico's exports somewhat tempered the reduction in the surplus in the balance of goods trade, from 0.9 to 0.3 per cent of GDP (ECLAC, 2014).

2. Services

Global exports of services expanded at around 5.5 per cent in 2013 (at current prices), and at about 7 per cent in the first quarter of 2014, compared with the same period of the previous year. It reached $4.7 trillion in 2013, representing 20 per cent of total exports of goods and services – a share that has been quite stable since the early 1990s.

The evolution of trade in services tends to be more stable than that of goods, as it reacts less abruptly to the economic situation. Its growth rate, which exceeded that of goods in 2012, 2013 and the first months of 2014, partly reflects its greater resilience to the slowdown in global output, but it may also be evidence of some structural factors that contribute to expanding trade in services. Among the most dynamic services sectors between 2008 and 2013 were computer and information services (with an average annual growth of 9.1 per cent), followed by personal, cultural and recreational services (8.9 per cent), and then by other business and professional services (6.8 per cent). The computer and information services sector in developing economies recorded the highest growth rates: 13 per cent on average annually since 2008, compared with 7.5 per cent in developed countries. Financial and insurance services are other fast-growing areas in developing countries, with an average annual increase of almost 11 per cent. Exports of these modern services also grew rapidly in the least developed countries (LDCs), although from very low levels. Since 2008, computer and information services, insurance services and construction in LDCs have recorded an average annual increase of close to 30 per cent. However, together they represented just 7 per cent of LDCs' total exports of services in 2013.

The two major components of world trade in services remain tourism and transport services. Exports in tourism generated earnings of $1.4 trillion in 2013. Receipts from international visitors grew 5 per cent (in constant dollars), exceeding its long-term trend. Tourist arrivals also grew by 5 per cent in 2013, to reach 1,087 million persons. Europe and Asia and the Pacific accounted for 42 per cent and 31 per cent of all international tourism receipts, respectively (World Tourism Organization, 2014). Tourism flows appear to be unaffected by slow economic growth, which may indicate participation by a larger proportion of the world's population, particularly from developing countries with a growing middle class. Of the $81 billion increase in international tourism expenditure in 2013, Brazil, China and the Russian Federation accounted for $40 billion.

International transport services – the second largest category of commercial services – also posted a positive but declining growth in 2013. Preliminary data indicate that world seaborne trade – a measure of demand for shipping, port and logistics services – increased by 3.8 per cent in 2013, compared with 4.7 per cent in 2012 (UNCTAD, 2014). This growth resulted from a 5.5 per cent increase in dry cargo shipping (including containerized trade and commodities carried in bulk), which accounts for 70 per cent of total shipping. Tanker trade, which constitutes the remaining 30 per cent, was flat compared with 2012 (Clarkson Research Services, 2014).

Developing countries continued to contribute larger shares to international seaborne trade. In terms of global goods loaded, their share increased from 60 per cent in 2012 to 61 per cent in 2013. Meanwhile, their import demand, as measured by the volume of goods unloaded, increased from 58 per cent to 60 per cent. These figures reflect growing South-South/intra-Asian trade, developing countries' increasing participation in the world trading system, and their rising consumption of commodities and consumption goods.

Developing countries have traditionally registered higher loaded volumes than unloaded ones owing to their supply of raw materials to developed economies. However, this trend has been changing over the years since developing countries have started to account for larger shares of imports (unloading). Thus, in these countries unloaded goods are steadily catching up with loaded ones, becoming almost on a par in 2013. This mirrors developing countries' urbanization process, their growing population and their emerging middle class, as well as the internationalization of supply chains and production processes. Nevertheless, the balance between loaded and unloaded volumes at regional levels remains uneven, and skewed to the loaded side in Africa, Latin America and the Caribbean and West Asia.

3. Trade and growth

Slow output growth is the main reason for virtually stagnant trade, especially in goods. Subdued international trade, in turn, is likely to hamper global economic growth in the long run, to the extent that the lower incidence of scale economies and specialization gains holds back the productivity frontier. Expanding trade should therefore be an important component of a process aimed at strong, sustainable and balanced growth. This, in part, is the logic behind efforts to conclude a development-friendly round of multilateral trade negotiations launched in 2001 in Doha. At the end of 2013, a multilateral framework on Trade Facilitation was reached at the IXth WTO Ministerial Conference in Bali to boost the multilateral trading system, and as a stepping stone to closing the more comprehensive Doha package. However, that agreement was not adopted by the membership in Geneva by the proposed deadline of 31 July. Given the insufficiency of global demand, it is anyway unlikely that international trade alone will be able to kick-start economic growth. Whatever the desirability of facilitating trade flows by modernizing customs procedures or further lowering tariffs, these would not, by themselves, be able to significantly change the situation, since they do not address the immediate main constraints on trade. International trade has not decelerated or come to a virtual standstill because of higher trade barriers or supply-side difficulties; its slow growth is the result of weak global demand. In this context, a lopsided emphasis on the cost of trade, prompting efforts to spur exports through wage reductions and an "internal devaluation", would be self-defeating and counterproductive, especially if such a strategy is pursued by several trade partners simultaneously.

The way to expand trade globally is through a robust domestic-demand-led output recovery; not the other way round. Moreover, if an individual country or group of countries were to try an exit from the crisis through net exports, this strategy would create a fallacy of composition if followed by many trading partners. A wider revival of economic growth and trade could conceivably follow from surging demand in a number of systemically important economies. However, demand must also be geographically distributed in a way that is consistent with the reduction of global imbalances. This requires that surplus countries take the lead in expanding domestic demand, so as to enable an expansionary adjustment, in contrast

with the recessionary bias of balance-of-payments adjustments, which, typically, place the entire burden on deficit countries.

Therefore, countries cannot passively wait for external sources of demand to revive growth. In the post-crisis environment, where there is less dynamic demand from developed economies, developing countries need to adopt a balanced approach that gives a larger role to domestic and regional demand and to South-South trade than in the past (*TDR 2013*). If many trading partners encourage domestic demand simultaneously, they would also be supporting each other's exports and the recovery of international trade. At the same time, production capacities should be expanded and adapted to the new demand pattern through appropriate, proactive industrial policies.

C. Recent developments in commodity markets

In 2013 and early 2014, most commodity prices continued their declining trend after their peaks reached in 2011, although the decline was at a slower pace than in 2012. The price of crude oil was a notable exception, since it has been relatively stable since 2011. In the second quarter of 2014, there appear to have been signs of stabilization, and even a recovery, in the prices of a number of commodities. In the tropical beverages and vegetable oilseeds and oils commodity groups, the price rebound began a few months earlier (chart 1.1). What is more, during the period 2012–2014 most commodity prices stayed, on average, at substantially higher levels than the average levels of the boom period of 2003–2008 (table 1.3). Prices of many commodities are still at levels close to their peaks of 2008.

While recent developments in commodity prices have differed by commodity group and for particular commodities, a common feature in the physical markets is that supply-side factors have played a predominant role in those developments. There are indications that changes in physical commodity demand factors had only a small influence on

the evolution of commodity prices in 2013 and early 2014. In general, demand for commodities continued to grow, although modestly because of the sluggish growth of the world economy. Contrary to widespread belief, the slowdown in the growth of China's GDP during this period does not seem to have made a major dent in global demand growth for many commodities.[3] Indeed, Chinese demand remained robust for most commodities in 2013, and there are indications that it is holding up in 2014, partly due to its Government's stimulus measures. A case in point is that of copper: there was a 12.2 per cent increase in refined copper consumption in China in 2012, with only a slight deceleration to 11.2 per cent in 2013, whereas worldwide refined copper consumption, increased by 4.8 per cent in 2013, compared with a 2.6 per cent rise in 2012 (Cochilco, 2014). However, it is not quite clear how much of the demand for copper in China is for actual consumption and how much is kept in bonded warehouses as collateral for financing deals.

Crude oil prices continued to oscillate within a narrow band in continuation of the trend they had exhibited since 2011. Between mid-2013 and mid-2014, the highest price of the monthly average of United Kingdom Brent (light), Dubai (medium) and Texas (heavy) equally weighted crude oil was $108.8 per barrel in September 2013, while the lowest price was $102.3 per barrel in January 2014. Nevertheless, there were signs of increased volatility during the second quarter of 2014 as geopolitical tensions in West Asia and in Ukraine raised risk perceptions in energy markets.[4] This volatility seems to be related more to market sentiment than to real production effects, as no significant disruption in production associated with these tensions had occurred by July 2014.

In general, the oil market was well supplied in 2013 and the first half of 2014, mainly due to increased production in the United States linked to the shale oil and gas boom. This has compensated for oil supply disruptions in other producing countries, such as the Islamic Republic of Iran, Libya, Nigeria and South Sudan (AIECE, 2014). Members of the Organization of the Petroleum Exporting Countries (OPEC) continue to play an important role in global markets, as reflected in the perceived impact of the tensions in the West Asian region. However, larger non-OPEC supplies have helped buffer the effect of those pressures. Indeed, only a few years ago similar events would most likely have led to substantial oil price hikes, while this time, although some volatility has emerged, price movements have been contained. After oil prices increased with the intensification of the conflict in Iraq, they fell back in response to indications that Libyan supply would return to the market soon. However, the supply picture remains uncertain and depends very much on the evolution of geopolitical conditions in some major producing countries. As for the demand side, growth of demand for oil continues to be driven by non-OECD countries, where it remained robust in 2013, at 3.1 per cent, with demand from China increasing by 3.8 per cent. However, there was no growth in demand for oil in OECD countries (BP, 2014).

Agricultural commodity prices have continued to display a high degree of volatility (Mayer, 2014). Their evolution has been strongly determined by weather conditions which have favoured or curtailed production, depending on the type of commodity. For food commodities, price developments have differed significantly by commodity group. In the case of cereals, bumper crops as a result of favourable weather conditions led to lower prices and healthy

Chart 1.1

MONTHLY COMMODITY PRICE INDICES BY COMMODITY GROUP, JAN. 2002–JUNE 2014

(Index numbers, 2002 = 100)

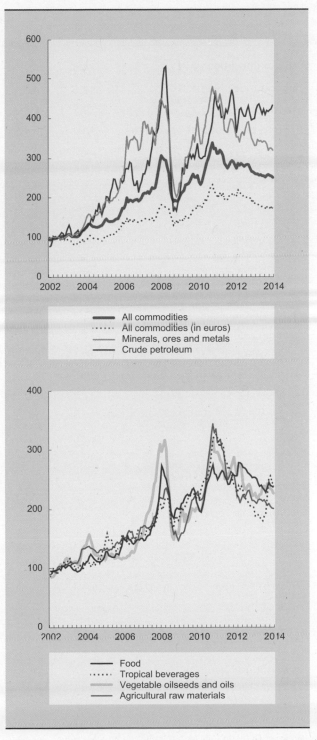

Source: UNCTAD secretariat calculations, based on UNCTAD *Commodity Price Statistics Online* database.

Note: Crude petroleum price is the average of Dubai/Brent/West Texas Intermediate, equally weighted. Index numbers are based on prices in current dollars, unless otherwise specified.

Table 1.3

WORLD PRIMARY COMMODITY PRICES, 2008–2014

(Percentage change over previous year, unless otherwise indicated)

Commodity groups	2008	2009	2010	2011	2012	2013	2014[a]	2012–2014 versus 2003–2008[b]
All commodities[c]	**24.0**	**-16.9**	**20.4**	**17.9**	**-8.3**	**-6.7**	**-3.9**	**55.6**
All commodities (in SDRs)[c]	**19.5**	**-14.5**	**21.7**	**14.1**	**-5.5**	**-6.0**	**-5.3**	**53.3**
All food	**39.2**	**-8.5**	**7.4**	**17.8**	**-1.4**	**-7.4**	**-2.0**	**68.8**
Food and tropical beverages	**40.4**	**-5.4**	**5.6**	**16.5**	**-0.4**	**-6.7**	**-2.5**	**70.8**
Tropical beverages	20.2	1.9	17.5	26.8	-21.5	-18.3	20.5	50.9
Coffee	15.4	-6.9	27.3	42.9	-25.7	-23.6	25.5	58.5
Cocoa	32.2	11.9	8.5	-4.9	-19.7	2.0	23.7	38.8
Tea	27.2	16.5	-1.0	11.4	0.8	-23.9	-11.5	31.9
Food	42.5	-6.0	4.4	15.4	2.0	-5.7	-4.3	72.8
Sugar	26.9	41.8	17.3	22.2	-17.1	-17.9	-1.8	86.1
Beef	2.6	-1.2	27.5	20.0	2.6	-2.3	5.5	64.2
Maize	34.0	-24.4	13.2	50.1	2.6	-12.1	-16.0	93.3
Wheat	27.5	-31.4	3.3	35.1	-0.1	-1.9	-0.8	51.6
Rice	110.7	-15.8	-11.5	5.9	5.1	-10.6	-18.1	52.2
Bananas	24.6	0.7	3.7	10.8	0.9	-5.9	1.3	55.2
Vegetable oilseeds and oils	**31.9**	**-28.4**	**22.7**	**27.2**	**-7.6**	**-12.6**	**2.1**	**55.1**
Soybeans	36.1	-16.6	3.1	20.2	9.4	-7.9	-1.7	66.7
Agricultural raw materials	**20.5**	**-17.5**	**38.3**	**28.1**	**-23.0**	**-7.4**	**-5.4**	**44.5**
Hides and skins	-11.3	-30.0	60.5	14.0	1.4	13.9	14.8	37.1
Cotton	12.8	-12.2	65.3	47.5	-41.8	1.5	3.2	46.2
Tobacco	8.3	18.0	1.8	3.8	-3.9	6.3	10.7	51.7
Rubber	16.9	-27.0	90.3	32.0	-30.5	-16.7	-21.8	62.4
Tropical logs	39.3	-20.6	1.8	13.8	-7.4	2.6	3.5	27.4
Minerals, ores and metals	**6.2**	**-30.3**	**41.3**	**14.7**	**-14.1**	**-5.1**	**-6.8**	**38.9**
Aluminium	-2.5	-35.3	30.5	10.4	-15.8	-8.6	-5.0	-11.3
Phosphate rock	387.2	-64.8	1.1	50.3	0.5	-20.3	-27.6	59.9
Iron ore	26.8	-48.7	82.4	15.0	-23.4	5.3	-17.6	10.1
Tin	27.3	-26.7	50.4	28.0	-19.2	5.7	2.7	110.4
Copper	-2.3	-26.3	47.0	17.1	-9.9	-7.8	-5.6	54.4
Nickel	-43.3	-30.6	48.9	5.0	-23.4	-14.3	10.2	-18.9
Lead	-19.0	-17.7	25.0	11.8	-14.2	3.9	-1.9	51.3
Zinc	-42.2	-11.7	30.5	1.5	-11.2	-1.9	7.4	0.6
Gold	25.1	11.6	26.1	27.8	6.4	-15.4	-8.5	163.7
Crude petroleum[d]	**36.4**	**-36.3**	**28.0**	**31.4**	**1.0**	**-0.9**	**0.9**	**78.1**
Memo item:								
Manufactures[e]	4.9	-5.6	1.9	10.3	-2.2	1.7	..	..

Source: UNCTAD secretariat calculations, based on UNCTAD, *Commodity Price Statistics Online* database; and United Nations Statistics Division (UNSD), *Monthly Bulletin of Statistics*, various issues.

Note: In current dollars unless otherwise specified.

   a Percentage change between the average for the period January to May 2014 and the average for 2013.
   b Percentage change between the 2003–2008 average and the 2012–2014 average.
   c Excluding crude petroleum. SDRs = special drawing rights.
   d Average of Brent, Dubai and West Texas Intermediate, equally weighted.
   e Unit value of exports of manufactured goods of developed countries.

levels of inventories. The situation in the rice market is highly dependent on the evolution of the Thai Government's rice reserves. Overall, ample supplies and weaker grain prices in 2013 helped improve the world food security situation; the United States Department of Agriculture (USDA, 2014a) projects that in 2014 the number of food-insecure people will fall by 9 per cent, to 490 million, in the 76 low- and middle-income countries it considers. The greatest decline of all the regions is expected to be in sub-Saharan Africa, where the number of food-insecure people is projected to fall by close to 13 per cent. Nevertheless, in early 2014, cereal markets were upset by some weather-related supply concerns, as well as by geopolitical tensions in the Black Sea region. This led to a temporary rebound in prices of wheat and maize, as there was increasing uncertainty about the impact of the conflict on cereal production in this major producing and exporting region. Dry weather in South America also led to increases in soybean prices in late 2013 and early 2014, in a context of solid growth of soybean consumption in China.

By contrast, the more recent price increases in the group of tropical beverages (chart 1.1) are mainly related to unfavourable weather conditions resulting in reduced harvests; for example, coffee prices surged due to dry weather in Brazil.[5] Similarly, cocoa production was affected by crop conditions in major producing countries in West Africa. As for sugar, weather-related production shortages in Brazil and increased demand contributed to the recent surge in prices, after a sharp decline in 2012−2013. Regarding agricultural raw materials, cotton prices were supported mainly by the stockpiling policy of China, which holds about 60 per cent of global cotton inventories (ICAC, 2014). The price of natural rubber fell due to plentiful supply.

The price index of the group of minerals, ores and metals exhibited the most pronounced declining trend in 2011−2013 (chart 1.1). This price deterioration was mainly due to moderate demand growth in a context of increasing supplies in response to the investments made during the period of rapidly increasing prices.[6] As a result, most metals markets have been in a surplus situation. In particular, abundant supplies in the copper market have continued to exert downward pressure on prices. Nonetheless, there have been price reversals in some metals in 2014. For nickel, a mineral ore export ban in Indonesia, a major producing and exporting country,

reduced global supplies, leading to a sharp increase in prices. Concerns on nickel supplies from the Russian Federation have also played a role. The price of aluminium also soared in the first half of 2014, primarily due to reduced supply as smelters shut down production following the low level of prices in 2012−2013. Renewed investor interest has added to these upward pressures on prices (see below).[7] In the precious metals group, gold prices bounced back slightly in early 2014, thanks to increased demand for it as a safe haven following geopolitical tensions in different parts of the world. However, physical demand remained weak. The prices of the platinum-group metals also rose as a result of strikes in the mining sector in South Africa, which is a major producing country together with the Russian Federation.

As in previous years, short-term developments in commodity prices continued to be influenced by the high degree of financialization of commodity markets during 2013 and the first half of 2014. Investments in commodities as a financial asset can take different forms, and for some of these, data are not readily available for providing an overall indication of magnitude. Thus the evolution of financial investments in commodities cannot be properly captured by a single variable. Nevertheless, as an illustration, Barclays' data[8] on commodity assets under management (AUM) indicated a marked drop in 2013. The decline of financial positions in commodity exchanges may have contributed to a weakening of commodity prices. Still, total AUM have remained at very high levels. After a sharp fall in the second half of 2008 following the onset of the global financial crisis, AUM had strongly recovered, reaching a peak of $448 billion in April 2011 (up from a trough of $156 billion in November 2008). The average AUM for January to May 2014 was $321 billion, which is significantly higher than the average of the same period in 2008, at $236 billion. The latter period of commodity price spikes prompted increased questioning about the role of financial investors in commodity markets. During the first half of 2014 there was some stabilization in the level of AUM, which may reflect a revival of investor interest in commodities as a financial asset. This interest has been fuelled by increased price volatility, improving returns on commodities and lower correlations with other financial assets, which encourage portfolio diversification. By 20 June 2014, Deutsche Bank (2014b) noted that commodities had been the world's best performing asset class since the end of 2013.[9]

In the first half of 2014 there were some episodes when investors may have contributed to amplifying commodity price movements beyond what would be warranted by supply and demand fundamentals. This may partly explain the price increases of cereals early in the year, following geopolitical tensions in the Black Sea region. Financial positions in wheat and maize on the Chicago Board of Trade rose strongly during the first four months of 2014 (Mayer, 2014). However, grain production was not affected by those tensions, as had been feared, and financial investors unwound their positions. Another example was the rapid decline in copper prices as a result of a copper sell-off in early March 2014 (AIECE, 2014). This was prompted by uncertainties about the possibility of an unwinding of inventories in China due to prospects of tightening credit conditions which could affect the use of copper as collateral in financing deals. Similarly, by mid-July 2014 big speculators slashed their long crude oil futures and options positions in what was the second largest decline since the United States Commodity Futures Trading Commission began reporting these data in 2009. Changes in position-taking most likely contributed to the gyrations in oil prices in June and July 2014, owing to uncertainties in oil production in connection with geopolitical tensions in Ukraine and West Asia.[10]

In a context of diminishing returns on commodities in 2013,[11] associated with declining prices and stricter financial regulations, including larger capital requirements, a number of major banks involved in commodity futures trading have either withdrawn from this activity or scaled it back substantially. However, this should not lead to the premature conclusion that financialization of commodity futures markets is no longer an influencing factor or an issue of concern for commodity price developments. Indeed, some other major banks have intensified their financial activity in this domain.[12] Moreover, trading in commodity futures does not stop as banks exit it; the banks basically sell their commodity units to other agents. There are indications that commodity trading companies are intensifying their participation in commodity futures trading. For example, the commodity trading firm Mercuria acquired the commodities unit of JP Morgan Chase.[13] As these commodity trading firms operate in a relatively less transparent and regulated environment than banks, this may create additional difficulties when considering possible regulation of the financialized commodity futures markets. In addition, media reports note that some

Chinese banks are also moving into this activity.[14] According to Futures Industry (2014) the Chinese commodity futures markets showed explosive growth in 2013, with the number of contracts traded on exchanges up 38.9 per cent from 2012. Furthermore, it is not only financial agents apart from banks, but also other actors, such as major commodity producing companies, that are entering this business; for example, Rosneft, the State-controlled oil enterprise of the Russian Federation, acquired the oil trading unit of Morgan Stanley in December 2013.

The progressively more entangled environment for commodity futures trading suggests that regulating the financialized commodity markets remains as relevant as ever. In considering regulation, this activity should be looked at in a broad sense, examining not just the agents that run the business, but also the kinds of financial activities. Furthermore, in order to prevent the commodity futures trading from moving to different locations where regulations might be weaker or absent, regulations should be global in scope and coverage.

Short-term prospects for commodity prices remain highly uncertain in view of the erratic global economic recovery and geopolitical tensions in different commodity-producing regions. Supply conditions, involving the emergence of new supplies, may continue to exert downward pressure on prices. In particular, there are expectations of another year of good crop conditions for maize and soybeans as a result of a successful planting season and higher yields in the United States.[15] However, the supply of agricultural commodities risks being negatively affected by unfavourable weather conditions associated with the "El Niño" phenomenon in the second half of 2014.[16] On the demand side, much depends on the evolution of the emerging market economies – particularly China – where commodity demand is more dynamic.

From a longer term perspective, the conclusion of the analysis of *TDR 2013* that commodity prices are set to remain high in historical terms, after some short-term corrections, remains valid. This is supported by recent studies by the World Bank and the IMF. According to Canuto (2014: 1), "it may be too soon to say that the commodities super-cycle phenomenon is a thing of the past"; and the IMF (2014b: 36) finds that "China's commodity consumption is unlikely to have peaked at current levels of income per capita". ◾

Notes

---

1 After defaulting on part of its external debt in December 2001, Argentina restructured 92.4 per cent of it with two debt swaps (2005 and 2010). It has, since, regularly serviced the new bonds. Part of the restructured debt was issued under the jurisdiction of the State of New York. A small number of institutional investors – so-called "vulture funds" – acquired part of the remaining bonds with deep discount and sought to obtain its full face value by filling a suit at the Southern District Court of New York. Based on an unprecedented interpretation of the *pari passu* clause of the debt contracts, a federal judge ruled not only that Argentina had to pay the full amount claimed by the vulture funds but he also forbade any new payments on the restructured 92.4 per cent of the debt unless the vulture funds were paid concurrently or in advance. The ruling was upheld by the Appeals Court of New York, and the Supreme Court declined to hear Argentina's request to review the case. On 30 June 2014, Argentina made a due payment of $539 million through the usual channel, the Bank of New York Mellon. But under the order of the New York District Court judge, that bank did not transfer the money to their owners, the exchange holders. The judge did not agree either to extend the "stay" that allowed bondholders to receive the payments while Argentina negotiated the means for paying the $1,350 million claimed by the vulture funds. Argentina needed to delay any agreement that would offer better conditions to the vulture funds, because the restructured debt has a clause ("rights upon future offers" – RUFO) which stipulates that if Argentina offered better conditions to any creditor in the future, those conditions would extend to all creditors agreeing to restructure their claims in 2005 and 2010. This RUFO clause is due to end on 31 December 2014, but the New York court has so far refused to allow any delay in the implementation of its ruling. This could cancel the successful debt restructurings of 2005 and 2010 and oblige Argentina to disburse more than $120 billion. See UNCTAD News Item on "Argentina's 'vulture fund' crisis threatens profound consequences for international financial system" (25 June 2014), available at: http://unctad.org/en/ pages/newsdetails.aspx?OriginalVersionID=783& Sitemap_x0020_Taxonomy=UNCTAD Home.

2 One explanation for the lack of exchange rate elasticity of Japanese exports is that the share of consumer durables (whose demand is price-elastic) in its exports has halved since the late 1980s, to about 15 per cent at present, while capital goods and industrial materials now account for about 80 per cent of Japan's export volumes. It might well be that Japan's exports will only increase when global investment recovers.

3 See IMF, 2014b, chart 1.2.2.

4 The potential impact on commodity markets of geopolitical tensions over Ukraine is analysed in more detail in IMF, 2014a; AIECE, 2014; and Deutsche Bank, 2014a.

5 Coffee crops in Central America were also damaged by disease (IMF, 2014a).

6 Data from SNL Metals & Mining (2014) show that worldwide metals and mining exploration budgets totalled $13.75 billion in 2008, up 677 per cent from the bottom of the cycle in 2002. While they dropped considerably after the global financial crisis in 2008, they quickly recovered to reach a record $20.53 billion in 2012. However, in 2013 they fell by 30 per cent. This may point to tighter metal supplies in the years to come.

7 See also, *Financial Times*, "Copper confounds bears with strong gains", 3 July 2014.

8 Data provided by Barclays (personal communication).

9 See also *Financial Times*, "Base metals return to investors' radar", 9 July 2014; Reuters, "Commodity investor inflows rebound as sector outperforms shares", 17 April 2014; *Financial Times*, "Sun finally shines on commodities", 30 June 2014; Reuters, "Rallies in energy, metals boost commodity funds in Q2-Lipper", 11 July 2014; and Reuters, "Investors swap grains for metals as flows trickle to commodities", 21 July 2014.

10 See Reuters, "Big funds slash oil bets by nearly $6 bln in biggest exodus-CFTC", 21 July 2014; *Futures Magazine*, "Crude specs cut off guard", 21 July 2014; and *Financial Times*, "Speculators cut bets on higher oil prices", 21 July 2014.

11   According to data from the business intelligence provider, Coalition, quoted in media reports, the revenues of the top 10 banks from commodities dropped by 18 per cent in 2013 to $4.5 billion, down from the record of over $14 billion they had reached in 2008, at the height of the commodity prices boom. See Reuters, "Major banks' commodities revenue slid 18 per cent in 2013", 18 February 2014; and Reuters, "Major banks' Q1 commodities revenue up 1st time since 2011", 19 May 2014.

12   See Reuters, "Amid frigid Winter, Goldman, Morgan Stanley see commodity gains", 17 April 2014; Bloomberg, "Goldman Sachs stands firm as banks exit commodity trading", 23 April, 2014; and *Financial Times*, "Goldman seeks commodities edge as rivals retreat", 15 July 2014.

13   See Financial Conduct Authority (2014); and *Financial Times*, "Banks' retreat empowers commodity trading houses", 31 March 2014.

14   See *Business Insider*, "Chinese banks are jumping into a business that Western banks are dropping left and right", 21 January 2014.

15   For projections on agricultural supply, see USDA (2014b). FAO (2014) also looks at short-term prospects of the world food situation.

16   The United States National Oceanic and Atmospheric Administration gives a 70 per cent probability for it to happen (World Bank, 2014).

References

AIECE (2014). *World Trade and Commodity Prices in 2014-2015*. Associations d'instituts européens de conjoncture économique. Louvain-la-Neuve. Working Group on Commodity Prices and Foreign Trade.

BP (2014). *Statistical Review of World Energy 2014*. London.

Canuto O (2014). The commodity super cycle: Is this time different? World Bank Economic Premise 150, Washington, DC.

Clarkson Research Services (2014). Dry Bulk Trade Outlook. London, Clarkson Research Services Limited, June.

Cochilco (2014). *Anuario de Estadísticas del Cobre 1994-2013*. Comisión Chilena del Cobre. Santiago, Chile.

Deutsche Bank (2014a). Ukraine & Global Commodities. Special Report. Deutsche Bank Markets Research, Frankfurt am Main, 3 March.

Deutsche Bank (2014b). *Commodities Weekly*. Deutsche Bank Markets Research, Frankfurt am Main, 20 June.

ECLAC (2014). Balance Económico Actualizado de América Latina y el Caribe 2013. Santiago, Chile, April.

FAO (2014). Crop Prospects and Food Situation. Rome, July.

Financial Conduct Authority (2014). *Commodity Markets Update*, London, February.

Futures Industry (2014). *FIA Annual Volume Survey*. Futures Industry Association. Washington, DC, June.

ICAC (2014). World prices high despite excess production. International Cotton Advisory Committee, Press Release, 13 February; available at: https://www.icac.org/Press-Release/2014/PR-3.

IMF (2014a). *Quarterly Review of Commodity Markets*, 2014 Q2. Washington, DC.

IMF (2014b). Special Feature: Commodity prices and forecasts. In: *World Economic Outlook 2014*. Washington, DC, April.

Mayer J (2014). Food security and food price volatility. In: Kathuria R and Nagpal NK, eds. *Global Economic Cooperation - Views from G20 Countries*. New Delhi, Springer (India), forthcoming.

OECD (2014). *Economic Outlook* No 95, May.

SNL Metals & Mining (2014). World Exploration Trends 2014. A Special Report from SNL Metals & Mining, for the PDAC International Convention, available at: http://go.snl.com/rs/snlfinanciallc/images/WETReport_0114.pdf.

UNCTAD (2014). *Review of Maritime Transport 2014*. United Nations publication, Geneva, forthcoming.

UNCTAD (*TDR 2013*). *Trade and Development Report, 2013. Adjusting to the changing dynamics of the world economy*. United Nations publication, sales no. E.13.II.D.3, New York and Geneva.

USDA (2014a). International food security assessment, 2014-2024. Washington, DC, United States Department of Agriculture, June.

USDA (2014b). World agricultural supply and demand estimates. Washington, DC, 11 July.

World Bank (2014). Commodity Markets Outlook. Global Economic Prospects. July, available at: http://www.worldbank.org/content/dam/Worldbank/GEP/GEPcommodities/commodity_markets_outlook_2014_july.pdf.

World Tourism Organization (2014). *UNWTO World Tourism Barometer*, vol.12. Madrid, April.

Chapter II

TOWARDS A SUSTAINED ECONOMIC RECOVERY: REVIEW OF POLICY OPTIONS

This chapter examines some of the main macro-economic policy stances in developed and developing countries and their policy options. It shows that not only is the recovery of global growth since the financial crisis rather weak, but also its drivers are inadequate. Indeed, in several major economies, policies intended to spur the recovery are similar to those that led to the latest global crisis in the first place, which raises justifiable doubts about the sustainability of the modest GDP growth attained so far. The chapter then undertakes an empirical modelling exercise to highlight the possible consequences of current policies, and offers an alternative set of policy options. This methodology helps to highlight issues of consistency (or the lack of it) between diverse policies applied at the national level, as well as the interrelationships between the outcomes of those policies in different countries and regions.

Section A analyses the policy approaches adopted by developed and developing countries. These policies consist of a varied mix of wage compression, reduced public sector spending, and a heavy reliance on liquidity expansion that causes asset appreciations and debt bubbles, especially in developed countries. While such policies may contribute to faster growth in a subset of countries in the short run, such a pattern of expansion sows the seeds of a future crisis. To the extent that labour incomes do not increase and public sector services and social protection are cut back, there can be no solid growth of real demand to fully absorb the additional liquidity created by expansionary monetary policies. To date, most of the extra liquidity has flowed instead into speculative activity or moved abroad. Policymaking in developing countries is further challenged by these trends, which have either distorted prices or shifted resource allocations away from primary development goals. Altogether, risks of a hard-landing are increasing, and if this occurs, it could have strong negative effects on global demand and financial stability.

Section B assesses this configuration of policies with the help of the United Nations Global Policy Model (GPM), and evaluates the macroeconomic implications for the medium term. It measures the impact of current policies on growth, demand, financial stability of the public and private sectors, and external balances. The modelling framework is then used to examine the impact of a different set of policy choices that replicate some of the more favourable conditions that prevailed not so long ago. This hypothetical exercise demonstrates that coordinated incomes policies which would restore the patterns of distribution of the mid-1990s, combined with supportive fiscal policies and investment promotion policies, could deliver a robust, sustained and more balanced growth performance than a baseline which assumes a prolongation of current policy stances.

A. Policy threats to a global economic recovery

To many observers, the improvement, albeit small, of the growth performance of some of the major economies in 2013 came as a pleasant surprise. That momentum is expected to continue through 2014. Meanwhile, projections for some developing and transition economies suggest that growth is likely to be slower than expected, but nevertheless considerably faster than in most developed economies. Overall, there is likely to be some improvement in global growth performance in 2014. At an initial glance, this would appear to be a welcome trend, but a deeper look at the nature of this growth revival raises concerns. The analysis that follows suggests that the recent growth in a number of important economies may not be based on sound policies. Thus, even if the current pace is maintained for some time, vulnerability to financial shocks persists, due to a repeat of the policy failings that led to the 2008 global crisis.

1. Policy stances in the developed world

(a) Synchronized premature fiscal contractions

In most developed economies, there was a sharp turnaround of fiscal policy in 2010, with the apparent withdrawal of fiscal stimuli, but which was effectively a contraction of government spending (chart 2.1). The chart shows the differences in real government spending on goods and services between the second quarter of 2010 and the last quarter of 2013, as a per cent of real 2010 Q2 GDP (thus reflecting the cumulative contribution of government spending to GDP growth). However, this may not be the ideal measure, since it assumes that zero growth of government spending is a neutral stance. In fact, after extraordinary measures, such as a fiscal stimulus, are

removed, a truly neutral stance would be to return to a "normal" growth path of real spending, which can be estimated in the form of a long-term trend.[1] Hence, chart 2.1 also compares the actual value of real government spending with what could have resulted if government spending had followed its long-term pace of growth, which is a more meaningful indication of the degree of the fiscal adjustment from mid-2010.

Chart 2.1 confirms that the most pronounced cases of fiscal austerity have been in the peripheral countries of the euro area. The negligible size of the European budget and the reluctance of the European Central Bank (ECB) to assume the role of lender of last resort affected the degree and timing of fiscal adjustments in these countries. Due to such institutional flaws, national governments had to absorb the costs of the crisis, in many cases leaving them little alternative but to subsequently squeeze public spending. By the last quarter of 2013, real government spending on goods and services in Greece, Ireland, Italy, Portugal, Slovakia and Spain was below the level of 2010, showing shortfalls in the range of roughly 1 per cent to 2.5 per cent of GDP over this period (2010 Q2–2013 Q4). Comparing these observed patterns with the long-term trend of government spending, the implied adjustment turns out to be more than twice those figures. Other economies in the euro area also changed their fiscal stance. Even if government spending in real terms remained close to the levels of 2010, when compared with the long-term trend, almost all these other economies effectively adopted a contractionary fiscal stance from 2010 Q2 to the end of 2013.

Several developed economies outside the euro area followed a similar path, prompted by the threat that fiscal deficits, whatever their cause, may be viewed as a sign of economic "indiscipline" and result in credit downgrades. It was feared that such downgrades might cause stampedes by concerned investors. Among these economies, a closer examination of the United Kingdom and the United States can offer some useful pointers. In the former, the fiscal stimulus adopted to avert a deeper recession after the financial crisis was reversed prematurely, causing a second recession. Initially, a recovery in exports helped weather the recession, but that recovery turned out to be short-lived. A moderate relaxation of the fiscal stance eventually followed in response to the weak growth performance. The cumulative effect of government spending from 2010 Q2 to 2013 Q4 accounted for a mere 0.6 per cent of GDP, and by the end of that period, real GDP in the United Kingdom remained below the level of 2007.[2]

In the United States, adjustments imposed upon financially stretched state and local governments started in 2009 Q4,[3] followed in 2010 by cuts in federal spending in the wake of discussions on the debt ceiling. Contributions of real spending to GDP growth by the government sector as a whole have been consistently negative since 2010 Q3, amounting to a cumulative negative contribution of 1.6 per cent by 2013 Q4. Compared with the long-term trend, there was a cumulative gap in real government spending of more than 3 per cent of real GDP from 2010 Q2 to 2013 Q4.

On the whole, governments in developed countries adopted contractionary fiscal stances from mid-2010 to the end of 2013, when compared with the long-term trend. Only Japan and France maintained the trend growth of spending over this period. The case of Japan is revealing. It experienced a long deflationary period before being adversely affected first by the global crisis and subsequently by the earthquake of 2011. The Government's adoption of strong monetary and fiscal stimuli over the past two years (referred to as "Abenomics") has met with some success so far. Domestic demand has been a more important driver of Japan's GDP growth than its net exports, which in turn implies a positive effect on global demand. This is the kind of adjustment that should be expected from a surplus country to help avoid a global deflationary trap.

Finally, in Sweden and Switzerland public spending increased above the trend after 2010, which is consistent with their slightly better growth performance compared with most EU countries.

Chart 2.1

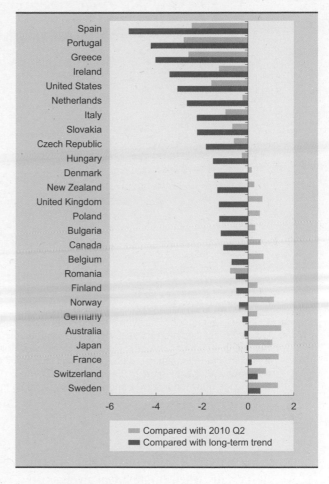

CHANGE IN REAL GOVERNMENT EXPENDITURE, SELECTED DEVELOPED COUNTRIES, 2010 Q2–2013 Q4

(Per cent of real 2010 Q2 GDP)

Source: UNCTAD secretariat calculations, based on Economist Intelligence Unit (EIU), *CountryData* database.

Note: Long-term trend is estimated by applying from 2010 Q2 onwards the average expenditure growth of the period 1997 Q1–2010 Q2.

(b) Mercantilist race to increase exports

In the aftermath of the financial crisis it is normal to expect subdued spending by households, which were affected by a fall in asset values and heavy debt burdens. This narrows the options for policymakers in attempting to revive aggregate demand. But if public sector demand is also suppressed, the only remaining alternatives are net export recovery or a revival of "animal spirits" that trigger a push in private investment.[4] Unless households' balance

Chart 2.2

**CHANGES IN REAL UNIT LABOUR COSTS AND EXPORTS,
SELECTED EUROPEAN COUNTRIES, 2010 Q3–2013 Q4**

(Per cent)

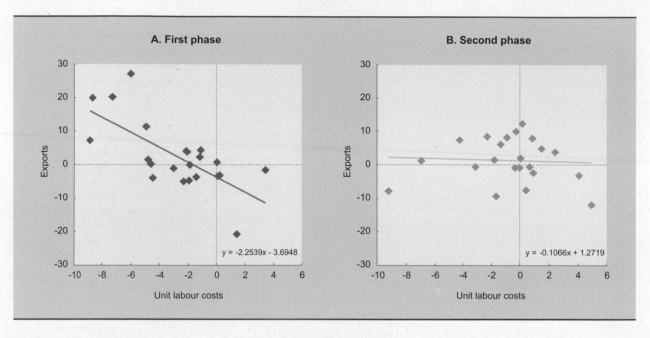

Source: UNCTAD secretariat calculations, based on *Eurostat*; *OECD.StatExtracts*; and *UNCTADstat*.
  Note: Countries included are Austria, Belgium, Czech Republic, Denmark, Estonia, Finland, France, Germany, Greece, Hungary, Ireland, Italy, Luxembourg, the Netherlands, Norway, Poland, Portugal, Slovakia, Slovenia, Spain, Sweden and the United Kingdom. In the first phase, data for real unit labour costs refer to the change between 2010 Q3 and 2012 Q1, while data for exports refer to the change between 2011 Q1 and 2012 Q3. In the second phase, data for real unit labour costs refer to the change between 2012 Q1 and 2013 Q2, while data for exports refer to the change between 2012 Q3 and 2013 Q4.

sheets regain strength and consumer confidence recovers, especially when employment levels are low, a resumption of productive investment for the domestic market seems unlikely. Given these constraints, any possible chance of success for this strategy rests on stimulating private investment in export sectors.

Over the years, *TDR*s and other studies have argued that relying on an export-led recovery cannot be a solution for all at the same time. Yet, in the current circumstances of minimal global coordination, aggregation issues are not a primary concern of policymakers; each country, individually, expects to become a winner. Accordingly, compression of wage incomes has become a key component of the prevailing "structural policies" aimed at increasing competitiveness. It is believed that such policies will induce investment, while a depreciation in the real exchange rate, derived from relatively lower wages, will help to gain market shares. The seeming success

of a handful of countries in translating improved cost competitiveness into export growth tends to reinforce such beliefs. There is also the added fear that countries that do not join this race risk being left behind.

Such beliefs call for a deeper examination of the empirical evidence. This can be done by taking the European countries as a sample. This choice offers the advantage of concentrating on the recent period in which there has been concurrent pressure in these countries to reduce labour costs in order to gain export shares. The additional advantage of taking Europe as a sample is that feedbacks similar to those found with global aggregation can be captured to a significant degree, since a fairly substantial proportion of trade in the region is internal to this market. The correlation between wage compression and export growth in the short run cannot be fully ignored, as reflected in chart 2.2A. Taking a two-year period starting in 2010, when policies shifted away from fiscal stimuli and towards a competitive race to gain export market shares, the scatter plot shows that, despite great diversity of outcomes, exports seem to have been inversely correlated with changes in real unit labour costs among the selected sample of developed economies. However, in most cases such an effect fades over time (chart 2.2B). Efforts towards achieving greater cost competitiveness through labour market flexibility and wage compression face known constraints: competition becomes harder, as there is a limit to how much labour costs can be cut without seriously affecting social stability and productivity. What is more, declining labour incomes affect revenues of households that have a higher propensity to spend, further eroding, in the aggregate, consumption and investment demand. This eventually has an adverse impact on imports, and thus on the exports of the whole set of countries.

These dynamics are captured in chart 2.3. Under normal conditions that would allow sustained demand expansion, real unit labour costs should at least be stable or rise, but starting in 2010, the index of real unit labour costs (weighted) contracted. Three or four quarters later, real GDP in these economies stopped growing, and as a result, import volumes decelerated sharply. In the aggregate, imports remained flat throughout 2013, with a small upturn in the last two quarters, largely in response to asset appreciations fuelling demand in the major economies (see below). The relevant point is that the ratio of imports to exports declined considerably. Hence, the apparent success of a net-export-oriented strategy mostly reflects, in the aggregate, an adjustment on the import side. In other words, a strategy based on a compression of labour incomes alone, if carried out by a significant number of countries, runs the risk of exacerbating a deflationary trap for all of them.

(c) Declining labour-income shares and global imbalances

Further clarifications can be provided from longer term analyses, as the most recent evolution of real unit labour costs and GDP growth in Europe suggests some ambiguity about the relationship between these variables (chart 2.3). Despite a seeming pause in wage compression in Europe, though no real growth in wages, GDP seems to be gaining traction. Likewise, there were periods in the past when GDP growth in developed countries remained

Chart 2.3

REAL GDP, REAL UNIT LABOUR COST AND RATIO OF IMPORTS TO EXPORTS IN EUROPE, 2009 Q4–2013 Q4

(Index numbers, 2009 Q4 = 100)

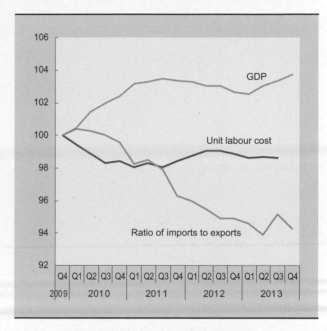

Source: UNCTAD secretariat calculations, based on *Eurostat*; *OECD.StatExtracts*; and *UNCTADstat*.

Note: Europe includes Belgium, Czech Republic, Denmark, Finland, France, Germany, Hungary, Ireland, Italy, the Netherlands, Poland, Portugal, Slovakia, Spain and the United Kingdom. Unit labour cost is weighted by imports.

relatively strong even though labour income shares in GDP were falling, or only marginally rising. At least from the early 1990s, there was a marked long-term tendency for wage shares to fall in a number of developed economies (see chart 2.4, where wage shares are the national accounts equivalent of real unit labour costs), though in a few of them some stabilization has taken place in recent years.

These data can be complemented with the historical investigation of Piketty (2014). His detailed analysis of tax returns and other datasets in a number of countries and across decades (and, in a few cases, centuries) has the advantage of showing the evolution of income not only among wage and profit-earners, but also across the distribution of households. The results point to the continuing stagnation in earning of low- and middle-income groups in a number of developed countries over time, together with a dramatic

Chart 2.4

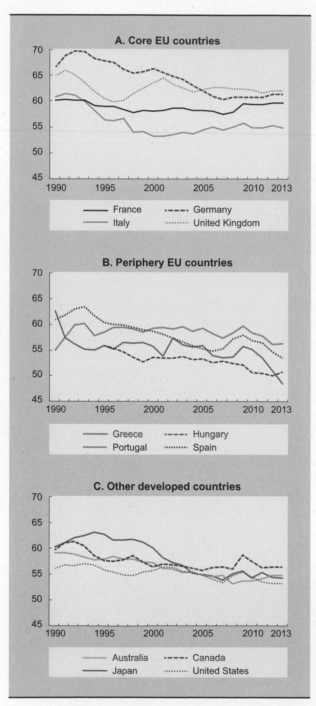

LABOUR INCOME SHARE IN GDP, SELECTED DEVELOPED COUNTRIES, 1990–2013

(Per cent)

A. Core EU countries

France — Germany — Italy — United Kingdom

B. Periphery EU countries

Greece — Hungary — Portugal — Spain

C. Other developed countries

Australia — Canada — Japan — United States

Source: UNCTAD secretariat estimates, based on UN-DESA, *National Accounts Main Aggregates* database; European Commission, *AMECO* database; Eurostat, *Annual National Accounts* database; University of California at Davis and University of Groningen, *Penn World Tables* version 8.0; United States Bureau of Economic Analysis, *National Income and Production Accounts*; and United Kingdom Office for National Statistics, *United Kingdom Economic Accounts*.

rise in the earnings of the top decile, and of the top percentile in the United States, but also in Australia, Canada, France, Japan, the United Kingdom and more than 20 other countries.[5] The rise at the very top of the distribution of earned incomes is so staggering that it is reasonable to suggest that such earnings should actually be conceptualized as "rents" from accumulated wealth.

Various implications of relevance to the policy diagnosis of this chapter can be extracted from Piketty's work. First, aggregate statistics of labour income shares based on national accounts do not fully capture the true extent of deterioration of the incomes of middle- and low-income wage earners. Removing the rising proportions of earned income of the top decile, and especially the top percentile in most, if not all, the developed economies, and characterizing them instead as profit earnings, would significantly accentuate the declining trends of labour income noted above.[6] Second, Piketty observes relatively constant patterns of worsening distribution over considerably long periods, measurable in decades, interrupted only by wars or serious crises. The author argues that returns on capital tend to increase at a faster rate than the growth of income and wages, particularly as GDP growth decelerates in the process of development.[7] The more that capital is accumulated at the top, the more the economic structure is likely to be shaped to favour rents and profits over wage income, which then reduces the reliance of the owners of capital on faster GDP growth. Policy-driven efforts to bring about wage competitiveness with the aim of triggering faster growth of GDP would exacerbate, rather than reverse, this trend. Third, Piketty advances a possible interpretation of the global financial crisis of 2008-2009 on this basis. In his opinion, the long-run tendency towards an increase in the wealth-to-income ratio, together with the rise of cross-border capital, which presumably took place as wealth-holders sought higher rents through a reallocation of their portfolios in global markets, contributed to greater global financial vulnerability and, eventually, to the global crisis.

A growing body of research has shed light on the global implications of worsening income and wealth distribution on growth and stability (Baker, 2009; Cripps et al., 2011; Galbraith, 2012). Based on this, it would seem that the tendency towards declining wage shares may not require an export boost to generate faster growth everywhere; as long as global imbalances are allowed to rise, a declining wage share can coexist with rising domestic demand in a number of economies where credit expansion can compensate for lower household incomes. This is confirmed by developments in the 1990s and 2000s, which were decades of fairly strong global growth in which wage shares consistently declined (chart 2.4). It is the combination of these patterns which brought about the large macro-financial imbalances and the subsequent collapse in the form of the global financial crisis.[8]

Some authors stress a more direct causal link between wage compression and the formation of credit bubbles: as the relative erosion of labour incomes creates insufficient real demand, capital is mostly diverted towards financial operations, which generate asset bubbles and volatility. This in turn becomes the source of temporary real economic expansion (Foster, 2010; Patnaik, 2010). The growing financialization of developed countries and "subordinate" financialization in developing countries (Epstein, 2005; Lapavitsas, 2013) can be explained in these terms. As a result, economies become more prone to crises, which adversely affect employment and productive activities, and also lead to greater concentrations of wealth and income. The resulting drag on GDP growth is ameliorated only by unsustainable episodes of debt-driven consumption booms.[9]

(d)   Asset appreciations and real balance effects

From the above arguments, it seems clear that the synchronized fiscal contraction and slow growth of labour income across many developed countries will likely lead to either of two outcomes: a protracted slowdown (secular stagnation), or a temporary growth spurt driven by an unsustainable expansion of demand through greater indebtedness in a few major economies. The latter situation characterized the pre-crisis years, and, to a lesser degree, it has been repeated in the recent past. Moreover, it has been exacerbated by the creation of liquidity by central banks, with a direct impact on asset markets across the world.

Elements of this situation appear to be most prominent in Australia, Canada, the United Kingdom and the United States. In these economies the mechanisms at work have strong commonalities: the expansion of liquidity has generated record highs in stock markets, and rapid price increases in real estate markets, particularly in the United Kingdom and, to some extent, in Canada. As a result, households are continuing to experience a positive shock on the asset side of their balance sheets and feel more encouraged to reduce their savings. If previous cycles are any guide, household lending capacity (total income minus total expenditure, including investment) may even turn negative, so that the additional spending will be fully financed by debt. The process can go on for as long as asset prices keep rising and liquidity is made available for the purchase of assets.

These mechanisms are illustrated empirically for the United States and the United Kingdom (chart 2.5).[10] Chart 2.5A shows the indices of stock market and house prices in the United States since the early 1990s, and tracks the dot-com boom, the recession of 2001 and the subsequent expansion leading up to the financial crisis of 2008. Since then, in the wake of an ultra easy monetary policy, stock market prices have climbed significantly, reaching unprecedented levels. The speculative nature of these patterns is highlighted in the chart by the inclusion of the New York Stock Exchange (NYSE) "margin debt" series (margin debt being the dollar value of the securities purchased with funds borrowed from investors' accounts at the NYSE), which have also risen to unprecedented levels. The housing market in the United States has started to recover, but has not yet displayed the exuberance of the mid-2000s.

Real holding gains[11] of the household sector have fluctuated considerably over the past few years (chart 2.5B). In the United States, balance sheets of households were subject to positive shocks equivalent to about 25 per cent of real GDP during the financial boom years, followed by negative shocks equivalent to almost 100 per cent of real GDP during the crisis. Asset prices recovered quickly in the wake of policy stimuli in 2009–2010, but fell once again in 2011 in response to "risk-on, risk-off" fluctuations in speculative markets, presumably reflecting changes in the level of confidence in the financial sustainability of the public sector and the banking sector in the United States and elsewhere. Since then, there has been a continuous recovery of asset prices and, to some extent, real estate prices following quantitative easing programmes. Real holding gains towards the end of 2013 can be estimated to equal about 50 per cent of real GDP, a non-negligible increase in the net worth of the household sector as a whole. Even though these

Chart 2.5

**ASSET PRICES, CHANGE IN HOUSEHOLD EXPENDITURE, AND HOUSEHOLD BORROWING
AND NET FINANCIAL SAVINGS IN THE UNITED STATES AND THE UNITED KINGDOM**

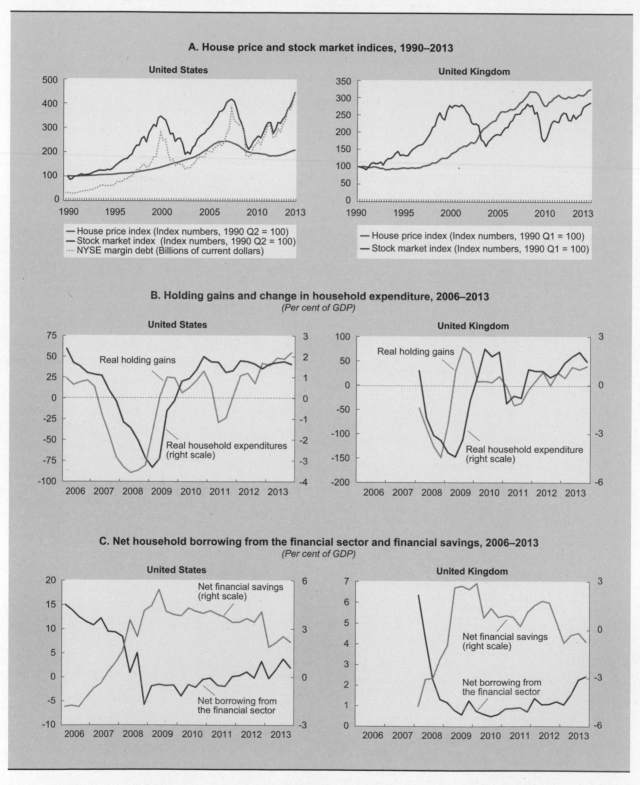

Source: UNCTAD secretariat calculations, based on BIS, *Residential property price statistics* database; Bloomberg; United States
        Federal Reserve, *Financial Accounts* database; United Kingdom Office of National Statistics and Bank of England databases.
  Note: Real holding gains refers to capital gains due to changes in asset values, after discounting CPI inflation (3-quarter centred
        moving average). Net savings refers to total disposable income less total spending (including investment) of the household
        sector.

holding gains are not cash-flow income, the rise in the value of net worth may induce a proportional increase in spending through wealth effects. With a moderate lag of one to two quarters, there is a fairly strong correlation between holding gains and real spending (chart 2.5B). In turn, the increments of real household spending represented a contribution to GDP growth of about 1.6 per cent in 2013, which is about 60 per cent of total growth.

Asset appreciations driven by liquidity expansions help to explain the recent recovery in the United States, despite the fall in fiscal spending and labour-income shares. However, these patterns also justify concerns about growth under such conditions. In the United States, net financial savings of the household sector, defined as total disposable income minus total expenditure (including consumption and investment spending),[12] peaked at 5.5 per cent of GDP in mid-2009, but then fell sharply following drastic deleveraging after the crisis (chart 2.5C). Subsequently, net financial savings moved back to close to 3 per cent of GDP, approaching what could be considered the long-term norm. However, over the last two years, it has dropped below 2 per cent of GDP, with the trend pointing downwards. At the same time, household net borrowing from the financial sector has started to climb from its unusually negative levels at the trough of the crisis (chart 2.5C). By the end of 2013, net borrowing by the household sector had not reached the extremes experienced at the onset of the crisis, but the direction was still upwards. Apart from the NYSE margin debt plotted in chart 2.5A, complementary data (not shown here) suggest that consumer credit accounted for the larger proportion of the increases in net borrowings of households. Mortgage debt has only recently stabilized, in aggregate terms, after years of adjustments in the housing market, but it is likely that rising house prices will trigger another debt expansion.

Asset appreciations, holding gains and debt dynamics of the United Kingdom can be assessed using the same methodology (chart 2.5). A most striking feature is the pattern of real estate appreciation, which was higher than in the United States and steeper than the appreciation in the stock market. But the combination of these price swings caused exceptionally high holding gains and losses during the booms and crises, respectively, showing a similar pattern to that of the United States. From 2011 onwards the real net gains of the household sector on account

of asset prices climbed continuously to reach about 40 per cent of real GDP by 2013. After a lag, there seems to have been a clear correlation between real holding gains of households in the United Kingdom and their pattern of spending (chart 2.5B). Despite the fact that labour income shares remained barely flat, asset appreciations appear to have led to a rise in household spending amounting to a contribution to GDP growth of about 1.5 per cent per annum in 2013. Further, the rise in household spending, to the extent that it was partly due to holding gains, was matched by a fall in net financial savings (chart 2.5C). Starting in the first quarter of 2013, the household sector in the United Kingdom shifted to a net deficit position: borrowing from the financial sector started to rise again, though not to the same degree as it did during the pre-crisis boom. As in the United States, the underlying growth dynamics in the United Kingdom point to patterns similar to those that preceded the financial crisis. Experience indicates that these are unsustainable processes, but it also shows that they can continue for a fairly long time. Preliminary investigation of growth dynamics in some other countries, such as Australia and Canada, suggests that they share some of these characteristics.

The rapid growth of household demand in this subgroup of developed countries provides a boost for the exports of other economies, particularly those seeking recovery based on net exports. At this juncture, the implied global macro-imbalances between surplus and deficit countries, as well as the internal imbalances between the asset and liability sides of household budgets in deficit countries, may not be alarming. But relying on these patterns is not a sustainable policy strategy, and a strategy from which it is not easy to exit without an alternative growth agenda.

2. Policy stances in developing and emerging economies in a context of growing vulnerability to external shocks

(a) The role of domestic demand and incomes policies

Many developing and emerging economies continued to support domestic demand after 2010, even as developed countries' policy stances shifted

Chart 2.6

CONTRIBUTION OF DOMESTIC DEMAND AND NET EXPORTS TO REAL GDP GROWTH, SELECTED COUNTRIES, 2011–2013

(Percentage points)

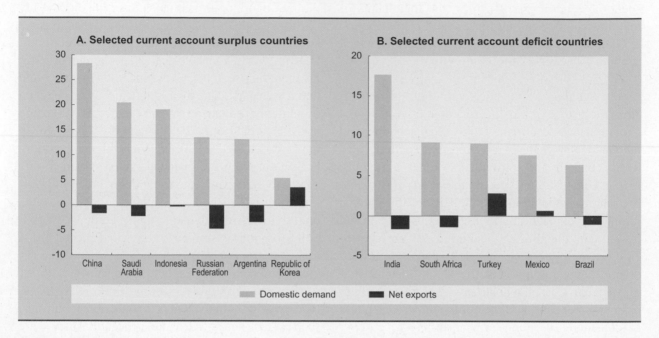

Source: UNCTAD secretariat calculations, based on UN-DESA, *National Accounts Main Aggregates* database and *World Economic Situation and Prospects: Update as of mid-2014*; *OECD.StatExtracts*; and EIU, *CountryData* database.
Note: Data refer to the 3-year cumulative contribution. The classification of the two groups of countries as surplus and deficit is based on their current account balance in 2010.

towards fiscal tightening. In the context of a global economy that was struggling to recover from the financial crisis, such support helped to maintain their pace of growth, which turned out to be significantly higher than that of developed economies despite a recent deceleration. To the extent that these countries as a group are becoming increasingly important in global trade, their performance contributed to global demand as well, providing growth opportunities for their trading partners.

UNCTAD has often insisted on the need for surplus countries to narrow their external balances by boosting domestic demand and increasing their imports at a faster pace than their exports, instead of forcing deficit countries to adjust and to rely on the compression of labour costs in the hope that this will lead to an export-led recovery. Net import demand from surplus countries would not necessarily make them more vulnerable, particularly if their contribution succeeds in generating new sources of income

in deficit countries, thereby eventually lifting global demand.

Examining macroeconomic indicators of the developing and emerging country members of the G20 is illuminating in this respect. Chart 2.6A shows the cumulative contributions to real GDP growth of countries which were in current account surplus in 2010. Cumulative contributions were calculated for a three-year period, from end-2010 to end-2013. In all these cases, GDP growth was significant, and the major driver was domestic demand, not net exports. Except for the Republic of Korea, which continued to rely on external demand as a significant source of its GDP growth, this subset of developing countries managed to sustain the growth of global demand during the process of recovery from the crisis. Chart 2.6B groups countries that were in current account deficit in 2010. In these countries, the standard approach would be to "adjust" by reducing spending until balance is achieved. But, except for Turkey and Mexico (which showed a relative improvement in their net trade balances), the other countries' trade deficits increased beyond 2010. In most of these countries, the standard approach was not followed, and their economies continued to be supported by domestic demand. But additional risks were involved, as discussed below.

On the basis of this decomposition alone it is difficult to assess whether the countries grouped in chart 2.6B were following sustainable growth strategies. As noted earlier, in some cases net trade gains may be the consequence of competitiveness achieved by wage compression, but this could eventually lead to demand and productivity bottlenecks. Conversely, trade deficits may be the result of an investment-driven strategy aimed at structural transformation, and, to the extent that such deficits are manageable in the medium term, they could result in considerable advantages in terms of long-term growth and development. However, if the trade deficits are the consequence of asset bubbles and excessive consumer borrowing, often accompanied or promoted by a bonanza of foreign capital inflows, they could have hazardous effects and create the need for harsh adjustment measures down the road.

Over the past few decades, in the process of integration into the world economy, many developing and transition economies have adopted policies to attract investors and/or gain market shares by reducing labour income shares (in some cases from already low levels). However, in more recent years these processes seem to have been contained, and in some cases reversed. Based on statistical information available, though incomplete,[13] it is found that here has been varied evolution in the shares of labour income (including mixed income)[14] in GDP (chart 2.7) in different groups of developing countries. The average for South America points to a sustained increase in labour income shares in GDP from the mid-2000s, which reflects an improvement in labour market conditions and deliberate income redistribution policies. The average for countries in Africa shows a similar pattern, albeit starting more recently and from a lower level, and it is less pronounced. Even so, in both regions, this has been insufficient to reach the labour income shares achieved in the past. Meanwhile, other regions in the developing world have managed to contain the deterioration of labour income shares. However, in some cases, such as West Asia, after a sharp decline in those shares, the

Chart 2.7

LABOUR INCOME SHARE IN GDP, SELECTED DEVELOPING-COUNTRY GROUPS, 1990–2012

(Per cent)

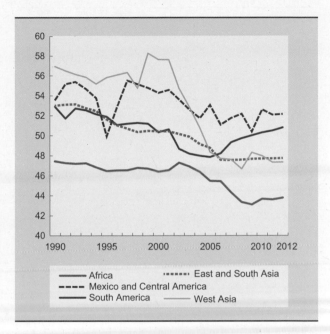

Source: UNCTAD Secretariat estimates based on UN-DESA, *National Accounts Main Aggregates* database; European Commission, *AMECO* database; and University of California at Davis and University of Groningen, *Penn World Tables* version 8.0.

trend has not significantly reversed. Hence, despite significant progress in several countries, the share of labour income needs to expand significantly if it is to provide the basis for a self-sustaining path of growth and development.

(b) Challenges from the external financial and trade environment

The vulnerabilities of developing and emerging economies have been heightened by weaknesses in the international financial architecture.[15] It was hoped that the global financial crisis would give rise to sufficient political motivation and intellectual strength to address these weaknesses in a more determined manner. But efforts in this direction, such as those promoted by the United Nations Commission of Experts of the President of the United Nations General Assembly (United Nations, 2009), have been stymied by pressures from global financial interests

Chart 2.8

TOTAL ASSETS OF MAJOR CENTRAL BANKS AND GLOBAL STOCK MARKET INDEX, JAN. 2009–DEC. 2013

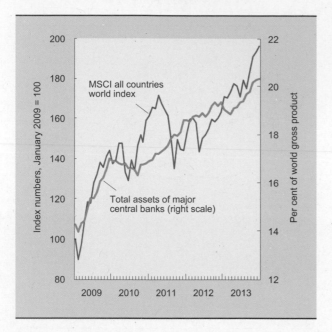

Source: UNCTAD secretariat calculations, based on United States Federal Reserve database; European Central Bank database; Bank of Japan Accounts database; IMF, *International Financial Statistics* and *World Economic Outlook* databases; and Bloomberg.

Note: Major central banks includes the Bank of England, Bank of Japan, European Central Bank, People's Bank of China and United States Federal Reserve.

seeking new investment opportunities, particularly in emerging markets. Justifications for resisting a systematic reform agenda have been widespread. They include the view that adverse financial conditions in major economies are not necessarily transmitted to developing and emerging economies which are virtually "decoupling" from the rest (see, for example, IMF, 2007; Blanchard et al., 2010; Leduc and Spiegel, 2013).

As noted in chapter VI of this *Report*,[16] developing and transition economies have remained susceptible to the kind of boom and bust cycles of capital flows which were commonplace during the period of finance-driven globalization. In the period prior to the crisis most capital flows were triggered by cycles of leveraging and deleveraging by private financial institutions in the developed economies. The last cycle that started in 2010 began with an extraordinary amount of liquidity creation by the central banks of the major

economies. Such monetary injections fuelled asset appreciations not only in the United States and the United Kingdom, as discussed above, but also in many other stock markets, as measured by the MSCI global index (see chart 2.8). Between mid-2010 and the last quarter of 2013, that global index more than doubled, while real economic activity remained subdued. But in some cases, as can be observed by stock market reactions to releases of employment data in the United States and elsewhere, good news on economic activity triggered a fall in the stock market, reflecting the anxiety of speculators about reversals of the liquidity expansion if economic activity and favourable employment conditions were to resume.

Unprecedentedly large volumes of liquidity are currently coursing through highly liberalized capital markets. In the absence of a corresponding increase of demand for credit for productive activities in most developed economies, financial flows are being diverted to portfolio operations within and beyond the issuing economies. In a few exceptional cases, policymakers who are aware of the potentially devastating effects of unfettered capital markets have tried to put in place regulatory measures to protect their macroeconomic environment. In most emerging and transition economies, however, the policy response has resembled more of a revival of the "Lawson doctrine", which was highly permissive of private capital flows and current account imbalances.[17] Provided that fiscal balances are kept in check, this doctrine recommends against interfering in the portfolio decisions of private agents. Lenders and borrowers, the argument goes, are fully capable of assessing the benefits and risks of their financial decisions. However, such a belief is at odds with the observed highly homogeneous and synchronized risk perceptions of international investors about a quite varied set of developing countries, as evidenced by the strong co-movements of EMBIG indices in chart 2.9. This suggests that investors do not undertake sophisticated analysis specific to very different countries, including the performance of their real economies and their financial structures.

The evidence confirms that many developing and transition economies have been subject to considerable cyclical fluctuations of capital flows, before and after the crisis (chart 2.10). These flows have in turn influenced speculative behaviour, reflected in the rises and falls of stock market indices. The flow series in the chart encompass portfolio flows to the private banking sectors, including FDI in the form of private equity channelled through domestic financial institutions. They do not include credit to the public sectors of these countries, which was relatively minor during the period under observation. With variations, inflows reached a peak before the crisis and collapsed at its onset in 2008. They resumed sharply after 2009, in some cases reaching new highs,[18] presumably reflecting the vast increase in global liquidity in comparison with previous cycles. Around the second quarter of 2013, with the first announcements of tapering by the Federal Reserve, and before any tapering actually took place, investors began to pull out funds, to varying degrees, from these countries.

The specifics of country experiences have been well documented and analysed elsewhere.[19] General patterns can be identified through both the upswings and downswings of the cycles. Though the inflows per se are not motivated mainly by the performance of the real economy, it is known that they can have the effect of altering exchange rates, price formation, spending behaviour, financial balances of institutions and policymakers' room for manoeuvre. It is also known that drastic capital reversals can take place for reasons that, again, have mostly to do with changes in the financial conditions of the creditor countries. But these outflows leave behind serious dislocations. Usually, capital reversals have an immediate effect on the exchange rate, making the servicing of the debt or repayment in a foreign currency more difficult. They also have knock-on effects on asset prices, significantly eroding balance sheets. Many of these cases may well represent systemic crises to the extent that the sectors most affected are corporations and financial institutions, with balance sheets which can be greater than a country's GDP. For example, by 2013, the value of assets of the banking sectors in the Republic of Korea, South Africa and Thailand were estimated to be close to three times the size of their respective GDPs, while in Brazil, Chile and Malaysia, bank assets represented about two times their GDP. Under these circumstances, public sector institutions are often forced to come to the rescue. Eventually, public sectors which are not themselves beneficiaries of the inflow bonanza, tend to assume the burden of bad debts once crisis conditions emerge, often leading them to adopt damaging fiscal austerity prescriptions.

Finally, policymakers should be aware of possible negative shocks originating from international trade, particularly in countries that rely on exports

Chart 2.9

SOVEREIGN BOND YIELD SPREADS, SELECTED DEVELOPING AND TRANSITION ECONOMIES, 2007 Q4–2014 Q2

(Basis points)

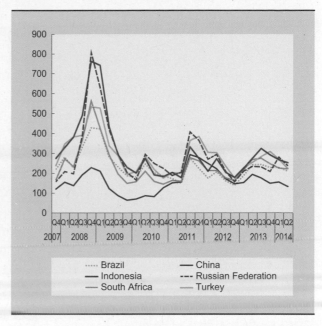

Source: Bloomberg; JP Morgan Emerging Markets Bond Index Global of sovereign dollar denominated bonds (EMBIG).

Note: Data refer to the last value of the quarter and reflect the spread to comparable United States Treasuries.

of only a few primary commodities or low-skill, labour-intensive manufactures. As further discussed in this *Report* (see particularly chapter V), proactive industrial policies need to aim at diversification and upgrading of exports. Indeed, diversification of their productive and export activities remains a pending task for many transition and developing economies. In a sample of relatively open developing economies the index of export concentration increased from the early 2000s (before the commodity boom) to 2012 (table 2.1). Admittedly, in Argentina, China and Mexico the increase in the concentration index was minor and the low value of their respective indices by 2012 suggests that these economies remain quite diversified, though the basket of their export revenues is slightly more dependent on fewer products. Meanwhile, dependence on a smaller set of export products has clearly increased in commodity exporters such as Colombia, Chile, Ecuador, the Bolivarian Republic of Venezuela and the group of transition economies as a whole.

Chart 2.10

CAPITAL INFLOWS TO THE PRIVATE BANKING SECTOR AND STOCK MARKET INDICES, SELECTED DEVELOPING AND TRANSITION ECONOMIES, 2005 Q1–2013 Q4

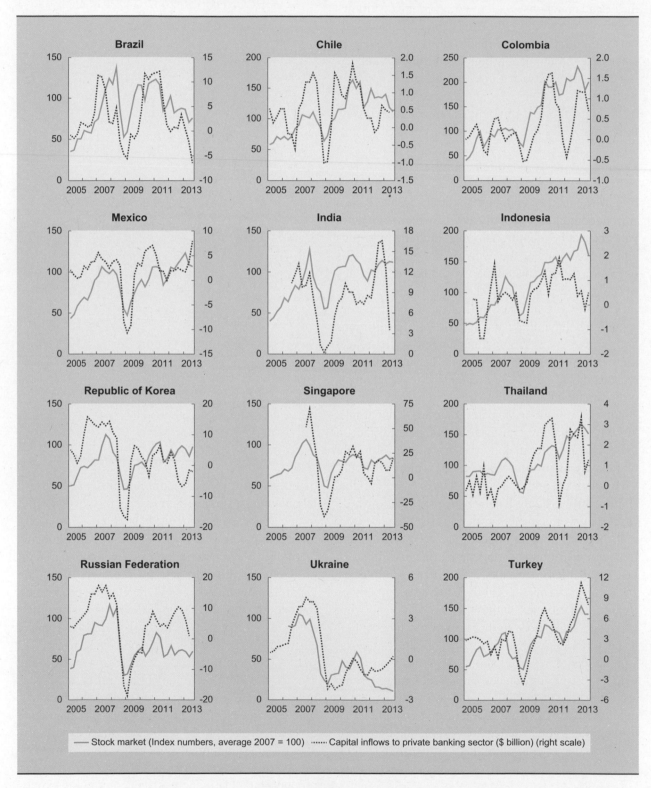

Stock market (Index numbers, average 2007 = 100) .... *Capital inflows to private banking sector ($ billion) (right scale)*

Source: UNCTAD secretariat calculations, based on IMF and World Bank, *Quarterly External Debt Statistics* database; and Bloomberg.
Note: The stock market index refers to the end-of-period price of the dollar-denominated MSCI index, except for the Republic of Korea, where it refers to the dollar-denominated KOSPI index. Capital inflows refer to 3-quarter centred moving average of the changes in the gross external debt position of the banking sector (except for India and Mexico where they refer to the sum of the banking and "other [private] sectors").

A complementary measure of the degree to which countries are better prepared to withstand trade shocks, using the UNCTAD Merchandise Trade Specialization Index, produces similar results.[20] The detailed examination of the indices across main categories of products over the period 1995–2012 confirms that, despite the rapid rate of growth of trade in many developing economies over the past two decades, the degree of specialization in the export structure of most developing economies has not varied significantly. Only in a few countries, mostly in East Asia, including China, Malaysia, the Republic of Korea and Singapore, has this structure progressed in the sense that trade balances of manufactures, and particularly of products with higher skill content, improved during this period. Elsewhere, in West Asia, Africa and Latin America, there have been few, if any, improvements, and in some even a clear deterioration, particularly in Africa and among oil exporters.

3. Current policies and outcomes from a global perspective

The review of economic policies proposed above suggests that there is need for caution in interpreting current developments. Contrary to the views of some observers, there is no convincing evidence that the world economy is in fact beginning a sustained recovery. The belief that growth in developed economies has finally picked up is overly optimistic; it only serves to claim success for pro-market reforms and to support arguments for a withdrawal of the precautionary measures and stimuli that still remain. This could have grave repercussions. For example, the recommendation that developing countries should pursue fiscal and labour market adjustments similar to those pursued in developed countries is of particular concern. In the light of the discussion in the previous subsection, developing countries could instead consider strengthening incomes policies that still have considerable possibilities to deliver, and could also introduce more effective precautionary measures to mitigate the effects of global financialization and enhance policies aimed at diversifying their economies.

Leaders from developed and developing countries deserve credit for the policies they promoted in 2009–2010. However, changes of policy stances

Table 2.1

EXPORT CONCENTRATION INDEX, SELECTED COUNTRIES, 2003–2012

	Change between 2003–2008 average and 2012 (Per cent)	Index average for 2011–2012
Colombia	18.7	42.0
Chile	10.0	37.1
Ecuador	9.1	50.0
Hong Kong, China	8.3	20.0
Brazil	7.1	15.8
South Africa	5.2	16.9
Indonesia	4.8	17.1
India	4.4	17.8
Bolivarian Republic of Venezuela	3.9	67.4
Peru	2.1	25.2
Mexico	1.7	15.0
China	1.3	10.0
Argentina	1.1	15.4
Memo item:		
Transition economies	10.2	33.0
Major oil and gas exporters	2.2	55.6

Source: UNCTAD secretariat calculations, based on *UNCTADstat.*
Note: The index ranges from 0 to 100 (maximum concentration).

after 2010, particularly in developed countries, which primarily include flexibilization of labour markets and restrained public spending, are factors that have delayed recovery. If, at present, there is a sense of a growth revival in some of these countries, the new growth patterns should rather be interpreted as reflecting structural problems of the kind already apparent in the years that preceded the global crisis. Under these conditions, economic growth seems to hinge again on excessive liquidity in the context of asset appreciations, which may drive up private expenditure for a while. As long as this can last, growth of consumer debt in deficit countries could fuel export demand in countries that are either leading exporters or opted more recently for promoting exports to exit from the crisis. However, by now it is known that such processes are unsustainable. Continuing on such a path, in the hope that things will work out differently this time appear to be short-sighted at best. It seems worthwhile aiming, instead, for a different strategy, a subject to which the next section turns.

B. Economic policies for a sustained global recovery

The previous section examined the main policy stances which have helped shape the current world economic situation. In some countries policymakers have aimed at boosting global demand; but, for the most part, macroeconomic policies have either exhibited deflationary tendencies or favoured short-term gains that lead to heightened risks in the long term. There are various reasons why the economic policy landscape remains disappointing, including a general mistrust in the feasibility of more proactive and inclusive policy approaches. The aim of this section is to show that a different set of policies could deliver better results, taking into account possible constraints and feedbacks, both domestic and international. Alternative policy scenarios for the global economy are examined using the United Nations Global Policy Model (GPM).[21]

1. Policies and outcomes

The scenarios produced with the GPM consider a "baseline", representing a continuation of the policy stances described in section A, and an alternative "balanced-growth" simulation. The baseline is not intended to be a forecast and the balanced-growth simulation is not the only measurable combination of policies and outcomes that could bring about the desired results. More importantly, the scenarios are highly stylized and contingent, for reasons given below. Their value resides in demonstrating, with rigorous empirical backing, the direction of change that could be expected from the two sets of policy assumptions. As such, their aim is to encourage policymakers to consider a different course of action.

(a) The baseline scenario

The baseline, which is a projection over the next 10 years, assumes a continuation of existing policies and no exogenous shocks. In particular, it does not include a financial crisis which, as the previous section argues, could result from the current policy stances. Admittedly, from the current combination of policies it is possible to highlight the structural flaws that could eventually cause a crisis. But it is not possible to determine in advance the timing of a crisis of this nature, the concrete measurement of its macro and global implications, and the nature of the recovery that may follow. This is because such a crisis is usually triggered by a sudden shift in market confidence, resulting from news, or even rumours, about signs of heightened financial fragility or losses of a relatively important institution. Likewise, a recovery from such a crisis is triggered by an even more complex combination of changes in the "state of confidence".[22]

Therefore, the baseline is a projection of current policies and their implied outcomes, assuming away the occurrence of a crisis, the timing and proportions of which are unknown. Accordingly, the baseline also assumes away the possibility that policymakers will decide to change course in order to avert a crash before it is too late. The concrete quantification of the outcomes of the baseline and how they are related to the assumed policy stances are discussed below in conjunction with those of the balanced-growth scenario.

(b) The balanced-growth scenario: Policy assumptions compared with the baseline

The balanced-growth scenario is proposed as a departure from the policies discussed in section A of this chapter. It focuses on the following aspects:

- Incomes policies to support growth of demand on a sustainable basis,

- Growth-enhancing fiscal policies,

- Industrial policies to promote private investment and structural transformation,

- Regulation of finance and capital controls to stabilize global financial markets, and

- Development-oriented trade agreements.

The latter two aspects are mostly qualitative in nature and contemplate varied modalities. In the model, regulation of finance and capital flows is imputed as exogenous conditions (usually called 'add-factors') to allow smooth adjustments of exchange rates and international prices of traded goods and services.[23] Likewise, development-oriented trade agreements are imputed as add-factors that replicate an expansion of the Generalized System of Preferences (GSP) between higher income economies on the one hand, and lower income economies on the other.[24] Among developing countries, the simulations impute an expansion of existing South-South trade agreements. Together with the other sets of policies proposed in the scenario, the result is an increase in exports of manufactures in low- and middle-income countries by 50–75 per cent in 10 years compared with the baseline. By contrast, trade-related aspects in the baseline are modelled as a continuation of existing conditions, mostly determined by bilateral trade agreements and prevailing investment patterns. As shown in section A, under these conditions, trade specialization does not improve, and the export concentration of very open economies in developing countries increases.

The other three sets of policy assumptions are summarized in table 2.2. The first columns show the evolution of the labour-income share as a percentage of GDP (labour share, for short) for both scenarios (baseline and balanced-growth). The simulation period is represented by five-year averages (2015–2019 and 2020–2024), while the historic period is represented by two points in time: 1990 and 2012.[25] As noted earlier, there was a continuous fall in the labour share for most regions until recently, with some indication that the trend was bottoming out in several regions. For the world as a whole, the labour share fell from about 59 per cent of GDP in 1990 to about 52 per cent in 2012. The baseline assumes that in all the 25 countries and country groups considered in the model, incomes of employees and self-employed informal workers will continue to remain depressed at around their prevailing low levels. By contrast, the

balanced-growth scenario assumes that policymakers in all countries will introduce incomes policies aimed at improving the functional distribution of income closer to the levels of the early or mid-1990s.[26] This degree of improvement seems essential for bringing about a robust growth of consumption, and, consequently, of private investment. It should be noted from the outset that the assumption that all countries proceed at a similar pace of improvement precludes unfair gains in competitiveness in export markets based on seeking advantage of labour costs by a few free-riders.[27]

The other sets of columns in table 2.2 show the growth patterns of government expenditure on goods and services and of private investment. The historic period is summarized by an average for the period 1990–2014, and the projections by averages for two five-year periods. Regarding government expenditure, the projected baseline shows a growth pattern similar to the average for the past 25 years. This means that in most developed countries, protracted fiscal austerity is assumed to imply a weak or negligible growth of expenditure, while in most developing countries the fiscal stance is assumed to be moderately expansionary. By contrast, the balanced-growth scenario assumes a more proactive fiscal policy in all countries, with a more marked increase, compared with the baseline, in developed countries. The assumed patterns of growth of government expenditure of most countries turn out to be closely aligned with the patterns of growth of GDP (discussed below).[28] It is also shown that these assumptions do not imply greater financial vulnerability.

The last columns of table 2.2 show that private investment is assumed to take on a greater role than public spending in developed countries during the projected baseline, leading to growing financial imbalances in the private sector. Private investment in developing countries, on the other hand, is not expected to grow at a similarly fast pace as the historic period. This is partly because demand stimulus remains subdued, but also because a large proportion of investment is related to exports to developed countries, which are expected to remain rather sluggish. Another major reason for the slowdown in private investment is the assumed continuation of China's policy shift, aimed at strengthening other sources of growth than private investment (which recently accounted for about 40 per cent of GDP). By contrast, the combined assumptions of proactive fiscal and

Table 2.2

MAIN ASSUMPTIONS OF THE MODEL SIMULATIONS
IN SELECTED REGIONS AND COUNTRIES, 1990–2024

	Scenario	Labour-income share in GDP (Per cent)				Government spending on goods and services (Average annual percentage growth)			Private investment (Average annual percentage growth)		
		1990	2012	Average 2015– 2019	Average 2020– 2024	1990– 2014	2015– 2019	2020– 2024	1990– 2014	2015– 2019	2020– 2024
Developed economies	Baseline	60.5	56.1	55.5	55.2	2.0	1.1	1.1	1.1	3.0	3.2
	Balanced growth	.	.	57.9	60.1	.	2.8	3.5	.	3.7	4.8
of which:											
United States	Baseline	56.1	53.2	53.3	53.5	2.4	1.8	2.2	2.0	3.6	4.0
	Balanced growth	.	.	55.4	58.2	.	4.9	3.9	.	3.8	4.4
CIS	Baseline	71.5	57.3	55.9	54.6	1.8	0.9	1.5	4.6	-0.7	1.7
	Balanced growth	.	.	61.1	63.4	.	2.8	4.8	.	0.3	6.6
Developing Asia	Baseline	55.2	48.8	50.6	50.8	6.7	6.3	6.1	7.7	3.9	4.6
	Balanced growth	.	.	53.2	55.9	.	7.9	7.2	.	4.3	5.7
of which:											
China	Baseline	61.0	49.7	52.6	53.4	10.3	7.7	7.0	12.4	4.2	4.8
	Balanced growth	.	.	55.1	58.1	.	9.0	8.1	.	3.7	5.0
India	Baseline	51.0	44.7	46.2	46.0	6.7	5.7	6.5	7.2	5.1	5.6
	Balanced growth	.	.	50.0	53.4	.	8.4	7.8	.	6.1	7.4
Africa	Baseline	47.5	43.8	44.6	44.7	4.3	4.5	4.8	4.8	2.0	3.1
	Balanced growth	.	.	46.4	47.0	.	6.4	7.0	.	5.2	7.7
Latin America and the Caribbean	Baseline	51.8	49.6	49.8	49.1	4.3	2.3	2.5	3.2	1.7	2.9
	Balanced growth	.	.	51.8	53.1	.	4.7	5.6	.	3.4	7.0

Source: UNCTAD secretariat calculations, based on GPM.
Note: CIS includes Georgia.

industrial policies in the balanced-growth scenario for all countries are consistent with a faster growth of private investment than that of the baseline in all regions.[29] Such an acceleration of private investment in developing countries is an essential component of a strategy of structural transformation, which is required both for sustained welfare as well as for fuller integration into the global trading system.

(c) Main outcomes of the simulations

Table 2.3 shows a summary of economic growth outcomes under both scenarios. In the baseline scenario, GDP growth, both globally and in most countries individually, is marginally faster than the historic average.[30] Since crises in the projection period are ruled out by assumption, as noted earlier,

Table 2.3

GDP GROWTH IN SELECTED REGIONS AND COUNTRIES, 1990–2024

	Scenario	Average annual growth of GDP[a] (Per cent)		
		1990–2014	2015–2019	2020–2024
World	Baseline	3.3	3.4	3.6
	Balanced growth	.	4.7	5.5
Developed economies	Baseline	1.9	1.8	2.0
	Balanced growth	.	2.8	3.5
of which:				
United States	Baseline	2.5	2.3	2.6
	Balanced growth	.	3.3	3.7
CIS	Baseline	2.7	2.0	2.1
	Balanced growth	.	3.3	4.9
Developing Asia	Baseline	6.3	5.5	5.4
	Balanced growth	.	6.7	7.2
of which:				
China	Baseline	9.8	7.1	6.7
	Balanced growth	.	8.1	8.3
India	Baseline	6.3	5.8	6.0
	Balanced growth	.	7.5	7.9
Africa	Baseline	3.8	3.9	3.9
	Balanced growth	.	6.1	7.0
Latin America and the Caribbean	Baseline	3.1	2.9	3.0
	Balanced growth	.	4.5	5.7
Memo item:				
World (based on market exchange rates)	Baseline	2.7	2.8	3.0
	Balanced growth	.	3.9	4.7

Source: UNCTAD secretariat calculations, based on GPM.
Note: CIS includes Georgia.
    a Data refer to PPP in constant 2005 international dollars, except in the memo item.

the implication is that structural imbalances will keep growing. Therefore, the baseline scenario, even if showing a moderate rate of growth, is increasingly vulnerable to shocks and financial instability. Given that financial institutions, households and governments in many countries have not yet succeeded in regaining financial strength, such a baseline suggests intolerable risks for weak institutions. The longer such imbalances remain unresolved, the harsher the consequences will be for the world economy.

The balanced-growth scenario, on the other hand, shows considerable improvements in growth rates. The average growth for the world economy (estimated in PPP terms) is significantly faster than it is under the baseline scenario. This partly reflects an effect of the PPP adjustments, since developing and emerging economies show a growth difference compared with the baseline which is nearly double that of developed economies.[31] More importantly, the faster growth rates for all regions are the result not only of policy stimuli in each country individually, but also of the strong synergy emerging from the coordination of pro-growth policy stances among all regions. Finally, improvements in growth rates for developing countries, especially in Africa, compared with those of developed countries, confirm the strong growth-convergence characteristic of the balanced-growth scenario. This is a most desirable objective to support development and welfare objectives.

Table 2.4 shows the most relevant aspects of financial stability resulting from the balanced-growth scenario, compared with the baseline. The first two sets of columns concentrate on financial conditions in the public sector and the other sets on private sector financial balances and the current account. It was argued in section A of this chapter that many countries, especially developed countries, have tightened their fiscal stance in order to improve financial stability. However, baseline results show that reducing fiscal deficits by cutting spending is a tortuous path with likely unsatisfactory results. Unless policies are effective in enhancing growth, and thus public revenues, fiscal deficits will remain high and reductions in public debt will be slow. In developing countries, the relatively moderate growth of public spending assumed in the baseline for India and Latin America does not lead to an improvement in the government's financial position either. In Africa, a slightly faster growth of public spending in the projected baseline than in the historic period leads to larger fiscal deficits and public debt ratios. This illustrates that, particularly for countries where fiscal policy space is limited, fiscal policies aimed at improving growth and stability could be more effective when accompanied by other, complementary policies.

On the other hand, fiscal deficits and debt ratios in the balanced growth scenario are smaller than in the baseline scenario.[32] This is not surprising, even if a critical ingredient of the policy mix is assumed to be faster growth of public spending on goods and services. Fiscal sustainability is the result of various converging policies, such as those proposed above. To the extent that fiscal support in the form of spending on social protection and infrastructure development is complemented by industrial promotion policies and by incomes policies, positive synergies are created. As a result of such synergies, consumption, private investment, and a more balanced growth of trade help to generate more government revenues. In addition, in order to ensure that the assumed improvements in the functional distribution of income are net (i.e. after taxes), greater progressiveness in direct tax collection is pursued, thus improving domestic resource mobilization. This in turn would contribute to reducing fiscal deficits and alleviating debt burdens.

The baseline results shown in the last two columns of table 2.4 confirm that private sector balances, as well as external balances of the various regions move in diverging directions. Developed countries as a whole, and particularly the United States (but also the United Kingdom and a few other major economies) tend to pursue policies that result in a continuing decline of net financial savings of the private sector (which also lead to heavier debt burdens).[33] This in turn translates into worsening external deficits, which, by the end of the simulation period, show similar magnitudes as those of the previous peak just before the onset of the financial crisis. Meanwhile, a number of other countries, typically those which accumulated large external surpluses during the pre-crisis period, show similar patterns in the projected baseline, as they will continue to rely on a recovery of their net exports and a relative increase in net financial savings, mostly by the private sector. By contrast, the balanced-growth scenario shows a significant reduction of external imbalances. More precisely, there are increases in the net financial savings of the private sector where originally there were deficits, and reductions of private surpluses where these were too large. Indeed, the proposed policy stimuli trigger robust growth of public and private spending, made possible by increased incomes and enhanced by improvements in the regulation of the financial system and of international transactions. In addition, trade imbalances of low- and lower-middle-income countries improve as a result of the assumed pro-development trade agreements.

2. Summing up: The need for policy consistency and macroeconomic coherence

The global modelling exercise synthesized above offers an evaluation of the favourable outcomes that can be broadly expected from a break with current policy stances. Clearly, these results cannot be achieved by means of market-driven adjustments. They reveal the need for explicit policy triggers that, estimated on a historical basis, are shown to yield more robust and stable growth patterns, particularly if policies worldwide are combined in a coordinated fashion. However, the use of this modelling tool does not mean that such policy choices will actually be undertaken. It requires a careful examination of what policy space is available, the possible constraints, and the political will of countries' leaders to break with most of the current approaches, all of which is discussed more thoroughly in the chapters that follow.

Table 2.4

FINANCIAL VARIABLES FOR SELECTED REGIONS AND COUNTRIES, 1990–2024

(Average in per cent of GDP)

	Scenario	Public sector balance			Public debt			Private sector balance			Current account balance		
		1990–2014	2015–2019	2020–2024	1990–2014	2015–2019	2020–2024	1990–2014	2015–2019	2020–2024	1990–2014	2015–2019	2020–2024
Developed economies	Baseline	-4.0	-4.0	-2.7	79.2	96.2	89.8	3.2	2.5	0.2	-0.5	-1.2	-2.1
	Balanced growth		-3.3	-2.8		91.2	79.7		2.3	1.7		-0.7	-0.8
of which:													
United States	Baseline	-4.3	-4.5	-3.1	71.1	87.1	78.7	1.4	0.3	-3.1	-2.9	-4.2	-6.2
	Balanced growth		-3.6	-3.0		83.1	72.5		0.8	0.7		-2.8	-2.3
CIS	Baseline	-0.6	1.9	3.0	57.7	22.7	22.2	4.3	2.5	4.3	3.8	4.4	7.3
	Balanced growth		1.3	2.0		26.6	27.2		1.5	0.9		2.7	2.9
Developing Asia	Baseline	-2.2	-1.3	-1.2	40.1	44.5	48.7	4.2	3.6	4.3	2.0	2.8	3.5
	Balanced growth		-1.2	-1.2		43.6	43.9		2.5	2.3		1.7	1.3
of which:													
China	Baseline	-1.8	0.7	1.9	16.3	29.0	32.4	5.1	2.7	3.8	3.3	3.4	5.8
	Balanced growth		-0.2	-0.0		28.8	29.3		1.7	1.5		1.5	1.5
India	Baseline	-7.7	-7.0	-6.5	76.0	77.6	80.3	7.2	5.1	5.4	-0.5	-2.0	-1.1
	Balanced growth		-3.9	-3.0		69.4	62.2		2.4	2.9		-1.4	-0.1
Africa	Baseline	-2.1	-3.8	-4.0	59.	59.6	64.3	2.6	0.3	0.4	0.3	-3.6	-3.6
	Balanced growth		-2.8	-1.9		57.8	55.9		-0.0	0.4		-2.8	-1.5
Latin America and the Caribbean	Baseline	-3.0	-4.3	-3.5	51.4	54.5	53.5	1.1	1.7	1.9	-1.9	-2.6	-1.6
	Balanced growth		-3.0	-2.4		51.0	48.2		0.7	1.5		-2.4	-0.9

Source: UNCTAD secretariat calculations, based on GPM.
Note: CIS includes Georgia.

In the realm of policymaking, what these model simulations underscore is the need to ensure policy consistency and macroeconomic coherence in order to obtain outcomes similar to those presented above. Policy consistency refers to preventing policy instruments from operating at cross purposes. Current inconsistencies in the configuration of fiscal and monetary policies of many economies after 2010 has been colourfully described as "driving the economic car with one foot on the brake and one foot on the pedal" (White, 2013:1). Instead, monetary expansion should be accompanied by fiscal expansion to prevent liquidity being hoarded or channelled to speculative uses; employment promotion programmes should be accompanied by income distribution policies so that aggregate demand is sustained by rising household incomes rather than debt; and policies targeting inflation should be accompanied by policies that address the causes of inflation, which in turn draws attention to incentives to domestic production and demand. These are but a few examples of policy consistency.

Pro-growth and rebalancing policies need to ensure macroeconomic coherence by addressing primarily the root problems that impede a solid and sustained global recovery. Until very recently, and even now in many developed economies, policymakers have seemed to be excessively concerned with fighting the threat of inflation and have been ignoring the reality of deflation. Likewise, policymakers in many countries have been advocating harsh adjustments in their governments' fiscal balances but have been neglecting to consider the potential effects on households and enterprises which would find it more difficult to rebuild their balance sheets when aggregate demand and income are depressed.

If the main problems of the post-crisis period have to do with insufficient aggregate demand and financial instability, the appropriate policy response should be not to inject more liquidity per se, but to encourage credit flows that generate productive activity, while boosting aggregate demand and designing income policies to make use of such credit flows in a sustainable manner.

There is another aspect of macroeconomic coherence that may easily be overlooked by policymakers when considering their options. In an increasingly interconnected global economy, policies have to be consistent for the world as a whole. There are several examples of why this matters, but two are discussed here. First, after taking into account real and financial feedbacks, it should be clear that a sustained and stable demand-led growth path has to start domestically, rather than each country individually pushing for competitive reductions of costs and imports in order to generate a net-export-led recovery. Robust domestic activity in a sufficient number of countries – a process in which, admittedly, surplus countries have much more to contribute – is the only truly sustainable basis for the recovery of global trade. Second, in the absence of a truly globally inclusive financial architecture, unfettered global financial markets without adequate regulatory control can be pernicious, as the 2008 financial crisis has amply demonstrated. The continuing inadequacy of institutions and mechanisms for international coordination of policy actions affects the rules of the game in fundamental ways, forcing policymakers to adopt strategies that may appear to be convenient for the moment, but which are effectively self-defeating in the medium term. It is essential to continue with efforts to devise a more effective set of globally inclusive institutions to regulate markets, help correct unsustainable imbalances when they emerge, and better pursue the aims of global development and convergence. This may be an ambitious undertaking, for which a great degree of perseverance and vision is required. But as chapter IV highlights, history shows that deep reforms of global scope similar to the ones mentioned here were seriously contemplated in the past. Meanwhile, far more meaningful efforts are needed to coordinate national policy strategies, to consider the implications of their interactions in a global setting, and to manage international transactions and flows accordingly. ■

Notes

1 The trend is estimated from the mid-1990s onwards to avoid giving excessive weight to the boom years preceding the crisis, which were deemed unsustainable, as well as to the immediate policy responses during the global crisis, which were clearly more expansionary than the norm.

2 At the time of writing, the United Kingdom's Office for National Statistics was in the process of revising its annual GDP statistics (in *United Kingdom National Accounts – The Blue Book, 2014 edition*), and preliminary reports suggest that by 2013 the level of real GDP may be marginally above the pre-crisis level.

3 State and local governments in the United States are required by statutory law to balance their primary budgets, which in practice imposes expenditure adjustments relative to tax collection and other revenues.

4 This term, which was used by Keynes in his General Theory, refers to a burst of optimism that affects the mood of private investors.

5 This confirms earlier work on the United States (Piketty and Saez, 2003) and across a large pool of countries in both developed and developing regions (see, for example, Cornia, 2004; and Milanovic, 2005).

6 From a different methodological perspective, and using industry-level datasets, other empirical studies suggest that a greater proportion of capital accumulation vis-à-vis wage-earners and the self-employed implies, when properly estimated, a tendency towards a sharper deterioration of labour income (Arpaia et al., 2009).

7 While there is broad agreement on the importance of Piketty's empirical findings about long-term trends of inequality, his theoretical explanation, which validates neoclassical growth theory, has been subjected to rigorous critiques (Patnaik, 2014; Taylor, 2014).

8 Similar conclusions with variations, depending on underlying economic structures of different countries, have been provided by analytical and empirical evaluations of the "wage-led" versus "profit-led" debate (Storm and Naastepad, 2012; Lavoie and Stockhammer, 2012).

9 See earlier *Trade and Development Reports*; also Turner, 2008.

10 These two cases together account for a significant share of global consumption, and could therefore have at least some influence in reigniting global imbalances. While other relatively large economies seem to show similar patterns, the investigation on these two countries is facilitated by the availability of detailed balance sheets and asset compositions of their household sectors.

11 This is an accounting term that refers to a positive shock to the net wealth of asset owners when asset prices rise. The shock can be estimated by imputing the price changes of the different assets to the underlying structure of the balance sheet. By further discounting consumer price inflation, a measure of real holding gains is obtained. See Izurieta (2005) for a formal methodological justification and earlier empirical estimates. The Financial Accounts of the Federal Reserve of the United States publishes the series of holding gains in nominal terms (see table R.100) before discounted by inflation. The nominal series generated here show a very close match with those of the Federal Reserve, with only negligible errors due to the aggregate nature of the asset prices used. This allows checking against such existing data the estimation methodology applied further below to the case of the United Kingdom, which does not publish holding gains of the household sector. It should be emphasized that these are accounting gains, rather than the gains actually realized through asset transactions.

12 "Net financial savings", attributed to Tobin (1982), is the equivalent of the more known concept of surplus or deficit, commonly used in reference to the public sector and the external sector (the current account). Its formal name in national accounts is "net lending" (or "net borrowing" when negative), but this term is not used in the text to avoid confusion with the also commonly used "lending" or "borrowing" in relation to the banking sector.

13 The series, which only run up to 2012, were compiled by combining national accounts statistics with survey data and imputed trends from the evolution of wage

or agricultural incomes when available. However, a large margin of error is possible, particularly for countries where the proportion of informal/mixed incomes is large.

14   Mixed income in the national accounts comprises incomes earned from the self-employed as well as all incomes earned by unincorporated enterprises and those classified as "non-market output".

15   See also *TDR 2001*; Akyüz, 2002; D'Arista, 2007; Ghosh and Chandrasekhar, 2001; Singh, 2003; Stiglitz, 1999.

16   See also Akyüz, 2013 and 2014; Ghosh, 2014; *TDR 2013*; UNCTAD, 2011.

17   See Lawson (2011), and also Obstfeld (2012) for a more general appraisal of similar views.

18   Ukraine, where capital inflows rose only marginally after 2009, is an example of how a shock like the financial crisis can hit vulnerable sectors causing systemic threats that require more lasting adjustments, often exacerbated by social tensions.

19   See, for example Chandrasekhar and Ghosh, 2013 and 2014; Lee, 2013; McKenzie and Pons-Vignon, 2012; Chang, 2013; Kang et al., 2011; Ffrench-Davis, 2012.

20   This index is available at: http://unctadstat.unctad.org/ wds/TableViewer/tableView.aspx?ReportId=30953. It measures, product by product, the evolution of (normalized) balances over time, while controlling for re-exporting activities. The dataset is very disaggregated and detailed, allowing a full mapping across the standard industrial classification, and it also specifies categories by the degree of labour skills within the manufacturing sector.

21   The GPM is a fully endogenous modelling framework based on water-tight accounting without "black-holes" and without unexplained residuals. Behavioural relations that determine the macroeconomic adjustments are estimated econometrically using panel (124 countries) and time series (period 1980 to 2012). The model covers 25 countries and country groups, and considers GDP in main sectors; public, private and financial institutions; employment; international trade (five main categories) and finance; and fiscal, monetary and industrial/ trade policy (see TDR 2013, annex to chapter I). For a more technical discussion, see website: http:// unctad.org/en/PublicationsLibrary/tdr2014_GPM_ TechnicalDescription.pdf.

22   As stated by Keynes (1936: 149), "The state of confidence is relevant because it is one of the major factors determining the former [the rate of investment], which is the same thing as the investment demand-schedule. There is, however, not much to be said about the state of confidence a priori. Our conclusions must mainly depend upon the actual observation of markets and business psychology."

Keynes further made a crucial observation to stress how much more difficult it is to know, a priori, about the conditions that enable a recovery after a crisis (1936: 158), "Thus we must also take account of the other facet of the state of confidence, namely, the confidence of the lending institutions towards those who seek to borrow from them, sometimes described as the state of credit. A collapse in the price of equities, which has had disastrous reactions on the marginal efficiency of capital, may have been due to the weakening either of speculative confidence or of the state of credit. But whereas the weakening of either is enough to cause a collapse, recovery requires the revival of both."

23   In this particular case there are only small differences of degree with the baseline. In its construction, in order to avoid crisis conditions, as explained above, the baseline imposes ceilings and floors on exchange rates and commodity prices which would have resulted from the imbalances discussed in section A.

24   In the GPM, these preferences apply to countries with a per capita income lower than $2,000 dollars in 2012.

25   The historic period runs up to 2014, but the latest verifiable figures for the share of labour income are not available beyond 2012 for most countries.

26   Incomes policies are assumed to be comparatively stronger in the United States, bringing its labour share closer to pre-1990 levels and closer to the levels of other developed economies. More importantly, households in the United States have accumulated serious financial imbalances over time, and the assumed improvement in the functional distribution of income is required in order to generate a sustained growth of private consumption without increasing households' financial vulnerabilities.

27   *TDR 2013* proposed an alternative simulation that assumed that all developing and emerging economies would engage in proactive incomes policies while developed countries would continue to seek net export advantages by compressing wage shares. The model showed that this would result in a net benefit for developed countries at the expense of developing and emerging economies. In this situation, the latter set of countries would naturally exercise considerable caution in adopting similar incomes policies, which, consequently, would result in a weaker impact on growth and distribution.

28   In the United States, and to a lesser degree in India, growth of government spending is assumed to be relatively stronger than in the historic period, and it also turns out to be marginally stronger than the growth of GDP in the first five years of the projections. This is because, as discussed earlier, debt-driven spending of the private sector was growing at a fast rate, and to achieve a financially stable path

of fast GDP growth the public sector had to make a larger contribution than the private sector.

29 An exception is China, where the policy shift away from investment growth towards faster growth of household incomes and consumption is assumed to be strengthened during the first few years of the simulation. Under these assumptions private investment in China would tend to stabilize at around 25 per cent of GDP towards the end of the simulation period.

30 An exception is China, where a deceleration of growth is expected by policy design, and for many of the periphery countries of Europe which continue to be under pressure by deflationary policies, as well as for many of the oil-exporting countries which will not benefit from a continuing rise in oil prices of the magnitude experienced over the past two decades.

31 The balanced-growth scenario has a pro-development bias (without disregarding growth in developed countries), and it is also known that the growth potential of developing and emerging economies is greater than that of developed economies. Regarding measurement, the PPP weights (base 2005 in these simulations) are not re-scaled each year, resulting in a greater weight of developing economies in global GDP along the entire period of the projection.

32 Exceptions include members of the Commonwealth of Independent States (CIS) and China. The CIS economies, instead of accumulating larger fiscal surpluses over time, would benefit from reducing surpluses in order to enhance the process of structural transformation. And in China, more emphasis is placed on strengthening social protection in order to promote the growth of household consumption.

33 Not all developed countries encourage debt-driven private sector spending. For example Germany and Japan significantly increase their external surpluses in the baseline. Thus, the group of developed countries as a whole does not show a strong pattern in one direction.

References

Akyüz Y (2002). Towards reform of the international financial architecture: Which way forward? In: Akyüz Y, ed. *Reforming the Global Financial Architecture, Issues and Proposals*. Geneva, Penang and London: UNCTAD, Third World Network and Zed Books: 1–27.

Akyüz Y (2013). Waving or drowning: Developing countries after the financial crisis. Research Paper No. 48, South Centre, Geneva.

Akyüz Y (2014). Crisis Management in the United States and Europe: Impact on Developing Countries and Longer-term Consequences. Research Paper No. 50, South Centre, Geneva.

Arpaia A, Pérez E and Pichelman K (2009). Understanding labour income share dynamics in Europe. Economic Papers 379, European Commission, Brussels.

Baker D (2009). *Plunder and Blunder: The Rise and Fall of the Bubble Economy*. Sausalito, CA, PoliPoint Press.

Blanchard O, Faruqee H, Das M, Forbes J and Tesar L (2010). The initial impact of the crisis on emerging markets. *Brookings Papers on Economic Activity*, Spring: 263–323

Chandrasekhar CP and Ghosh J (2013). The looming banking crisis. *Business Line*, 2 September; available at: http://www.thehindubusinessline.com/opinion/columns/c-p-chandrasekhar/the-looming-banking-crisis/article5086242.ece.

Chandrasekhar CP and Ghosh J (2014). How vulnerable are emerging economies? *Business Line*, 3 March; available at: http://www.thehindubusinessline.com/opinion/columns/c-p-chandrasekhar/emerging-economies-in-a-vulnerable-phase/article5746927.ece.

Chang KS (2013). *South Korea in Transition*. New York, NY, Routledge.

Cornia GA (2004). *Inequality, Growth and Poverty in an Era of Liberalisation and Globalisation*. Oxford, Oxford University Press.

Cripps F, Izurieta A and Singh A (2011). Global imbalances, under-consumption and over-borrowing: The state of the world economy and future policies. *Development and Change*, 42(1): 228–261.

D'Arista J (2007). U.S. debt and global imbalances. *International Journal of Political Economy*, 36(4): 12–35.

Epstein G, ed, (2005). *Financialization and the World Economy*. Cheltenham and Northampton: Edward Elgar.

Ffrench-Davis R (2012). Employment and real macroeconomic stability: The regressive role of financial flows in Latin America. *International Labour Review*, 151(1-2): 21–41. International Labour Office, Geneva.

Foster JB (2010). The financialization of accumulation. *Monthly Review*, 62(5): 1–17.

Galbraith J (2012). *Inequality and Instability*. Oxford and New York, Oxford University Press.

Ghosh J (2014). Emerging markets: Déjà vu all over again? *Triple Crisis Blog*, 3 February; available at: http://triple crisis.com/emerging-markets-deja-vu-all-over-again/.

Ghosh J and Chandrasekhar CP (2001). *Crisis as Conquest: Learning from East Asia*. New Delhi, Orient Longman Limited.

IMF (2007). *World Economic Outlook*, Washington, DC. October.

Izurieta A (2005). Hazardous inertia of imbalances in the US and world economy. *Economic and Political Weekly*, 40(34): 3739–3750.

Kang J, Lee C and Lee D (2011). Equity fund performance persistence with investment style: Evidence from Korea. *Emerging Markets Finance and Trade*, 47(3): 111–135.

Keynes JM ([1936], 1997). *The General Theory of Employment, Interest and Money*. Amherst, NY, Prometheus Books.

Lapavitsas C (2013). *Profiting without Producing: How Finance Exploits Us All*. London and New York, Verso.

Lavoie M and Stockhammer E (2012). Wage-led growth: Concept, theories and policies. Conditions of Work and Employment Series No. 41, International Labour Office, Geneva.

Lawson N (2011). Five myths and a menace. *Standpoint*, January/February 2011; available at: http://stand-pointmag.co.uk/node/3644/full.

Leduc S and Spiegel M (2013). Is Asia Decoupling from the United States (Again)? *Federal Reserve Bank of San Francisco Working Paper Series* 2013-10, San Francisco, CA.

Lee KK (2013). The end of egalitarian growth in Korea: Rising inequality and stagnant growth after the 1997 crisis. Paper presented at the World Economics Association Conferences on Inequalities in Asia: The Interaction with Growth, Structural Change, Economic Openness and Social and Political Structures, 12 May–8 June; available at: http://iiaconference2013.worldeconomicsassociation.org/wp-content/uploads/WEA-IIAConference2013-3_lee.pdf.

McKenzie R and Pons-Vignon N (2012). Volatile capital flows and a route to financial crisis in South Africa.

MPRA paper 40119, University Library of Munich, Munich.

Milanovic B (2005). *Worlds Apart: Measuring International and Global Inequality*. Princeton, NJ, Princeton University Press.

Obstfeld M (2012). Does the Current Account Still Matter? *American Economic Review: Papers & Proceedings*: 102(3): 1–23.

Patnaik P (2010). The myths of the subprime crisis. *Networkideas.org*, 13 August; available at: http://www.networkideas.org/news/aug2010/print/prnt13082010_Crisis.htm.

Patnaik P (2014). Capitalism, inequality and globalization: Thomas Piketty's "Capital in the Twenty-First Century". Networkideas.org; available at: http://www.networkideas.org/featart/jul2014/fa18_Thomas_Piketty.htm.

Piketty T (2014). *Capital in the Twenty-First Century*. Cambridge, MA, Harvard University Press.

Piketty T and Saez E (2003). Income inequality in the United States, 1913–1998. *Quarterly Journal of Economics*, 118(1): 1–39.

Singh A (2003). Capital account liberalization, free long-term capital flows, financial crises and economic development. *Eastern Economic Journal*, 29(2): 191–216.

Stiglitz J (1999). Reforming the global economic architecture: Lessons from recent crises. *Journal of Finance*, 54(4): 1508–1521.

Storm S and Naastepad CWM (2012). *Macroeconomics Beyond the NAIRU*. Cambridge, MA, Harvard University Press.

Taylor L (2014). The triumph of the rentier? Thomas Piketty vs. Luigi Pasinetti and John Maynard Keynes. Institute for New Economic Thinking blog; available at: http://ineteconomics.org/blog/institute/triumph-rentier-thomas-piketty-vs-luigi-pasinetti-and-john-maynard-keynes.

Tobin A (1982). Money and finance in the macroeconomic process. *Journal of Money, Credit and Banking*, 14(2), May: 171–204.

Turner G (2008). *The Credit Crunch*. London, Pluto Press.

UNCTAD (2011). *Report of the Secretary-General of UNCTAD to UNCTAD XIII. Development-led Globalization: Towards Sustainable and Inclusive Development Paths*. New York and Geneva.

UNCTAD (*TDR 2001*). *Trade and Development Report, 2001. Global Trends and Prospects, Financial Architecture*. United Nations publication, sales no. E .01.II.D.10, New York and Geneva.

UNCTAD (*TDR 2013*). *Trade and Development Report, 2013. Adjusting to the Changing Dynamics of the World Economy*. United Nations publication, sales no. E.13.II .D.3, New York and Geneva.

United Kingdom Office for National Statistics (2014). *United Kingdom National Accounts: The Blue Book: 2014 edition*. London.

United Nations (2009). *Report of the Commission of Experts of the President of the United Nations General Assembly on Reforms of the International Monetary and Financial System*. New York.

White W (2013). Overt monetary financing (OMF) and crisis management. *Project Syndicate*, June 12; available at: http://www.project-syndicate.org/commentary/overt-monetary-financing--omf--and-crisismanagement.

Chapter III

POLICY SPACE AND GLOBAL GOVERNANCE: ISSUES AT STAKE

The discussions now under way on a post-2015 development agenda are aiming for an ambitious narrative that goes beyond "business as usual" to establish a more universal, transformative and sustainable approach than the one advanced through the Millennium Development Goals (MDGs) (United Nations, 2012). As such, it will play a key role in setting new goals and targets for policymakers, both at the national and international levels. The 17 goals (and related targets) agreed to at the United Nations Open Working Group on Sustainable Development point to a level of ambition and complexity well beyond the MDGs (United Nations, 2014). The international community faces three principal challenges in fashioning this new approach.

The first challenge is aligning goals and targets to a policy paradigm that can help raise productivity and per capita incomes everywhere, generate decent jobs on a scale needed to meet a rapidly growing and urbanizing global labour force, establish a stable international financial system that boosts productive investment, and deliver reliable public services that leave no one behind, particularly in the most vulnerable communities. The economic paradigm of market liberalism that has been in the ascendency for the past three decades has disappointed in most of these respects (UNCTAD, 2011; Caritas in Veritate Foundation, 2014).

The second challenge facing any new development agenda is the massive rise in inequality, which has accompanied the spread of market liberalism. This is important because, in addition to ethical considerations, and unlike the simple textbook trade-off

between growth and equality, growing inequality can threaten economic progress and social stability, and undermine political cohesion (*TDRs 1997* and *2012*; Wilkinson and Pickett, 2009; Piketty, 2014). The rising income share (and political influence) of the top one per cent has already helped revive this discussion; and figures such as the wealth of the 85 wealthiest individuals surpassing that of the bottom half of the world's population provide the desired shock effect. But for a full understanding of the recent rise of inequality, it is necessary to look more carefully at functional income dynamics and, in particular, at the divergence between wage and productivity growth, the imperatives of shareholder value and executive compensation in shaping corporate behaviour, and the regressive turn in taxation. Greater capital mobility has made it harder to tax some, often the largest, firms. In addition, it has reduced the bargaining power of labour and increased the State's reliance on regressive taxes and bond markets, and further amplified the adverse distributive impact of unregulated financial activity. A growing body of research has begun to tie the scale of the recent crisis to these inequalities, pointing to their skewed impact on the composition of demand and their links to an increasingly fragile, debt-driven growth model (Kumhof and Rancière, 2010; Stiglitz, 2012; Mian and Sufi, 2014).

The third challenge is to ensure that effective policy instruments, and the space to use them, are available to countries to enable them to achieve the agreed goals and advance the development agenda. This is very much the focus of this *Report*. The appeal but also the weaknesses of the MDGs[1] stem, in part, from their singular emphasis on clearly defined social outcomes, while giving virtually no consideration to either economic outcomes or the policy instruments required for achieving any of the set goals at the national and international levels. Only MDG 8 on a global partnership for development allowed for a discussion of those policy instruments, but it has proved much weaker and less specific than any of the other goals (UNCTAD, 2013).[2]

Addressing these three challenges would be a formidable task even under ideal circumstances, but it is all the more daunting now because of changes to the global economic environment resulting from the financial crisis in 2008–2009. Initial efforts to meet the MDGs took place in a generally supportive external economic environment: not only were aid flows growing, but there was also strong market demand in both developed and emerging economies, commodity prices were rising and access to external capital proved easier than before for many developing countries. These factors have contributed to strong growth across the developing world since 2002, where growth rates have been consistently higher than those in the developed world.

These trends were interpreted as part of a new era for the world economy, combining a "great moderation" in macroeconomic circumstances with a "great convergence" in global incomes, with expectations for sustained future growth linked to the rapid emergence of a "global middle class". Concomitantly, calls for stronger global governance of an increasingly interconnected world economy, diminished. For a time, it also encouraged a belief that growth in the poorer countries had decoupled from trends in the developed world (Canuto, 2012). However, recent events suggest that this is a premature conclusion (Akyüz, 2013).

The new development agenda is likely to face a harsher external environment in the years ahead. Some of the potential difficulties are outlined in chapter II of this *Report*, and they confirm the prolonged and fragile nature of the post-crisis recovery, particularly if a "business-as-usual" macroeconomic scenario continues. The financial crisis also revealed a set of persistent and highly interrelated economic and social imbalances that will inevitably have a strong bearing on efforts to design new development strategies aimed at tackling issues relating to a growing urban-rural divide, formal and informal livelihoods, access to affordable energy sources that minimize environmental damage, and food and

water security. These will need to be resolved by both developed and developing countries if a more inclusive and sustainable global economy is to be achieved by 2030.

Rebalancing on these many fronts will require an integrated policy framework encompassing more viable and inclusive national development strategies, along with changes in the governance of the global economic system to accommodate and support them. If progress on social and economic goals is not underpinned by effective national strategies for sustainable and inclusive development, or if the global economy is incompatible with such strategies, progress towards achieving more ambitious development goals will, in all likelihood, be frustrated. Last year's *Trade and Development Report* argued that mobilizing greater domestic resources and building markets at the national and regional levels were likely to be key to sustained growth in many developing countries in the years ahead. Maximizing the contribution of national resources for achieving the economic and social goals envisaged in the post-2015 agenda will certainly require a more assertive macroeconomic policy agenda. Such an agenda would need to include the use of a broad array of fiscal, financial and regulatory instruments in support of capital accumulation, proactive labour market and incomes policies to generate more decent jobs, and effective control of the capital account to limit potential damage from external shocks and crises. But economic sustainability will also require diversification and upgrading of the productive structures and capabilities from which wealth is created and distributed (Salazar-Xirinaches et al., 2014). Building more competitive firms, moving resources into higher value-added sectors and strengthening national technological capabilities cannot rely on market forces alone; effective industrial policies and dedicated efforts to support and coordinate private- and public-sector activities will also be crucial.

Any such broadening and strengthening of national development strategies will need to be accompanied by institutional changes. Markets are rarely "free", and never operate in isolation; they require a framework of rules, restraints and norms to operate effectively (Polanyi, 1944). As such, the market economy is always embedded in a wider legal, social and cultural setting, and is sustained by a panoply of political forces. The search for profits by private firms implies that individual businesses are constantly testing the limits of these wider rules and restraints, and mobilizing for changes that give them more space to undertake that search, such as exerting pressure to reduce what they see as the "burden" of red tape, "excessive" taxes, the "strictures" of banking and accounting rules, the "biases" in labour and consumer laws, and the "constraints" on moving money in and out of a country. Most governments understand that the profit motive brings benefits but also entails costs. Accordingly, they strive to seek a balance between corporate interests and those of their other constituencies. How and to what extent the framework of rules and regulations for markets to operate is strengthened or weakened is part of a complex political process specific to each society, but it cannot be entirely dispensed with without threatening a breakdown of the wider economic and social order. A basic and dangerous flaw in market fundamentalism, as recently argued by Mark Carney, Governor of the Bank of England, is its denial of these complexities in the design and implementation of economic policies (Carney, 2014).

Historically, the evolution of today's successful economies has, above all, been marked by what has been described as "adaptive efficiency" (North, 2005); that is, the capacity to develop institutions that provide a stable framework for economic activity, but which are also flexible enough to provide the maximum leeway for the adoption and tailoring of strategies and choices to meet the specific challenges of a given time and situation. In the particular case of State institutions, the notion of adaptive efficiency implies that policymakers must have the requisite space to articulate priorities, choose their preferred policy instruments and implement what they consider to be the most appropriate policy mix. Some time ago, the eminent Dutch economist, Jan Tinbergen, established that for the mix to work at an aggregate level there have to be at least as many policy instruments as there are goals. If a programme includes more goals than instruments, at least one goal will not be met; whereas if it contains more instruments than goals, there will be more than one way of achieving the combination of goals.

Arguably, and as is certainly the case with most development strategies where a variety of microeconomic, macroeconomic, structural and strategic goals are pursued simultaneously, maximizing the number of instruments would seem to be the sensible option. However, simply reducing the issue of policy space to the number of instruments and goals is not sufficient for an understanding of the complexities involved. Different instruments are likely to have different degrees of effectiveness in meeting a particular goal; but also, because goals are interdependent, a particular instrument can potentially influence many goals at the same time, and not always in the expected or desired direction. Moreover, the distinction between goals and instruments is neither entirely unambiguous nor obvious. What is a target for one set of policymakers (or in one set of circumstances) may well be an instrument for another set of policymakers (or in another set of circumstances).

Policy space essentially refers to the freedom and ability of a government to identify and pursue the most appropriate mix of economic and social policies to achieve equitable and sustainable development that is best suited to its particular national context. It can be defined as the combination of de jure policy sovereignty, which is the formal authority of national policymakers over policy goals and instruments, and de facto national policy control, which involves the ability of national policymakers to set priorities, influence specific targets, and weigh possible trade-offs (Mayer, 2008). Both are affected by the external environment, albeit in different ways, and there is well-recognized tension between the consequences of external economic integration and national policy flexibility (Panic, 1995).

* * * *

Restoring a development model that favours the real economy – and the constituencies that depend on it for their livelihoods and security – over financial interests, will almost certainly require adding more instruments to the policy toolkit than is currently contemplated by economic orthodoxy. However, broadening development strategies in this way must still recognize the contingent and uncertain effects of particular policy instruments, as well as the potential trade-offs and adjustment costs of choosing one set of policies over another. Typically, policy goals are rarely of the "either-or" type (e.g. employment or inflation, open or closed economies, State or private ownership, fixed or flexible exchange rates), but of various shades in-between. This would already suggest that learning to mix objectives and instruments is an unavoidable component of policymaking, and that experimentation becomes all the more important, given that there are different ways of achieving faster growth, macroeconomic stability, openness and a more equitable distribution of income (World Bank, 2005).

Moreover, at any particular time, there is an unwritten social contract about the rules that make an economy work and which set boundaries to the State's economic role. The process whereby a consensus is forged, priorities are set and attitudes are shaped is just as important a part of defining policy space as technocratic competence. Deciding on the appropriate policy mix will also involve judgements and quantitative estimates about the likely magnitude of the adjustments arising from a particular programme. In any event, the combination of leadership, judgement and experimentation is certain to make for an open-ended policymaking process.

The State's capacity to coordinate different interest groups, generate confidence in its actions and behaviour, and establish national development as an urgent, overarching project continues to distinguish those countries that have promoted catch-up growth and sustained structural transformation from those that have not. Successful States have enhanced their competencies through the development of structures of accountability; through continuous improvements to staff recruitment, promotion, compensation and training; and through the creation of (semi-) public institutions and other types of partnerships, particularly with industry associations, but also with trade unions, universities and research bodies. They have also established regulatory and supervisory bodies, often with significant degrees of independence from the political process, to provide the rules, disciplines, incentives and surveillance that help markets to operate, while seeking to minimize possible microeconomic and macroeconomic distortions. In the context of the structural, technological and social deficits that need to be corrected in all developing countries, albeit to varying degrees, UNCTAD has associated these various institutional elements with the efforts of a "developmental State" to oversee successful transformation.

* * * *

In an increasingly globalizing world, no less than at the domestic level, market activity also requires a framework of rules, restraints and norms. And, no different from the domestic level, the weakening and strengthening of that framework is a persistent feature. However, there are two important differences. The first is that the international institutions designed to support that framework depend principally on negotiations among States with regard to their operation. Essentially these States must decide on whether and how much of their own policy space they are willing to trade for the advantages of having international rules, disciplines and support. Inevitably, in a world of unequal States, the space required to pursue their own national economic and social development aspirations varies, as does the likely impact of an individual country's policy decisions on others. Managing this trade-off is particularly difficult at the multilateral level, where the differences among States are the most pronounced. Second, the extent to which different international

economic forces can intrude on a country's policy space also varies. In particular, cross-border financial activities, as Kindleberger (1986) noted in his seminal discussion of international public goods, appear to be a particularly intrusive factor. But in today's world of diminished political and legal restraints on cross-border economic transactions, finance is not the only such source; as chapter V notes, there are also very large asymmetries in international production, in particular with the lead firms in international production networks, which are also altering the space available to policymakers.

The growing interdependence among States and markets provides the main rationale for a well-structured system of global economic governance with multilateral rules and disciplines. In principle, such a system should ensure the provision of global public goods such as international economic and financial stability and a more open trading system. In addition, it should be represented by coherent multilateral institutional arrangements created by intergovernmental agreements to voluntarily reduce sovereignty on a reciprocal basis. The guiding principle of such arrangements should be their ability to generate fair and inclusive outcomes. This principle should inform the design, implementation and enforcement of multilateral rules, disciplines and support mechanisms. These would contribute significantly to minimizing adverse international spillovers and other negative externalities created by national economic policies that focus on maximizing national benefits. From this perspective, how these arrangements manage the interface between different national systems (from which they ultimately draw their legitimacy), rather than erasing national differences and establishing a singular and omnipotent economic and legal structure, best describes the objectives of multilateralism.

The extent to which national development strategies respond to national needs and priorities can be limited or circumscribed by multilateral regimes and international rules, but equally, they can be influenced by economic and political pressures emanating from the workings of global markets, depending on the degree of integration of the country concerned. While the extent and depth of engagement with the global economy may result from domestic economic policy choices, subsequent policies are likely to be affected by that engagement, sometimes in a way and to an extent not anticipated. As noted in *TDR 2006*, it is not only international treaties and rules, but also global market conditions and policy decisions in other countries that have an impact on policy space. Global imbalances of power (both economic and political) also remain undeniably significant in affecting the capacities of governments of different countries to engage in the design and implementation of autonomous policies.

There are valid concerns that the various legal obligations emerging from multilateral, regional and bilateral agreements have reduced national policy autonomy by restricting both the available range and the efficacy of particular policy instruments. At the same time, multilateral disciplines can operate to reduce the inherent bias of international economic relations in favour of countries that have greater economic or political power (Akyüz, 2007). Those disciplines can simultaneously restrict (particularly de jure) and ease (particularly de facto) policy space. In addition, the effectiveness of national policies tends to be weakened, in some instances very

significantly, by the global spread of market forces (especially financial markets) as well as by the internalization of markets within the operations of large international firms.

It is important to consider whether, how and to what extent policy space is reduced and reconfigured. Limits on policy space resulting from obligations or pressures to deregulate markets tend to circumscribe the ability of governments to alter patterns of market functioning to meet their broader social and developmental objectives. Yet unfettered market processes are unlikely to deliver macroeconomic and financial stability, full employment, economic diversification towards higher value added activities, poverty reduction and other socially desirable outcomes.

But while national policies are obviously affected by the extent of policy space available, as determined by the external context, they are also – and still fundamentally – the result of domestic forces. These include, among others, politics and the political economy that determine the power and voice of different groups in society, domestic expertise and capacities, the nature of institutions and enforcement agencies, the structure of the polity (e.g. degree of federalism), and prevailing macroeconomic conditions. Even when policymakers have full sovereign command over policy instruments, they may not be able to control specific policy targets effectively.

Furthermore, the interplay between these internal and external forces in determining both policymaking and implementation within countries in today's globalized world is an increasingly complex process. The emergence in the 1980s and 1990s, and the growing acceptance by policymakers throughout the world, of what could be called a standard template for national economic policies – irrespective of the size, context and nature of the economy concerned – was certainly influential (even if not always decisive) in determining patterns of market liberalization. But even as waves of trade liberalization and financial deregulation swept across the world, culminating in what we experience as globalization today, variations across individual countries suggest that they have retained some degree of policy autonomy, along with relatively independent thinking.

Certainly, for the more developed countries, globalization *à la carte* has been the practice to date, as it has been for the more successful developing countries over the past 20 years. By contrast, many developing countries have had to contend with a more rigid and structured approach to economic liberalization. This one size-fits-all approach to development policy has, for the most part, been conducted by or through the Bretton Woods institutions – the World Bank and the International Monetary Fund (IMF) – whose surveillance and influence over domestic policymakers following the debt crises of the 1980s were considerably extended giving them greater authority to demand changes to what they deemed to be "unsound" policies. Countries seeking financial assistance or debt rescheduling from the Bank or the IMF had to adopt approved macroeconomic stability programmes and agree to "structural" and political reforms, which extended the influence of markets – via liberalization, privatization and deregulation, among others – and substantially reduced the economic and developmental roles of the State. Similarly, and as discussed in greater detail in the next chapter, the Uruguay Round of trade negotiations extended the authority of the World Trade Organization (WTO) to embrace services, agriculture, intellectual property and trade-related investment measures, thereby restricting, to varying degrees, the policy space available to developing countries to manage their integration into the global economy.

Emphasizing the role of policy, and of the international economic institutions in promoting one set of policies over another, is an important correction to the view that globalization is an autonomous, irresistible and irreversible process driven by impersonal market and technological forces. Such forces are undoubtedly important, but essentially they are instigated by specific policy choices and shaped by existing institutions. It is also misleading to think of the global economy as some sort of "natural" system with a logic of its own. It is, and always has been, the evolving outcome of a complex interaction of economic and political relations. In this environment, multilateral rules and institutions can provide

incentives and sanctions that encourage countries to cooperate rather than go their own way. And as the world has become increasingly interdependent, it is more challenging for countries to build institutional structures and safeguard remaining flexibilities in support of inclusive development. To the extent that markets and firms operate globally, there are grounds for having global rules and regulations. Moreover, international collective action is needed to help provide and manage global public goods that markets are unable or unwilling to provide. Dealing effectively with emerging threats, such as climate change, also requires appropriate global rules, regulations and resources. However, it goes without saying that governance at the international level is very different from governance at the national level, given that governments are being asked to surrender some measure of their sovereignty and responsibility to support collective actions and goals. It is imperative, therefore, and all the more so in a world of interdependent but unequal States and economies, for international measures to be designed in such a way that they complement or strengthen capacities to achieve national objectives and meet the needs of their constituencies.

The system that has evolved under finance-led globalization has led to a multiplicity of rules and regulations on international trade and investment that tend to excessively constrain national policy options. At the same time it lacks an effective multilateral framework of rules and institutions for ensuring international financial stability and for overseeing extra-territorial fiscal matters. Within this imperfect system, policymakers in developed countries are aiming to tackle a series of interrelated macroeconomic and structural challenges, while those from developing countries are trying to consolidate recent gains and enter a new phase of inclusive development. It is therefore more important than ever before for national policy space to be made a central issue on the global development agenda.

* * * *

Subsequent chapters of this *Report* address a number of these issues in detail. Chapter IV looks at the origins of the post-Second World War multilateral system and, in particular, at efforts to ensure that the

space for a new State-led policy consensus that avoided the mistakes of the inter-war years would be consistent with multilateral arrangements and disciplines in support of a more open, stable and interdependent world economy. It contends that the partial efforts to internationalize the New Deal in the 1940s eventually gave rise to a more inclusive multilateral agenda that was championed by the developing world. Chapter V reviews the mostly de jure policy constraints on developing countries, associated with multilateral, regional and bilateral agreements on trade and investment, which hamper their efforts to advance and direct the structural transformation of their economies. It presents some of the options that are still available to these countries in the areas of trade and industrial policy, and discusses how a further shrinking of their policy space can be avoided. It also highlights the importance of policy space in relation to the spread of global value chains. Chapter VI discusses the mostly de facto constraints on policies aimed at securing macroeconomic and financial stability in developing countries. Such stability is a prerequisite for achieving a high level of productive capital formation and productivity gains, which can benefit entire populations of these countries.

In addition, the chapter examines efforts to strengthen capital account management, and considers various options to avoid the destabilizing effects of short-term flows. Further, it considers the impact of international investment agreements on policy space, particularly through dispute settlement mechanisms that favour private over public law and interests, and examines the possible options to redress that anomaly without foregoing the potential benefits accruing from hosting foreign direct investment (FDI). Chapter VII deals with the factors that are limiting the scope of governments to use fiscal instruments for pursuing their development objectives, and provides some ideas on how fiscal space could be enlarged through national and global reforms. In particular, it looks at the economic costs resulting from the surge in tax evasion by individuals and corporations that use secrecy jurisdictions, as well as the specific challenges facing commodity-dependent economies in bargaining over the distribution of resource rents. ∎

Notes

1   For a discussion on whether and which of the Millennium Development Goals has been attained, see UNCTAD, 2014.

2   Employment targets, which were added somewhat later to Goal 1, have contributed to opening up the discussion to wider policy issues.

References

Akyüz Y (2007). *Global rules and markets: Constraints over policy autonomy in developing countries.* Penang, Third World Network.

Akyüz Y (2013). Drowning or waving? Developing countries after the financial crisis. South Centre Research Paper, no. 48. Geneva, South Centre.

Canuto O (2012). Recoupling or switchover: Developing countries in the global economy. In: Canuto O and Giugale M, eds. *The Day After Tomorrow: A*

Handbook on the Future of Economic Policy in the Developing World. Washington, DC, World Bank.

Caritas in Veritate Foundation (2014). Beyond the financial crisis: Towards a Christian perspective for action. Working paper, Geneva.

Carney M (2014). Inclusive capitalism: Creating a sense of the systemic. Speech delivered at the Conference on Inclusive Capitalism, London, May.

Kindleberger C (1986). International public goods without international government. *The American Economic Review*, 76(1): 1–13.

Kumhof M and Rancière R (2010). Inequality, leverage and crises. IMF working paper WP/10/268, November, Washington, DC, International Monetary Fund.

Mayer J (2008). Policy space: What, for what and where? UNCTAD Discussion Paper no. 191, Geneva.

Mian A and Sufi A (2014). *House of Debt: How They (and You) Caused the Great Recession, and How We Can Prevent It from Happening Again*. Chicago, IL, University of Chicago Press.

North D (2005). *Understanding the Process of Economic Change*. Princeton, NJ, Princeton University Press.

Panic M (1995). International economic integration and the changing role of national governments. In: Chang H-J and Rowthorn R, eds. *The Role of the State in Economic Change*. Oxford, Clarendon Press: 51–80.

Piketty T (2014). *Capital in the Twenty-First Century*. Cambridge, MA, Harvard University Press.

Polanyi K (1944). *The Great Transformation: The Political and Economic Origins of Our Time*. New York, NY, Farrar and Rinehart.

Salazar-Xirinachs J, Nübler I and Kozul-Wright R, eds. (2014). *Transforming Economies: Making Industrial Policy Work for Growth, Jobs and Development*. Geneva, International Labour Office.

Stiglitz J (2012). The Price of Inequality: How Today's Divided Society Endangers Our Future. New York, NY, W.W. Norton and Co.

United Nations (2012). *Realizing the Future We Want for All*. United Nations publications, New York.

United Nations (2014). Outcome document. Open Working Group on Sustainable Development Goals, United Nations, New York.

UNCTAD (2011). Report of the Secretary-General of UNCTAD to UNCTAD XIII, Development-led Globalization: Towards Sustainable and Inclusive Development Paths. United Nations, New York and Geneva.

UNCTAD (2013). UNCTAD and the post-2015 Development Agenda. Post-2015 Policy Brief 1, Geneva.

UNCTAD (2014). *Least Developed Countries Report 2014*. United Nations publications, New York and Geneva, forthcoming.

UNCTAD (*TDR 1997*). *Trade and Development Report, 1997. Globalization, Distribution and Growth*. United Nations publication, sales no. E.97.II.D.8, New York and Geneva.

UNCTAD (*TDR 2006*). *Trade and Development Report, 2006. Global Partnership and National Policies for Development*. United Nations publication, sales no. E.06.II.D.6, New York and Geneva.

UNCTAD (*TDR 2012*). *Trade and Development Report, 2012. Policies for Inclusive and Balanced Growth*. United Nations publication, sales no. E.12.II.D.6, New York and Geneva.

UNCTAD (*TDR 2013*). *Trade and Development Report, 2013. Adjusting to the changing dynamics of the world economy*. United Nations publication, sales no. E.13.II.D.3, New York and Geneva.

Wilkinson R and Pickett K (2009). *The Spirit Level: Why Equality is Better for Everyone*. London, Penguin.

World Bank (2005). *Economic Growth in the 1990s: Learning From a Decade of Reform*. Washington, DC.

Chapter IV

POLICY SPACE AND THE ORIGINS OF THE MULTILATERAL ECONOMIC SYSTEM

A. Introduction

The challenge of reconciling the requirements of national policy sovereignty with the imperatives of an interdependent world economy may seem today to be relatively new – an outcome of advances in information and communications technologies (ICTs) and the spread of global market forces. In fact, it is a long-standing challenge that has been discussed extensively, and from many different angles, for almost two centuries (Mazower, 2012). This chapter takes a historical look at some of the debates around this issue in the mid-twentieth century, when much of the current multilateral economic architecture was being constructed.

The architects of the post-Second World War multilateral system were principally concerned with the economic challenges facing the leading industrialized countries. But in a profound break with the actions of policy-makers after the end of the First World War, they recognized that the modern State was "splendidly equipped" to undertake the challenges of attaining higher standards of living, full employment and economic and social security.[1] Moreover, in light of the changing contours of the global economy,

> Controlling potentially destructive financial forces was central to the discussions of the architects of the post-Second World War multilateral system.

development challenges facing poorer countries were also part of the discussions of State-driven international cooperation. Indeed, not only did those issues have a more important place in negotiations over the future direction of international cooperation than is generally recognized, they also focused attention on the question of policy space in achieving the goals and objectives of the new multilateral order.

The outcomes of the negotiations, in terms of institutions, rules and disciplines, reflected both decisions taken by nation States and the lobbying efforts of various interest groups within the major economic powers. In particular, the shifting coalition of interests that underpinned the New Deal in the United States had a very strong bearing on multilateral discussions that began even before the start of the Second World War. Those who supported efforts to internationalize the New Deal provided an initial opening for a more inclusive multilateralism that could accommodate the needs and concerns of developing countries. However, several promising initiatives in this direction were dropped from the Bretton Woods negotiations and their influence diminished further following the death of United States President Roosevelt, giving way to a more technocratic multilateralism which proved less accommodating to those needs.

One central feature of the discussions of the time, which was relevant for both developed and developing countries, was the imperative of controlling potentially destructive financial forces. Politicians and policymakers from across the developed countries (and the political spectrum) recognized the importance of making finance a servant, rather than the master, of their economic destiny. At the end of the First World War, financial interests had been quick to reassert their influence over economic policymaking, calling for a restoration of market confidence as the only assured way to "return to normalcy" (James, 2001: 25). This effectively meant not just a rapid dismantling of wartime controls, but an unqualified commitment to the gold standard, the establishment of independent central banks and the adoption of austerity policies, all of which reduced the possibilities of moving towards a more managed economy that would support new social and political demands. Financial interests were in a strong position to define what was acceptable policy; and they were also the big winners from the resulting surge of short-term capital flows (and accompanying toxic financial instruments), which picked up rapidly from the mid-1920s, leading to an increasingly skewed pattern of income distribution in many countries (Kumhof et al., 2013; Piketty, 2014). These trends, in combination with highly fragile banking systems, culminated in the Great Depression and the international economic disintegration that followed. Against this backdrop, expanding policy space to meet the new post-war challenges and reducing the profit space of the "rentier" financial class was uppermost in the minds of negotiators at Bretton Woods.[2]

The rules and measures eventually adopted to limit the destructive tendencies of unregulated finance certainly helped open up policy space for developing countries to establish independent growth paths. However, the scale of financial resources made available to developing countries through new multilateral mechanisms never matched their aims of radically transforming the economic structures inherited from their previous colonial or peripheral status. This meant that international trade assumed greater importance in the design of post-war development strategies, but at the same time technological gaps and structural asymmetries in production between developed and developing countries made the trading system a more contested terrain. Moreover, in contrast to the discussions around international finance, strong corporate interests linked to an export-led growth agenda, particularly in the United States, were better positioned to influence the outcomes of multilateral trade discussions in a more liberal direction. The resulting unwillingness of developed countries to address the pervasive gaps and asymmetries in production eventually galvanized developing countries into promoting a development agenda more in line with their needs and demanding sufficient policy space to pursue that agenda. From the early 1960s, UNCTAD was at the centre of those efforts, often pursuing a mix of multilateral support measures and policy space initiatives that had previously been proposed by the international New Dealers. Despite major transformations in the global economy and in different developing regions since then, the arguments made during these decades still have powerful contemporary resonance, as will be evident in the subsequent chapters of this *Report*.

This opening chapter is structured as follows. Section B examines the wider historical context that influenced the debates on international cooperation in the 1940s. It notes that these debates were heavily informed by the failure of the neo-liberal agenda that had dominated policy thinking in the 1920s. This agenda is contrasted with that of the Roosevelt Administration, which tried to internationalize the New Deal during the Bretton Woods negotiations. Section C examines the neglected role of development issues in subsequent accounts of the Bretton Woods discussions, recalling the importance of New Deal and Keynesian thinking in taming the role of international finance and its strong links to development policy debates in Latin America under Roosevelt's "Good Neighbor Policy". It then looks at the way in which discussions of a new international trade architecture were constrained by the political alliances that underpinned the New Deal, with very different outcomes for the direction of trade policy

> UNCTAD played a pivotal role in promoting a development agenda in line with the needs of developing countries, and in pushing for sufficient policy space to pursue it.

in Europe and the developing world respectively. Section D describes subsequent efforts by developing countries to make multilateralism more inclusive, including their revival of elements of the New Deal's international agenda in support of State-led industrialization and their push for stronger recognition of the interdependence of trade and financial issues, which was at the heart of UNCTAD's mandate. The final section concludes with a discussion on the re-emergence of international finance, the associated "softening" of multilateralism and the resulting impact on contemporary policy space.

B. Debates on the emerging international economic order in the mid-twentieth century

1. The rise and fall of the inter-war liberal policy agenda

The inter-war period was a time of sharp economic contrasts across countries, with prolonged economic stagnation in some contrasting with boom-bust cycles in others. However, in almost all cases, severe and highly contagious shocks and crises in the late 1920s and early 1930s ushered in a period of deep global economic distress and uncertainty which had a profound effect on politicians and policymakers. The economic problems of the inter-war period are often ascribed to the pervasive influence of isolationist and protectionist ideologies, particularly in the United States, which are deemed to have been responsible for blocking a return to the liberal internationalism that had supported growth and stability before 1914 (Wolf, 2003; Eichengreen and Kenen, 1994). Such an interpretation is misleading. In fact, tariffs had been steadily rising almost everywhere in the "high growth" decades prior to 1914, in some cases reaching very high levels (Bairoch, 1995). And while tariff barriers increased immediately after the war, this was followed by a mixture of protectionist and liberalizing measures, which included the use of surtaxes and anti-dumping legislation, but also the removal of quantitative trade controls, promotion of the most-favoured-nation (MFN) principle, the lifting of restrictions on capital exports and a return to the

gold standard. It is true that with the adoption of the Smoot Hawley Act in June 1930 United States tariffs rose to unprecedented levels, triggering reprisals from 25 countries over the subsequent 18 months, with damaging consequences for exports (Bairoch, 1995). However, in terms of both timing and scale, the collapse in output and employment during the early 1930s cannot be attributed to this policy shift. Besides, growth in many countries recovered rapidly under these same tariff structures, albeit under the stewardship of very different macroeconomic policy regimes.[3]

Contrary to a good deal of narrative on this period, liberalism was the dominant economic ideology of the 1920s. Therefore, examining its influence, in particular through its promotion of conservative macroeconomic policies, is key to understanding the decade that followed (Polanyi, 1944: 231–36; Boyce, 2009: 6–7). Following the sharp global downturn of 1920-1921, official support for independent central banks, flexible labour markets, lightly regulated capital markets and the gold standard was in full ascendancy in all the leading economies. As Eichengreen and Temin (1997: 38) have observed, the gold standard rhetoric not only "dominated discussions of public policy ... and sustained central bankers and political leaders as they imposed ever greater costs on ordinary people", it also provided a "one-size fits all" policy agenda, to which, those same voices insisted, there was no alternative. From this perspective, adopting the gold standard was seen both as a commitment to "responsible" policymaking, by limiting the scope for independent government monetary and fiscal actions, and as a way of attracting foreign capital inflows by strengthening investor confidence. The result was not only a recovery of pre-war globalization trends, but a concomitant loss of policy autonomy and increased vulnerability to events elsewhere in the world.

Trade and capital flows picked up rapidly from the mid-1920s, reaching (and, in certain instances, surpassing) pre-war levels towards the end of the decade.[4] Moreover, and again contrary to conventional opinion, discussions on international economic cooperation were widespread (but relatively unfruitful) during the 1920s (Boyce, 2009). Indeed, as James (2001: 25) notes, "Rarely had there been so much enthusiasm for internationalism and international institutions as in the 1920s". The United States was actively engaged in debt renegotiations through the Dawes and Young Plans, which led to the creation of the Bank for International Settlements (BIS). The BIS was at least partly created to depoliticize those negotiations, but it was also seen as an instrument of central bank cooperation (James, 2001: 41). In addition, a series of international conferences were organized to promote trade liberalization and the protection of intellectual property, most notably the World Economic Conferences of 1927 and 1933 (Kindleberger, 1986). Towards the end of the 1920s, there was also a strong push for greater regional cooperation (Boyce, 2009).

With investor confidence serving as the policy lodestone, fiscal austerity was seen as the right approach for returning to normalcy in the early 1920s, and also for correcting the imbalances that had begun to emerge towards the end of the decade.[5] In reality, the turn to austerity and the instability surrounding the flows of short-term capital (encouraged by disparities between national inflation and interest rates) gave rise to mutually inconsistent stabilization plans, misaligned exchange rates and persistent frictions in the trading system. The associated imbalances in real economies (including those in agriculture and industry), combined with the debt overhang from the war and highly fragile banking systems, interacted with these trends, eventually culminating in the Great Depression.[6] This in turn generated further pressure for governments to adopt measures to cope with severe balance-of-payments problems, which eventually led to beggar-thy-neighbour exchange rate policies and trade and payments restrictions on a quid pro quo basis. A crucial aggravating factor was the absence of adequate public policy at national, regional and international levels to correct internal and external imbalances in an orderly and equitable manner.

The lack of either a "benevolent" hegemon or viable international cooperation was certainly critical to the international transmission of adverse shocks and eventual global depression (Kindleberger, 1986).[7] However, the absence of a hegemon that could defend the global public interest should not be considered independently of the policy choices taken at the time. The return to the gold standard was itself a de facto commitment to a certain type of international coordination that was in line with liberal principles as well as with the needs of finance. Indeed, the financial lobby was the most ambitious of the internationalist interest groups within the leading powers, and prevailed against other groups, including more dynamic segments of the manufacturing sectors (Boyce, 2009).

The links between economic instability, international disintegration and political polarization were certainly apparent to some observers at the time. Keynes, in his *Economic Consequences of the Peace*, had already warned that the onerous debt payments imposed by the Treaty of Versailles (as well as outstanding debts between the victorious allied powers), in a context of excessively volatile short-term capital flows, would make it impossible for each country to put its own house in order without damaging others. Moreover, and despite the narrowness and conservative nature of economic thinking, alternative policy approaches began to emerge towards the end of the decade, as the scale of the damage resulting from the liberal economic agenda became impossible to ignore (Kozul-Wright, 1999; Crotty, 1999).

> The absence of adequate public policy to correct internal and external imbalances in an orderly and equitable manner was a strong aggravating factor in the Great Depression.

This context necessarily shaped economic perceptions at the international level as well. Biltoft (2014) has noted that after the Great Depression, even the economists at the League of Nations, who essentially favoured the creation of a relatively liberal and open world order, began to question the monetary orthodoxy of adherence to the gold standard and recognized the need for selective trade interventions, such as for commodity price stabilization. Even as Ohlin and others developed theories to show how international gains from specialization could address the problem of global imbalances, other economists associated with the League, such as Mikhail Manoilescu and Ragnar Nurkse, highlighted potential problems of unequal exchange and the need to increase domestic savings and investment "to expand domestic markets and decouple them from foreign capital and tight and inequitable global market structures" (Biltoft, 2014).

However, it was political changes in the United States, associated with Roosevelt's New Deal, that signalled a dramatic break with the orthodox way of looking at economic policy choices and trade-offs.[8] The New Deal involved a rejection of the ideas that the free market is intrinsically self-correcting and geared to generating the most economically and socially optimal outcomes, that fiscal austerity and budget cuts provide the only reliable way out of a crisis, and that government intervention distorts and damages future economic prospects. By adopting an expansionary economic agenda through targeted support for different regions and sectors of the economy (most notably through the creation of the Tennessee Valley Authority), redistribution measures, strengthened regulation of markets (particularly financial markets) and belated but expansive fiscal measures, the New Deal demonstrated a willingness to make job creation and social security the responsibility of government policy. It also set out to promote a public sphere that did not respond simply to market forces, but could also act as a countervailing power to private interests, particularly in the financial sector, whose behaviour and actions were seen as the real causes of the crisis.[9] Similar moves in the direction of what subsequently became known as "welfare Keynesianism" were taking place in other countries, albeit drawing on their own intellectual and political traditions (Hall, 1989; Temin, 1991; Blyth, 2002).

> Economic crises and contagion could not be managed in isolation.

2. Internationalizing the New Deal

Given the broad agreement amongst the democratic powers that economic crises and contagion could not be managed by countries in isolation, the search for a form of domestic economic governance "between the anarchy of irresponsible individualism and the tyranny of state socialism"[10] was bound to have a profound impact on the discussions around a new international economic order which began soon after the outbreak of the Second World War.

The principle objective of the architects of Bretton Woods was to design a post-war international economic structure that would prevent the recurrence of the opportunistic actions and damaging contagion that had led to the breakdown of international trade and payments in the 1930s and its destructive aftermath.[11] This involved a radical break with the approach that had followed the First World War and the misguided and unsuccessful efforts to return to normalcy at that time. The two most well-known protagonists in the discussions were John Maynard Keynes, representing the waning (but still imperial) power of the heavily-indebted United Kingdom, and Harry Dexter White, negotiating on behalf of the dominant industrial and creditor economy of the United States. They recognized that establishing conditions both for global economic stability and security, and for sustained and broad-based growth in incomes and employment, required a number of measures. These included dismantling the ad hoc exchange controls and discriminatory trade barriers introduced after the Great Depression, "conferring autonomy on national policies" to the extent needed to pursue full employment, and building in additional supports and safeguards to ensure the efficient operation of the international economic system (Eichengreen and Kenen, 1994: 34).

Mindful that the inter-war economic disintegration was due to uncorrected market failures, excessive competition and unchecked contagion, the restoration of a stable global economic system was understood to require a shift from purely national policy formulations to a multilateral system based on the recognition of economic interdependence, enhanced cooperation and supportive multilateral institutions. Exchange rate stability and sustained expansion of output and employment were seen as essential for avoiding tensions and disruptions in international trade. This, in turn, required global arrangements based on three ingredients: multilateral discipline over exchange rate policies, mechanisms for the provision of international liquidity, and restrictions on destabilizing capital flows. Controlling finance at home had its international analogue in restricting the ability of financial markets to make profits abroad through short-term speculative capital flows. Keynes (1944), in defending the final arrangements negotiated at Bretton Woods, was clear that taming finance was at the heart of any stable post-war multilateral order:

> Whilst other schemes are not essential as prior proposals to the monetary scheme, it may well be argued, I think, that a monetary scheme gives a firm foundation on which the others can be built. It is very difficult while you have monetary chaos to have order of any kind in other directions... [I]f we are less successful than we hope for in other directions, monetary proposals instead of being less necessary will be all the more necessary. If there is going to be great difficulty in planning trade owing to tariff obstacles, that makes it all the more important that there should be an agreed orderly procedure for altering exchanges... [S]o far from monetary proposals depending on the rest of the programme, they should be the more necessary if that programme is less successful than we all hope it is going to be.

Thus, controls on finance were seen as the essential basis for enlarging policy space at home to meet the newly defined goals of full employment, economic and social security, and higher living standards for the majority of the population, as well as for building a form of "constructive internationalism" that could underpin a more stable economic environment in support of this shared policy agenda. However, from the outset, United States policymakers (more so than Keynes) made it very clear that the development implications of taming financial interests at home and abroad should also be addressed at the international level. According to Oliver (1975: 4),

> White was convinced that private investors could not be relied upon to provide the capital that would be needed for postwar reconstruction. He also felt that even after the postwar transition period, the normal flow of capital from rich to poor could not be left solely to the

private investment markets of the world. The lessons of the twenties had been that long-term private capital movements tended to enforce, rather than mitigate, the spread of international business fluctuations and that the high interest rates and the relatively short-term maturities of private portfolio investments tended to make unproductive what might otherwise be productive international ventures.

Also from the very start, Roosevelt and his administration officials favoured the establishment of public international financial institutions whose membership would be open to all "the United and Associated Nations".[12] The New York financial community opposed this idea, preferring a "key currency" plan that would re-establish international financial stability through a bilateral loan to the United Kingdom. In rejecting that plan, United States Treasury Secretary Morgenthau highlighted the need to avoid a "dictatorship of the world's finances by two countries", insisting instead that "the problems considered at Bretton Woods are international problems, common to all countries, that can be dealt with only through broad international cooperation" (Morgenthau, 1945: 192). Moreover, Morgenthau stressed that the Bretton Woods framework was designed not just to meet developed countries' goals of full employment, but also to address less developed countries' objectives of raising levels of industrialization and standards of living:

> Unless some framework which will make the desires of both sets of countries mutually compatible is established, economic and monetary conflicts between the less and more developed countries will almost certainly ensue. Nothing would be more menacing to have than to have the less developed countries, comprising more than half the population of the world, ranged in economic battle against the less populous but industrially more advanced nations of the west. The Bretton Woods approach is based on the realization that it is to the economic and political advantage of countries such as India and China, and also of countries such as England and the United States, that the industrialization and betterment of living conditions in the former be achieved with the aid and encouragement of the latter (Morgenthau, 1945: 190).[13]

But even before this approach began to inform the Bretton Woods negotiations, it had helped to reshape United States engagement with developing countries, in particular through Roosevelt's "Good Neighbor Policy" with Latin America. This policy aimed to promote development in poorer countries in a way that was not just consistent with United States geopolitical interests at the time, but also with the aims and values of the New Deal. As such, this implied a clear break with the conventional policy advice that had been promoted by United States academic advisers to Latin American governments in the 1920s (often informally backed in the United States by the State Department, the Federal Reserve Bank of New York and banking interests). Those earlier advisers had advocated adherence to the gold standard, the establishment of independent central banks, open markets for goods and capital, and a minimal role for the State (Helleiner, 2014).

By contrast, many New Deal economists saw Latin American countries as victims of the same financial elite that had pushed their own economy into crisis and depression. The region had been the recipient of very large capital inflows in the 1920s, resulting from aggressively marketed bonds issued mainly in New York, as well as short-term loans to both governments and corporations. With the sharp drop in commodity prices in the late 1920s, an already deteriorating debt-to-export ratio – reaching triple digits in some countries – was made considerably worse. As new inflows dried up, servicing the debt became a huge burden for many governments. At the same time, deteriorating, and ultimately unsustainable, current account positions forced countries to abandon the gold standard, adding further to their debt burden (in terms of national currency). The combination of growing government deficits and a fragile banking system, which lacked a lender of last resort, meant that the risk of a financial panic increased significantly. The first default occurred in Bolivia in January 1931, and with the United States Government refusing to lend support to the region, contagion quickly spread across Latin America. A combination of defaults and devaluations induced a strategy

> There was broad agreement that private capital on its own could not be relied upon to achieve national or global goals...

> ... and that there should be sufficient policy space for countries to achieve an appropriate level of economic security by aiming at full employment and extended social protection.

of export-led recovery while also forcing countries to substitute imported goods with domestically produced goods (Fishlow, 1985). Argentina was the only major country in the region not to default, but it endured a very slow recovery (James, 2001).

In a series of economic policy missions to the region in the late 1930s and early 1940s, most notably to Cuba and Paraguay, New Deal economists from the United States supported the creation of publicly controlled central banks that would have a much more active monetary policy agenda. They also recommended the creation of more specialized development banks, managed exchange rates and the use of exchange controls as part of a development agenda in support of structural transformation and catch-up growth (Helleiner, 2014).[14] In addition, these same economists supported the extension of loans to various Latin American governments for development projects, as well as for currency stability, through the newly created Export-Import Bank. Furthermore, they explored possible financing mechanisms that could support commodity price stabilization, and engaged in lengthy discussions to promote an Inter-American Bank (IAB) as the world's first multilateral financial institution. The latter project did not take off at the time, but it had clearly innovative features, in marked contrast to the much less ambitious BIS established in 1930. These included a mandate to provide public international loans to achieve development objectives, provisions to address capital flight from poorer countries, and control and ownership of the institution by the concerned governments (Helleiner, 2014). Together these initiatives defined a distinctly new and engaged form of international economic cooperation.

Even before the United States entered the Second World War, Roosevelt, in his famous "four freedoms" speech of January 1941, made it clear that "freedom from want" was a goal for people "everywhere in the world". Just as his New Deal had promised greater economic security to Americans, Roosevelt now saw the improvement of standards of living in poorer regions of the world as a crucial foundation for post-war international peace and political stability (Borgwardt, 2005). This was combined with recognition of the positive role such an approach could play in sustaining economic prosperity in developed countries as well. Treasury Secretary Henry Morgenthau provided an early statement of global Keynesianism when presenting a proposal for what eventually became the World Bank, arguing that "the investment of productive capital in undeveloped and capital-needy countries means not only that those countries will be able to supply at lower costs more of the goods the world needs but that they will at the same time become better markets for the world's goods" (quoted in Helleiner, 2014: 117).

The emphasis by the Roosevelt Administration on a strong *public* dimension in the management of financial institutions was evident in the Bretton Woods agreement. The IMF was created to ensure an orderly system of international payments at stable, but multilaterally negotiated, adjustable exchange rates under conditions of strictly limited international capital flows. Its most important function was to provide international liquidity, not only to avoid deflationary adjustments and trade and exchange restrictions in deficit countries, but also to help maintain stable exchange rates during temporary payments disturbances.

Modalities of liquidity provisioning were one of the most controversial issues in the negotiations leading up to the Bretton Woods Conference in 1944. The plans independently prepared by White and Keynes both provided for international liquidity to enable countries to stabilize their currencies. Keynes's plan for an international clearing union, based on the "bancor" as international liquidity, effectively proposed that the reserves of surplus countries should be automatically available to deficit countries for meeting their current account needs (Mikesell, 1994; Dam, 1982; Oliver, 1975). However, it was White's scheme that eventually prevailed, reflecting the greater economic and political power of the United States. This led to the establishment of a fund, with contributions from countries partly in gold and partly in their own currencies, which would be available for drawing by those in need of international reserves.

Despite the differences in institutional detail, there was broad agreement that private capital on its own could not be relied upon to achieve national or global goals, and that there should be sufficient policy space for countries to achieve an appropriate level of economic security through the pursuit of a full-employment agenda and extended social protection (Martin, 2013). Thus a key assumption behind the Bretton Woods Conference was that the leading countries, in particular the United States and the United Kingdom whose financial centres would continue to dominate once the war ended, would be willing to forego, or attenuate, the pursuit of immediate economic interests in favour of a larger concern for systemic stability. The original institutional contours of the IMF were very much in line with those goals and assumptions. In a particularly telling remark, White insisted that "To use international monetary arrangements as a cloak for the enforcement of unpopular policies, whose merits or demerits rest not on international monetary considerations as such but on the whole economic programme and philosophy of the country concerned, would poison the atmosphere of international financial stability" (cited in Felix, 1996: 64).

C. Development voices

1. *Pursuing a development agenda*

The Bretton Woods negotiations are generally described as an "Anglo-American" affair in which the leading officials – Keynes and White – showed little interest in international development issues and the concerns of poorer countries. Even the significance of their endorsement of the International Bank for Reconstruction and Development (IBRD) is downplayed. Yet well over half of the governments invited to Bretton Woods were from the poorer regions of the world.[15] Moreover, whatever the strategic realpolitik that ultimately drove the agenda, the United States was committed to a form of procedural multilateralism which recognized a place for all the participating countries in the discussions.[16]

Particularly active in the conference discussions were officials from Latin America, China (which had the second largest delegation to the conference) and India (whose delegation was divided equally between British and Indian officials because of its colonial status at the time). Many of them expressed their view of the Bretton Woods negotiations as an opportunity to construct a development-friendly international financial regime that would be supportive of their State-led efforts to raise standards of living and begin to industrialize. The developing countries were also in agreement with the broad aims of the IMF to support managed currency regimes and provide short-term loans to manage balance-of-payments difficulties. However, they called for a more flexible use of its resources to deal with the special needs of primary commodity exporters. Indeed, their support was key to including a "waiver clause" that would allow the Fund, under specified circumstances, to overrule its regular lending limits (Helleiner, 2014: 166–168).

The birth of the IBRD (now the World Bank) is generally thought to have been easier and less controversial than that of the IMF. But it too was contested along two important axes: whether long-term financing should be private or public, and the relative importance given to reconstruction versus development.[17] The Europeans, who focused on the latter, saw a trade-off between financing for reconstruction and that for development, and emphasized the urgency of projects in war-torn areas. However, post-war reconstruction was a transitory requirement, and given the necessary financing, it could be completed in a relatively short period of time, since the required complementary skills, know-how, infrastructure and institutions were largely in place. This was not the case in much of the developing world, which therefore had different but equally, if not more, pressing financing requirements. The compromise was that there "should be equitable consideration to projects for development and projects for reconstruction alike" (Oliver 1975). In any case, after 1947, the dramatic increase in United States financing to Europe under the Marshall Plan effectively eliminated the trade-off.

It was recognized that the terms and conditions of private financing, notably market interest rates, would not be appropriate for the conditions prevailing in the borrowing countries. Consequently, even

> Developing countries saw the Bretton Woods negotiations as an opportunity to construct a development-friendly international financial regime that would be supportive of their State-led efforts to raise standards of living and industrialize.

though such provisions were not explicitly included in the Articles of Agreement of the IBRD, the original intention was for the Bank to finance projects that, while not considered profitable by financial markets, would be beneficial to the world as a whole. The initial drafts of the Articles of Agreement prepared by White included an explicit mandate to promote "development", and one of its core purposes was to "raise the productivity and hence the standard of living of the peoples of the United Nations", as well as to encourage the movement of capital from "capital-rich to capital-poor countries" (Helleiner, 2014: 121, 102–105).

It was believed that this capital would aid structural transformation, just as public investment in the United States had done in its own poor regions. Domestically, the New Deal had experimented with government initiatives which combined long-term financing with structural transformation. One such initiative was the Tennessee Valley Authority (TVA), whose apparent success encouraged United States policymakers to consider "international TVA" initiatives to raise living standards abroad through a more active public sector, including through industrial support measures.[18] This approach also reflected some of the lessons of the United States' Good Neighbor policy, which had encouraged many Latin American governments to become increasingly committed to State-led development and industrialization strategies to raise living standards, address high levels of indebtedness and reduce dependence on commodity exports (Bertola and Ocampo, 2012).

The resulting multilateral development vision included the IBRD's commitment to mobilize long-term development lending. This feature was highly novel: no international financial institution had ever been created with the purpose of supporting long-term development loans to poorer countries, although this idea built directly on the previously noted, but ultimately unsuccessful, initiative of 1939-1940 to create an Inter-American Bank (IAB). The IMF's short-term lending for balance-of-payments purposes also effectively borrowed from the experience of United States bilateral loans to Latin American countries, whose dependence on commodity exports

– and unstable capital inflows – left them vulnerable to unexpected seasonal fluctuations and price swings and boom-bust financial cycles.[19] Efforts to curtail capital flight from poorer countries were highlighted in early draft proposals and were supported by developing-country representatives. In the Fund's proposed charter, White included a provision that all member countries would undertake commitments to help enforce each other's controls by agreeing "(a) not to accept or permit deposits or investments from any member country except with the permission of that country, and (b) to make available to the government of any member country at its request all property in form of deposits, investments, securities, safety deposit vault contents, of the nationals of member countries" (cited in Helleiner, 2014: 111). In subsequent drafts, he also added the idea that countries receiving capital flows would commit to sharing information about those flows with the sending countries. White argued – as did Keynes at the time – that countries experiencing illegal outflows of capital would have a greater chance of making their controls effective with these kinds of international assistance. As White put it later, "Without the cooperation of other countries such control is difficult, expensive and subject to considerable evasion" (cited in Helleiner, 1994: 38).

> Before the IBRD's inception, no international financial institution had ever been created with the purpose of supporting long-term development loans to poorer countries.

Two trade issues of significance for international development were also addressed in initial drafts. One was a proposal that the Bank "organize and finance an International Commodity Stabilization Corporation for the purpose of stabilizing the price of important commodities" (Helleiner, 2014: 112–113). The second was explicit support for poorer countries' use of tariff protection for infant industries. White argued that the belief that trade liberalization would generate higher standards of living in poor countries made the mistake of assuming "that a country chiefly agricultural in its economy has as many economic, political and social advantages as a country whose economy is chiefly industrial, or a country which has a balanced economy". He added, "It assumes that there are no gains to be achieved by diversification of output. It grossly underestimates the extent to which a country can virtually lift itself by its bootstraps in one generation if it is willing to pay the price. The view further overlooks the very important fact that political relationships among countries being what they are vital considerations exist in the shaping of the economic structure of a country other than that of producing goods with the least labor" (cited in Helleiner, 2014: 113).

Taken together, these provisions outlined a highly innovative vision for international policy coordination that was supportive of development. Never before had this kind of multilateral framework been proposed with the explicit purpose of supporting the development of poorer countries.

2. From an international New Deal to technocratic multilateralism

Given this history, it is striking that so many scholars have overlooked the international development content of Bretton Woods. The neglect is, however, understandable considering that this content was dramatically watered down, and some of it even eliminated, during the negotiations and in subsequent discussions on other aspects of the international economic system soon after the war ended.

Within the United States, political support for the international development goals of Bretton Woods unravelled in the wake of Roosevelt's death in April 1945. In the new, more conservative Truman Administration, many of the key architects of those goals were marginalized, including both Morgenthau (who resigned in July) and White (who left government service in March 1947 and died shortly afterwards), while figures close to the New York financial community assumed more prominent positions in United States foreign economic policy-making (Helleiner, 2014). Since members of this community had been sceptical of the Bretton Woods plans and institutions – and of the New Deal more generally – they now lobbied to reduce the powers and degree of ambition of those plans and institutions.[20] The leadership of the IBRD, with increasing links to Wall Street, became reluctant for the institution to extend large-scale development loans, particularly to countries that had not reached debt settlements with foreign creditors. As Latin America's strategic significance declined with the war's end, United States policymakers also ended the Good Neighbor policy of bilateral public lending that had supported Latin American development since the late 1930s. Indeed, officials in the new administration were generally more critical of State-led development policies, arguing that private investment flows and free trade should serve as the main engines of development.

The internationalist spirit of the New Deal did enjoy a final flourish in the Marshall Plan launched in June 1947. The Plan was restricted in geographical coverage, but remarkably generous in terms of both money and policy space, providing Western Europe with some $12.4 billion over a four-year period. Most of it was in the form of grants rather than loans, amounting to just over 1 per cent of the GDP of the United States and over 2 per cent of the GDP of the recipients. However, the Marshall Plan did much more than supply Europe with scarce dollars; in line with the Bretton Woods Consensus, it also introduced a framework of organizing principles intended to ensure that the aid was used to forge a new kind of "social contract" that would be radically different from the deflationary and divisive actions of the inter-war period (Mazower, 1998). Marshall insisted that the required policies, together with estimates of the need for assistance, be drawn up by the West Europeans themselves, thereby acknowledging national sensibilities and recognizing that the recipient countries were better informed about the facts of their situation than outsiders, and generally showing deference towards European traditions and preferences.

The architects of the Marshall Plan regarded it as a long-term investment in structural transformation.

Crucially, the provision of financial assistance to deal with long-term imbalances was not seen as condoning weak commitment to reform or encouraging loss of discipline by postponing necessary adjustments. Rather, the architects of the Marshall Plan regarded such assistance as a long-term investment in structural transformation, and as being necessary for providing governments with the breathing space required to bring difficult and often painful policy objectives to fruition. Indeed, when such policies threatened to cause social upheaval on a scale that might upset the adjustment process, as was the case in post-war Italy at one point, Marshall Aid was available to support government budgets in order to cushion the social costs.

The scale of assistance mobilized under the Marshall Plan meant that there was little need for IBRD assistance in European reconstruction. However, and despite its clearly stated mandate to encourage "international investment for the development of the productive resources of members, thereby assisting in raising productivity, the standard of living and conditions of labour in their territories", the new leadership of the IBRD was reluctant to fund the kind of big investment push which New Deal economists had envisaged. Rather, because it was not a "bank", in the sense that it could independently create finance, its attention turned to the challenges of safeguarding its own creditworthiness by securing triple-A status for its bonds and reviving international private finance. This included promoting a more market-friendly business climate in host countries (Toye and Toye, 2004: 76). In both respects, its fledgling leadership sought to win over the confidence of financial markets as a priority. Thus, Latin American policymakers' proposal for a Marshall-type plan at the Bogota conference that created the Organization of American States in 1948 was rejected; instead, emphasis was given to the importance of a liberalized regime for foreign investments.

In many respects, however, the retreat from inclusive multilateralism was more visible in the evolution of the post-war international trade architecture. Trade issues were under discussion quite early in the allied wartime alliance. However, while both the Fund and the Bank recognized their role in supporting the trading system, trade policy issues were deemed too controversial for the Bretton Woods negotiations. Eventually, this role was handed over to the United Nations in the form of a proposal for an International Trade Organization (ITO).[21]

The negotiations on the shape of the post-war trading system got under way in the early 1940s, and were intended to create a third institution alongside the IMF and the World Bank, though this was not to emerge until more than half a century later. A United Nations Conference on Trade was first proposed in

> They also saw the Plan as providing governments with the necessary breathing space for achieving difficult and often painful policy objectives.

1946 by the United States, in part to justify negotiations that were already under way among a select group of countries to reduce trade barriers. However, the United States delegation's attribution of the "economic anarchy" of the inter-war years to protectionist measures, and the breakdown of the trading system to blind nationalism, provoked an immediate response from developing countries. The Colombian delegate, picking up a theme he had previously raised during the Bretton Woods negotiations, immediately asserted that employment goals in developing countries would hinge on a State-led industrialization strategy that would require managed trade. He pointed out that this was precisely how the more advanced countries had built their own productive capacities over the previous decades. With support from other countries, the issue of State-led industrialization (which had been left out of Bretton Woods discussions) was tabled at the Conference (Toye and Toye, 2004).[22]

The United States agreed to the addition of economic development and industrialization on the agenda, which already included infant industry protection. It also agreed that the proposed ITO should be responsible for judging the distinction between "wise" and "unwise" protection. With this, and as the United Kingdom's representative (and future Prime Minister), Harold Wilson, acknowledged in his closing speech, policy space became a key element in the discussions on the ITO. The head of the United States delegation noted, "The most violent controversies at the conference and the most protracted ones were those evoked by issues raised in the name of economic development" (Wilcox, 1949: 46). However, it would be wrong to suggest that policy space in the context of the governance of international trade was only a developing-country concern. Anticipated balance-of-payments problems and issues of State trading were also on the minds of many European policymakers as the war was drawing to an end, and these were certainly familiar challenges to the British drafters of the ITO Charter (Toye and Toye, 2004). Indeed, as Gardner (1995) has noted, the initial reaction to the emerging multilateral order was particularly negative in the United Kingdom, not only because of lingering concerns about having to give up colonial preferences, but also because of a more general worry that any commitment to rapid trade liberalization would undermine the competitiveness of its industries. As *The Times* of London put it at the time, "We must reconcile ourselves once and for all to the view that the days of *laissez-faire* and the unlimited division of labour are over; that every country – including Great Britain – plans and organizes its production in the light of social and military needs; and that the regulation of this production by such 'trade barriers' as tariffs, quotas, and subsidies is a necessary and integral part of this policy".

In the end, the Havana Charter that was signed in 1948 represented a compromise between the demands of economic liberalism, especially with regard to free trade, and the requirements of domestic policy autonomy, including for industrialization and development. Article 2 of that charter, the first substantive article, explicitly states that "the avoidance of unemployment or underemployment, through the achievement and maintenance in each country of useful employment opportunities for those able and willing to work and of a large and steadily growing volume of production and effective demand for goods and services, is not of domestic concern alone, but is also a necessary condition for the achievement of the general purpose and the objectives… including the expansion of international trade, and thus for the well-being of all other countries".

> The Havana Charter was a compromise between the demands of economic liberalism, especially in terms of free trade, and the requirements of domestic policy autonomy, including for industrialization and development.

While the Havana Charter did not meet the more ambitious requirements mooted by developing countries, it nevertheless did incorporate some crucial concerns. Thus, while import quotas were the subject of bitter controversy, they were eventually approved for a range of purposes, including the protection of industries established during the war, industries devoted to processing primary commodities and infant industries. Similarly, it included provisions to facilitate the establishing of commodity agreements to stabilize primary commodity prices. Significantly, the Charter implicitly recognized the right of expropriation of foreign investment by host countries, with due compensation, and entitled them to impose specific requirements on any foreign investment. Host countries would also be able to use "any appropriate safeguards" to prevent foreign direct investment

from interfering in their domestic policies, and could decide whether to approve or deny access to future investments (Graz, 2014).

In the event, the ITO project did not endure, as the Truman Administration lost interest in it in the face of aggressive opposition by United States business interests. Graz (2014) notes that the ITO "did not survive American trade politics because it faced up to the impossibility of reaching a broad international understanding on the proper balance between market rules and State intervention". It was not ratified by the United States Congress, and other countries therefore abandoned the idea. One of the early chapters survived in the form of the General Agreement on Tariffs and Trade (GATT), a much more limited treaty. The critical factor appears to have been the shifting New Deal alliance which accompanied the recovery of business confidence following the end of the war, and a shift towards growth as a policy priority and as a way to deflect attention from the earlier focus on redistribution. This was consistent with a greater emphasis on building overseas markets for a range of products in which United States firms had a significant advantage – an emphasis that converged with the traditional free trade agenda of the Democratic Party, particularly as driven by representatives from the country's southern States (Katznelson, 2013).[23]

As the threat of a post-war depression receded, giving way to a period of unprecedented growth, the institutional framework established at Bretton Woods proved sufficiently adaptable to guarantee enough policy space for developed countries to pursue their post-war economic goals. A more expansionary policy orientation combined with a stable financial system to support the recovery of trade. A rapid pace of capital formation was key to this, along with the widespread adoption of industrial policies (Eichengreen and Kenen, 1994).

Global trade grew, on average, more quickly than global output, much of it in the form of intra-industry trade amongst rich countries, and particularly within Western Europe.[24] In the process, the procedural multilateralism that had helped shape the early discussions about the international economy gave way to a more technocratic multilateralism in which routine problems and marginal changes were left to experts from the various international secretariats. This also applied to development issues. United States policymakers were still willing to pursue the Marshall Plan model (which provided aid in the context of locally formulated national development plans) for some development challenges, notably in East Asian countries where a combination of large aid flows and generous policy space allowed those countries to undertake a more sustained transformation of their economic and social structures.[25] However, it remained uncertain whether the multilateral architecture was sufficiently adaptable to support the new aims and ambitions of developing countries. In particular, there were doubts whether it would support a development policy agenda that recognized the limits of purely market-based incentives for bringing about structural transformation, and which acknowledged the need for more activist States, albeit functioning in different ways according to varying national contexts.

D. The unsteady rise of inclusive multilateralism

The onset of the Cold War in the late 1940s renewed United States interest in international development, as evidenced by President Truman's well-publicized commitment in January 1949 to support "underdeveloped areas" as part of the struggle against communism. However, his "Point Four" programme was focused primarily on the provision of large-scale technical assistance, with a particular emphasis on scientific knowledge and expertise, in contrast to the broader vision of the Bretton Woods architects. Multilateral development assistance, as well as other bilateral programmes, moved in a similar direction, particularly as European countries progressed from recovery to more sustained economic growth. Together with the shift from the bigger issues of designing and negotiating rules and institutions to their more day-to-day operation, this marked the arrival of a more technocratic and market-friendly form of multilateralism.[26]

The 1950s witnessed a series of further retreats from the inclusive multilateral development agenda. Truman's inaugural speech had stressed the central role of private investment in development finance, which was at odds with the earlier idea of a "big investment push" with a prominent public component to galvanize more transformative changes in the economies of the emerging South. In particular, the World Bank's re-engagement with developing countries was made subordinate to its desire to fend off efforts by the United Nations to expand its reach into development finance (Mazower, 2012). This included strong opposition from developed countries to a proposal for a Special United Nations Fund on Economic Development (SUNFED) to offer long-term concessional loans to developing countries. Such a fund had been proposed by the Indian economist VKRV Rao in 1949, further developed by United Nations economists led by Hans Singer, and championed by India and other developing countries from 1951. A formal vote on the proposal only took place several years later, splitting along North-South lines, with the General Assembly voting by a 2 to 1 majority to establish it. However, it was effectively blocked, with a final compromise in the shape of the International Development Association (IDA), a soft

> Closing the gaps between developed and underdeveloped regions was in the interests of the former, and would require dedicated international cooperation through large-scale international public investment.

loan window of the World Bank. Meanwhile, the United Nations was left to fund much less ambitious "pre-investment activities" (Toye and Toye, 2004).

From the late 1950s, IMF lending conditions, notably in loans to Latin America, took a more orthodox turn; they prescribed tighter credit constraints, cuts in public expenditure, partial wage freezes and repeal of subsidies as a means to combat inflation (Felix, 1961). Finally, the GATT commissioned a group of eminent economists to examine the way the institution dealt with development issues. The resulting Haberler Report, published in 1958, criticized some of the tariff and non-tariff barriers erected by rich countries, but rejected the idea that structural differences between developed and developing countries required different rule-making (UNCTAD, 1964; Arndt, 1987). At the same time, while the GATT secretariat rebuffed Latin American efforts to advance regional trade ties, it adopted an accommodating stance on the European Economic Community (EEC).

As the 1950s drew to a close, the widening gap between the ambitions of the growing number of independent developing countries and the reluctance of technocratic multilateralism to embrace their demands became a growing source of tensions in a world already split along East-West lines. In a series of high-profile gatherings, developing countries began to highlight gaps and biases in the workings of the international economy which they saw as impeding their development efforts. And with United Nations membership approaching the 100 mark, the "Third World" was fast becoming a pivotal force for change at the multilateral level.

Concomitantly, a remarkable body of economic research emerged during the 1940s and 1950s in support of industrialization in "backward areas" (Rosenstein-Rodan, 1944). It provided analytical depth to what many policymakers saw as the obvious (and mutually reinforcing) connections between the rise of manufacturing, the spread of markets, technological progress and rapid capital formation. Rosenstein-Rodan's theory of the "big push" had a profound influence on development thinking along with other important work, by Hirschman on

unbalanced growth and by Kalecki and Gerschenkron on financing for development. These economists also argued that closing the gaps between developed and underdeveloped regions was in the interests of the former, and would require dedicated international cooperation through large-scale international public investment programmes. The concepts of balanced and unbalanced growth, increasing returns, linkages, learning by doing, and complementarities in production and consumption, which helped frame the emergence of a new discipline of development economics, were based on the idea that industrial development was the most reliable engine of sustainable and inclusive growth. Moreover, this research made the very strong case that economic development could not be left to market forces alone, and that an activist State was crucial for escaping low-income traps.[21]

> Economic development could not be left to market forces alone; an activist State was considered crucial for escaping low-income traps.

Practical efforts to build industrial capacity were also beginning to provide useful lessons. As noted in section B above, the economic crisis of the 1930s had proved deeply damaging for primary commodity exporters due to the collapse of traditional markets and unfavourable terms-of-trade movements, leading to deteriorating balance-of-payments positions. Under these circumstances, and with protectionist policies spreading across the developed countries, some developing countries had little option but to raise tariffs and to switch expenditure towards domestic substitutes. The resulting pattern of economic transformation was as much a spontaneous response to external shocks as the product of well thought out policy efforts. However, by the late 1940s, this experience had begun to stimulate analysis by academics from within and outside developing regions, as well as by the fledgling multilateral development agencies.

Further research, some conducted within United Nations agencies, on the terms of trade of developing countries was one outcome of these developments (Toye and Toye, 2004). But the big idea that galvanized subsequent development policy debates was "import substitution industrialization". While in some ways this was a response to the model of development that countries had felt forced to adopt following the shocks of the early 1930s and the exigencies of the wartime economies from the late 1930s, this idea also provided a more systematic framework for promoting policies aimed at structural transformation and economic diversification.

The most prominent figure linking the debates of the 1930s with the emerging developing-country concerns of the late 1950s was the Argentine economist, Raul Prebisch. His work in the Central Bank of Argentina and in developing an economic recovery plan for his country had required engagement with new macroeconomic thinking as well as with the asymmetries of the global trading system.[28] This was reinforced by his experience in the Economic Commission for Latin America (ECLA), one of the fledgling regional bodies created by the United Nations system (along with other economic commissions for Europe and Asia) as global interest in development issues flagged with the decline of New Deal internationalism and the lingering death of the ITO. To some extent, these regional bodies adopted the development discourse that had failed to capture the multilateral imagination, especially the policy challenges raised by economic diversification and industrialization (Berthelot, 2004).

Import substitution industrialization (ISI) has often been rather simplistically portrayed as a failed strategy of self-reliance. In actual fact, industrial growth rates during the period from the end of the Second World War to the early 1970s, when ISI was in the ascendency, have not been matched before or since (Bénétrix et al., 2012). Moreover, it enabled several developing countries to achieve significant degrees of economic diversification. In practice, ISI covered a broad range of strategies and policy measures, and the countries that implemented it most successfully were simultaneously actively engaged in export promotion. However, even by the late 1950s it was apparent to economists in the different developing regions that there were limits to these strategies, particularly to the extent that they produced unbalanced development patterns which continued to rely heavily on essential imports that could only be funded through increased exports. There were also concerns about the dangers of excessive or prolonged protectionism, as well as growing recognition that State-led industrialization was constrained by both weak demand and by insufficient levels of productive investment (Ocampo, 2014; Toye and Toye, 2004).

As a result, there was growing momentum for developing countries to re-engage actively at the multilateral level, with a growing emphasis on promoting exports of manufactures within regional trading arrangements as well as through the provision of favourable treatment for developing-country manufactured exports in the expanding markets of developed economies. However, much as in the 1940s, the rules of the trading system, which now included over a decade of experience with the GATT, were seen as an obstacle because of the reluctance of the rule makers to accommodate the ambitions of developing countries. This contrasted sharply with their continued willingness to make exceptions to allow adequate policy space for developed countries (Dosman, 2008).

In 1962, 36 developing countries from all regions of the world organized a conference in Cairo to discuss the economic challenges facing developing countries, including in international trade. The conference ended with a call to convene a United Nations conference on trade and development.[29] This was subsequently endorsed by the General Assembly. The first UNCTAD conference held in 1964, led by Raul Prebisch, provided some key elements of the demands that developing countries would see as important in subsequent decades. Some of the major issues included how to address terms-of-trade losses of primary exporters through commodity agreements or compensatory financing; how to ensure the necessary financing for development; and how to enable a sustainable export-oriented strategy for developing countries that included manufactured goods aimed at developed-country markets. Prebisch's report to the Conference addressed all these issues based on three essential premises: the necessity of industrialization, the need to counter external imbalances and the forces that generate them, and the need for different treatment for structurally different economies (UNCTAD, 1964).

Accordingly, Prebisch re-emphasized the limitations of the GATT principles for developing countries "based on the abstract notion of economic homogeneity which conceals the great structural differences between industrial centres and peripheral countries

> By the early 1960s, the rules of the trading system were seen as obstacles due to the reluctance of the rule makers to accommodate the ambitions of developing countries.

with all their important implications" (UNCTAD, 1964: 6). But he also highlighted the close interdependence of trade and finance in rebalancing the agenda for international cooperation. His report to the conference highlighted the mutually reinforcing nature of savings and foreign exchange constraints on the desired growth target for many developing countries. Based on the then recently established growth target of 5 per cent per annum and a population growth rate of 2.5 per cent, UNCTAD economists argued that developing countries would need investment rates well above what most of them had reached and savings well above their current savings rates. Moreover, a 5 per cent growth rate could not be sustained unless imports by developing countries (principally capital goods) grew at 6 per cent. With projected exports from developing countries growing at 4 per cent per annum, the estimated trade gap would reach some $20 billion by 1970. If the resources were not found to fill this gap, growth would have to be reduced. This meant that developing countries would need determined political efforts, domestically and internationally, to remove the obstacles to more sustained and inclusive growth.

> The creation of UNCTAD as a permanent body set the stage for developing a more inclusive trade and development agenda.

The creation of UNCTAD as a permanent body following the end of the first conference set the stage for developing a more inclusive trade and development agenda. The purpose was to move beyond negative policies aimed simply at removing trade barriers to a more positive agenda. Such an agenda would include assisting the trade of developing countries through measures to stabilize and boost the revenues of primary exporters (including through compensatory financing for terms-of-trade losses), mobilizing more reliable resources for productive investment, and enhancing policy space to support exports of manufactures from developing countries aimed more broadly at their structural transformation. In the decade following the conference, UNCTAD advanced this agenda through its efforts to extend supplementary financing, improve the mechanisms of international liquidity, help create commodity agreements, and advocate tariff preferences, increased flows of official development assistance (ODA) and debt relief (Toye, 2014).

Despite these efforts and the fact that development issues were more vociferously raised at international meetings and discussions, the institutional and other arrangements that determined the functioning of global markets did not fundamentally change. From the late 1960s, as economic tensions within and between the developed economies began to grow and spread across the global economy, the calls for a new international economic order (a term reminiscent of the call by the Group of 77 (G77) for "a new and just world economic order" at UNCTAD I) became steadily louder. The growing strains on the Bretton Woods system, the oil price shocks and their stagflationary impact on the developed countries, provided further opportunities for developing countries to push for a more inclusive multilateralism. Negotiations on a New International Economic Order (NIEO) were launched at a special session of the United Nations in 1974. The thrust of the initiative, to break the international constraints on growth in developing countries, had much in common with the earlier efforts of the international New Dealers and with reform proposals advanced by UNCTAD.[30] However, the political context of the time encouraged a broader agenda which included regulation and supervision of transnational corporations (TNCs) – and the possibility of nationalization when required (Helleiner, 2014) – the promotion of greater economic cooperation among developing countries, and, very explicitly, the protection of policy autonomy. Many of the measures that formed an integral part of the NIEO discussions had already been proposed in debates in the 1930s and 1940s, as noted in the previous section.

The NIEO negotiations were seen at the time as a further substantial challenge to the economic order created by the Bretton Woods system, which had already been weakened by the collapse of dollar convertibility and the fixed exchange rate system in 1971. However, the geopolitical and global economic situation was only briefly favourable to such demands. They quickly came up against more inward-looking policies and "aid weariness" in the developed countries. Indeed, as firms in the United States and Europe saw their profits squeezed at home, they sought greater support from their governments to find new profit opportunities abroad. Moreover, a recovery of growth in some developing countries generated tendencies to downplay their shared structural

asymmetries at the international level even as growing economic divergences in the South undermined
their political solidarity built around a common
agenda (Arndt, 1987).

In fact, beginning in the late 1970s, international
economic relations took a very different turn from
what had been envisaged in the NIEO, with a policy
backlash in the industrialized countries against the
post-war Keynesian policy consensus. The initial
response of policymakers in these countries to the
breakdown of the Bretton Woods system, two oil
shocks, rising labour militancy, a loss of control over
inflation and, to some extent, government budget
deficits, had been a series of ad hoc adjustments that
aimed to contain the threat of "stagflation" (Bruno

and Sachs, 1985). However, as governments and
business groups increasingly viewed redistribution
measures and monetary disorder as the root of a wider
socio-political malaise, moves to cut welfare provision, control the money supply, liberalize financial
flows and use unemployment as a tool of adjustment
crystallized into an alternative policy paradigm. That
paradigm sought to shift the distribution of income
back towards profits through a withdrawal of the
State from the economy and a dismantling of the
post-war political and social compromise (Mazower,
1998). President Reagan's refusal in 1981 to give any
credence to the Report of the Brandt Commission at
a meeting in Cancun effectively ended the North-
South dialogue and, with it, any lingering hopes of
negotiating an NIEO (Toye and Toye, 2004).

E. Profits and policies: The dangers of amnesic globalization

As noted in the previous section, the weaknesses
of the post-war growth model that emerged in the
late 1960s were reflected in distributional struggles,
energy crises, inflationary pressures and balance-
of-payments difficulties. This ultimately led to the
collapse of the Bretton Woods system in the early
1970s and to a series of policy responses and adjustments in developed countries that eventually came to
be associated with the emergence of finance-driven
globalization (UNCTAD, 2011).

It also anticipated a very different approach to
international economic relations from the one that had
underpinned the post-war consensus. The international system that emerged after 1945 was, inevitably, a
compromise dominantly among developed countries
with shared histories and similar levels of economic
development. It was based on a common view of what
needed to be avoided, namely the incoherence and
turmoil of the 1930s, and it was characterized by a
broad tolerance of different national policy choices
(and the requisite policy space) so long as they did not
risk damaging the economies of the other members

of the system. Its subsequent evolution, to include
countries at very different levels of development,
was more punctuated and ad hoc.

The emerging multilateral arrangements were
premised on a broad political consensus that considered growth and employment as priorities, for which
a high rate of investment was seen as key, and a range
of macroeconomic and structural policy measures
were accepted as necessary. Those measures included
the effective regulation of finance and proactive
industrial policies, which were deemed essential to
ensure that profits were channelled into productive
activities. These premises were well accepted by both
the North and the South. It was also accepted that the
difficulties facing most developing countries seeking to integrate into the global economy could best
be managed by allowing some derogation from the
rules that essentially had been agreed upon by, and
in the interests of, the richest countries. However, in
contrast to the generosity of the Marshall Plan that
had helped European economies make a swift post-
war recovery, the resources needed for effectively

tackling the deep-seated structural problems facing most of the developing countries were never made available.

Initially, it was believed that the breakdown of the Bretton Woods system and the shift to floating exchange rates allowed a much looser form of monetary cooperation that gave policymakers in developed countries more room to take independent policy action. The British economist, Fred Hirsch, welcomed this, hoping that a "controlled disintegration of the world economy" would provide more policy space to address the varied challenges posed by a world of economic stagflation. But the more likely alternative, as noted by the United States central banker, Paul Volcker, was a different kind of market-led integration in a multi-polar world. Volcker's solution was to build into the system of flexible exchange rates more informal coordination among central bankers, and to provide the IMF with the disciplines to ensure that the "right" kinds of policies could be pursued at home. An unspoken corollary of this was that "the guardians of the world's money would in the future have a greater role to play internationally, and national legislatures and electorates a smaller one" (Mazower, 2012: 317).

> Trade liberalization has been given priority over economic growth and full employment, thereby rekindling mercantilist agendas, not least in developed countries.

The international trade and finance system that has evolved since the debt crisis of the early 1980s has broken with the working principles of the post-war system. Indeed, under present arrangements and policies, developing countries almost invariably have found themselves obliged to adjust to international imbalances through cuts in domestic spending. The IMF, having abandoned the objective of ensuring stable exchange rates in an orderly international financial system, has, instead, actively promoted the spread of "an open and liberal system of capital movements" (Camdessus, 1997: 4). International financial flows have been allowed to return to the kinds of levels that had caused instability during the inter-war period. The result has been exchange rate instability and misalignments leading to sudden disruptions in the pattern of international competitiveness. In contrast to its early history, the IMF has shifted its lending portfolio substantially to developing countries, blurring the distinction between the short-term liquidity requirements of a stable financial system and the long-term financing requirements for the development of lower income countries.[31] The World Bank has also shifted its emphasis away from longer term infrastructure projects, and now concentrates on "structural adjustment" lending and poverty reduction.

The governance of international trade has moved towards a single-tier system of rights and obligations, in which developing countries are expected, generally, to commit to a level of obligations much closer to those of developed countries. The former have managed to retain certain flexibilities (as discussed in later chapters) within the system and have benefited from the predictability of a rules-based system. However, the recognition that employment creation and structural diversification should be key measures of the success of an increasingly free trade system has been weakened. Trade liberalization has been given priority over economic growth and full employment, thereby rekindling mercantilist agendas, not least in developed countries. A range of issues of interest to developing countries, including changes in their terms of trade, technology transfer, non-tariff barriers and restrictive business practices, have fallen down the negotiating agenda at the international level or disappeared altogether (UNCTAD, 2011). Trade agreements, particularly at the regional and bilateral levels, have increasingly extended their reach into areas of policy earlier confined to national borders. Much of national and global economic policy has progressively been driven by an aggressive agenda of "deep" integration, including the elimination of barriers to trade and capital flows, and enlargement of the space in which corporations can make profits through privatization, deregulation and flexibilization of labour markets.

In effect, the collapse of the Bretton Woods system paved the way for the global dominance of financial markets. The earlier compromise between private profits and national policies that had determined the multilateralism of the first two post-war decades was deemed no longer valid from the 1980s. What emerged was a new international financial and economic order built on a strong ideological faith in the inherent efficiency and stability of markets, which opened up new profit-making opportunities for an increasingly unregulated financial sector. The policy space for countries with different histories, contexts and institutional structures that was at the heart of the Bretton Woods arrangements was replaced with a one-size-fits-all policy agenda of so-called "sensible economic policies" which bore a close resemblance to the policy agenda of the 1920s (Temin, 2010, Blyth, 2013). Like then, this agenda was premised on the assumption of the inherent efficiency and stability of market forces, and was, above all, driven by the rapid deregulation of finance.

The extensive deregulation of the financial sector in developed countries, along with the dismantling of controls on cross-border financial activities, which led to a surge in capital flows, marked a radical break with the post-war international policy framework. The rapid ascent of financial interests eroded the checks and balances that had previously helped to channel market forces into the kind of creative and productive activities needed for long-term growth. Instead, it encouraged short-term, and at times destructive, behaviour by banks, businesses and households. Ideological support for all this came from the efficient market hypothesis, which makes the case for a hands-off policy agenda applicable to all economic circumstances and challenges.

In some cases that agenda was pushed by the policy conditionalities of IMF lending to developing countries, but its reach was much wider, extending to many countries that had no need for IMF support. Thus, the IMF's original role as a guarantor of international financial stability became secondary to the promotion of financialization, defined as the increasing importance of financial markets, financial motives, financial institutions and financial elites in the operation of the economy and its governing institutions, both at the national and international levels (Epstein, 2006). This has been associated with the undermining of the countervailing power of the public sector, and has converted ever-increasing areas of public life into potential sources of profit (Sandel, 2010). It is worth noting that the one-size-fits-all message was in some ways a return to the policies that were dominant in developed countries in the 1920s, and resulted – just as it did then – in a steady erosion

of the abilities of States to take independent policy action (Temin, 2010).

As observed in Section B above, the "return to normalcy" in the 1920s led to global economic volatility, crisis and depression; and the post-war recovery required a reorientation of policies at both national and international levels. The financialization trends that had been building up after the collapse of the Bretton Woods system coincided with a period of growing imbalances, instability and inequality. As discussed extensively in previous *Trade and Development Reports*, developing countries were often the first to experience these problems. However, the most destructive impact of the financial arrangements linking uneven demand growth, debt and unstable capital flows was felt in developed countries, as ongoing concerns over subprime lending in the United States, combined with the collapse of the investment bank, Lehman Brothers, led to a freezing of credit markets in September 2008 and to a slump in equity prices. With contagion and panic spreading through markets, leading financial institutions began to fail, while others turned to their governments for support.

The multilateral arrangements designed at Bretton Woods did not include a global regime for regulating capital movements, as capital mobility was assumed to be limited by the wider workings of the international system. Neither did such a regime emerge after the breakdown of these arrangements, despite the growing importance of private capital flows. And even the grave economic and political impacts of the latest financial crisis have failed to produce such a regulatory regime. This failure points to a larger deficit in global governance. The Doha Round is fast approaching its fifteenth anniversary, with few signs of imminent completion, despite the positive steps taken in the Bali Ministerial Conference in 2013. Progress on reducing greenhouse gas emissions has stalled following the failure to reach a comprehensive deal in Copenhagen. Finally, even before the latest crisis, keeping the Millennium Development Goals on track was a struggle: their achievement by 2015 now seems increasingly unlikely. It is telling that even a small proportion of the resources used to

> Policy space for countries with different histories, contexts and institutional structures that was at the heart of the Bretton Woods arrangements was replaced with a one-size-fits-all policy agenda.

save financial institutions deemed "too big to fail" could never be found in better economic times for social and economic development, infrastructure building and social welfare, or to address environmental challenges.

Pointing to the "trilemma" of policy choice under globalization, Dani Rodrik (2002: 2) has argued that "'deep' economic integration is unattainable in a context where nation states and democratic politics still exert considerable force". Even if his contention were to be accepted, it can certainly be argued that there are ways to forge international arrangements that encourage more cross-border economic activity in general (including the movement of goods, services and people) without necessarily sacrificing the policy autonomy that enables a nation State to respond to the developmental and social needs of its own citizenry in a flexible manner. Indeed, the experience of rapidly growing and "globalizing" economies in East Asia, and the more varied and inclusive policies adopted by several countries in Latin America and some in Africa over the past decade, all demonstrate that successful external economic integration can take many different forms and need not always be associated with the standard policy package. A critical element of these more inclusive growth strategies has been the priority given to the needs and rights of States and citizens, rather than to strategies that privilege profitability.

> The growing financialization trends following the collapse of the Bretton Woods system coincided with a period of greater imbalances, instability and inequality.

It is therefore necessary to examine the extent to which various forces have reshaped policy space in the era of finance-driven globalization. Subsequent chapters of this *Report* explore different aspects of this in the areas of trade, capital flows and macroeconomic policies. This in turn enables a consideration of elements of a new development strategy for reviving a more inclusive form of multilateralism that can tackle contemporary challenges. ■

Notes

1   See Mazower (2012: 202), quoting Gilbert Murray, an Oxford scholar, who, as an early supporter of the League of Nations, had helped to found it and had participated in the League as a delegate for South Africa.

2   Most famously Keynes, in his *General Theory of Employment, Interest and Money* (chap. 24), had called for the "euthanasia of the rentier". In equally strident language, President Roosevelt variously compared Wall Street financiers to economic royalists and to a plague of locusts, and insisted that social values needed to be given priority over monetary profits. United States Secretary of the Treasury, Henry Morgenthau, was just as clear in his closing remarks at the Bretton Woods Conference, that "The institution proposed by the Bretton Woods Conference would indeed limit the control which certain private bankers have in the past exercised over international finance" (Morgenthau, 1945), and his insistence on locating the institution in Washington rather than in New York reflected his concern to bring it closer to democratic politics and further from the influence of Wall Street bankers.

3   Price rises during and immediately after the war did, of course, mean that specific duties had, by 1920, lost much of their effectiveness as measures of protection, and this was not reversed significantly by the worldwide price deflation in 1920-1921. On trade policy during the inter-war years, see Gordon, 1941; Bairoch, 1995, chap. 1; and James, 2001, chap. 3. On the links between trade policy and economic growth, see Bairoch, 1995.

4 The movement of people was the exception, with immigration sharply curtailed in comparison to the pre-1914 world (see James, 2001, chap. 4).

5 This restrictive monetary policy and fiscal austerity of the 1920s, resulting from what Keynes referred as the "Treasury View", was accompanied by the political message that government policy could do nothing to alter the state of an economy for the better. On the debate between Keynes and the Treasury, see Clarke, 1988.

6 The cycle was dominated by short-term capital flows from and back to the United States. James (2001, 30–31) clearly describes the setting in of a vicious circle thus: "Fiscal and financial crises reinforced each other: fiscal difficulties led to capital flight, and the withdrawal of capital weakened banks and created a potential or actual fiscal burden. Banking problems thus led to fiscal problems, because the cost of taking over bad banks strained the budget. But budget imbalances were interpreted by investors, foreign and domestic, as meaning that there were limits to the government's ability realistically to offer support for banks, and that it was therefore time to get out".

7 Kindelberger (1986: 11) defines an economic hegemon as "a country that is prepared, consciously or unconsciously, under some system of rules that it has internalized, to set standards of conduct for other countries and to seek to get others to follow, and in particular to take on an undue share of the burdens of the system, and in particular to take on its support in adversity by accepting its redundant commodities, maintaining a flow of investment capital, and discounting its paper". Kindelberger's analysis of the inter-war years hinges on the idea that the United Kingdom was no longer able to play the role of economic hegemon after the First World War, while the United States was reluctant to do so until the mid-1930s.

8 In the United States, those policy choices and trade-offs were essentially based on "a commitment to free markets that limited the role of government to the protection and enforcement of contracts; antitrust laws that sought to maintain efficient market competition; and guidelines for what President Hoover had called 'associationalism', a policy that used the federal government to collect and disseminate information to firms and economic leaders in order to confront the worry that insufficient information could lead to market failure" (Katznelson, 2013: 234).

9 On the construction of the New Deal alliance, see Badger, 1989 and 2008; and Katznelson, 2013.

10 "Quoting" Donald Richberg, the general counsel of the National Recovery Administration in the United States (see Katznelson, 2013: 237). The Atlantic Charter issued in August 1941 was among the first attempts to set out some of the aims and principles of the Allied powers for a post-war world. It emerged out of discussions between the United States and the United Kingdom over funding for the latter's war efforts. Three of its eight points dealt with the following economic issues: lowering trade barriers, the need for global economic cooperation to advance social welfare and a world free of fear and want, in the context of the Anglo-American discussions (see Mazower, 2012: 194–200). The discussions also revealed areas of likely contention, particularly international trade.

11 For a brief account of these problems, see Oliver, 1975, chap. I; and Dam, 1982, chap. III.

12 "Associated" nations referred to countries that had broken diplomatic relations with the Axis powers but had not joined the United Nations.

13 See also Helleiner, 2014: 117–132.

14 The first mission to Cuba, under Dexter White, took place in the latter half of 1939, although informal discussions with Cuban, Paraguayan and Brazilian officials had taken place earlier. A similar mission to Honduras took place in 1943 and to Paraguay in the same year (the latter under the Belgian economist, Robert Triffin, which also included Raul Prebisch – who had been constrained to leave his position at the Argentine central bank, following a military coup – in the follow-up mission in 1944). Subsequently, there were similar missions to Costa Rica, Bolivia, the Dominican Republic (again involving Prebisch), Guatemala and Ecuador (also led by Triffin who was by then working at the International Monetary Fund) (Helleiner, 2014). The aim of all these missions was to help domestic policymakers fashion monetary policy in line with the domestic needs of their countries.

15 All countries from Latin America, except Argentina, were invited and attended. Others included were representatives from four African countries (Egypt, Ethiopia, Liberia and South Africa) and five delegations from Asia (China, India, Iran, Iraq and the Philippines). Also represented were four countries from Eastern Europe (Czechoslovakia, Greece, Poland and Yugoslavia), a region that many (including its representatives) saw at the time as facing similar economic problems as those of other poor regions. Altogether, there were 32 delegations from these regions comprising 173 people, compared with the 140 from delegations of the other 12 countries (Australia, Belgium, Canada, France, Iceland, Luxembourg, the Netherlands, New Zealand, Norway the United Kingdom, the United States and the Union of Soviet Socialist Republics) (Schuler and Rosenberg, 2012, appendix A).

16 The numerical dominance of Latin American countries was a particular worry to the delegation from the United Kingdom at Bretton Woods. On Keynes's and the wider British attitude towards development

issues in the run-up to and during the Bretton Woods conference, see Helleiner, 2014, chap. 8.

17 An early dilemma was one of reconciling the means with the objectives of the Bank; that is, its capital base would need to be provided by the very same countries whose reconstruction and development it was designed to help. This was resolved by an agreement which provided that each member country would pay only 20 per cent of its subscription to the Bank's capital, with the rest being callable as the Bank ran out of resources (paid in capital plus reserves) to meet its obligations on funds borrowed from international markets. This guarantee provided by its shareholders greatly helped the Bank in subsequent decades to raise funds at highly favourable terms, thereby introducing an additional subsidy element to its loans and reducing the cost to its borrowers.

18 See Helleiner 2014a, chaps. 1–3. Such thinking can be clearly detected in Morgenthau's closing speech at Bretton Woods. He argued that "Long-term funds must be made available also to promote sound industry and increase industrial and agricultural production in nations whose economic potentialities have not yet been developed. It is essential to us all that these nations play their full part in the exchange of goods throughout the world. They must be enabled to produce and to sell if they are to be able to purchase and consume. The Bank for International Reconstruction and Development is designed to meet this need". On the significance of the TVA to the New Deal agenda, see Badger, 2008, chap. 5; and Bateman et al., 2009.

19 See: Black, 1991: 35; Gold, 1988; Bordo and Schwartz, 2001.

20 Strong opposition from financial interests had already led White to drop the idea of mandatory international cooperation to enforce capital controls from the Bretton Woods discussions, and replace it with a provision simply permitting such cooperation among countries.

21 The importance attached to favourable trading conditions for attaining rapid growth and full employment is reflected in the statement of the objectives of the IMF: "To facilitate the expansion and balanced growth of international trade, and to contribute thereby to the promotion and maintenance of high levels of employment and real income and to the development of the productive resources of all members as the primary objectives of economic policy".

22 At Bretton Woods, the same Colombian delegate, Carlos Restrepo, had insisted that the commercial agreements should allow "the necessary protection which must be given in the new countries to their infant industries during their first steps in industrial development" (cited in Helleiner, 2014: 170). The preparatory committee for the Conference first met in London in October 1946 to discuss the charter of an international trade organization previously proposed during loan negotiations between the United States and the United Kingdom. Following Bretton Woods, full employment and the stability of global demand were high on the committee's agenda, but the issue of industrialization was pushed by the Australian delegation, backed by Brazil, Chile, China, India and Lebanon.

23 Tensions in the Roosevelt Administration over trade issues were already apparent at the World Economic Conference in London in 1933 (see Kindleberger, 1986). Advocates of free and non-discriminatory trade, under Cordell Hull, successfully pushed through legislation on "Reciprocal Trade Agreements" in 1934, which gave the President much greater authority for bilateral tariff bargaining. Some 21 agreements were struck between 1934 and 1940. However, its impact was quite limited in terms of overall tariff reductions, while other parts of the New Deal constituency and legislation were pushing in a different direction (see Irwin, 1997).

24 In Western Europe, the share of intraregional trade in world trade rose from 18.3 per cent in 1953 to 31.2 per cent in 1973 (WTO, 2008: 15).

25 On the links between the Marshall Plan, policy space and development challenges, see Kozul-Wright and Rayment, 2007: 283–294.

26 See Arndt (1987) for a further discussion. One of the lasting consequences of this shift was a stronger focus on human capital and education as an integral part of the development agenda. As Mazower (2012) notes, Truman's inaugural address signalled that the United States would work with a range of United Nations agencies, such as the Food and Agriculture Organization (FAO), the World Health Organization (WHO) and the International Labour Organization (ILO), providing both resources and staff. Moreover, this more technocratic multilateralism harked back to the League of Nations whose technical services had been transferred from Geneva to the United States in 1940. Truman's 1949 proposal to make technical assistance the centre-piece of United States development assistance, and to encourage the use of the United Nations for this purpose, offered agencies such as the WHO and the FAO "a practical and modest alternative to more ambitious and more socialized approaches to aid that had run afoul of Congress" (Mazower, 2012: 277).

27 For a history of these ideas, see Toner, 1999; Taft and Adelman, 1988; Kohli, 2004; and Jomo, 2005.

28 Raul Prebisch's entry onto the policy stage began as head of research at the National Bank of Argentina, in which capacity he also participated in the London World Economic Conference of 1933. There, he became familiar with the new policy ideas of Keynes, and was also exposed to the asymmetries of the

trading system through negotiations on the bilateral trade agreement between Argentina and the United Kingdom. On his return to Argentina he helped design the government's Economic Recovery Plan which signalled a new and less orthodox shift in the country's policy direction. It combined public debt restructuring, currency devaluation, tariff measures and public work schemes in an effort to turn the economy round. Subsequently, he prepared the legislation to establish a central bank, with powers to manage the business cycle and oversee the stability of the entire financial system rather than merely fight inflationary pressures. As its first General Manager in 1935, Prebisch pursued a countercyclical monetary policy, reinforced exchange controls and adopted a supportive credit policy (Prebisch, 1972, vol. 2, chap. XIV). While Argentina's growth rates did not return to their levels of the 1920s, its GDP in 1930 was nevertheless 17 per cent higher than its 1929 level. Moreover, it was widely viewed as a stable international financial centre, and Prebisch's own professional standing, at home and abroad, rose significantly during this period (see Dosman, 2008, chap. 5).

29 For a more detailed history of the rising voices of developing countries on the international stage during the 1950s and 1960s, see Prashad, 2007.

30 Arndt (1987: 140) rather dramatically describes the NIEO as an internationalisation of the welfare state, an internationalisation of protection and an internationalisation of class conflict. For a more measured account of the links between UNCTAD and the NIEO discussions, see Toye and Toye, 2004, chap. 10.

31 This pattern changed following the 2008 crisis, when a number of developed countries once again turned to the IMF for funding.

References

Arndt H (1987). *Economic Development: The History of an Idea*. Chicago, IL, University of Chicago Press.

Badger A (1989). *The New Deal, the Depression Year, 1933–1940*. Chicago, IL, Ivan R Dee.

Badger A (2008). *FDR, the First Hundred Days*. New York, NY, Hill and Wang.

Bairoch P (1995). *Economics and World History*. Chicago, IL, University of Chicago Press.

Bateman F, Ros R and Taylor J (2009). Did New Deal and World War II public capital investments facilitate a "big push" in the American South? *Journal of Institutional and Theoretical Economics*, 165(2): 307–341.

Bénétrix A, O'Rourke K and Williamson J (2012). The spread of manufacturing to the poor periphery, 1870-2007. NBER Working Paper no. 18221, NBER, Cambridge, MA.

Berthelot Y (2004). Unity and diversity of development: The regional commissions' experience. In: Berthelot Y, ed. *Unity and Diversity in Development Ideas: Perspectives from the UN Regional Commissions*. Bloomington, IN, Indiana University Press: 1–50.

Bertola L and Ocampo JA (2012). *Economic Development of Latin America since Independence*. Oxford, Oxford University Press.

Biltoft CN (2014). The League of Nations and alternative economic perspectives. In: Reinert E, Kattel R and Ghosh J, eds. *Handbook of Alternative Theories of Economic Development*. Cheltenham, Edward Elgar Publishing, forthcoming.

Black S (1991). *A Levite Amongst Priests: Edward M Bernstein and the Origins of the Bretton Woods System*. Boulder. CO, Westview Press.

Blyth M (2002). *Great Transformations: Economic Ideas and Institutional Change in the Twentieth Century*. Cambridge, Cambridge University Press.

Blyth M (2013). *Austerity: The History of a Dangerous Idea*. Oxford, Oxford University Press.

Bordo M and Schwartz A (2001). From the Exchange Stabilization Fund to the International Monetary Fund. NBER Working Paper no. 8100, NBER, Cambridge, MA.

Borgwardt E (2005). *A New Deal for the World: America's Vision for Human Rights*. Cambridge, MA, Harvard University Press.

Boyce R (2009). *The Great Interwar Crisis and the Collapse of Globalization*. New York, NY, Macmillan.

Bruno M and Sachs J (1985). *The Economics of Worldwide Stagflation*. Cambridge, MA, Harvard University Press.

Camdessus M (1997). Global capital flows: Raising the returns and reducing the risks. Speech to Los Angeles World Affairs Council, 17 June.

Clarke P (1988). *The Keynesian Revolution in the Making, 1924–36*. Oxford, Oxford University Press.

Crotty J (1999). Was Keynes a corporatist? Keynes's radical views on industrial policy and macro policy in the 1920s. *Journal of Economic Ideas*, 33(3): 555–578.

Dam K (1982). *The Rules of the Game. Reform and Evolution in the International Monetary System*. Chicago, IL, University of Chicago Press.

Dosman E (2008). *The Life and Times of Raul Prebisch, 1901–1986*. Montreal, McGill-Queen's University Press.

Eichengreen B and Kenen PB (1994). Managing the world economy under the Bretton Woods System: An overview. In: Kenen PB, ed. *Managing the World Economy: Fifty Years After Bretton Woods*. Washington, DC, Institute for International Economics: 3–57.

Eichengreen B and Temin P (1997). The gold standard and the Great Depression. NBER Working Paper no. 6060, NBER, Cambridge, MA.

Epstein G (2006). Introduction: Financialization and the World Economy. In: Epstein G, ed. *Financialization and the World Economy*. Cheltenham, Edward Elgar.

Felix D (1961). An alternative view of the monetarist-structuralist controversy. In: Hirschman A, ed. *Latin American Issues: Essays and Comments*. New York, NY, The Twentieth Century Fund.

Felix D (1996). Financial globalization versus free trade: The case for the Tobin Tax. *UNCTAD Review* (UNCTAD/SGO/10), Geneva.

Fishlow A (1985). Lessons from the past, capital markets and international lending in the 19th century and the interwar years. In: Kahler M, ed. *The Politics of International Debt*. Ithaca, NY, Cornell University Press: 37–94.

Gardner (1995). Establishing a vision for promoting economic development. In: Boughton J and Latef K, eds. *Fifty Years After Bretton Woods: The Future of the IMF and the World Bank*. Washington, DC, IMF/World Bank.

Gold J (1988). Mexico and the development of the practice of the International Monetary Fund. *World Development*,16(10): 1127–1142.

Gordon M (1941). *Barriers to World Trade: A Study of Recent Commercial Policy*. New York, NY, The Macmillan Company.

Graz JC (2014).The Havana Charter: When state and market shake hands. In: Reinert E, Kattel R and Ghosh J, eds. *Handbook of Alternative Theories of Economic Development*. Cheltenham, Edward Elgar Publishing, forthcoming.

Hall P, ed. (1989). *The Political Power of Economic Ideas: Keynesianism Across Nations*. Princeton, NJ, Princeton University Press.

Helleiner E (1994). *States and the Reemergence of Global Finance*. Ithaca, NY, Cornell University Press.

Helleiner E (2014). *Forgotten Foundations of Bretton Woods International Development and the Making of the Postwar Order*. Ithaca, NY, Cornell University Press.

Irwin D (1997). From Smoot Hawley to reciprocal trade agreements: Changing the course of US trade policy in the 1930s. NBER Working Paper no. 5895, NBER, Cambridge, MA.

James H (2001). *The End of Globalization: Lessons from the Great Depression*. Cambridge, MA, Harvard University Press.

Jomo KS, ed. (2005). *Pioneers of Development Economics*, London, Zed Press.

Katznelson I (2013). *Fear Itself: The New Deal and the Origins of Our Times*. New York, NY, WW Norton and Co.

Keynes JM (1944). Letter to Lord Addison, May 1944. In: Moggridge D, ed. (1980). *The Collected Writings of John Maynard Keynes*, Volume XXVI: Activities 1941-1946, Shaping the Post-War World, Bretton Woods and Reparations. London, The MacMillan Press Ltd.

Kindleberger C (1986). *The World in Depression 1929-1939*. Harmondsworth, Penguin Books.

Kohli A (2004). *State-Directed Development: Political Power and Industrialization in the Global Periphery*. Cambridge, Cambridge University Press.

Kozul-Wright R (1999). On dentists, dreamers and defunct economists. In: Sardoni C and Kriesler P, eds. *Keynes, Post-Keynesianism and Political Economy: Essays in honour of Geoff Harcourt*, Vol. 3. London and New York, NY, Routledge: 131–150.

Kozul-Wright R and Rayment P (2007). *The Resistible Rise of Market Fundamentalism: Rethinking Development Policy in an Unbalanced World*. London, Zed Press.

Kumhof M, Rancière R and Winant P (2013). Inequality, leverage and crisis: The case of endogenous default. IMF Working Paper 249. International Monetary Fund, Washington, DC.

Martin J (2013). Were we bullied? *London Review of Books*, 21 November.

Mazower M (1998). *Dark Continent. Europe's Twentieth Century*. London, The Penguin Press.

Mazower M (2012). *Governing the World: The History of an Idea*. London, Penguin Books.

Mikesell R (1994). The Bretton Woods debates: A memoir. *Essays in International Finance* No. 192. Princeton University, Department of Economics, Princeton NJ.

Morgenthau II (1945). Bretton Woods and International Cooperation. *Foreign Affairs*, 23(2): 182–194.

Ocampo JA (2014). Latin American structuralism and productive development strategies. In: Salazar-Xirinachs J, Nübler I and Kozul-Wright R, eds. *Transforming Economies: Making Industrial Policy*

Work for Growth, Jobs and Development. Geneva, UNCTAD and ILO: 41–64.

Oliver R (1975). *International Economic Cooperation and the World Bank*. London, Macmillan.

Piketty T (2014). *Capital in the Twenty-First Century*. Cambridge, MA, Harvard University Press.

Polanyi K (1944). *The Great Transformation: The Economic and Political Origins of Our Time*. New York, NY, Farrar and Rinehart.

Prashad V (2007). *The Darker Nations: A People's History of the Third World*. New York, NY, The New Press.

Prebisch R (1972). *La creación del Banco Central y la experiencia monetaria argentina entre los años 1935-1943*. Buenos Aires, Central Bank of Argentina.

Rodrik D (2002). Feasible Globalizations. NBER Working Paper no. 9129, NBER, Cambridge, MA.

Rosenstein-Rodan P (1944). The international development of economically backward areas. *International Affairs*, 20(2): 157–165.

Sandel M (2010). *What Money Can't Buy: The Moral Limits of the Market*. London, Penguin.

Schuler K and Rosenberg A (2012). *The Bretton Woods Transcripts*. New York, NY, Center for Financial Stability.

Taft C and Adelman I (1988). *Comparative Patterns of Economic Development, 1850-1914*. Baltimore, MD, Johns Hopkins University Press.

Temin P (1991). *Lessons from the Great Depression*. Boston, MA, MIT Press.

Temin P (2010). The Great Recession and the Great Depression. NBER Working Paper no. 15645, NBER, Cambridge, MA.

Toner P (1999). *Main Currents in Cumulative Causation: The Dynamics of Growth and Development*. London, Macmillan.

Toye J and Toye R (2004). *The UN and Global Political Economy: Trade, Finance, and Development*. Bloomington, IN, Indiana University Press.

Toye J (2014). *UNCTAD at 50: A Short History*. New York and Geneva, United Nations.

UNCTAD (1964). *Towards a New Trade Policy for Development*. Geneva.

UNCTAD (2011). *Report of the Secretary-General of UNCTAD to UNCTAD XIII, Development-led Globalization: Towards Sustainable and Inclusive Development Paths*. New York and Geneva, United Nations.

Van Dormeal A (1978). *Bretton Woods: Birth of a Monetary System*. London, Macmillan.

Wilcox C (1949). *A Charter for World Trade*. New York, NY, Macmillan.

Wolf M (2003). Is globalisation in danger? *World Economy*, 26(4): 393–411.

WTO (2008). *The World Trade Report 2008*. Geneva, World Trade Organization.

Chapter V

TRADE AND INDUSTRIAL POLICIES IN AN EVOLVING GLOBAL GOVERNANCE REGIME

A. Introduction

As the international community rethinks its goals for a post-2015 development agenda to succeed the Millennium Development Goals, it is imperative to ensure that effective policy instruments are available to countries to enable them to achieve the agreed goals and advance the agenda. This chapter argues that recent experience, historical evidence and theoretical insights all point to the role that proactive trade and industrial policies must play in that agenda.

The role of such policies in development strategies has been extensively discussed and debated. Developed countries adopted a variety of industrial policies during their period of industrialization, and continued to do so after the Second World War in their pursuit of sustained economic growth, full employment and accelerated technological progress. Subsequently, industrial policy was also high on the agenda of many developing-country governments that saw industrialization as key to unlocking underutilized resources, addressing long-standing structural weaknesses and social deficits, and closing the technological gap with the developed economies. This post-war policy consensus on the utility of proactive trade and industrial

> The availability of effective policy instruments is imperative to advance a post-2015 development agenda and achieve its goals.

policies also informed the debates about reforming the multilateral trade and financial systems in a way that would allow developing countries the policy space[1] to adopt the measures and instruments they deemed necessary to foster rapid productivity growth and industrial development (see chapter IV).

From the early 1980s, industrial policy largely disappeared from the development agenda of many countries, particularly in Africa and Latin America. This was partly a reaction to evidence of specific policy mistakes and abuses, but it was also due to a more ideologically driven debate that blamed government failures much more than market failures for slow economic development and emphasized the need for market liberalization. Just as important, in several developing economies the debt crisis eroded the ability of States to pursue proactive policies. Not only did they suffer from macroeconomic and fiscal constraints, but also they had to submit to the growing policy conditionality attached to loans extended to them by the Bretton Woods institutions. Furthermore, many observers saw the period of economic stagnation following the debt crisis as the inevitable outcome of distortions associated with State-led industrialization, rather than as a consequence of deflationary macroeconomic policies, and supply-side shocks due to badly designed adjustment programmes. As a consequence, many countries reduced or abandoned proactive trade and industrial policies and began to favour unfettered markets and transnational firms, as endorsed by the so-called "Washington Consensus".

Interest in proactive trade and industrial policies has revived since around the turn of the millennium, for a variety of reasons. First, and probably most important, was the accumulation of overwhelming evidence that the most successful developing countries – notably the newly industrializing economies in East Asia followed by China – were the ones that had systematically followed a pragmatic approach to promoting industrial development through a combination of macroeconomic and structural policies, measured protectionism while gradually opening up to trade and investment, and effective collaboration between the private and public sectors.[2] Second, it was increasingly recognized that the policies associated with the Washington Consensus were doing little to support economic upgrading and diversification, which meant that countries would risk falling into a "middle-income trap" (see, for example, Felipe et al., 2012). Third, mainstream economists started to accept some of the insights into economic development from classical economics, such as the recognition that economic development has a "structural" dimension, the importance of linkages and learning for accelerating productivity growth, and the key role of demand. This greater acceptance was helped by translating classical economists' "intuitive insights into clear-cut models that could serve as the core of an enduring discipline" (Krugman, 1993: 26).[3] For these reasons, there is now wider interest in industrial policy (Naudé, 2010). This has moved the debate to a more pragmatic level, with discussions focusing not so much on whether industrial policies are needed as on how best to pursue such policies (e.g. Rodrik, 2008; Salazar-Xirinachs, et al., 2014), and what lessons can be learned (and transferred) from the experiences of the successful industrializers.

It is clear that specific policy measures adopted by some of the successful industrializing countries cannot easily be replicated by other countries. This is not only because individual countries' success stories are invariably linked to special economic and institutional conditions that are unlikely to exist in other countries; it is also because changes in the external economic environment affect both the availability and effectiveness of specific policy instruments (Akyüz et al., 1998). At present, four elements of the changing dynamics of the world economy are crucial for the way in which proactive trade and industrial policies can spur economic development, as discussed below.

(i) International economic governance has increasingly restricted the options available for conducting the kinds of trade and industrial policies that individual countries are legally allowed to pursue.

This is in contrast to conditions prevailing at the time of the export-oriented revival of Japan's manufacturing base after the Second World War and the rapid economic catch-up of the so-called "Asian tigers" (Hong Kong, the Republic of Korea, Singapore and Taiwan Province of China) between the 1960s and 1980s. Although these economies periodically encountered protectionist barriers on developed-country markets, such as high tariffs and tariff escalation, as well as so-called "voluntary" export restraints, the Multi-Fibre Arrangement and other non-tariff barriers, they enjoyed significant flexibility in pursuing their own trade and industrial policies that helped them achieve rapid structural transformation.

This situation changed with the Uruguay Round Agreements (URAs), resulting from multilateral trade negotiations, and the creation of the World Trade Organization (WTO) in 1995. As discussed in some detail in *TDR 2006*, these agreements came with some significant restrictions on the conduct of trade and industrial policies of all WTO member States. Further restrictions followed with the proliferation of regional trade agreements (RTAs) and international investment agreements (IIAs), many of which contain rules and regulations that go beyond the URAs.

(ii) Under the increasing influence of financial markets and interests, many countries have been experiencing unbalanced economic growth, both internally and externally, and many policymakers have recognized a link between structural problems in their economies and a heightened vulnerability to shocks and crises (UNCTAD, 2011a). In this environment, the challenge for policymakers is to make economic growth and development more inclusive − ensuring that all social groups enjoy the benefits of economic growth − by complementing the market mechanism with policy measures and institutional support aimed at the creation of decent jobs, and at achieving more equal income distribution and poverty reduction. There is an ongoing search for policy measures that can bring about such outcomes without putting a large additional burden on government budgets.

(iii) Developments in the global economy since the onset of the economic and financial crisis in 2008–2009 have thrown new light on prevailing challenges to export-led industrialization models.

It is well known that export-led industrialization strategies must sooner or later reach their limits when many countries pursue them simultaneously, as competition among economies based on low unit labour costs and taxes faces a fallacy of composition that leads to a race to the bottom (e.g. *TDR 2002*). At the present juncture, when developing countries' opportunities to increase exports of manufactures to developed countries are likely to remain weak for some time, the limitations of such a growth strategy are becoming even more obvious. A rebalancing of developing countries' growth strategies towards a greater emphasis on domestic and regional demand could reduce this risk (e.g. *TDR 2013*). It is true that the combination of faster growth of domestic demand and slower growth of external demand could lead to a deterioration of the trade account. This means that such a shift would require proactive trade and industrial policies that strengthen domestic supply capacities in order to contain trade deficits, which otherwise would have to be redressed through foreign capital inflows.

(iv) In some developing countries, the fear that the strong increase in primary commodity prices

> Trade negotiations need to refocus on multilateral agreements which recognize the legitimate concerns of developing countries.

since 2002 may cause or accelerate deindustrialization has given greater urgency to the question of how to foster industrialization. Several developing countries have, moreover, found that their apparently successful structural transformation by promoting manufacturing through participation in international production networks is linked to only "thin" industrialization. That is, they have succeeded in participating in manufacturing networks, but only in low-skill activities without the ability to upgrade. In many cases, this has yielded lower than expected economic benefits, besides hampering both social upgrading and inclusive industrialization. In many such economies, as in others where structural transformation is even less developed, there are growing demands by their societies, and especially by the increasingly more educated youth, for policies and economic outcomes that meet their aspirations for greater economic opportunities and better lives.

Against this background, this chapter examines how systems of global economic governance (both private and public) have constrained proactive trade and industrial policies, and highlights how some countries have managed to implement policies to foster structural transformation despite these constraints. It also considers what additional challenges could impede the effective pursuit of such policies in the years ahead. It concludes that, in order to pursue rapid and inclusive economic growth and meet future global development goals, developing countries will need sufficient policy space at the national level to undertake the necessary structural transformation of their economies. At the international level, the multilateral governance framework will need to be more permissive and coherent if it is to facilitate such structural transformation.

The chapter is structured as follows. Section B discusses the impacts of the various trade, investment and comprehensive economic partnership agreements on national trade and industrial policy space. It highlights areas where provisions in URAs and RTAs have constrained such policy space for developing countries, as well as areas where flexibilities remain intact. The factors that prompt developing countries to engage in RTAs and effectively renounce policy space are also considered. Such engagement is paradoxical, especially as it is evident that many of these countries have been investing considerable efforts at the multilateral level to preserve such space, for example by rejecting developed-country proposals to deepen rules concerning international investment, intellectual property rights (IPRs), government procurement and financial services. The section concludes by addressing recent tendencies towards broadening the notion of "protectionism" and denouncing as "murky" those behind-the-border measures that are designed to advance and direct structural transformation but which could hamper the opportunities for profit-making by transnational corporations (TNCs).

> WTO-plus and WTO-extra provisions should be abandoned, while fostering the developmental aspects of the Doha Round.

Section C begins with a brief discussion of the meaning of industrial policy. It then provides some recent country-specific examples of industrial policies, especially those aimed at creating and strengthening domestic linkages and fostering innovation within the context of what remains legally possible. Section D discusses two elements of the changing dynamics of the world economy that pose additional challenges to the effectiveness of proactive trade and industrial policies in spurring economic development. The first is a potential decline in export opportunities for developing countries.

While exporting can be a powerful driver of productivity growth in manufacturing, slow growth in developed countries is causing them to reduce their imports from developing countries. This suggests that export-oriented industrial policies are becoming less effective, and reinforces the need for developing-country governments to strengthen industrial policies directed at fostering domestic and regional linkages and innovation. The second challenge relates to tendencies to move away from a coherent multilateral governance system towards a multitude of initiatives that are introducing ever-growing constraints on the ability to use national policy instruments.

The concluding section E argues that developing countries require greater policy space to enable them to continue their rapid growth trajectory of the past 15 years and make such growth more equitable and sustainable. Strengthened global economic governance that refocuses trade negotiations on multilateral agreements which recognize the legitimate concerns of developing countries, abandons WTO-plus and WTO-extra provisions and fosters the developmental character of the Doha Round would be an important step in this direction. Leveraging the greater economic and political power that developing countries have achieved over the past two decades could strongly support this process.

B. The evolving global governance framework: Implications for national trade and industrial policies

Successful development experiences have generally been associated with structural transformation (see box 4.1). This section examines the constraints faced by developing countries in adopting the trade and investment policies they deem to be the most suitable for structural transformation. In particular, it focuses on the multiplicity of trade agreements (multilateral, bilateral and regional) and how they restrict national policy space. Multilateral agreements maintain some flexibilities and incorporate some special and differential treatment (SDT) for least developed countries (LDCs); however, they typically limit or forbid the kinds of policies that played an important role in successful processes of

Box 5.1

STRUCTURAL TRANSFORMATION IN DEVELOPING COUNTRIES: THE ROLE OF THE MANUFACTURING SECTOR

At relatively early stages of economic development, per capita income growth results from capital accumulation that allows a fuller use of underutilized labour and natural resources without necessarily altering the efficiency of use of these factors of production. As economic development proceeds, further growth of per capita income has generally been associated with sustained productivity gains based on structural transformation, i.e. moving labour and other resources from relatively less productive activities, such as in agriculture, to more productive activities in the formal manufacturing and services sectors.[a]

Manufacturing plays a central role in this structural transformation. Activities in this sector are more conducive to specialization and the division of labour, and offer greater potential for innovation and increasing returns to scale than other sectors (Kaldor, 1968). Moreover, in contrast to the primary sector, and especially the extractive industries, most manufacturing activities are labour-intensive, so that, given the right wage and labour market policies, productivity growth has the potential to benefit a large proportion of the population. The ensuing, relatively more equal distribution of income growth, combined with the high income elasticity of demand for manufactured goods, ignites a virtuous process of cumulative causation between supply and demand effects that further supports structural transformation. The central development challenge for policymakers, therefore, is to achieve an intersectoral shift of productive employment towards high-productivity activities combined with productivity growth within each economic sector, particularly manufacturing, while ensuring a broad distribution of the benefits of productivity growth.

Once developing countries have succeeded in establishing a manufacturing base, and the intersectoral productivity gaps have narrowed, their ability for further catch-up with richer countries increasingly depends on sustained improvements in productivity within the manufacturing sector, such as through technological advances and the creation of new products and processes, along with the development of related technological and social capabilities.[b]

Success in achieving structural transformation and the policy strategies contributing to that success have varied significantly across countries. As discussed in previous *TDRs* (in particular *TDRs 1996, 2003* and *2006*), the pace of structural transformation in developing economies in East Asia – especially the Republic of Korea and Taiwan Province of China between the 1960s and the 1990s, and China since the 1990s – has outperformed that in other developing countries. Proactive trade and industrial policies, rather than a reliance on unfettered market forces, have generally played a key role in their success, just as they did during the process of industrialization in the now developed countries.[c]

Country-specific factors, including not only different initial economic conditions but also less developed administrative and institutional capabilities, partly explain the limited ability of other developing countries to emulate the successful structural transformation experiences of some East Asian economies and China. But also, and equally important in this context, the other developing countries are likely to have been constrained by less room for manoeuvre in their trade and investment policies.

---

[a]   The classic references for this so-called "dual economy" approach include Lewis (1954), and Ranis and Fei (1961), while the more recent literature, reviewed by Roncolato and Kucera (2014), also includes McMillan et al. (2014). For a more detailed discussion and evidence up to the turn of the millennium, see also *TDR 2003*, chap. V. This distinction between traditional and modern economic sectors contrasts with growth models in the neoclassical tradition, which consider such structural differences sufficiently small to allow all economic activities to be aggregated into just one sector.

[b]   While this chapter emphasizes the role of manufacturing, successful structural transformation in Asia (such as observed first in, Japan, then in the Republic of Korea and Taiwan Province of China, and most recently in China) suggests the importance of two other elements. The first relates to the maximization of agricultural output, while the other relates to the government's role in directing investment towards activities that have the fastest possible productivity growth potential, and hence promise large future profits. The first of these two elements was discussed in detail in *TDRs 1995, 1996* and *1998*, while *TDRs 2003* and *2013* addressed the second one. On both elements, see also Studwell, 2013.

[c]   For detailed empirical evidence on structural transformation over the past four decades, see UNIDO, 2013, and for a more general discussion of developmental success stories see, for example, Fosu, 2013.

structural transformation in the past. This process of limiting national policy space began with the URAs, which included several rules that were not directly related to trade flows. Subsequent bilateral and regional trade agreements have increasingly included rules that can be important for the design of comprehensive national development strategies, such as government procurement, capital flows, trade in services, and environmental and labour issues. Many of them have also included disciplines concerning IPRs and investment-related measures that are more stringent than those already incorporated in multilateral agreements. In a sense, these bilateral and regional agreements are no longer "trade agreements"; they are more comprehensive economic integration treaties, often referred to as economic partnership agreements.

1. Multilateral trade agreements: Constraints on policy choices and remaining flexibilities

The multilateral trade regime comprises a set of negotiated, binding and enforceable rules and commitments that are built on the core principles of reciprocity and non-discrimination, as reflected in the most-favoured-nation (MFN) treatment and the commitment to national treatment (i.e. equal treatment for domestic and foreign goods and enterprises in domestic markets) requirements. Together, these rules and commitments may be considered a global public good, as they inject certainty and predictability in international trade and limit adverse international spillovers that may result from beggar-thy-neighbour policies (i.e. discriminatory or mercantilist trade policies whereby economically or politically powerful countries seek to obtain benefits at the expense of less influential countries). This trade regime has granted developing countries some important exceptions. For example, exceptions to the MFN rule accord developing countries preferential and more favourable market access, and exceptions to the reciprocity principle allow developed countries to grant their developing-country partners less than full reciprocity in multilateral trade agreements. Prior to the URAs, these exceptions, which are generally known as special and differential treatment (SDT) provisions, were couched in developmental terms; they were seen as recognition by the international

community of the differences between developed and all developing countries in terms of economic structures and levels of development.

While maintaining some exemptions for LDCs (and, in some cases, other low-income countries), the URAs represented a step towards a single-tier system of rights and obligations. The SDT was modified to accord developing countries time-limited derogations and longer transition periods, as well as technical assistance for the implementation of multilateral agreements (such as through the WTO-led Aid for Trade initiative). However, eventually these countries will need to fully comply with all the rules and commitments embodied in the URAs.[4] This reinterpretation of SDT was part of the grand bargain behind the URAs and the establishment of the WTO which, more generally, aimed at providing developing countries improved access to developed-country markets, particularly in agriculture and textiles and clothing, in exchange for some important concessions by developing countries in terms of market opening and, in particular, their acceptance of a wide range of rules and commitments (*TDRs 1994* and *2006*).

For example, the Agreement on Trade-related Investment Measures (TRIMs)[5] prohibits the discriminatory imposition of requirements on foreign investors such as local-content and trade-balancing requirements, as well as foreign-exchange restrictions. These instruments had often been used by policymakers in the past to increase the linkages between foreign investors and local manufacturers in the context of structural transformation.[6] Under this agreement, it is also difficult for countries to make support conditional on reaching certain export targets. This means that policy measures that were important for controlling performance, such as withdrawing support from producers that fail to achieve international competitiveness within a predefined period of time, are no longer possible.[7] However, measures that do not impose quantitative restrictions and do not treat foreign investors less favourably than domestic ones do not violate the agreement; nor does a potential race to the bottom in according foreign investors ever larger concessions that may well harm domestic investors, and even drive them out of the market, especially as there are no effective multilateral codes of conduct for foreign investors. Furthermore, policymakers may continue to impose sector-specific entry conditions on foreign investors, including industry-specific limitations.[8] They may also apply local-content requirements for the procurement of services, including technology and data flows, unless such measures have been prohibited through commitments in the General Agreement on Trade in Services (GATS).

A second set of obligations results from the Agreement on Trade-related Aspects of Intellectual Property Rights (TRIPS), which establishes multilateral minimum standards for granting and protecting the use of intellectual property (IP) (e.g. copyrights, patents and trademarks) in foreign markets. The agreement severely restricts reverse engineering and other forms of imitative innovation which previously were used by many countries, including the now developed ones, for their structural transformation processes. This has also adversely affected competitive conditions in all countries, as it has been found that patents "are increasingly used as strategic assets to influence the conditions of competition rather than as a defensive means to protect research and development outcomes" (Max Planck Institute for Innovation and Competition, 2014: 2). Moreover, the recent rapid rise in the number of patent filings and grants has led to an increase in costs that disproportionally benefits TNCs at the expense of smaller enterprises and individual inventors.

There is some flexibility in the TRIPS Agreement through its mechanisms of compulsory licensing and parallel imports.[9] In addition, varying patentability standards, such as the granting of narrow patents for incremental innovations that build on more fundamental discoveries, may be useful for adapting imported technologies to local conditions.[10]

The Doha Declaration on the TRIPS Agreement and Public Health, which was adopted at the WTO Ministerial Meeting in 2001, clarified some of these flexibilities. Even though the Declaration focused on public health issues, many of its clauses have broader implications and concern IP in any field of technology. Therefore, they may also be used to promote domestic production (Correa, 2014). However, there is little evidence to suggest that these flexibilities have been incorporated into national laws and regulations and put to effective use (Deere, 2009). This may be because of the proliferation of RTAs, many of which incorporate more stringent provisions than the TRIPS Agreement. But it could also be because it is not always clear which IPR regime is appropriate at a given stage of development. This lack of clarity makes it difficult for policymakers to determine how the flexibilities available could be used in industrial policy instruments to suit the requirements of national technological capabilities and social priorities.

In this context, it may be useful to identify three stages of industrial development: *initiation*, *internalization* and *generation*. At the early or *initiation* stage, mostly mature technologies are incorporated into domestic production through informal channels of technology transfer (such as the acquisition of machinery and equipment, reverse engineering and subcontracting) as well as through formal modes of transfer (such as turnkey agreements and foreign-direct investment (FDI)). At this stage, the IPR regime has little or no positive impact on local innovation, although it may affect access to goods by the local population. Thus, the IPR regime should allow as much margin as possible for the absorption and diffusion of acquired technologies. This is the situation in LDCs, where technology efforts typically focus on mastery of operation and low-level design technology. Similarly, in other developing countries strong IPR protection most probably will not allow for more technology transfer or local innovation. At the *internalization* stage, some low-intensity research and development (R&D) industries emerge, and local producers are able to develop "minor" or "incremental" innovations, mostly from routine exploitation of existing technologies rather than from deliberate R&D efforts. Strong IP protection may have little or no impact on innovation, while reducing the diffusion of foreign inputs and technologies and increasing their costs. A flexible system is ideal at this stage, but at the very least the design of IPR legislation should aim to allow reverse engineering and technology diffusion by making full use of the remaining flexibilities in the TRIPS Agreement and in various RTAs. Finally, at the *generation* stage, some industries may benefit from IP protection to consolidate their innovation strategies domestically or internationally, as is the case in some of the more advanced developing countries such as Brazil and India. However, there will

The URAs have reduced the policy space available to WTO members while leaving some flexibilities intact.

still be some tension between the interests of local innovators and the society at large, since increased levels of IP protection may reduce technology diffusion by restricting the access of other local producers, as well as access by local consumers to the products of innovation because of consequently higher prices.

A third example of additional commitments through the URAs relates to the GATS, which has extended the most-favoured-nation and national treatment principles from trade in goods to trade in a wide range of services, such as finance, tourism, education and health provision. The GATS provisions are based on a "positive-list" approach, i.e. countries list their liberalization commitments in terms of mode and sequencing, but retain autonomy over all other sectors. In principle, this should allow countries to retain some of their policy space. However, some observers have expressed concern about the full reach of GATS regulations and argue that the GATS effectively covers regulations as wide-ranging as domestic laws, guidelines, unwritten practices, subsidies and grants, licensing standards and qualifications, and economic needs test (Chanda, 2002), making it applicable to all regulations and measures by governments at all levels (central, state, provincial, local and municipal), even when they are for the purposes of environmental and consumer protection or universal service obligations. There are also persistent ambiguities about the extent to which "non-commercial" government services are excluded from the GATS, since most such service delivery today contains a mix of public and private involvement (Chanda, 2002).

A fourth set of obligations can be found in the Agreement on Subsidies and Countervailing Measures (SCM), which significantly strengthens disciplines relating to subsidies.[11] The agreement covers two categories of subsidies, and regulates the use of countervailing measures on subsidized imports that are found to hurt domestic producers. "Prohibited" subsidies are those that are contingent upon the use of domestic over imported goods or export performance.[12] Yet, making subsidies conditional on export performance was a crucial monitoring device in East Asian countries' outward-oriented strategies to ensure that support was given only to those enterprises that were able to compete in international markets.

> WTO members can still use tariffs to protect certain sectors, and they have some flexibility in the use of both IP and FDI regulatory measures.

Under the SCM Agreement, all other subsidies, including those for production, are "actionable". They are not prohibited, but are subject to challenge through the Dispute Settlement Mechanism (DSM) or to countervailing action. Such a challenge would need to be based on the finding that a subsidy causes any of the following three adverse effects for a member State: first, nullification or impairment of tariff concessions or other benefits accruing under the GATT 1994; second, injury to a domestic industry caused by subsidized imports in the territory of the complaining member, where such injury can be the basis for countervailing action; and third, serious prejudice, which constitutes the broadest form of adverse effect (e.g. export displacement) in the market of the subsidizing member or in a third-country market. Until the expiration of article 6.1 of the SCM Agreement at the end of 1999, a serious prejudice claim could be related to four situations, but whether such claims still apply remains unresolved (Coppens, 2013: 91).[13]

A major flexibility retained by the SCM Agreement concerns the granting of export credits.[14] While Annex I explicitly identifies export credits as prohibited subsidies, its item (k) includes a safe-haven clause stipulating that "an export credit practice which is in conformity with … [the interest rate] provisions … of an international undertaking … to which at least twelve original Members to this Agreement are parties as of 1 January 1979 … shall not be considered an export subsidy prohibited by this Agreement."[15] While not explicitly naming it, this clause refers directly to the Arrangement on Officially Supported Export Credits of the Organisation for Economic Co-operation and Development (OECD). The purpose of that Arrangement is to provide an institutional framework for the orderly use of publicly supported export credits relating to exports of goods and/or services and to financial leases with a repayment term of two or more years. Through its implicit inclusion in the SCM Agreement, this framework has become a benchmark for all WTO members applying the interest rate provisions of the Arrangement (Coppens, 2009).[16] A reflection of this is the complaint "Brazil-Aircraft" (1996–2001) brought to the WTO dispute settlement panel by Canada, where Brazil, as a non-signatory to the OECD agreement, successfully claimed that its revised financing programme (PROEX III) supporting its aircraft industry was in accordance with the SCM's safe-haven provision (WTO, 2013b).

Country-specific schedules annexed to the Marrakesh Protocol of the GATT 1994 have governed the commitments relating to tariff reductions resulting from the Uruguay Round negotiations. These schedules have committed developing countries to a larger coverage of tariff bindings (e.g. all tariffs on agricultural products have been bound) as well as to significant reductions in their previous bound rates of industrial tariffs. Nevertheless, developing countries have preserved some degree of flexibility with regard to tariff policy, as they have left part of their tariffs unbound, and bound other tariffs at sometimes relatively high levels. As a result, there are sometimes rather wide differences between bound and applied rates (often referred to as "tariff binding overhang"), and between those tariff rates across individual tariff lines.[17] However, those large differences are also indicative of the considerable trade liberaliza tion that has occurred on a unilateral basis outside the multilateral trade regime, including through conditionalities associated with loans extended by the International Monetary Fund (IMF) and the World Bank to developing countries.

The remaining flexibility for developing countries' tariff policies may well be reduced, or even eliminated, by the Doha Round negotiations on non-agricultural market access (NAMA). It may be argued that further constraints on tariff policy would do little harm, because it is generally recognized that in many respects tariffs are not the best tool to promote structural transformation, that developing countries have rarely used this remaining flexibility, and that the "tariff wars" of the 1930s amply demonstrate their potential harm. However, tariffs remain an important source of fiscal revenues for many developing countries. Moreover, modulating the level of applied tariffs may be an important tool for sector-specific support policies, especially because the SCM Agreement has circumscribed the use of subsidies, which, in many instances, have been a preferred instrument to support structural transformation.

In this context, it is important to bear in mind that structural transformation is a cumulative process

> WTO members can also continue to use certain subsidies and standards to promote R&D and innovation activities.

in the course of which an economy moves from one stage of industrialization to another through the establishment of new and more productive manufacturing activities. Successful experiences of structural transformation, as in the Republic of Korea, point to the importance of flexibility in sector-specific public support policies.[18] Applied to tariffs, this would imply changing the sector-specific level and structure of tariffs over time, while maintaining considerable dispersion of tariffs across economic sectors.[19]

Yet, in addition to aiming at full binding coverage, the NAMA negotiations have been pursued on a line-by-line basis, which implies tariff cuts in all product categories, subject to some country-specific provisions, some of which are still under negotiation, and a considerable decline in tariff dispersion across products. This contrasts with the approach adopted during the Uruguay Round "when commitments by developing countries were for an average level of tariffs without any obligation to apply reductions to all tariff lines" (Akyüz, 2005: 6). Equally important, the negotiations have been based on using a formula for tariff reductions, rather than the previously used request-and-offer approach, with a view to reducing more than proportionally higher tariffs and therefore achieving greater harmonization of industrial tariffs across countries. Attaining the latter objective would imply deeper cuts by developing than by developed countries, since tariffs in developing countries are typically higher. Indeed, the approach adopted for modalities of industrial tariff reductions, as contained in the latest negotiated text of December 2008, stipulates an increase in binding coverage and a reduction in tariffs according to a simple Swiss formula, with separate coefficients for developed- and developing-country members (WTO, 2008).[20]

This section has shown that the URAs have reduced the policy space available to WTO member States, but also that the multilateral trade regime has preserved policy space in some areas. In terms of constraints, the URAs have placed restrictions on the imposition on foreign investors of performance requirements on exports, on domestic content and on technology transfer, all of which have historically been very important in promoting late industrialization. They also make it more difficult or costly for domestic producers to undertake reverse engineering and imitation through access to technology that is covered by patent or copyright protection.

However, WTO members retain the possibility of using tariffs to protect certain sectors, and have some flexibility in the use of both IP and regulatory measures concerning FDI. Perhaps most importantly, WTO members can continue to use certain kinds of subsidies and standards aimed at fostering structural transformation that involves the generation of new productive capacity by helping to promote R&D and innovation activities. Some examples of how countries have used such flexibilities are discussed in section C.

2. Regional trade agreements: Additional constraints on policy choices

Since the early 1990s, a wave of RTAs (i.e. regional trade agreements with reciprocal commitments between two or more partners) has eroded a considerable degree of policy space that was preserved under the multilateral trade regime.[21] This has happened by strengthening enforcement, eliminating exceptions or demanding commitments not included in the URAs. RTAs also have increasingly incorporated investment provisions, which, traditionally, were dealt with in separate bilateral investment treaties (BITs). This trend is reflected in the declining number of new investment treaties concluded since the mid-1990s, and especially the early 2000s (UNCTAD, 2014: 115), and a growing number of RTAs with investment provisions (Miroudot, 2011). RTAs may be considered as constituting steps in the direction of so-called "deep integration" – economic integration that goes well beyond the reduction or elimination of tariffs, quotas and other barriers to trade at the border, and covers measures such as government procurement, investment, competition policy and the mutual recognition or harmonization of standards.[22]

By 15 June 2014, the GATT/WTO had been notified of some 585 RTAs, of which 379 were in force.[23] Article XXIV of the GATT 1994 and article V of the GATS permit RTAs between developed- and developing-country partners (North-South agreements) within the multilateral trade regime, provided they do not raise the overall level of protection against non-participants, liberalize "substantially all" trade in goods and attain substantial sectoral coverage in trade in services. The Enabling Clause of the GATT 1979 (in particular, its paragraph 2(c)) permits preferential arrangements among developing countries (South-South agreements) in goods trade, even in the absence of such liberalization commitments. The number of South-South agreements has grown significantly over the past two decades, with a particularly sharp increase during the 1990s. According to WTO estimates, roughly 200 such agreements were in force worldwide in 2010 compared with only about 30 in 1990 (WTO 2011: 55).

The measures included in RTAs are often analysed in terms of whether they are "WTO-plus" (i.e. more stringent than provisions already covered by the multilateral trade regime) or "WTO-extra"(i.e. deal with provisions that go beyond current multilateral trade agreements) (see, for example, Horn et al., 2010; WTO, 2011; Dür et al., 2013; Kohl et al., 2013).[24] A large proportion of these agreements include either the EU or the United States as a partner, and both have come to be identified as the two main "hubs" in the pattern of RTAs, with their various partner countries being the "spokes".

Regarding the scope of RTA provisions, the evidence shows that they have become more comprehensive over the past 20 years (Dür et al., 2013), and many are now formally described as comprehensive economic partnership agreements. It also seems that North-South agreements generally contain a larger number of both WTO-plus and WTO-extra provisions than either North-North or South-South agreements (WTO, 2011). For the inclusion of WTO-extra provisions in South-South agreements, WTO (2011: 133) notes that some developing countries may attempt to export their regulatory regimes just as developed countries do. This may raise concern as to the extent to which South-South agreements follow an approach that prioritizes development-oriented trade and investment promotion. On the other hand, the

> RTAs have eroded considerable policy space that was preserved under the multilateral trade regime.

detailed comparison of WTO-plus and WTO-extra provisions in North-South and South-South agreements in Thrasher and Gallagher (2008) suggests that South-South agreements maintain ample policy space for industrial development. However, these authors also note that the greater flexibilities in South-South agreements do not derive from a lack of affirmative trade disciplines but from the attempt of these agreements to combine substantial trade liberalization with regional protection to promote regional growth.

Evidence for North-South agreements shows that agreements with the EU include substantially more WTO-extra provisions than agreements with the United States. However, many provisions in RTAs with the EU are not legally enforceable, so that, overall, provisions in agreements with the United States would appear to be stricter (WTO, 2011).[25]

Tariff regulations are but one example of WTO-plus provisions. RTAs typically demand reductions of applied tariffs, rather than referring to the often much higher bound rates as in the NAMA negotiations. Regulating applied tariffs results in significantly lower flexibilities in developing countries' tariff policies, in particular when reductions lead to free trade agreements (FTAs) or even customs unions. A second example concerns trade in services. GATS-plus commitments may take the form of either stricter bindings in sectors already committed under the GATS with a view to guaranteeing a minimum level of treatment, or new bindings or commitments. The latter may result from the adoption of a negative-list approach, as used in the North American Free Trade Agreement (NAFTA), meaning that obligations in the respective RTA fully apply to all sectors, subject only to explicitly listed reservations. By contrast, some RTAs, such as the Common Market of the South (MERCOSUR) and the Framework Agreement on Services of the Association of Southeast Asian Nations (ASEAN), maintain the positive-list approach of the GATS.

Third, regarding TRIPS-plus commitments, RTAs generally include more stringent enforcement requirements or provide fewer exemptions (such as allowing compulsory licensing only for emergency situations). They also prohibit parallel imports, and extend obligations to cover additional IP issues (such as life forms, counterfeiting and piracy) or exclusive rights to test data (such as those relating to pharmaceuticals).[26] Furthermore, they may contain more detailed and prescriptive IP provisions, and reduce the possibility for States to tailor their IP laws to their specific domestic environments or adapt them to changing circumstances.

A fourth example is TRIMs-plus commitments. Some RTAs have broadened the definition of investment such that the principle of non-discrimination extends to forbidding export-performance requirements, demands for technology and knowledge transfer, as well as preconditions concerning the nationalities of senior management and personnel. RTAs may also extend TRIMs provisions to cover taxes and charges or distribution activities (such as warehousing, unloading, storage and shipment of goods). Indeed, given that the investment chapters in RTAs often draw on pre-existing BITs, rather than on the TRIMs Agreement, their provisions may be considered WTO-extra commitments (discussed in greater detail below).[27]

A final example of WTO-plus provisions in RTAs relates to technical barriers to trade (TBTs), which concern the cost of adapting foreign goods to the importing countries' standards and technical regulations. While the latter involve barriers such as testing and certification, standards may be broadly distinguished as applying to products, processes or management systems, all of which have the effect of discriminating between those firms that respect certain standards and those that do not. In the context of fostering structural transformation of the domestic economy, such discrimination may be considered a benefit for domestic firms, as it would increase the cost for foreign firms to adapt their operations and demonstrate conformity with a view to penetrating domestic markets. While WTO agreements provide rules for the design and implementation of standards, as well as guidelines and recommendations for WTO members to base their measures on international standards, several RTAs refer to the main instruments of liberalization in this area, namely harmonization and mutual recognition (Maur and Shepherd, 2011). TBT provisions in existing RTAs with the United

> North-South agreements contain a larger number of both WTO-plus and WTO-extra provisions than either North-North or South-South agreements.

States tend to include mutual recognition, meaning that countries agree to recognize each other's regulations, standards or conformity assessment procedures as equivalent, thus facilitating the unimpeded flow of goods into partner markets even though standards may continue to differ.

RTAs involving the EU typically prefer harmonization, which enhances compatibility between imported and domestically produced goods, and facilitates substitution (Disdier et al., 2013). To the extent that harmonization requires conformity with EU standards, this region's firms will realize economies of scale by gaining access to a larger market with the same standards. More generally, mutual recognition and harmonization may introduce de facto discrimination against developing countries, which may lack the capacity and resources required to achieve conformity with given technical standards. It was observed, for example, that the harmonization of the EU's electronics standards with international ones in the 1990s induced entry by new United States exporters but resulted in a withdrawal of some developing-country exporters from EU markets (Reyes, 2012). There may be an additional adverse effect on both South-South exports and on production for a country's home markets, given that "once the Southern-based producer has been forced to adapt its production processes to Northern regulations for products bound to that market, it is likely to adopt the same processes for all of its production to avoid separate production chains and higher fixed costs. When those processes are more costly due to stringent Northern regulations, one can expect the Southern country's trade flows to be affected with all partners" (Disdier et al., 2013: 11).

Turning to WTO-extra provisions, these commitments largely concern competition policy, investment and the movement of capital. A smaller number of RTAs have also extended their coverage to include issues such as government procurement, labour mobility[28] and environmental standards (Kohl et al., 2013). Provisions relating to competition policy attempt to dilute or prevent the abuse of market power by requiring commitments to the adoption and/or application of competition law and closer cooperation among the competition authorities of RTA partners. The areas most often affected include concerted actions, abuse of a dominant position and State aid, but they may also relate to monopolies and State-owned enterprises. For example, provisions may require the progressive dismantling of any State-owned commercial monopoly, so as to ensure that there is no discrimination between nationals of RTA members in terms of the conditions under which goods or services are produced and marketed.[29] This may have asymmetric effects because developing countries tend to have more State-owned enterprises, partly owing to the absence of private entrepreneurs willing and capable of providing certain goods or essential services.

The investment chapters in RTAs generally combine provisions on the protection and promotion of investment with provisions on the liberalization of foreign investment (such as the prohibition of local-content and trade-balancing requirements), as well as comprehensive disciplines on trade in services. They thereby cover rules and commitments included in BITs and, multilaterally, in the TRIMs Agreement and in the GATS. They serve to facilitate company strategies that combine FDI and trade in international production networks and liberalize trade and investment to a greater extent than is done at the multilateral level (Miroudot, 2011). An important reason for the wider coverage of these commitments is their application of the principle of non-discrimination to foreign investors, combined with a broad, asset-based definition of investment. In addition to FDI, the latter also covers some types of portfolio investment, such as equities and real estate, and in some instances even extends to IPRs (Fink, 2011).[30]

Moreover, several RTAs include investment provisions that cover both the pre-establishment phase (i.e. market access) and the post-establishment phase (i.e. protection of investment, including in the event of nationalization or expropriation, and the right of temporary entry of managers and key personnel of a foreign investor). The rules also provide for a standard of fair and equitable treatment, which, contrary to the relative standards of national

> WTO-extra provisions largely cover competition policy, investment and capital movement, but some also cover government procurement, labour mobility and environmental standards.

and third-country MFN treatment, is an absolute standard that confers the right to a certain minimum level of treatment. Some of them also provide for the unrestricted flow of transfers, including all kinds of fees and returns on investment.

Another key commitment concerns dispute settlement. While traditional trade agreements follow the paradigm of State-to-State resolution of disputes, some RTAs (i.e. those following the NAFTA approach) include an investor-State dispute settlement mechanism. The latter feature, common in investment treaties, allows foreign investors to seek compensation for perceived damages resulting from measures implemented by host governments, typically through the International Centre for Settlement of Investment Disputes (ICSID).[31]

The inclusion of investment chapters in some RTAs also implies that these provisions govern the movement of capital under a negative-list approach. This extends beyond WTO provisions where capital flows are treated under the positive-list approach of the GATS. Besides, most RTAs do not provide exceptions in the case of serious balance-of-payments and external financing difficulties (as allowed multilaterally in article XII of the GATS).[32]

With regard to government procurement policies, RTAs generally address social, environmental and national security concerns, as well as issues related to good governance, but, historically, they have also been used to support industrial and regional development. Government procurement is excluded from the national treatment obligation of GATT article III (8)(a), and of the GATS, though the latter calls for multilateral negotiations on government procurement in services. This means that at the multilateral level, government procurement policies are governed only by the WTO Agreement on Government Procurement (known as GPA) – a plurilateral agreement that currently covers only 42 WTO members (including the 27 member States of the EU), most of which are developed countries. However, some RTAs affect non-GPA signatories through provisions such as reciprocity and transparency, and may even extend to non-discrimination. The latter implies granting partner countries' firms access to contract award procedures on conditions no less favourable than those accorded to firms from any other country. Such provisions would be violated, for example, through "buy national" provisions in fiscal stimulus packages, as were used by many countries in 2008–2009, unless the government entities administrating such stimulus programmes remain outside GPA coverage.[33]

3. The rising restrictiveness of policy commitments and international production networks

(a) Why developing countries engage in RTAs

From the above discussion, the question arises as to why developing-country governments continue to enter into RTAs despite the existence of a multilateral trade regime that supports international cooperation and limits the opportunities for beggar-thy-neighbour policies. This question becomes even more pertinent given that, by signing RTAs, these governments relinquish some of the policy space they have been struggling hard to preserve at the multilateral level.

The economic literature has discussed several motives that may induce developing-country policymakers to sign RTAs. One is to enhance policy predictability. For example, more liberal-minded governments might seek to engage in RTAs with a view to tying the hands of future governments that are perceived as being more easily influenced by domestic interest groups lobbying for protection (Maggi and Rodriguez-Clare, 1998) or that have different ideologies. RTAs may also be considered a fallback option in case multilateral negotiations are caught in a prolonged stalemate. Additionally, policymakers may wish to stabilize and secure the preferential market access that developed countries have granted them unilaterally and temporarily through the Generalized System of Preferences (GSP) and related programmes (Manger and Shadlen, 2014).[34]

> By signing RTAs, developing-country governments relinquish some of the policy space they have been struggling hard to preserve at the multilateral level.

Further, there may be a "domino effect", with the proliferation of RTAs increasing the likelihood of further RTAs being formed as a result of some governments fearing exclusion when other countries gain preferential market access and become more attractive as destinations for FDI (Baldwin and Jaimovich, 2012). This is related to the emphasis on export promotion as a development strategy that makes securing and increasing access to developed-country markets, including relative to other developing countries, almost an end in itself. On the other hand, the sizeable reduction of MFN tariffs has led to very low levels of applied tariffs, and applied MFN rates have been reduced to zero for many tariff lines. At the same time, the wave of preferential trade agreements has allowed a very wide range of countries to enjoy preferential access, further eroding any country's preference margin over other countries. Hence, from a global perspective, the importance of tariff preferences has been greatly reduced (Fugazza and Nicita, 2013).

However, these factors cannot fully explain why the wave of RTAs has been accompanied by an increasing number of provisions that lead to deep economic integration which extends beyond border measures such as tariffs. Such provisions include a wide range of domestic policies and regulations, particularly those that protect tangible and intangible assets (such as foreign capital and intellectual property), facilitate the coordination of dispersed production activities (such as the flow of investment, know-how and people), and govern product and process standards. Developing-country policymakers may well believe that locking in preferential market access is necessary in exchange for policy and regulatory commitments seemingly required for attracting FDI and for enabling their firms to join international production networks.

Empirical evidence on the link between RTAs and international production networks indeed shows that two countries that already engage in trade within production networks are more likely to sign a deep RTA. This is a prominent feature in agreements of developed countries with developing countries in East and South-East Asia, the region where international production sharing has increased the fastest (Orefice and Rocha, 2014). Related empirical

> Empirical evidence that strict investment provisions stimulate FDI is ambiguous.

evidence for BITs and investment chapters in RTAs that regulate the treatment of FDI, "whose protection is a core element of the package used by many developing nations to join international supply chains" (Baldwin, 2014: 31), shows that the strictest investment provisions are often signed by developing countries under economically weak conditions in the hope that increased FDI inflows will help resolve their economic problems (Simmons, 2014). But while the empirical evidence that such provisions are effective in stimulating FDI is ambiguous, the more general trend towards agreements with stricter investment rules is driven by competitive diffusion; that is, defensive moves on the part of developing countries concerned that FDI will be diverted to competing host countries. Importantly, contagion may also help explain the increasing severity of provisions, with developing countries caught in a race to conclude not only more such agreements but increasingly more stringent ones (Neumayer et al., 2014).

(b) Tendencies towards further reductions of policy space

The onset of the global crisis and the ensuing collapse in global trade in 2008–2009 prompted various attempts to document changes in trade and investment policy measures. In part this was a response to widespread fears that the Great Recession would lead to a sharp increase in protectionism and would cause further fragmentation of the world trade regime, as well as a sharper decline of economic activity and a slower trade-related recovery. It was also felt that documenting the changes could increase transparency relating to the adoption of trade-related policy measures that may make the inclusion of developing-country firms in international trade more difficult.

The fear that the Great Recession would trigger a sharp rise in protectionism was based on the comparison often made between the Great Recession and the Great Depression that started in 1929, which led to a wave of protectionism during the 1930s as part of more general beggar-thy-neighbour policies (see chapter IV and Eichengreen and Irwin, 2010). Successive declarations by G20 leaders sought to allay this fear, starting at the Washington summit in

November 2008, where the leaders declared that they would maintain open trade and investment regimes and eschew protectionism (with the qualifier "in all its forms" added at the Los Cabos summit in November 2012). They also proposed the establishment of a (non-binding) monitoring mechanism.

Evidence shows hardly any increase in industrial tariffs, even though a large number of countries, and especially developing countries, could have used their so-called "tariff binding overhang" to raise applied tariffs by fairly wide margins without violating their WTO commitments (Baldwin and Evenett, 2012). It is debatable whether policymakers voluntarily renounced use of this policy option that is still available to them because they found WTO commitments sufficiently persuasive, or because many crisis-hit countries had the possibility to let their currencies depreciate, contrary to the 1930s when this option was not available for countries unless they abandoned the gold standard. In any case, economic historians have long pointed out that economic crises generally spark innovative policy measures, implying a divergence in the character of pre- and post-crisis protectionisms. The 1930s, for example, witnessed a substantial resort to voluntary export restraints, implying that documentation of trade policy measures concentrating on traditional instruments, such as tariffs and quotas, would have missed the shift to protectionism (Eichengreen and Irwin, 2010; Evenett, 2013a).

There have been various attempts to assess different countries' use of trade and investment policy measures in response to the crisis in order to evaluate the extent to which such measures may have worsened the relative treatment of "foreign commercial interests". The Global Trade Alert (GTA) finds that in this respect, France, Germany, Italy and the United Kingdom are among the world's 10 most protectionist countries (Evenett, 2013b).[35] More traditional trade policy measures like tariff increases and trade defence measures (such as anti-dumping policies) have accounted for less than half of all recorded actions.

> Characterizing some recent trade and industrial policy measures as "murky protectionism" is problematic, since several of those measures have an important public policy purpose.

Evidence from developing countries, particularly in Asia, suggests that those countries that have lower levels of tariff binding overhangs have used "non-traditional" policies, such as bailouts, more than other countries that have tended to employ tariff increases and trade defence measures. However, countries that had undertaken the largest tariff reductions in the pre-crisis period tended to adopt trade defence measures, rather than reversing those tariff cuts. On the other hand, countries that were able to adopt larger fiscal stimulus packages were less likely to use some of these trade and investment measures (Evenett, 2013b and c).

The very broad characterization of "murky protectionism" in the GTA is problematic, since it also includes several measures that have an important public policy purpose, not only for promoting financial stability and preventing drastic declines in employment, but also for building domestic productive capacity and protecting consumers. These include health and safety regulations, stimulus packages that earmark public spending for domestic products, bank bailouts, industrial and innovation policies, and many other policies that do not violate any current international agreements or other legal provisions. Some of these measures have played important roles in allowing developing countries to recover from the global crisis and to continue their process of structural transformation. Moreover, the GTA's assessments of the impact of these measures rely entirely on subjective judgement. The combination of these factors raises serious questions about the GTA's sometimes alarmist conclusion that protectionism has increased over the past five years (Evenett, 2012 and 2013b). More importantly, the close relationship between the measures denounced as "protectionist" by the GTA and its recommendations on how policymakers should embark on the "fast route" to industrialization by including domestic firms in international production networks, risks giving such assessments undue prominence on the agenda of trade negotiations in the future.[36] This relationship is addressed in section D.

C. Industrial policy in an era of reduced policy space

In recent years there has been a global revival of interest in industrial policy. A number of developing countries, including the largest ones, have reassessed the benefits of industrial policy for structural transformation and economic growth. In fact, countries such as Brazil, China and South Africa never really abandoned the use of policy measures aimed at accelerating industrialization. Instead, over the past decade or so, they have even adopted new initiatives. Some of these initiatives may be seen as a response to the various financial shocks that hit a number of developing countries at the end of the 1990s and at the turn of the millennium, while others may have resulted from a growing recognition that the policies associated with the Washington Consensus had failed to deliver structural transformation (*TDR 2003*). Yet others may have been prompted by the sharp increase in commodity prices that started around 2002–2003, raising fears of premature deindustrialization in some developing countries.

Reassessments of the potential benefits of industrial policy have not been limited to developing countries only. Many developed countries have begun to explicitly acknowledge the important role that industrial policy can play in maintaining a robust manufacturing sector, with the associated benefits in terms of productivity growth, innovation and employment creation. This has been the case especially following the global financial crisis and the Great Recession, when developed countries whose economies are based mainly on services – such as the United Kingdom and the United States – appeared to be much more vulnerable to adverse external shocks than most of those that have a sizeable manufacturing base.

There is no generally accepted definition of industrial policy. This could be mainly because industrial policy has been based on a wide variety of economic perspectives with different rationales, targets and scopes, and reliance on a diverse mix of policy measures (see, for example, Salazar-Xirinachs et al., 2014). However, there is probably a general consensus that "industrial policy is basically any type of selective intervention or government policy that attempts to alter the sectoral structure of production toward sectors that are expected to offer better prospects for economic growth than would occur in the absence of such intervention" (Pack and Saggi, 2006: 2). Usually, measures aimed at diversifying the production structure and contributing to creating capacities in new economic sectors or in new types of activities are part of what is called "vertical" or "selective" industrial policy.[37] These measures include support in the form of sector-specific subsidies, tariffs and investment-related performance requirements that have generally been associated with successful industrialization in East Asia, where they have been combined with control mechanisms, such as export requirements (*TDRs 1996* and *2006*). They also include measures that target variations in different sectors' potential to generate, absorb and commercially use knowledge, and, in particular, their potential to help countries catch up with (and then push beyond) the technological frontier through direct support for innovation

> Many developed countries have acknowledged the important role of industrial policy in maintaining a robust manufacturing sector, and in boosting productivity growth, innovation and employment creation.

and learning. Examples of such measures include the establishment of national innovation systems and improvements in education and vocational training (Nübler, 2014).

It is the use of this form of industrial policy that has been the most constrained by the increasing number of rules and regulations in international economic governance. However, constraint does not imply interdiction and the remainder of this section provides country-specific examples of industrial policy measures. It begins by discussing how the United States and the EU have tried to foster their manufacturing sectors. It then looks at the measures taken by developing countries, which combine creative market forces with State activities to promote manufacturing and raise living standards.

1. Recent proactive policies for reindustrialization in developed economies

(a) United States: Multiple initiatives of a vertical industrial policy

The United States is often portrayed as a country that takes a hands-off approach to industrial policy. However, several authors have recently argued that the United States has consistently pursued an industrial policy with a view to maintaining a strong manufacturing base and securing the country's global technological leadership. In recent years, United States policymakers have not focused on the formulation of national visions and national programmes by centralized coordination agencies to develop specific industries, even though this has been the model followed at times in the past (Kozul-Wright, 1995; Rohatyn, 2009). Rather, they have used a more decentralized approach wherein a variety of Federal and State-led initiatives and programmes have lent support to strategic industries, both traditional and emerging (Ketels, 2007; Block, 2008; Schrank and Whitford, 2009; Di Tommaso and Schweitzer, 2013; Mazzucato, 2013; Wade, 2014).

> The United States can be viewed both as an "entrepreneurial State" and a "coordinating State" in the way it conducts industrial policy.

As such, two overlapping elements have characterized industrial policy in the United States, so that it is viewed both as an "entrepreneurial State" and a "coordinating State". As an "entrepreneurial State" it acts as a leading risk taker and market shaper in the development and commercialization of new technologies that are considered essential for the country. By funding very risky research, the "entrepreneurial State" reduces the risk to private investors, thus making it indispensable as an enabler of significant innovation. According to Mazzucato (2013), in the United States, the State is the primary source of funding in the early stages of innovation, with the public sector accounting for over 50 per cent of spending on basic research, compared with less than 20 per cent by the private sector. This type of public investment covers different types of research, much of which has particularly uncertain prospects in terms of returns.[38]

As a "coordinating State" it creates and manages networks between the different actors in innovation systems (e.g. firms, financial and research institutions and public sector funds), as well as within organizations and institutions. It thereby encourages firms of different types to be embedded in a decentralized system of innovation spanning the sectoral, regional and national levels.[39] Given this network character of industrial policy, and the associated absence of a single agency that would be responsible for that policy, this kind of State action in pursuing industrial policy has sometimes been called "the hidden developmental state" (Block, 2008; Schrank and Whitford, 2009).

The onset of the Great Recession heralded the adoption of a wide range of more visible policies having the common objective of bringing about the "renaissance of American manufacturing" (Sperling, 2012). These measures are not usually specified as being part of an industrial policy, because their immediate objective is to prevent bankruptcies and large scale unemployment. However, many of them target domestic manufacturing because of its crucial role in innovation, exports and the creation of well-paid jobs, which makes "manufacturing an essential component of a competitive and innovative economy" (Sperling,

2012: 1). These long-term measures may be considered part of a broader strategy adopted to forestall the perceived risk of the country losing its position as a global technology leader, as well as to correct structural problems in the United States economy that were revealed by the crisis, such as the decline in the importance of manufacturing with its associated adverse impacts on employment (Sperling, 2013; Warwick, 2013).[40]

The initiatives that directly address concerns about the United States' loss of global technological leadership have two main components.[41] The first includes a range of R&D programmes which are grouped under the Advanced Manufacturing National Programme whose key element is the National Network for Manufacturing Innovation (NNMI). This network consists of regional manufacturing institutions which are public-private partnerships designed to bring together the best talents and capabilities from its three partners (industry, academia and government, notably the Ministries of Defence and Energy).[42]

The second component is the American Recovery and Reinvestment Act of 2009, which is endowed with about $800 billion to be spent over the period 2009–2019. The immediate objective of this economic stimulus package was to smooth the adverse effects of the Great Recession. But its longer term goal is to use vertical industrial policy measures to strengthen the domestic manufacturing sector and encourage its structural adjustment to better withstand international competition. For example, the Act allocated funds to re-start the production of advanced batteries with the objective of increasing its share in global production from 2 per cent in 2009 to 40 per cent in 2015 (Sperling, 2012). This is part of the more general objectives of (i) repatriating offshore manufacturing activities back to the United States based on the notion that geographic proximity of production and design activities facilitates the task of engineers to solve problems brought to them by technicians on the factory floor, and hence strengthens the link between manufacturing and innovation; and (ii) promoting clean energy industries,

> The United States has skilfully used the policy space not circumscribed by the URAs to support its manufacturing sector ...

> ... and the vertical nature of its industrial policy has helped attain at least some of its objectives.

such as wind and solar power, as well as more fuel-efficient vehicles. In the same vein, the bailout of General Motors and Chrysler, using the Troubled Assets Relief Program (TARP) had the immediate effect of saving thousands of jobs and reducing the adverse impacts of the Great Recession. However, entitlement to these funds was tied to environmental considerations, such as commencing production of more fuel-efficient vehicles, and thus helped to address broader sectoral restructuring concerns. In addition, in 2009, the Environmental Protection Agency allowed California to impose tougher emission standards for cars (Brunel and Hufbauer, 2009), and the General Services Administration announced that it would use funds under the Act to purchase $300 million worth of energy-efficient and alternative fuel vehicles,[43] in line with the Act's more general Buy American Provision.

Taken together, these measures reflect the United States Government's support for industries that were hit particularly hard by the global economic slowdown, and, more generally, for activities intended to assist United States enterprises in competing in innovative sectors. However, the question arises as to whether such support is compatible with multilateral trade and investment provisions. In particular, support under the Buy American Provision may be considered a prohibited subsidy under the SCM Agreement. Similarly, the bailout of the automobile industry under the TARP may constitute a subsidy under the SCM Agreement, given that the environment-related provisions under article 8 of the SCM Agreement regarding a non-actionable subsidy lapsed five years after the Agreement's entry into force (i.e. on 1 January 2000). However, it may be justified under the GATT article XX due to the environmental conditions attached to these measures, which, it could be argued, "relate to" the conservation of an exhaustible reserve.[44]

However, it should be pointed out that WTO rules and commitments only carry the *threat* of sanctions. Any eventual imposition by trading partners of retaliatory tariffs or other measures depends on the actual damage. As long as the damage caused by the infringement of rules is small, a WTO member State is unlikely to invoke the DSM and initiate the imposition of sanctions. Invoking the DSM will also be unlikely if determination of the actual damage caused is difficult to establish, and also because several countries are simultaneously adopting similar measures for similar objectives. For instance, a wide range of countries have adopted measures designed to support their automobile industries.[45] In any case, the above examples show that the United States has skilfully used the policy space not circumscribed by the URAs to support its manufacturing sector. They also show that the country has employed an industrial policy, and that its vertical nature has helped attain at least some of its objectives.

(b) European Union: Limited effectiveness of a horizontal industrial policy

Fostering industrial production has been among the major policy objectives of European economic integration since the end of the Second World War. Nonetheless, the related scope, instruments and institutional setups have varied significantly across countries and over the course of time. Fostering industrial development through sector-specific measures was pursued energetically during post-war reconstruction under the auspices of the Marshall Plan, and continued well into the 1970s through various national and regional initiatives (Eichengreen and Kenen, 1994). In the early 1980s, many countries adopted liberal policy agendas that considerably limited the scope of proactive government measures (Grabas and Nützenadel, 2014; Owen, 2012). In 1990, the European Commission outlined its industrial policy, which was the first time a common industrial policy approach was adopted for the then European Community as a whole (European Commission, 1990).[46] The general aim of this approach was to improve the competitiveness of European industry and speed up industrial adjustments to structural changes, including through innovation and technological development. The emphasis was microeconomic (i.e. using enterprise and competition policies), and predominantly horizontal in that it favoured the creation of general conditions for entrepreneurs and business undertakings, particularly small and medium-sized enterprises.[47]

Various strategies have been adopted to ensure better framework conditions for European industry. The Lisbon Strategy, adopted in 2000, formulated some quantitative goals at the national level (such as augmenting R&D expenditure to reach 3 per cent of gross domestic product (GDP)), but it has generally been considered a failure in terms of meeting its multiple goals of increasing productivity, employment and convergence across the member countries (e.g. Tilford and Whyte, 2010; Copeland and Papadimitriou, 2012). The Europe 2020 Strategy implemented since 2010 has objectives similar to those of recent initiatives in the United States, as it refers to strengthening innovation and creating exports and jobs, but it places greater emphasis on cost-related "competitiveness". The Horizon 2020 Programme introduced in 2014 includes complementary and more targeted measures to foster investment in innovation, such as €80 billion earmarked for research and innovation to support key enabling technologies[48] with a view to redefining global value chains and enhancing resource and energy efficiency.[49] The Programme also finances prototypes and demonstration projects in order to facilitate commercialization of innovations.

Despite these measures, EU industrial policy remains less comprehensive than that of the United States. Budget allocations appear to be too small to effectively overcome not only short-term constraints on growth but also longer term efforts to boost innovation. Limited funding for programmes is likely to result in a smaller stock of knowledge and fewer innovations that could be commercialized, compared with the much larger resources dedicated to innovation in the United States. Furthermore, using only horizontal industrial policy measures, without accompanying vertical measures, as in the United States, may impede achievement of the declared objective of maintaining a strong manufacturing base in Europe.[50] However, the adoption of more specific – vertical – support

> EU intergovernmental agreements illustrate how the policy choices of national policymakers can be constrained and how horizontal measures alone are insufficient in the pursuit of industrial policy objectives.

measures may not be possible under current EU legislation. For example, in response to the bailout of the automobile industry in the United States, several EU member States adopted measures in favour of their own automobile industries. Such measures may be in conflict with article 107 of the Treaty on the Functioning of the EU, which stipulates that "any aid granted by a Member State ... which distorts or threatens to distort competition by favouring certain undertakings or the production of certain goods shall ... be incompatible with the internal common market". However, the recent global financial crisis could be considered a special event that may require greater flexibility in applying these rules. Paragraph 3 of article 107, which refers to the existence of a "serious disturbance in the economy", ensures that such flexibility would remain temporary and exceptional.[51] Such exemptions are unlikely to be made in the future, because, according to the current European Guidelines on Restructuring Aid (European Commission, 2004: paragraphs 72 and 73), the granting of rescue or restructuring aid is a one-off operation and can, in principle, be granted only once every 10 years. Moreover, in its new draft guidelines on State aid, the European Commission considers that "rescue and restructuring aid are among the most distortive types of State aid" (European Commission, 2013: paragraph 6).

The EU situation illustrates how intergovernmental agreements can constrain the policy choices of national policymakers, and how industrial policies that are limited to the adoption of only horizontal measures may hamper achieving the objectives of those policies. Further, given these constraints and limitations, EU policymakers may believe that, in order to maintain a healthy manufacturing base, it will be necessary to increase exports to developing countries. Hence the Union's common international trade policy – which is one key policy area for which Community institutions have exclusive responsibility – and the associated objective of continued market opening in developing countries may end up playing a crucial role in plans for the reindustrialization of Europe.

> The nature and scope of recent industrial policies in developing countries reflect changes in the global trade and economic governance regimes with which their policies must conform ...

2. Developing countries: Recent experiences with national policies for industrial development

The extensive use of proactive trade and industrial policies in the successful transformation of East Asian economies has been discussed at length in previous *Trade and Development Reports* (in particular *TDRs 1994, 1996* and *2003*) and elsewhere (e.g. Akyüz et al., 1998; World Bank, 2005a; Chang, 2011). However, the nature and scope of recent industrial policies in developing countries have been strongly affected by changes in the global trade and economic governance regimes with which their policies must conform. Most important among such changes has been the accession of various countries to the WTO and/or their participation in RTAs. At the same time, developing-country policymakers have sought to adjust their industrial policies in response to structural vulnerabilities that have surfaced in their economies at times of change in the global economic environment, including economic crises and changes in their country's terms of trade. This section discusses, through country-specific examples, how such changes have affected various countries' policy mix, especially since the turn of the millennium.

Improvements in the terms of trade of economies that have benefited from higher global commodity prices since the early 2000s is one factor that has sparked increased interest in industrial policy. Soaring commodity prices and the associated strong improvements in the terms of trade of natural-resource-rich countries facilitated their attempts to improve their macroeconomic policy stances and fiscal accounts. However, this should not lead to complacency in the design of development strategies in these countries. Their main challenge remains that of appropriating a fair share of the resource rents (see also chapter VII of this *Report*), avoiding an appreciation of the real exchange rate, which would weaken the competitiveness of their tradable manufacturing activities, and channelling revenues towards investment in the real economy in order to spur diversification and upgrading of their production and exports. Diversification and industrialization are the best means in the long run for countries to reduce their vulnerability to the adverse effects of commodity price volatility and unfavourable price trends. Accelerating the movement of labour from low-productivity activities in the primary sector towards high-productivity activities in manufacturing boosts overall productivity and income growth. Meeting the challenge of diversification requires a high level of investment and the creation of a virtuous link between trade and capital accumulation. Policymakers could greatly facilitate these efforts by pursuing an industrial policy that supports the private sector in identifying and expanding activities with greater value added, as well as sectors with potential for more rapid productivity growth, along with the production of goods for which demand elasticities in world markets are higher. In particular, such measures would help reverse the trend of labour flows from high to low productivity sectors observed for the period 1990–2005 in African and Latin American countries, most of which have abundant natural resources (McMillan et al., 2014).

In 2004, Brazil established a new institutional framework for industrial policy through the adoption of three sets of policies aimed at increasing investment, innovation and international competitiveness of its manufacturing activities, as well as of its energy-related industries. It has prioritized the development of key industries and sectors, of companies that succeed as "national champions", and of infrastructure projects, in part through public-private partnership councils. The provision of long-term investment financing through the country's development bank (Banco Nacional de Desenvolvimento Econômico e Social, BNDES) has been an important instrument for implementation of these policies. For example, the BNDES has provided direct financial support to large-scale industrial and infrastructure projects as well as support for the export of certain goods and services (Ferraz et al., 2014). In order to promote economic upgrading in Brazil, the BNDES has been supporting the automotive, information technology, aeronautics and petroleum sectors through loans, long-term and equity financing, guarantees, grants and credit insurance. Unlike several other developing countries, Brazil has not signed on to any RTAs, which gives it greater flexibility in promoting such activities through its development bank.

In South Africa, the conviction that the country could no longer continue to rely as heavily as in the past on traditional commodities and non-tradable services as the basis for its growth and development led to the adoption of the National Industrial Policy Framework in 2007 (Department of Trade and Industry, 2007: 10). As a result, a range of both horizontal and vertical measures were implemented, such as sector-specific tariff changes and fiscal incentives, with a view to intensifying the industrialization process and making it more inclusive. However, the adopted measures have yielded somewhat fewer benefits than expected, partly because industrial policy was not properly aligned with the country's broader macroeconomic framework, and there were insufficient linkages created between megaprojects and smaller enterprises operating upstream and downstream (Zalk, 2014).

The constraints on a country's policy choices caused by its accession to the WTO may be illustrated by the experience of Viet Nam.[52] Viet Nam gained WTO membership in January 2007, which intensified its shift from an import-substituting to an export-promotion strategy. This shift was initiated with the introduction of the *Doi Moi* ("renovation") economic reform programme in 1986, and was reinforced by the signing of bilateral agreements with the country's major trading partners, including the EU, Japan, the United States and a number of countries in Asia during the 1990s and early 2000s. The associated reforms led to a complex system that promoted a dual industrialization strategy. That strategy was based on the simultaneous development of private, export-oriented, labour-intensive manufacturing industries (by attracting foreign investors, establishing export-processing zones and creating duty drawback systems for imported inputs) and of import-substituting industries (through investment in heavy industries and resource-based sectors where State-owned enterprises continued to play an important role).[53]

Already in the run-up to its formal accession to the WTO, Viet Nam had adjusted some aspects of

> ... as well as awareness of structural vulnerabilities that have surfaced due to changes in the global economic environment.

its industrial policy, including phasing out explicit export-performance requirements, local-content-related subsidies and tax incentives. The country's WTO accession was followed by a reduction in the simple average tariff rate from 18.5 per cent in 2007 to 10.4 per cent in 2013, and by liberalization of the services sector.

At the same time, Viet Nam has been using some of the flexibilities still allowed under WTO rules and commitments. For example, the difference between bound and applied tariff rates has enabled Viet Nam to modulate its applied tariffs with a view to controlling energy prices and protecting certain industries from import competition. It has also imposed tariff rate quotas on certain food commodities. In addition, it has provided sectoral support in the form of preferential import duties, tariff exemptions, reduced taxes on corporate income and land-use, and subsidized loans and investment guarantees aimed mainly at encouraging R&D and the development of infrastructure, training and enterprises in disadvantaged areas of the country. Although the services sector has undergone extensive liberalization, most of Viet Nam's current bilateral agreements follow a positive-list approach (i.e. signatories list only the sectors they wish to liberalize leaving all other sectors unaffected). As a result, Viet Nam has maintained foreign ownership ceilings in telecommunication services, it can impose higher fees on foreign firms in shipping and require an economic-needs test for foreign-owned retail outlets (beyond the first ones already established). The Government has also used procurement measures to support local suppliers.

However, these policy measures appear to have been insufficient for helping private enterprises overcome their capital constraints and reach sufficiently large economies of scale to achieve international competitiveness. Also, the dual track strategy has been only partially successful in speeding up desired spillovers from FDI, especially in the form of technology transfer and the creation of linkages between export-oriented industries and domestic supply firms (Nguyen et al., 2014). If initiatives such as the Trans Pacific Partnership materialize, they may carry even

> A wide range of measures can facilitate adjustments in developing countries' production structures, such as environmental regulations, government procurement and tax policies ...

stricter rules on investment and IPRs, which could further limit the possibility of domestic linkages and technological adaptation.[54]

China's accession to the WTO has also had a significant impact on the nature and scope of its industrial policy. Owing to its commitments to abide by the TRIMs Agreement, it had to discontinue certain policies towards FDI, including measures aimed at encouraging technology transfer and enhancing linkages, such as through local-content requirements. It also had to phase out other elements of its earlier industrial policy, in particular trade protection measures, and preferential interest and lower tax rates for its infant industries, as well as some forms of direct financial assistance to some of its other industries (*TDR 2006*).

Nevertheless, China has continued to pursue a strategic approach towards FDI which distinguishes between sectors that are seen as generating significant foreign exchange and employment, and those that are more involved in upgrading domestic productive capacities and capabilities in key areas of the economy (Poon, 2014). The former, efficiency-seeking type of FDI has benefited from the kinds of incentives generally associated with activities located in special economic zones, such as selective value-added tax rebates, corporate tax holidays and the provision of infrastructure that facilitates international trade (Zeng, 2011). By contrast, the latter, market-seeking type of FDI has been subject to varying foreign ownership limits, such as minority equity stakes in the steel and banking sectors or 50–50 joint ventures in the automobile industry. Encouraging several joint ventures in the automobile sector has been used as an instrument to maintain that sector's competitiveness, making it more attractive for foreign investors to transfer and upgrade their technologies used in production in China. This has been further supported by massive increases in the Government's R&D expenditures. Moreover, government procurement and State investment in infrastructure, such as the building of a highway system, have been used to boost the demand for cars (Lo and Wu, 2014). China began to publish FDI guidance catalogues (which list industries in which foreign investment is "encouraged", "restricted" or "prohibited") in the mid-1990s, which have been revised over time by applying more demanding technical thresholds to reflect improvements in domestic production capacities. For instance, in the 2011 version of the FDI catalogue, the joint-venture stipulation was removed from automobile manufacturing and was applied instead to the undertaking of R&D and manufacturing of automobile electronic devices, as well as to some key parts and components of "new energy vehicles", such as high energy power batteries (Dezan Shira & Associates, 2011: 8–9).[55]

The Chinese Government has also retained an important guiding role, especially in upstream heavy industries and producer goods sectors, in which a number of relatively large, Government-linked enterprises are involved.[56] While the size of these enterprises poses obstacles for other (including foreign) enterprises to enter these sectors, there appears to be a sufficiently large number of these enterprises to ensure competition, and hence economically efficient production. Public sector manufacturers are also subject to export disciplines, which are enforced by monitoring concessionary access to loans, for example from the China Development Bank. These enterprises are overseen by the National Development and Reform Commission (NDRC), which is the country's key industrial planning agency. The NDRC itself has also provided support, such as by formulating a policy on green energy technologies, which led the Government to provide environment-related subsidy support to wind turbines. Previously, this support was combined with local-content requirements that may have been deemed to violate China's WTO commitments. However, the measure is reported to have already attained its goal and was withdrawn before other WTO members could file a case before the DSM (Studwell, 2013).

Environmental regulations could play a major role more generally in facilitating adjustments in developing countries' production structures. One reason for this is that so-called "green growth" features prominently in the likely next big technological frontiers, where developing countries' technological backwardness may be an advantage, as they will have fewer incumbent carbon-intensive technologies to

> … and development banks may be well placed to extend the long-term loans that such adjustments require.

amortize. Besides, given the imperative of climate change mitigation and increasingly recognized ecological limitations to the use of traditional energy, it is unlikely that rapidly growing consumption in developing countries, emanating from income growth and from attempts to strengthen the contribution of domestic demand to growth, can be satisfied by pursuing the same materials- and energy-intensive path that the developed economies have followed so far (*TDR 2013*). Indeed, turning newly emerging consumption and production patterns into challenges for innovation in green technologies could be a powerful driver of structural transformation and the creation of employment and wage opportunities.[57]

Similar to the role played by State agencies in developed countries (such as the Defense Advanced Research Projects Agency in the United States), development banks in developing countries (such as BNDES and China's Development Bank), may be well placed to extend the long-term loans that such fundamental reorientations require (Chandrasekhar, 2014). This would not only reduce the risk of complementary private funding at initial stages of such reorientations; it could also induce private investment eventually to assume a leadership role in fundamental structural transformation. Supportive demand-side policies could include energy-intensity targets, for example for automobiles and buildings, with a view to creating demand for more energy-efficient systems and clean energy production. To support domestic firms in satisfying such emerging domestic demand, these policies could be supported on the supply side through WTO-compatible subsidies and tax credits, in addition to the funding of clean-energy-related innovations.[58]

To spur innovation more generally, the presence of suitable institutions, such as industry-specific bodies that provide testing facilities to ensure safety and compliance with product standards, can also play an important role. For instance, evidence suggests that economies that successfully developed domestic automobile industries (such as China, the Republic of Korea and Taiwan Province of China) had well-resourced auto industry research institutes. By contrast, such institutes were either lacking or poorly resourced in other countries, such as Malaysia and Thailand, where attempts to create a dynamic auto industry were less successful (Ravenhill, 2014).

Government procurement can also be an important instrument of industrial policy, especially to create demand on a scale that would be sufficiently large for domestic firms to establish profitable production facilities. Tax policy is another instrument that can be used in industrial policy. In China, it has been observed that tax policies favour export-oriented firms, whereas enterprises catering to the domestic market are subject to a substantially wider range of taxes, including import duties, a value-added tax and a consumption tax (Yang, 2014). Thailand supplemented tariff protection with excise tax reductions and corporate tax exemptions for particular car models with a view to creating specific domestic sales opportunities. Such measures were introduced in 2002 for pick-up trucks, followed in 2007 by similar measures for eco-cars. Some of these tax policies were linked to local-content requirements (Natsuda and Thoburn, 2013).

In Brazil, the main objectives of tax reduction measures adopted in 2012 in a five-year programme known as Inovar Auto have been to slow down import growth and encourage the development of local suppliers in the automobile sector. The policy implies a 30 percentage point increase in the excise tax on industrial products (*Imposto sobre Produtos Industrializados*, IPI) levied on cars imported from outside MERCOSUR, and specifies the eligibility requirements for firms to join the programme and be granted IPI tax credits. Some of these requirements are linked to domestic content and investment in innovation (ICCT, 2013). These measures complement other support policies for the domestic automobile industry, such as relatively high tariffs on automotive parts imported from outside MERCOSUR. This proactive approach towards the development of a domestic automobile industry has allowed Brazil to attract additional FDI by new vehicle assemblers and a progressive delegation of innovation activities to Brazilian affiliates and their local suppliers (UNCTAD, 2014).

D. Current challenges to proactive trade and industrial policies

1. A potential decline in developing countries' export opportunities

The wide variation across countries in the pace and scale of development of their manufacturing activities indicates that country-specific factors – such as resource endowments, size of the domestic market, geographical location and institutional development – are likely to have a strong bearing on the timing and extent to which labour shifts towards more productive activities, both across and within economic sectors. But the size and direction of any such impacts are also influenced by policies that affect macroeconomic developments, as well as by the pace and nature of investment and integration into the global economy.

Clearly, policies can play an important role, as reflected, for example, in the growth of manufacturing through an explicit policy of promoting export orientation in some developing countries, especially since the 1980s. Indeed, the sizeable increase in the share of manufactures in those countries' exports has been a notable feature of the more general rapid expansion of the volume of world trade and the growing share of developing-country exports in total world exports during the two decades prior to the onset of the global crisis in 2007–2008. As noted in *TDR 2013*, the share of developing countries in global manufactured exports increased from about one fourth in 1995 to about one third in 2007, with trade in manufactures between developing countries playing an important role.

Exporting may foster structural transformation in several ways. From a macroeconomic perspective, it allows sectoral expenditure patterns to deviate from sectoral production patterns. As a result, the level of manufacturing production can exceed the limits set by the domestic market. And the high income elasticity of demand for manufactured goods usually provides favourable global market conditions. This means that an increase in manufactured exports can be expected to result in larger export revenues, unless many countries follow this strategy for the same products at the same time. Whereas a fast-growing world market allows many countries to expand their exports, in a stagnating global market an individual country can only expand its exports if it gains market shares at the expense of others. In the latter situation, attempts to continuously expand export volumes may cause adverse price effects and reduce, or even eliminate, the expected increase in export earnings.

Moreover, it has long been recognized that a country's pace of growth will face a balance-of-payments problem unless exports earn a sufficiently large amount of foreign exchange to pay for the substantial capital goods and intermediate goods – and their embodied technologies – that must be imported to build industrial activities and strengthen their international competitiveness (Thirlwall, 1979). Countries at the initial stages of structural transformation will have the greatest need for such imports. But even though the pace at which a domestic capital goods industry can be established will determine how fast the gap in machinery and equipment requirements can be bridged, a considerable volume of imports of such goods will still be needed.

In addition, as per capita incomes rise, the more affluent domestic consumers increasingly demand more discretionary consumer manufactures and services, rather than basic necessity goods such as food. Such rapidly increasing domestic demand for manufactures will lead to balance-of-payments difficulties and threaten sustained economic growth unless the structural composition of domestic production changes in response to that of domestic demand, or unless exports from the primary sector continue to provide the necessary foreign exchange earnings. Failing this, the country will end up accumulating external debt, absorbing a rising amount of net capital inflows or letting the real exchange rate depreciate.[59] Of course, changing the structure of domestic output to meet changing domestic demand also requires the economy to be large enough for domestic production to be on a scale that is competitive.

In addition to these macroeconomic effects, developments at the firm level also affect the impacts of factor reallocation and accumulation on aggregate productivity. Taking account of the heterogeneity of firms, even within narrowly defined industries, productivity gains can occur in any sector from shifting resources away from less-productive towards more-productive firms. Exporting may play an important role in this context, as it has been observed that manufacturing firms that export are generally more productive than those that do not. However, there is strong theoretical support (e.g. Redding, 2011) and significant empirical evidence (e.g. Wagner, 2012) which indicates that only relatively few firms are directly involved in trade, and that high productivity is a prerequisite for export participation, rather than its outcome. It is self-selection that makes more productive firms engage in export activities, as it is only those firms that can absorb the additional sunk costs associated with learning about demand and setting up distribution networks on export markets.

Once such firms engage in exporting, they may further improve productivity through learning effects. Such effects occur to the extent that exposure to international buyers and competitors enables these firms to achieve better quality and product upgrading by learning how to use more expensive and higher quality inputs and selling the resulting higher priced and better-quality goods to the more demanding customers on export markets.

> Exporting boosts developing countries' growth most when developed countries experience rapid economic growth along with a high elasticity of their demand for imports from developing countries ...

> ... however, neither of these conditions appears to have been present since the Great Recession.

Chart 5.1

GDP AND IMPORT VOLUME GROWTH, DEVELOPED ECONOMIES, 2001–2013

(Annual average percentage change)

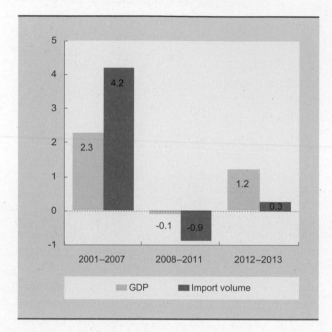

Source: UNCTAD secretariat calculations, based on table 1.1; and *UNCTADstat*.

Note: Developed economies comprises Australia, Canada, Denmark, the euro area (excluding Latvia), Iceland, Japan, New Zealand, Norway, Sweden, Switzerland, the United Kingdom and the United States. Data shown are based on weighted averages.

While, overall, "there is little evidence supporting 'learning-by-exporting'" effects (WTO, 2013c: 87), two additional results from the empirical literature are noteworthy. First, most of the benefits from productivity increases as a result of being able to export are passed on to buyers in the form of lower prices (Marin and Voigtländer, 2013). Consequently, only a small proportion, if any, of those benefits is passed on to workers in the form of higher wages, or transformed into higher profits that could be used for further investment. Second, some studies indicate that the size of any such learning effects greatly depends on the income level and market size of the destination countries. This is because exporters adjust the quality of their products across destinations by varying the quality of their inputs. Thus, productivity gains are persistently higher for firms that export higher quality

goods to high-income and larger countries (Manova and Zhang, 2012). This means that variation in the export performance of different firms depends not only on heterogeneity across firms but also across trade partners.

Thus, the favourable effects on the productivity of developing-country exporters are greatest when developed countries experience rapid economic growth, and when such growth has a high elasticity of demand for imports from developing countries. However, neither of these conditions appears to have been present since the Great Recession.

It is well known that the rate of income growth in developed economies since 2008 has been significantly lower than it was prior to the crisis, and statistical evidence also points to a considerable weakening of import elasticity of demand in these countries. Their volume of imports increased almost twice as rapidly as their income during the pre-crisis period, but it has barely changed since then, even during the slight recovery of income growth in 2012–2013 (chart 5.1). What is more, while there was a strong positive correlation between GDP growth in developed countries and developing-country exports during the pre-crisis period, this correlation became practically nil, or even negative thereafter (chart 5.2).[60]

Taken together, this evidence shows that the impact of developed economies' GDP growth on their imports is becoming smaller, and that the positive effect of their income growth on developing-country exports is also weakening. The challenges that developing countries face in achieving structural transformation under favourable global demand conditions are even greater when they are unable to rely as much as before on growing manufactured exports to developed countries to support such transformation. This may require a rebalancing of their growth strategies by according greater importance to domestic and regional demand, with the ensuing need to align their production structure more closely with their demand structure, as discussed in *TDR 2013*. In other words, the current global economic situation increases the policy challenges facing developing countries and necessitates the deployment of creative industrial policies.

Chart 5.2

DEVELOPED ECONOMIES' GDP GROWTH AND DEVELOPING ECONOMIES' EXPORT GROWTH, 2000–2013

(Per cent)

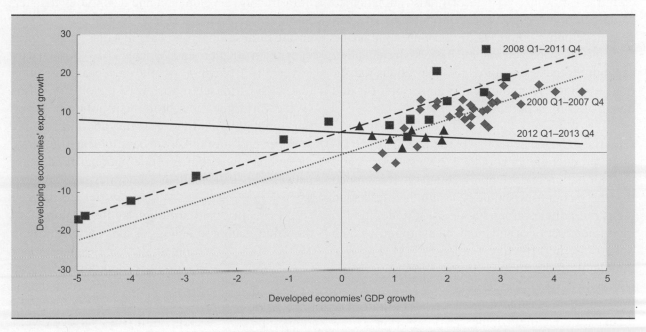

Source: UNCTAD secretariat calculations, based on *UNCTADstat*; Netherlands Bureau for Economic Policy Analysis (CPB); OECD, *Main Economic Indicators*; and *Eurostat*.

Note: The data shown are year-on-year growth rates based on quarterly data. See note to chart 5.1 for a listing of the developed economies; the group of developing economies is defined as emerging economies by the CPB. The data shown are weighted averages. Calculating the non-parametric Spearman's rank correlation coefficient indicates that there is no correlation between the growth of developed economies' GDP and of developing countries' exports during the period 2012–2013.

2. Production networks and the role of industrial policies

International production has often been considered an advanced form of mainly bilateral trade, where a foreign affiliate of a TNC imports parts and components that embody the parent firm's know-how and other production factors and transforms these imports into an assembled, final good for sale in the local market, or exports back to the home country or to a third market. Developing countries' participation in such production networks has been limited mainly to low-wage, labour-intensive activities, sometimes with some local sourcing of parts and components, depending on their level of industrial sophistication and the adopted trade policy strategy. However, the combination of rapid trade liberalization and the revolution in information and communications technologies (ICTs) has made possible a more fragmented

form of production sharing. It is characterized by firms from high-wage countries with advanced technologies combining their managerial, marketing and technical know-how with production and distribution tasks in other developed countries, as well as with low-wage labour tasks in several developing-country locations. All of this results in a more continuous movement across national borders of capital, services and skilled personnel, rather than just of goods.[61] Consequently, these production networks now span multiple national borders.

There have been some strong proponents of participation in international production networks on the grounds that this can open a new and "fast-track" to industrial development (e.g. Baldwin, 2014; WEF, 2012). This argument holds that such networks enable participating developing-country firms to specialize in specific segments of the production process instead of being obliged to simultaneously master all stages of production and build a full, vertically integrated industry. Moreover, by opening access to new – and often higher value – markets, participation in international production networks can provide an opportunity for nascent industries in developing countries at an early stage of industrialization to engage in higher value-added production. This can help developing countries to expand employment, raise incomes and accumulate basic skills and other capabilities that are required to pursue industrialization involving technologically more sophisticated manufacturing activities.

Based on the belief that participation in international production networks will help spur structural transformation in developing countries, it is argued that these countries should redesign their trade and industrial policies around a nexus of trade, foreign investment, services and intellectual property, which underpins the effective functioning of production networks (Baldwin, 2014). Essentially, this would mean that governments wanting their domestic firms to join such networks would need to align their policy measures to the interests of the networks' lead firms (Milberg et al., 2014). It implies that they would need to remove all measures that are deemed to be obstacles to the efficient connection of local factories with the relevant international production network, and adopt measures that protect the lead firms' proprietary assets. In practical terms, facilitating entry into these networks would require a policy that allows more foreign equity in domestic companies, eases the movement and employment of key personnel, relaxes local-content rules and rules relating to foreign exchange and repatriation of profits, strengthens investor protection (including the right to challenge domestic regulations and decisions), develops alternative dispute resolution mechanisms available to foreign investors, and adjusts domestic laws pertaining to such aspects as nationalization and expropriation (Taglioni and Winkler, 2014; Cattaneo et al., 2013).

Many who favour this approach recognize that an open trade and investment regime is not enough on its own to enable countries to benefit from insertion into global value chains (WEF, 2012: 8; OECD, 2013). They even acknowledge that the "problem is

that foreign investors do not actively pursue – and sometimes resist – such integration" (Taglioni and Winkler, 2014: 6). However, they offer only a limited solution to this problem by suggesting the need for horizontal policy measures including education, infrastructure development and technology transfer, in order to enhance access to global value chains, ensure local spillovers and avoid a bias against local integration (Taglioni and Winkler, 2014). As noted by Ravenhill (2014: 265), "despite the repeated assertion that we now inhabit a post-Washington Consensus (WC) world, the most prominent policy prescriptions mimic those of the WC era" and these policy prescriptions "are unlikely to be sufficient to generate the upgrading within … [international production networks] that developing economies seek".

In reality, and although adding "global" to the value chain terminology is almost obligatory in some policy circles, most international production networks are regional in nature, and their recent spread across developing countries has been very heavily skewed towards East Asia (UNCTAD, forthcoming). Moreover, lead firms are still predominantly from developed countries and from a small number of sectors such as clothing and textiles, electronics and the automotive sectors (Nolan, 2012; Starrs, 2014). While these features do not necessarily negate the calls for new thinking on policy related to international production networks, they should serve as a warning against designing strategies for structural transformation based exclusively on the opportunities linked to global value chains. In particular, the need for import promotion should not be used as a reason for downplaying the continued importance of a mix of proactive measures in support of import substitution and export promotion tailored to local conditions and constraints.

Moreover, the extent of the potential benefits from participating in international production networks remains an open empirical question. Those benefits, which will vary considerably across countries, as will the various costs entailed, will have to be weighed carefully when devising specific policies linked to participation in such networks (*TDRs 2002, 2006* and *2013*). In particular, there is a risk of developing countries becoming locked into

> The extent of the potential benefits from participating in international production networks is an open empirical question.

low-value-added activities due to strong pressure from lead firms and other suppliers to keep labour costs low. And they could be blocked from moving up the supply chain by the expensive and successful branding strategies of the lead firms, which are usually from a developed country (Milberg and Winkler, 2013), as well as by the fact that the various links in supply chains have become characterized by a sizeable concentration of business power, and the organization of a supply chain has evolved into a comprehensively planned and coordinated activity (Nolan, 2012).[62] These developments have strongly increased the competitive challenges not only for firms trying to move up the value chain, but also for those trying to enter the production networks. It will be difficult for developing-country firms to overcome these challenges without support through their government's trade and industrial policies.

> Domestic value added as a share of GDP in developing countries that mainly export primary commodities is considerably higher than it is in those that are heavily involved in international production networks engaged in manufacturing.

The extent to which a country's exports, including within international production networks, contain domestic value added has been difficult to assess empirically. This is because exports have traditionally been reported in terms of gross values (i.e. the sum of domestic value added and the value of re-exported inputs).[63] Recently, a number of initiatives have sought to assess the value-added content of international trade.[64] One immediate outcome of these initiatives has been a broader and more nuanced analysis of different types of international production networks, including in agriculture and the extractive industries. An important finding to emerge from this analysis is that domestic value added as a share of GDP in the group of transition economies and in developing regions that mainly export primary commodities, such as Africa and West Asia, is considerably higher than it is in those developing regions that are heavily involved in international production networks engaged in manufacturing, such as East and South-East Asia and the Caribbean (UNCTAD, 2013: 130).[65] This suggests that participating in international production networks does not necessarily ensure GDP growth through an increase in the share of domestic value added.[66] The analysis identifies two factors that are more closely correlated with domestic value added measured as a share of GDP: the nature of countries' exports (especially natural resources, services or final-demand goods), and the degree of self-sufficiency in production for export, which is generally correlated with the size of an economy. These findings raise doubts about the argument that joining international production networks is a "fast route" to industrialization.

Besides, it has long been known that the very logic of the business model underlying international production networks is built on asymmetric governance relations, where lead firms shape the distribution of risks and profits in their favour (e.g. Gereffi, 2014). A recent examination of the national profit shares of the top 2000 corporations by sector shows, on this measure, the continuing dominance of firms from the advanced countries, particularly the United States (Starrs, 2014). Despite the appearance of firms from some emerging economies, mainly China, in select sectors, their ability to climb the value chain remains a challenge. The electronics sector is telling; despite being the largest exporter, China accounts for just 3 per cent of the share of profits derived from this sector (Starrs, 2014: 91). Related empirical evidence suggests that even where developing countries can achieve economic upgrading, this may be linked to a significant deterioration in labour conditions and other forms of social downgrading (Milberg and Bernhardt, 2013).

> The business model underlying international production networks is built on asymmetric governance relations, where lead firms shape the distribution of risks and profits in their favour.

Perhaps most importantly, there is every reason to believe that the previously mentioned behind-the-border reforms considered necessary for inclusion in international production networks are most likely to cement such asymmetries at the expense of developing countries. For example, product standards and their harmonization through trade and investment agreements could play an important role in determining developing countries' production and trade patterns within international production networks.[67] It is true that compliance by developing-country exporters with the standards of their developed-country trading partners is likely to lead to quality upgrading and improved management and production processes. Hence, matching the more stringent standards of developed-country markets will confer the kind of learning-by-exporting benefits discussed in the previous section, including "moving up the quality ladder", by facilitating developing-country exports to markets with richer consumers. However, standards matching is likely to become increasingly difficult as developing-country firms try to continue to progress up the value chain, and at some point it will no longer be possible, which will halt this progression.

Harmonization of product standards also opens the developing-country market to imports from developed-country firms. Such imports will increase significantly if the less productive firms in the developing country, such as those that do not export but only produce for the home market, are unable to match the more demanding product standards. It will also mean that these firms will no longer be able to provide inputs to exporting firms, which will have an adverse effect on domestic production linkages and reduce the domestic value-added content of exports. Moreover, harmonization of product standards will harm developing countries' trade with other countries that are not included in the trade or investment agreement that requires such harmonization.

Taken together, the discussion in this section suggests that international production networks may provide opportunities for countries at an early stage of structural transformation to accelerate industrial development in some sectors. But participating in such networks should not, in most cases, be seen as the only element in a country's industrial development strategy. Developing countries that have achieved some degree of industrial development will need to weigh very carefully the costs and benefits associated with renouncing remaining policy flexibility when participating in international production networks, particularly in terms of the extent to which this contributes to economic and social upgrading.

Moreover, the importance of international production networks may well shrink to the extent that there is a prolonged period of slow growth in developed countries and/or a decline in the positive effects from their income growth on developing-country exports, documented in the previous section. This is more than a transitory phenomenon. The benefits that developed-country enterprises reaped from offshoring have declined as a result of higher transportation costs following the rising price of oil since the early 2000s. This may reinforce tendencies towards reshoring manufacturing activities back to developed countries and efforts in those countries to strengthen their own manufacturing sectors.[68] On the other hand, the importance of South-South production networks, which are currently poorly developed in most developing regions, will increase if developing countries rebalance their growth strategies by giving greater importance to domestic and regional demand (*TDR 2013*). The main point is that none of these shifts provides a rationale for renouncing policy space to the benefit of developed-country firms.

> Developing countries that have achieved some degree of industrial development will need to weigh the costs and benefits associated with renouncing remaining policy flexibility when participating in international production networks.

E. Conclusions

Implementation of effective policy strategies with a view to meeting the global development goals that are likely to emerge from discussions on a post-2015 development agenda will not be feasible without the availability of greater flexibilities in policymaking. Building sustainable and inclusive growth paths will certainly require devising a more effective macroeconomic policy mix and addressing the major systemic issues in the financial system. However, improving the governance of global trade will need to be part of a more comprehensive and integrated package to help preserve the policy space for proactive trade and industrial policies, and should complement the macroeconomic and financial reform agenda.

> Meeting the global development goals of a post-2015 development agenda will not be feasible without the availability of greater flexibilities in policymaking.

What steps could be taken towards strengthening global trade governance in support of development? Most important would be a strengthening of multilateral mechanisms. Multilateral rules provide a compass for national policymakers to ensure the consistency of rules across countries. Capitalizing on the new momentum from the WTO's Bali Ministerial Conference in December 2013, the Doha Round negotiations should progress in a manner that would justify its being dubbed a "development round". Steps in this direction would include an emphasis on implementation issues (paragraph 12 of the Doha Ministerial Declaration). They would also need to maintain the principle of a single undertaking (as stated in paragraph 47 of the Doha Declaration), rather than moving towards a variable geometry whereby a range of mandatory core commitments is supplemented by plurilateral agreements made by only some members. The most important benefit from all this may well be simply maintaining the public good character of multilateral rules and precluding powerful countries from coercing others into competitive liberalization that may be ill-suited to their development prospects.

Second, refocusing trade negotiations on multilateral agreements would imply a reconsideration of WTO-plus and WTO-extra provisions, as well as allowing greater flexibility in the application of the URAs. This could respond to a number of recent developments. In the area of IPR protection, for example, the role of patents in promoting innovation (i.e. the commonly cited basic rationale for the adoption of strict rules on such protection) has increasingly been challenged. Some observers have noted that "historical evidence suggests that patent policies, which grant strong intellectual property rights to early generations of inventors may *discourage* innovation", while "policies that encourage the diffusion of ideas and modify patent laws to facilitate entry and encourage competition may be an effective mechanism to encourage innovation" (Moser, 2013: 40).[69] It has also been suggested that patent laws may influence the direction of technical changes, because secrecy, lead time and other alternatives to patents in protecting IPRs may play a greater role in some industries than in others (Moser, 2013). Moreover, parallel imports and compulsory licensing may be easier to apply to some industries than to others (Max Planck Institute for Innovation and Competition, 2014). This implies that it may be advisable for developing countries to maintain a flexible system of IPR protection while being given appropriate technical support to make full use of the available flexibilities in order to support technology adoption and innovation at all stages of structural transformation.

With regard to subsidies, a wide range of countries have made use of the flexibilities that have remained under the SCM Agreement which allow export credits and measures for promoting "green growth". This might be understood as signalling an acknowledgement of the value of the policy space left by the URAs. It is worth noting that, in response to the Great Recession, a wide range of countries have adopted measures that broadly fall into the category of environment-related subsidies and whose compatibility with existing rules remain a grey area. Perhaps for this reason they have not been challenged before the DSM. This may even indicate that many countries consider some of the rules established by the URAs as inappropriately constraining their policy choices.

A reconsideration of WTO-plus and WTO-extra provisions would also imply renouncing investment provisions that go beyond the TRIMs Agreement. Arguments that international production networks provide a rapid path to structural transformation, and that joining such networks requires a hands-off approach to international business, have recently given new impetus to making such provisions more restrictive. Yet, for countries at early stages of structural transformation, it is far from clear how adopting far-reaching investment provisions would allow, or even foster, the developmental gains to be had from their industries joining such networks, particularly beyond the benefits of increased low-skill employment and initial experience in producing manufactures. The risk of being trapped in some low-level niche of the value chain, and not being able to upgrade, may be too high for countries to give up the possibility of using instruments that in the past have proved to be effective in supporting industrialization and overall production. ∎

> Improving the governance of global trade will need to be part of a more comprehensive and integrated package.

Notes

1   In this chapter, the term "policy space" refers to the availability and effectiveness of policy instruments in attaining policy targets, as introduced in *TDR 2006*. Given the chapter's focus on rules and regulations in trade and investment agreements, it concentrates on the *de jure* components of policy space. UNCTAD (2009) discusses LDCs-specific issues in this area.

2   For example, in its reassessment of growth experiences, the World Bank (2005a: 83) concluded that the "role of activist industrial policies is still controversial but is likely to have been important". See also Commission on Growth and Development, 2008, and *TDRs 1996, 2002* and *2006*.

3   For a discussion of the theoretical arguments in favour of proactive trade and industrial policies, see *TDR 2006*. That report emphasizes that much of the success of industrial policy depends on implementation and it examines institutional complements to industrial policy designs.

4   For a detailed discussion on implementation of current SDT provisions, see WTO, 2013a.

5   Some of the discussion in this section draws on Thrasher and Gallagher (2014), as well as on *TDR 2006* chap. V, which examined these issues in more detail. A range of other Uruguay Round agreements are of limited importance in the context of structural transformation, such as the Sanitary and Phytosanitary Measures Agreement (SPS), which sets out basic rules designed to protect human, animal or plant life and health. Other agreements concern measures that nowadays are rarely used. For example, import licences and bans, which were frequently deployed in the past to protect domestic industry and stabilize economies, are governed by the Agreement on Import Licensing Procedures.

Its objectives are to simplify, clarify and minimize the administrative requirements necessary to obtain import licences, and make sure that the procedures used for granting such licences do not in themselves restrict trade. To ensure transparency, import licensing is reviewed annually by the Committee on Import Licensing. Quantitative restrictions and import bans are generally prohibited under the GATT 1994, except, for example, to address balance-of-payments problems (articles XII and XVIII: B), but such exceptions, as well as other safeguard measures, are further restricted in some RTAs (for details, see Prusa, 2011).

6 Local-content requirements are closely related to rules of origin in preferential trade agreements between developed and developing countries. The developed-country partners to such agreements can tailor the rules of origin to their needs.

7 It is clear, however, that such performance requirements can be brought to dispute settlement only when they are published, which is unlikely to be the case for private understandings between governments and firms.

8 Moreover, Article 4 of the TRIMs Agreement sets out certain conditions under which developing countries can "deviate temporarily from the provisions of the Agreement".

9 Compulsory licensing defines a situation when authorities license companies or individuals other than the patent owner to use the rights of the patent – to make, use, sell or import a product under patent (i.e. a patented product or a product made by a patented process) – without the permission of the patent owner. Parallel imports refer to imports of branded goods into a market, which are then sold there without the consent of the owner of the trademark in that market.

10 This and the following discussion of the TRIPS Agreement are based on Correa, 2014.

11 The SCM Agreement replaced the Tokyo Round Subsidies Code, a plurilateral agreement accepted by only 24 countries, which virtually exempted developing countries from all new subsidy disciplines. Article 1 of the SCM Agreement defines a subsidy as a financial contribution or price support given by a government, which confers a benefit on domestic firms. Agricultural subsidies are governed by the WTO Agreement on Agriculture.

12 The SCM Agreement does not apply to LDCs. Moreover, countries that were WTO members when the URAs were concluded are excluded from this commitment until their per capita income reaches $1,000, in constant 1990s dollars, and remains at that level for at least three consecutive years. By contrast, newly acceding countries are not exempt even if they fall below this threshold, such as Viet Nam. For a detailed discussion on SDT under the SCM Agreement, see Coppens, 2013.

13 These four situations are: (i) the total ad valorem subsidization of a product exceeds 5 per cent; (ii) the subsidy covers operating losses sustained by an industry; (iii) the subsidy covers operating losses sustained by an enterprise, other than one-time measures; or (iv) direct forgiveness of debt owed by a domestic enterprise to the government.

14 Article 27 of the SCM Agreement covers the provisions governing SDT for developing countries in the SCM Agreements, including flexibilities following the expiration of the transition period.

15 Moreover, annex VII lists a range of countries, such as the LDCs, which, under certain circumstances, can use subsidized export credits as an instrument to promote exports.

16 Some observers argue that this flexibility provides relatively larger benefits to the signatories of the OECD Arrangement, for example because the provisions may be considered as being tailored to meet the policy objectives of its members, rather than those of developing countries. Moreover, other countries would have trouble securing agreement on an alternative arrangement, as it would be difficult for the signatories of the OECD Arrangement to subscribe to such an alternative (Coppens, 2009).

17 For country-specific illustrations, see Nicita et al., 2014.

18 For illustration, see *TDR 2006*, figure 5.1.

19 As explained by Akyüz (2005: 29, 31) "this kind of flexibility is best accommodated by binding the average tariff without any line-by-line commitment; that is, to leave tariffs for individual products unbound, subject to an overall constraint that the average applied tariffs should not exceed the bound average tariff ... [Because] of different initial conditions [this approach] ... is unlikely to be compatible with any formula-based procedure".

20 This negotiated text (WTO, 2008) also discusses flexibilities for various categories of developing countries subject to the formula. The Swiss formula is $t_{new}=(t_{old}M)/(t_{old}+M)$, where t indicates tariffs, in percentages, and M is a coefficient that indicates the maximum level of reduced tariffs. It reduces tariffs and harmonizes them at the same time. For further details, see: http://www.wto.org/english/tratop_e/dda_e/status_e/nama_e.htm.

21 This tipping point has often been attributed to the efforts of member States of the European Union (EU) and European Free Trade Association (EFTA) to stabilize trade relations with Central and Eastern European countries after the dismantling of the Council for Mutual Economic Assistance (Comecon) in 1991, and competition for market access motivated other countries to follow suit (Baldwin and Jaimovich, 2012).

22 For discussion of the great diversity regarding specific rules and provision in RTAs, see, e.g., World

Bank (2005b) on services, investment and intellectual property; te Velde and Fahmbulleh (2006) on investment-related provisions; various chapters in Estevadeordal et al. (2009) on market-access provisions, technical barriers to trade, and provisions on services and on competition; Prusa and Teh (2011) on contingent protection rules; and UNCTAD (2011b) on customs and trade facilitation.

23 It should be noted that these statistics refer to notification requirements, rather than simply the number of RTAs. This means that an RTA that covers both goods and services necessitates two notifications. For regular updates, see: http://www.wto.org/english/tratop_e/region_e/region_e.htm.

24 Assessing the scope and depth of these agreements requires screening the very large number of RTAs on the basis of item codes, and the scope and coverage of existing databases vary widely. Dür et al. (2013) claim that their dataset on the Design of Trade Agreements (DESTA), which is based on 587 agreements coded for more than 1,000 items, is the most comprehensive one. However, Kohl et al. (2013) claim that, in spite of covering fewer agreements, their dataset, which builds on those used by Horn et al. (2010) and WTO (2011), is superior because it explicitly identifies whether provisions are legally enforceable. Horn et al. (2010) indicate that legal enforceability may be judged according to how precisely the agreements are drafted (e.g. use of the word "shall"), and whether the agreements' terminology indicates the intent to have them "governed by international law". The complexity of these agreements is evident on examining the dataset of Horn et al. (2010), which is updated by WTO (2011) and synthesizes RTA provisions into 14 WTO-plus and 38 WTO-extra areas. Kohl et al. (2013) provide a wide range of detailed examples of enforceable and non-enforceable provisions of the 13 WTO-plus and 4 WTO-extra areas that their study emphasizes. For a comparison between legally enforceable and other provisions of RTAs with the EU, Japan and the United States, see also Baldwin, 2012.

25 According to Horn et al. (2010: 1587), who use the term preferential trade agreements (PTAs) instead of the term RTAs adopted in this chapter, "the fact that much of the 'legal inflation' occurs in development-related provisions, which are unique to the EC agreements, suggests that the EU has a greater need than the US to portray its PTAs as not driven solely by commercial interests." However, from the political science perspective, it could also be argued that this feature may reflect the objective of the EU to use RTAs as an instrument of foreign policy, thus serving as a precursor of political integration.

26 For further details, see Fink, 2011.

27 For a more detailed discussion, see also chapter VI of this *Report*.

28 Labour mobility is covered in the GATS, but several RTAs offer greater liberalization by including (i) full national treatment and market access for service suppliers as well as facilitation for groups, including those other than service providers; (ii) access to the labour market; (iii) temporary movement of business persons, including those involved in investment or trade in goods; (iv) non-discriminatory conditions for workers; and (v) labour mobility for business visitors, independent professionals, intra-corporate transferees and contractual services suppliers. For assessments of the effects of RTAs on labour mobility, see, for example, Goswami and Saéz, 2013; and Orefice, 2014.

29 For further discussion see, for example, Brusick et al., 2005; Dawar and Holmes, 2011; and WTO, 2011.

30 See also chapter VI of this *Report*.

31 Issues relating to the settlement of investment disputes are further discussed in chapter VI of this *Report*.

32 It is also interesting to note that a recent study which presents the IMF's institutional view indicates that "most of the current bilateral and regional agreements addressing capital flow liberalization do not take into account macroeconomic and financial stability" (IMF, 2012: 33). Indeed, they pose serious challenges to macro-prudential policies that receiving countries may want to apply, as further discussed in chapter VI of this *Report*.

33 For a discussion regarding the United States American Recovery and Reinvestment Act of 2009, see Cimino et al., 2014.

34 These preference programmes have two aspects in common: they are conditional and discretionary. The preference-granting country can establish, according to its own political choices, the programme's eligibility criteria and related concessions, as well as the procedures through which exceptions and waivers to country- and product-specific limitations and ceilings are granted, modified or withdrawn. Since unilateral and voluntary concessions are not bound under the WTO, developing countries have no recourse to challenge such changes. One example in this context is the United States' suspension of Argentina's designation as a GSP beneficiary developing country in March 2012 following Argentina's alleged non-compliance with provisions in a bilateral investment treaty (White House, 2012).

35 Evenett (2013b) provides a detailed assessment of the measures taken by the G20 countries that were denounced by the GTA as "murky protectionism". He also compares these with the measures taken by the "next 10 largest trading nations", comprising Chile, the Islamic Republic of Iran, Israel, Malaysia, Norway, Singapore, Switzerland, Thailand, the United Arab Emirates and Viet Nam.

36 For example, in May 2012, the then Director General of the WTO, Pascal Lamy, promoted the idea of

exploring this relationship as a way to break the stalemate in the Doha Round; see http://www.wto.org/english/news_e/news12_e/gc_rpt_01may12_e.htm. Henn and McDonald (2014) use GTA data to investigate the effect of policy measures implemented since 2008 on global trade flows, with the implicit suggestion that these data be used in future trade negotiations.

37   From a traditional, neoclassical perspective, this is in contrast to "horizontal" or "functional" industrial policies, which aim at a general improvement of economic conditions for all sectors and firms, such as improving a country's infrastructure, regulatory and competition environments, and the general business climate. However, any of these measures may effectively have sector-specific impacts. This is because specific sectors have different characteristics, so that functional policies applied economy-wide are likely to affect different sectors in different ways (Chang, 2011). Moreover, since their implementation may be too expensive, even policymakers who want to implement sectorally neutral policies will need to take sector-specific decisions. For example, for infrastructure development, it will be necessary to consider whether to focus, for example, on urban or rural areas; on ports that will favour industries producing bulky goods (such as motor vehicles and machinery) or on airports that will favour goods with high unit values (such as pharmaceuticals). More nuanced variants of this approach (e.g. Lin and Treichel, 2014) recognize the important role of government agencies in overcoming market failures by addressing information, coordination and externality issues inherent in the development of new activities and sectors, but emphasize that such structural change should follow the trajectory of "latent comparative advantage", rather than "defying comparative advantage".

38   For example, the National Institutes of Health, which are State-funded, constitute a major knowledge base in the biopharmaceutical sector. They produce about three-fourths of all new molecular entities, while private laboratories essentially produce minor variations of existing drugs. Mazzucato (2013) also credits this kind of State-funded research for several innovations – such as the Internet, the global positioning system (GPS) and a virtual personal assistant known as SIRI – that allowed, for example, Apple to develop the iPhone and several other products. In these three cases, the State funded the risky early stages of their development from its military budget.

39   The main institutions associated with this type of industrial policy have been (i) the Defense Advanced Research Projects Agency, created in 1958 in response to the launching of Sputnik by the then Soviet Union with a view to maintaining global technological leadership by having its officials "working directly with firms in identifying and pursuing the most promising innovative paths" (Mazzucato, 2013: 79); (ii) the Small Business Innovation Research (SBIR) programme, created in 1982, which has required government agencies with large research projects to earmark part of their research funding to support small firms for which SBIR has often been the first source of funding for technological innovations; (iii) the Orphan Drug Act, adopted in 1983, which provides tax incentives, subsidies and fast-track approval for drugs for treating rare conditions; and (iv) the National Nanotechnology Initiative, launched in 2000. Other developed countries have also adopted SBIR programmes. For example, in 2009 the United Kingdom reformed its SBIR programme, established in 2001, to resemble more closely that of the United States. In addition to some tangible effects in the pharmaceutical industry, this programme has been particularly successful in indicating the sectors where potential follow-on investment from the private sector may be profitable (Bound and Puttick, 2010).

40   According to Sperling (2013: 7), "The actual loss in *absolute* manufacturing jobs over the past 50 years primarily took place [in the] last decade, where we lost over 5 million manufacturing jobs, roughly one third of the manufacturing workforce. From 1965 until 2000, we steadily grew manufacturing production at roughly 4 percent per annum, in line with real GDP growth. From 2000 to 2010, our production stagnated and underperformed the economy by a consistent margin for the first time" (emphasis added).

41   In addition, in February 2012 President Obama created the Interagency Trade Enforcement Center to monitor and enforce trade provisions through, for example, the use of safeguard measures and initiating a range of cases against China before the WTO's DSM (Sperling, 2013).

42   In addition to the NNMI, the Advanced Manufacturing National Programme launched by President Obama includes three other main initiatives: the National Nanotechnology Initiative (NNI), the Materials Genome Initiative (MGI) and the National Robotics Initiative (NRI). The NNI is a multi-agency initiative that expedites the discovery, development and deployment of nanoscale science, engineering and technology to serve the public good through a programme of coordinated research and development. Besides advancing a world-class nanotechnology research programme, the NNI has the primary mandate to foster the transfer of new nanotechnologies to products for commercial and public benefit. A major aim of the Materials Genome Initiative is to create new knowledge, tools and infrastructure that will enable domestic industries to discover, manufacture and deploy advanced materials twice

as fast as today. In particular, this initiative intends to accelerate the lower cost insertion of advanced materials into United States manufacturing. The goal of the National Robotics Initiative is to accelerate the development and use of robots in the United States that work beside, or in cooperation with, people. It addresses the entire life cycle, from fundamental research and development to manufacturing and deployment. This programme strives to develop the next generation of robotics and to encourage existing and new communities to focus on innovative application areas. For a detailed discussion of the National Network for Manufacturing Innovation, see, for example, Hart et al., 2012.

43 See: http://www.gsa.gov/portal/content/103527.

44 For a discussion of these legal issues, see, for example, Brunel and Hufbauer, 2009, and Chukwumerije, 2010.

45 According to Warwick (2013), a number of countries responded to the global economic and financial crisis in 2008–2009, by providing direct support to the automotive industry and encouraging car sales, including Canada, China, Estonia, France, Israel, Japan, the Netherlands, Norway, Portugal, the Republic of Korea, Spain, the United Kingdom and the United States.

46 Under the umbrella of this EU-wide framework, many EU members have continued to design and implement their own national industrial strategies, in part because "the EU was less and less regarded as having solutions and progressively seen as an impediment to industrial restructuring" (Cohen, 2007: 222–223). For example, France complemented the Lisbon Strategy with a package of national measures in the early 2000s (*TDR 2006*). More recently, France launched a programme for "industrial renaissance" that follows similar concepts and ideas as the Horizon 2020 in that it intends to promote key technologies and facilitate their commercialization. For further details, see: http://www.redressement-productif.gouv.fr/files/nouvelle_france_industrielle_english.pdf.

47 European Parliament, General principles of EU industrial policy; available at: http://www.europarl.europa.eu/aboutparliament/en/displayFtu.html?ftuId=FTU_5.9.1.html# (accessed 9 April 2014).

48 Key enabling technologies "are knowledge and capital-intensive technologies associated with high research and development (R&D) intensity, rapid and integrated innovation cycles, high capital expenditure and highly skilled employment. Their influence is pervasive, enabling process, product and service innovation throughout the economy. They are of systemic relevance, multidisciplinary and trans-sectorial, cutting across many technology areas with a trend towards convergence, technology integration and the potential to induce structural change" (European Commission, 2011: 10).

49 For details on the allocation of these €80 billion and the principles governing their distribution, see http://europa.eu/rapid/press-release_MEMO-13-1085_en.htm.

50 In addition, EU industrial policy seems notable for the absence of a specific pattern or common strategy for adoption by all the member countries. This is because the Treaty on the Functioning of the EU (see: http://old.eur-lex.europa.eu/en/treaties/new-2-47.htm) treats industrial policy as an area where the Union may only "carry out actions to support, coordinate or supplement the actions of the member states, without thereby superseding their competence" and where legally binding acts of the Union "shall not entail harmonisation of member states' laws or regulations" (articles 6 and 173).

51 For this motivation see, for example, European Commission, Europa press release, "State aid: Commission authorises Romanian temporary aid scheme to grant compatible aid of up to €500 000"; available at: http://europa.eu/rapid/press-release_IP-09-1876_en.htm. See also Heimler and Jenny (2012), who discuss the provisions that govern the granting of State aid in the EU in non-exceptional circumstances. Views on the appropriateness of these provisions may differ widely across member States (see, for example, "Aides publiques: Montebourg dénonce les 'talibans du droit' à Bruxelles", *Le Monde*, 20 February 2014; available at: http://www.lemonde.fr/economie/article/2014/02/20/aides-publiques-montebourg-denonce-les-talibans-de-droit-a-bruxelles_4370721_3234.html).

52 This and the following two paragraphs are based on Thoburn, 2013, Nguyen et al., 2014, and Thrasher and Gallagher, 2014.

53 Nguyen et al., (2014: table 1) provide an overview of Viet Nam's industrial policy matrix.

54 With regard to IPRs, for example, Fergusson et al. (2013: 34) point to "negotiation of provisions that go beyond the level of protection provided in the WTO Trade Related Aspects of Intellectual Property (TRIPS) Agreement, most recently with the TPP negotiations. For example, the United States has sought to have its partner countries sign the World Intellectual Property Organization's (WIPO's) Performances and Phonograms Treaty, an agreement to which Brunei, Malaysia, New Zealand, and Vietnam are not parties."

55 China's treatment of FDI is an important issue in the current negotiations of a United States-China BIT, as discussed, for example in Price and Smart, 2013.

56 For more detailed accounts of China's industrial policy, see, for example, Studwell, 2013; Wu, 2013; and Lo and Wu, 2014.

57 Moving towards a so-called "circular economy" has become an official development strategy in China, as explained, for example, by Su et al., 2013.

58 For example, such measures may fall under the environment-related provisions of article 8 of the

SCM Agreement, mentioned above (discussed in detail in *TDR 2009*: 156–159).

59 The length of time any of these alternatives to changing the composition of domestic output can be pursued largely depends on the external economic environment, and they can quickly spiral into a balance-of-payments crisis as well. For further discussion, see *TDR 2013,* chap. II.

60 A recent paper by Cubeddu et al. (2014) provides econometric support for this evidence. It highlights the sizeable contribution of external demand from developed economies to the growth performance of non-commodity-exporting developing countries during the first decade of the 2000s. On the other hand, for the commodity exporters among developing countries, it was external demand from large emerging economies that played a more important role as a growth driver. The paper also shows that the contribution from external demand was greatest for those developing countries which had the largest share of exports in GDP, and that, despite the increase in South-South trade, their growth remained more sensitive to demand from developed than from developing countries.

61 This form of trade within production networks has been called the "second unbundling". The "first unbundling" referred to the progressive integration of national economies through a reduction in trade costs, mainly resulting from lower transportation costs, which allowed the production and consumption of goods to be geographically separated but maintained production stages bundled spatially in factories in order to minimize communication and coordination costs. The "second unbundling" refers to the unbundling of factories as a result of the spatial dispersion of production stages. This was made possible by a reduction in the costs of communication and information-sharing and associated changes in working methods and product designs that make production more modular (Baldwin, 2006).

62 Nolan (2012: 21) indicates, for example, "that just two firms produce 75 per cent of the global supply of braking systems for large commercial aircraft, ... three firms produce 75 per cent of the global supply of constant velocity joints for automobiles, [and] ... three firms produce 80 per cent of the global supply of industrial gases".

63 For an early assessment of the domestic value-added content of developing-country manufactured exports, see *TDR 2002.* Analysing data for the period 1980–1997, the assessment's main conclusion was that developing countries were "trading more but earning less". In other words, their share in global manufactured exports had increased, but their share in global manufacturing value added had fallen.

64 These initiatives for measuring value-added trade rely partly on reported statistics provided in the Trade in Value Added (TiVA) Inter-Country Input-Output model, operated by the OECD and the WTO, and the World Input-Output Database (WIOD) funded by the European Commission, which is based on supply-use tables from national statistics compiled by a consortium of 11 institutions and available from the University of Groningen. These data, on 18 industrial sectors, cover 57 economies (including all OECD countries, Brazil, China, India, Indonesia, the Russian Federation and South Africa) spanning the period 1995–2009. They have been used, for example, to assess the extent to which individual countries are involved in vertically fragmented production processes (e.g. Backer and Miroudot, 2013). By contrast, the data used in UNCTAD (2013) rely on input-output tables derived from the Eora project's global multi-region input-output (MRIO) table. This dataset relies on reported data with interpolations and exploratory estimates to provide continuous time series for the period 1990–2010 on 187 countries, including a large number of developing, and sometimes data-poor, countries. For details on the trade-offs between data coverage and statistical rigor, see UNCTAD (2013: 124).

65 The same phenomenon can be observed within Latin America and the Caribbean, where the share of domestic value added in a country's exports is significantly higher for the more resource-based economies in South America than it is for countries in Central America and the Caribbean, whose participation in value chains is based more on manufacturing (UNCTAD, 2014: figure II.12).

66 Given its focus on developed economies, the TiVA database offers limited evidence for developing countries. However, the OECD (2013: 56) shows that "China's exports currently involve assembly work with a high level of foreign content, leading to a significant fall in its domestic value added to output ratio between 2005 and 2009." On the other hand, the domestic content of China's exports has increased. The reason for this is closely related to the declining importance in China's total trade of processing trade with its high levels of foreign content (OECD, 2013: 147). However, domestic value added in China's processing trade increased only slightly, from about 38 per cent to about 40 per cent between 2007 and 2011. The same source does not provide data for Mexico for the same period, but it does show that Mexico's share of domestic value added in processing trade also increased slightly between 2000 and 2006, though it remained below 30 per cent (OECD, 2013: 147). Even though the economic outcomes during the two different time periods were clearly also affected by different external economic environments, taken together, this evidence would suggest that the larger share of domestic value added in China's exports of processed goods was associated

with China's more proactive trade and industrial policies. This argument receives further support from the different outcomes in the automobile industries in Mexico and Brazil (UNCTAD, 2014: 65–69).

67   Part of this paragraph draws on Disdier et al., 2013.
68   For example, reshoring of manufacturing operations in the United States is expected to occur as a result of falling prices in that country's gas market, as noted by UNCTAD (2014: 12).
69   According to Moser (2013: 40), "Historical evidence suggests that in countries with patent laws, the

majority of innovations occur outside of the patent system. Countries without patent laws have produced as many innovations as countries with patent laws during some time periods, and their innovations have been of comparable quality." This may be taken to indicate that "[p]atents as such do not create innovation incentives. They respond to incentives that result from market opportunities, which patentees may or may not capture by virtue of their exclusive rights" (Max Planck Institute for Innovation and Competition, 2014: 3).

References

Akyüz Y (2005). The WTO negotiations on industrial tariffs: What is at stake for developing countries? Trade & Development Series No. 24. Penang, Third World Network.

Akyüz Y, Chang HJ and Kozul-Wright R (1998). New perspectives on East Asian development. *Journal of Development Studies*, 34(6): 4–36.

Backer KD and Miroudot S (2013). Mapping global value chains. Trade Policy Paper No. 159. OECD, Paris.

Baldwin RE (2006). Globalisation: The great unbundling(s). Geneva, Graduate Institute of International Studies; available at: http://graduateinstitute.ch/files/live/sites/iheid/files/sites/ctei/shared/CTEI/Baldwin/Publications/Chapters/Globalization/Baldwin_06-09-20.pdf.

Baldwin RE (2012). WTO 2.0: Global governance of supply-chain trade. Policy Insight No. 64, Centre for Economic Policy Research (CEPR), London, December.

Baldwin RE (2014). Multilateralising 21st century regionalism. OECD Global Forum on Trade, 11 February; available at: http://www.rieti.go.jp/en/events/bbl/13070401.html.

Baldwin RE and Evenett SJ (2012). Beggar-thy-neighbour policies during the crisis era: Causes, constraints, and lessons for maintaining open borders. *Oxford Review of Economic Policy*, 28(2): 211–234.

Baldwin RE and Jaimovich D (2012). Are free trade agreements contagious? *Journal of International Economics*, 88(1): 1–16.

Block FL (2008). Swimming against the current: The rise of the hidden developmental state in the United States. *Politics and Society*, 36(2): 169–206.

Bound K and Puttick R (2010). Buying power? Is the Small Business Research Initiative for procuring R&D driving innovation in the UK? Research Report, National Endowment for Science, Technology and the Arts (NESTA), London; available at: http://www.nesta.org.uk/sites/default/files/buying_power_report.pdf.

Brunel C and Hufbauer G (2009). Money for the auto Industry: Consistent with WTO rules? Policy Brief No. 09-4. Peterson Institute for International Economics, Washington DC, February.

Brusick P, Alvarez AM and Cernat L, eds. (2005). *Competition Provisions in Regional Trade Agreements: How to Assure Development Gains*. UNCTAD/DITC/CLP/2005/1, New York and Geneva, United Nations.

Cattaneo O, Gereffi G, Miroudot S and Taglioni D (2013). Joining, upgrading and being competitive in global value chains. Policy Research Working Paper No. 6406, World Bank, Washington, DC.

Chanda R (2002). GATS and its implications for developing countries: Key issues and concerns. Discussion Paper No. 25. ST/ESA/2002/DP.25, United Nations Department of Economic and Social Affairs, New York.

Chandrasekhar CP (2014). National Development Banks in a Comparative Perspective. Jawaharlal Nehru University, New Delhi, February.

Chang HJ (2011). Industrial policy: Can we go beyond an unproductive confrontation? In: Lin JY and Pleskovic B, eds, *Lessons from East Asia and the Global Financial Crisis*. Proceedings of the Annual World Bank Conference on Development Economics – Global 2010. Washington, DC, World Bank: 83–109.

Chukwumerije O (2010). Obama's trade policy: Trends, prospects, and portends. *Journal of International Law and Policy*, 16(1): 39–79.

Cimino A, Hufbauer GC and Schott JJ (2014). A proposed code to discipline local content requirements. Policy Brief 14-6, Peterson Institute for International Economics, Washington, DC.

Cohen E (2007). Industrial policies in France: the old and the new. *Journal of Industry, Competition and Trade*, 7(3–4): 213–227.

Commission on Growth and Development (2008). *The Growth Report. Strategies for Sustained Growth and Inclusive Development*. Washington, DC, World Bank.

Copeland P and Papadimitriou D, eds. (2012). *The EU's Lisbon Strategy: Evaluating Success, Understanding Failure*. London, Palgrave Macmillan.

Coppens D (2009). How much credit for export credit support under the SCM Agreement? *Journal of International Economic Law*, 12(1): 63–113.

Coppens D (2013). How special is the special and differential treatment under the SCM Agreement? A legal and normative analysis of WTO subsidy disciplines on developing countries. *World Trade Review*, 12(1): 79–109.

Correa C (2014). Intellectual property: How much room is left for industrial policy? Background paper for the *Trade and Development Report 2014*. Geneva, UNCTAD.

Cubeddu L, Culiuc A, Fayad G, Gao Y, Kochhar K, Kyobe A, Oner C, Perrelli R, Sanya S, Tsounta E and Zhang Z (2014). Emerging markets in transition: Growth prospects and challenges. Staff Discussion Note 14-06, IMF, Washington, DC.

Di Tommaso MR and Schweitzer SO (2013). *Industrial Policy in America: Breaking the Taboo*. Cheltenham and Northampton, Edward Elgar.

Dawar K and Holmes P (2011). Competition policy. In: Chauffour JP and Maur JC, eds, *Preferential Trade Agreement Policies for Development. A Handbook*. Washington, DC, World Bank: 347–366.

Deere C (2009). *The implementation game: The TRIPS Agreement and the global politics of intellectual property reform in developing countries*. Oxford, Oxford University Press.

Department of Trade and Industry (South Africa) (2007). *National Industrial Policy Framework*. Pretoria.

Dezan Shira & Associates (2011). *Foreign Investment Industrial Guidance Catalogue* (2011 version). Hong Kong (China SAR).

Disdier AC, Fontagné L and Cadot O (2013). North-South standards harmonization and international trade. Policy Research Working Paper No. 6710, World Bank, Washington, DC.

Dür A, Baccini L and Elsig M (2013). The design of international trade agreements: Introducing a new dataset. *The Review of International Organizations*: 1–23; available at: http://rd.springer.com/article/10.1007/s11558-013-9179-8.

Eichengreen BJ and Irwin D (2010). The slide to protectionism in the Great Depression: Who succumbed and why? *The Journal of Economic History*, 70(4): 871–897.

Eichengreen BJ and Kenen PB (1994). Managing the world economy under the Bretton Woods system: an overview. In Kenen PB, ed, *Managing the World Economy: 50 Years After Bretton Woods*. Washington, DC, Institute for International Economies: 3–57.

Estevadeordal A, Suominen K and Teh R, eds. (2009). *Regional Rules in the Global Trading System*. Cambridge, Cambridge University Press.

European Commission (1990). Industrial policy in an open and competitive environment: Guidelines for a Community approach. Document COM(1990) 556, Brussels.

European Commission (2004). Community guidelines on State Aid for rescuing and restructuring firms in difficulty. *Official Journal of the European Union*, 2004/C 244/02, October; available at: http://eur-lex.europa.eu/LexUriServ/LexUriServ.do?uri=OJ:C:2004:244:0002:0017:EN:PDF.

European Commission (2011). High Level Expert Group on Key Enabling Technologies: Final Report; available at: http://ec.europa.eu/enterprise/sectors/ict/files/kets/hlg_report_final_en.pdf.

European Commission (2013). Draft guidelines on State aid for rescuing and restructuring non-financial undertakings in difficulty; available at: http://ec.europa.eu/competition/consultations/2013_state_aid_rescue_restructuring/draft_guidelines_en.pdf.

Evenett SJ (2012). Executive summary. In: Evenett SJ, ed, *Débâcle: The 11th GTA Report on Protectionism*. Centre for Economic Policy Research, London.

Evenett SJ (2013a). *What Restraint? Five years of G20 Pledges on Trade. The 14th GTA Report*. Centre for Economic Policy Research, London.

Evenett SJ (2013b). Mapping crisis-era protectionism in Latin America and the Caribbean. Discussion paper no. 9782. Centre for Economic Policy Research, London.

Evenett SJ (2013c). Mapping crisis-era protectionism in the Asia-Pacific region. Discussion paper no. 9783, Centre for Economic Policy Research, London.

Felipe J, Abdon A and Kumar U (2012). Tracking the middle-income trap: What is it, who is in it, and why? Working paper no. 715, Levy Economics Institute of Bard College, Annandale-on-Hudson, NY.

Fergusson IF, Cooper WH, Jurenas R and Williams BR (2013). The Trans-Pacific Partnership (TPP) negotiations and issues for Congress. Document R42694, Congressional Research Service, Washington, DC; available at: http://fas.org/sgp/crs/row/R42694.pdf.

Ferraz JC, Kupfer D and Marques FS (2014). Industrial policy as an effective developmental tool: Lessons from Brazil. In: Salazar-Xirinachs JM, Nübler I and Kozul-Wright R, eds, *Transforming Economies. Making Industrial Policy Work for Growth, Jobs and Development*. Geneva, International Labour Organization (ILO): 291–305.

Fink C (2011). Intellectual property rights. In: Chauffour JP and Maur JC, eds, *Preferential Trade Agreement Policies for Development. A Handbook*, Washington, DC, World Bank: 387–405.

Fosu AK, ed. (2013). *Achieving Development Success. Strategies and Lessons from the Developing World*. Oxford, Oxford University Press.

Fugazza M and Nicita A (2013). The direct and relative effects of preferential market access. *Journal of International Economics*, 89(2): 357–368.

Gereffi G (2014). Global value chains in a post-Washington Consensus world. *Review of International Political Economy*, 21(1): 9–37.

Goswami AG and Sáez S (2013). How well have trade agreements facilitated temporary mobility? In: Sáez S, ed. *Let Workers Move: Using Bilateral Labor Agreements to Increase Trade in Services*. Washington, DC, World Bank: 17–38.

Grabas C and Nützenadel A, eds. (2014). *Industrial Policy in Europe after 1945: Wealth, Power and Economic Development in the Cold War*. Basingstoke, Palgrave Macmillan.

Hart DM, Ezell SJ and Atkinson RD (2012). Why America needs a national network for manufacturing innovation. Washington, DC, The Information Technology & Innovation Foundation; available at: http://www.itif.org/publications/why-america-needs-national-network-manufacturing-innovation.

Heimler A and Jenny F (2012). The limitations of European Union control of state aid. *Oxford Review of Economic Policy*, 28(2): 347–367.

Henn C and McDonald B (2014). Crisis protectionism: The observed trade impact. *IMF Economic Review*, 62(1): 77–118.

Horn H, Mavroidis PC and Sapir A (2010). Beyond the WTO? An anatomy of EU and US preferential trade agreements. *The World Economy*, 33(11): 1565–1588.

ICCT (2013). Brazil's Inovar-Auto incentive program. International Council on Clean Transportation; available at: http://www.theicct.org/sites/default/files/publications/ICCTupdate_Brazil_InovarAuto_feb2013.pdf.

IMF (2012). *The Liberalization and Management of Capital Flows: An Institutional View*. Washington, DC, International Monetary Fund.

Kaldor N (1968). Productivity and growth in manufacturing industry. A reply. *Economioa*, 35(140): 385–391.

Ketels CHM (2007). Industrial policy in the United States. *Journal of Industry, Competition and Trade*, 7(3–4): 147–167.

Kohl T, Brakman S and Garretsen H (2013). Do trade agreements stimulate international trade differently? Evidence from 296 trade agreements. University of Groningen, unpublished; available at: http://www.tristankohl.org/site/KohlBrakmanGarretsen_296Agreements.pdf.

Kozul-Wright R (1995). The myth of Anglo-Saxon Capitalism: Reconstructuring the history of the American State. In: Chang HJ and Rowthorn R, eds. *The Role of the State in Economic Change*. Oxford, Clarendon Press: 235–251.

Krugman PR (1993). Toward a counter-counterrevolution in development theory. In: Summers LH and Shah S, eds. *Proceedings of the World Bank Annual Conference on Development Economics 1992, Supplement to The World Bank Economic Review and The World Bank Research Observer*. Washington, DC, World Bank: 15–62.

Lewis WA (1954). Economic development with unlimited supplies of labour. *The Manchester School*, 22(2): 139–191.

Lin JY and Treichel V (2014). Making industrial policy work for development. In: Salazar-Xirinachs JM, Nübler I and Kozul-Wright R, eds. *Transforming Economies: Making Industrial Policy Work for Growth, Jobs and Development*. Geneva, ILO: 65–78.

Lo D and Wu M (2014). The State and industrial policy in Chinese economic development. In: Salazar-Xirinachs JM, Nübler I and Kozul-Wright R, eds. *Transforming Economies. Making Industrial Policy work for Growth, Jobs and Development*. Geneva, ILO: 307–326.

Maggi G and Rodriguez-Clare A (1998). The value of trade agreements in the presence of political pressures. *Journal of Political Economy*, 106(3): 574–601.

Manger MS and Shadlen KC (2014). Political trade dependence and North–South trade agreements. *International Studies Quarterly*, forthcoming.

Manova K and Zhang Z (2012). Export prices across firms and destinations. *Quarterly Journal of Economics*, 127(1): 379–436.

Marin AG and Voigtländer N (2013). Exporting and plant-level efficiency gains: It's in the measure. Working paper no. 19033, National Bureau of Economic Research, Cambridge, MA.

Maur JC and Shepherd B (2011). Product standards. In: Chauffour JP and Maur JC, eds. *Preferential Trade Agreement Policies for Development. A Handbook*. Washington, DC, World Bank: 197–216.

Max Planck Institute for Innovation and Competition (2014). Declaration on patent protection: Regulatory sovereignty under TRIPS; available at: http://www. ip.mpg.de/en/pub/news/patentdeclaration.cfm.

Mazzucato M (2013). *The Entrepreneurial States. Debunking Public vs. Private Sector Myths*. London, Anthem Press.

McMillan M, Rodrik D and Verduzco-Gallo I (2014). Globalization, structural change, and productivity growth, with an update on Africa. *World Development*, forthcoming.

Milberg W and Bernhardt T (2013). Does industrial upgrading generate employment and wage gains? In: Bardhan A, Jaffee D and Kroll C, eds. *The Oxford Handbook of Offshoring and Global Employment*. Oxford, Oxford University Press: 490–531.

Milberg W and Winkler D (2013). *Outsourcing Economics: Global Value Chains in Capitalist Development*. Cambridge, Cambridge University Press.

Milberg W, Jiang X and Gereffi G (2014). Industrial policy in the era of vertically specialized industrialization. In: Salazar-Xirinachs JM, Nübler I and Kozul-Wright R, eds. *Transforming Economies. Making Industrial Policy work for Growth, Jobs and Development*. Geneva, ILO: 151–178

Miroudot S (2011). Investment. In: Chauffour JP and Maur JC, eds. *Preferential Trade Agreement Policies for Development. A Handbook*. Washington, DC, World Bank: 307–326.

Moser P (2013). Patents and innovation: Evidence from economic history. *Journal of Economic Perspectives*, 27(1): 23–44.

Natsuda K and Thoburn J (2013). Industrial policy and the development of the automotive industry in Thailand. *Journal of the Asia Pacific Economy*, 18(3): 413–437.

Naudé W (2010). Industrial policy: Old and new issues. Working paper no. 2010/106, UNU-WIDER, Helsinki.

Neumayer E, Nunnenkamp P and Roy M (2014). Are stricter investment rules contagious? Host country competition for foreign direct investment through international agreements. Working paper ERSD-2014-04, WTO, Geneva.

Nguyen TTA, Luu MD and Trinh DC (2014). The evolution of Vietnamese industry. Working paper 2014/076, World Institute for Development Economics Research (WIDER), Helsinki.

Nicita A, Olarreaga M and Silva P (2014). Cooperation in the tariff waters of the World Trade Organization. Policy Issues in International Trade and Commodities Study Series No. 62. UNCTAD, Geneva.

Nolan P (2012). *Is China Buying the World?* Cambridge and Malden, Polity.

Nübler I (2014). A theory of capabilities for productive transformation: Learning to catch up. In: Salazar-Xirinachs JM, Nübler I and Kozul-Wright R, eds. *Transforming Economies. Making Industrial Policy Work for Growth, Jobs and Development*. Geneva, ILO: 113–149.

OECD (2013). *Interconnected Economies. Benefiting from Global Value Chains*. Paris.

Orefice G (2014). International migration and trade agreements: The new role of PTAs. *Canadian Journal of Economics*, forthcoming.

Orefice G and Rocha N (2014). Deep integration and production networks: An empirical analysis. *The World Economy*, 37(1): 106–136.

Owen G (2012). Industrial policy in Europe since the Second World War. What has been learnt? Occasional paper no. 1/2012, European Centre for International political Economy, Brussels.

Pack H and Saggi K (2006). The case for industrial policy: A critical survey. Policy Research Working Paper No. 3839, World Bank, Washington, DC.

Poon D (2014). China's development trajectory: A strategic opening for industrial policy in the South. UNCTAD discussion paper, forthcoming. Geneva, UNCTAD.

Price DM and Smart MJ (2013). BIT by BIT: A Path to Strengthen US-China Economic Relations. Paulson Policy Memorandum. Chicago, The Paulson Institute; available at: http://www.paulsoninstitute. org/media/102532/bit_by_bit_pricesmart_english_final.pdf.

Prusa TJ (2011). Trade remedy provisions. In: Chauffour JP and Maur JC, eds. *Preferential Trade Agreement Policies for Development. A Handbook*. World Bank, Washington, DC: 179–196.

Prusa TJ and Teh R (2011). Contingent protection rules in regional trade agreements. In: Bagwell KW and Mavroidis PC, eds. *Preferential Trade Agreements. A Law and Economics Analysis*. Cambridge, Cambridge University Press.

Ranis G and Fei JC (1961). A theory of economic development. *American Economic Review*, 51(4): 533–565.

Ravenhill J (2014). Global value chains and development. *Review of International Political Economy*, 21(1): 264–274.

Redding SJ (2011). Theories of heterogeneous firms and trade. *Annual Review of Economics*, 3: 77–105.

Reyes JD (2012). The pro-competitive effect of international harmonization of product standards. In: Cadot O and Malouche M, eds. *Non-tariff Measures: A Fresh Look at Trade Policy's New Frontier*. London and Washington, CEPR and World Bank, 167–185.

Rodrik D (2008). Industrial policy: Don't ask why, ask how. *Middle East Development Journal*, Demo Issue, 1–29.

Rohatyn FG (2009). *Bold Endeavors: How Our Government Built America, and Why It Must Rebuild Now*. New York, Schuster & Schuster.

Roncolato L and Kucera D (2014). Structural drivers of productivity and employment growth: A decomposition analysis for 81 countries. *Cambridge Journal of Economics*, forthcoming.

Salazar-Xirinachs JM, Nübler I and Kozul-Wright R (2014). Industrial policy, productive transformation and jobs: Theory, history and practice. In: Salazar-Xirinachs JM, Nübler I and Kozul-Wright R, eds. *Transforming Economies. Making Industrial Policy Work for Growth, Jobs and Development*. Geneva, ILO: 1–38.

Schrank A and Whitford J (2009). Industrial policy in the United States: A neo-Polanyian interpretation. *Politics and Society*, 37(4): 521–553.

Simmons BA (2014). Bargaining over BITS, arbitrating awards: The regime for protection and promotion of international investment. *World Politics*, 66(1): 12–46.

Sperling G (2012). Remarks by Gene Sperling at the conference on the Renaissance of American Manufacturing; Washington DC, The National Press Club; available at: http://www.whitehouse.gov/sites/default/files/administration-official/sperling_-_renaissance_of_american_manufacturing_-_03_27_12.pdf.

Sperling G (2013). The case for a manufacturing renaissance. Remarks at the Brookings Institution; available at: http://www.whitehouse.gov/sites/default/files/docs/the_case_for_a_manufacturing_renaissance_gene_sperling_7-25-2013_final_p....pdf.

Starrs (2014). The Chimera of Global Convergence. *New Left Review*, 87(May/June): 81–96.

Studwell J (2013). *How Asia Works: Success and Failure in the World's Most Dynamic Region*. London, Profile Books.

Su BW, Heshmati A, Geng Y and Yu XM (2013). A review of the circular economy in China: Moving from rhetoric to implementation. *Journal of Cleaner Production*, 42(March): 215–227.

Taglioni D and Winkler D (2014). Making global value chains work for development. Economic Premise No. 143, World Bank, Washington, DC.

te Velde DW and Fahnbulleh M (2006). Investment-related provisions in regional trade agreements. In: te Velde DW, ed. *Regional Integration and Poverty*. Aldershot, Ashgate.

Thirlwall AP (1979). The balance of payments constraint as an explanation of international growth rate differences. *Banca Nazionale del Lavoro Quarterly Review*, 128: 45–53.

Thoburn J (2013). Vietnam as a role model for development. In: Fosu AK, ed. *Achieving Development Success: Strategies and Lessons from the Developing World*. Oxford, Oxford University Press: 99–118.

Thrasher RD and Gallagher K (2008). 21st century trade agreements: Implications for long-run development policy. The Pardee Papers, No. 2, Boston University, Boston, MA; available at: http://www.bu.edu/pardee/files/documents/PP-002-Trade.pdf.

Thrasher RD and Gallagher K (2014). The soft foundations and hard consequences of "soft protectionism". Background paper prepared for UNCTAD's *Trade and Development Report 2014*. Boston University, Boston, MA, unpublished.

Tilford S and Whyte P (2010). The Lisbon Scorecard X: The road to 2020. London, Centre for European Reform; available at: http://www.cer.org.uk/sites/default/files/publications/attachments/pdf/2011/rp_967-251.pdf.

UNCTAD (2009). *The Least Developed Countries Report 2009 – The State and Development Governance*. United Nations publication, sales no. E.09.II.D.9, New York and Geneva.

UNCTAD (2011a). Report of the Secretary-General of UNCTAD to UNCTAD XIII, Development-led Globalization: Towards Sustainable and Inclusive Development Paths. Document UNCTAD (XIII)/1, United Nations, New York and Geneva.

UNCTAD (2011b). Trade Facilitation in Regional Trade Agreements. Document UNCTAD/DTL/TLB/2011/1, United Nations, New York and Geneva.

UNCTAD (2013). *World Investment Report 2013 – Global Value Chains: Investment and Trade for Development*. United Nations publication, sales no. E.13.II.D.5, New York and Geneva.

UNCTAD (2014). *World Investment Report 2014 – Investing in the SDGs: An Action Plan*. United Nations publication, sales no. E.14.II.D.1, New York and Geneva.

UNCTAD (forthcoming). Global Value Chains and the Growth of South-South Trade. United Nations publication, New York and Geneva.

UNCTAD (*TDR 1994*). *Trade and Development Report, 1994*. United Nations publication, sales no. E.94.II.D.26, New York and Geneva.

UNCTAD (*TDR 1995*). *Trade and Development Report, 1995*. United Nations publication, sales no. E.95.II.D.16, New York and Geneva.

UNCTAD (*TDR 1996*). *Trade and Development Report, 1996*. United Nations publication, sales no. E.96.II.D.6, New York and Geneva.

UNCTAD (*TDR 1998*). *Trade and Development Report, 1998. Financial instability. Growth in Africa*. United Nations publication, sales no. E.98.II.D.6, New York and Geneva.

UNCTAD (*TDR 2002*). *Trade and Development Report, 2002. Developing Countries in World Trade*. United Nations publication, sales no. E.02.II.D.2, New York and Geneva.

UNCTAD (*TDR 2003*). *Trade and Development Report, 2003. Capital accumulation, growth and structural change*. United Nations publication, sales no. E.03.II.D.7, New York and Geneva.

UNCTAD (*TDR 2006*). *Trade and Development Report, 2006. Global Partnership and National Policies for Development*. United Nations publication, sales no. E.06.II.D.6, New York and Geneva.

UNCTAD (*TDR 2009*). *Trade and Development Report, 2009. Responding to the Global Crisis: Climate Change Mitigation and Development*. United Nations publication, sales no. E. 09.II.D.16, New York and Geneva.

UNCTAD (*TDR 2013*). *Trade and Development Report, 2013. Adjusting to the changing dynamics of the world economy*. United Nations publication, sales no. E.13.II.D.3, New York and Geneva.

UNIDO (2013). *Industrial Development Report 2013. Sustaining Employment Growth: The Role of Manufacturing and Structural Change*. Vienna, United Nations Industrial Development Organization.

Wade R (2014). The paradox of US industrial policy: The developmental state in disguise. In: Salazar-Xirinachs JM, Nübler I and Kozul-Wright R, eds. *Transforming Economies. Making Industrial Policy Work for Growth, Jobs and Development*. Geneva, ILO: 379–400.

Wagner J (2012). International trade and firm performance: A survey of empirical evidence since 2006. *Review of World Economics*, 148(2): 235–267.

Warwick K (2013). Beyond industrial policy: Emerging issues and new trends. Science, Technology and Industry Policy Paper No. 2, OECD, Paris.

White House (2012). To modify duty-free treatment under the Generalized System of Preferences and for other purposes. Proclamation of the Office of the Press Secretary, The White House, Washington, DC; available at: http://www.whitehouse.gov/the-press-office/2012/03/26/modify-duty-free-treatment-under-generalized-system-preferences-and-othe.

World Bank (2005a). *Economic Growth in the 1990s: Learning from a Decade of Reform*. Washington, DC, World Bank.

World Bank (2005b). *Global Economic Prospects. Trade, Regionalism, and Development*. World Bank, Washington, DC.

WEF (2012). The Shifting Geography of Global Value Chains: Implications for Developing Countries and Trade Policy. Geneva, World Economic Forum.

WTO (2008). Fourth revision of draft modalities for non-agricultural market access. TN/MA/W/103/Rev.3, Geneva.

WTO (2011). *World Trade Report 2011. The WTO and Preferential Trade Agreements: From Co-existence to coherence*. Geneva.

WTO (2013a). Special and differential treatment provisions in WTO agreements and decisions. WT/COMTD/W/196, Geneva.

WTO (2013b). WTO Dispute Settlement: One-Page Case Summaries (1995–2012). Geneva.

WTO (2013c). *World Trade Report 2013. Factors shaping the future of world trade*. Geneva.

Wu HX (2013). Rethinking China's path of industrialization. In: Szirmai A, Naudé W and Alcorta L, eds. *Pathways to Industrialization in the Twenty-First Century: New Challenges and Emerging Paradigms*. Oxford University Press, Oxford: 155–192.

Yang C (2014). Market rebalancing of global production networks in the post-Washington Consensus globalizing era: Transformation of export-oriented development in China. *Review of International Political Economy*, 21(1): 130–156.

Zalk N (2014). Industrial policy in a harsh climate: The case of South Africa. In: Salazar-Xirinachs JM, Nübler I and Kozul-Wright R, eds. *Transforming Economies. Making Industrial Policy Work for Growth, Jobs and Development*. Geneva, ILO: 327–354.

Zeng DZ (2011). How do special economic zones and industrial clusters drive China's rapid development? Policy Research Working Paper No. 5583, World Bank, Washington, DC.

Chapter VI

INTERNATIONAL FINANCE AND POLICY SPACE

A. Introduction

To be fully effective, policies aimed at structural transformation require a favourable macroeconomic framework. This means economic policy must aim to keep the key macroeconomic prices (interest rates, wages and exchange rates) at levels that favour robust capital accumulation, domestic market growth and trade competitiveness. Macroeconomic policy must also avoid excessive instability or unsustainable domestic and external imbalances. In all these areas, international finance can play an important, but sometimes disruptive, role. Indeed, foreign capital inflows, depending on their size and composition, may increase or reduce economic policy's room for manoeuvre and, more generally, support or undermine growth and development.

Regarding size, neither extreme scarcity nor an overabundance of foreign capital contributes positively to policy space. On the one hand, scarcity may restrict the volume of imports of goods that are essential for speeding up the development process, in particular capital goods that cannot be produced domestically, to the extent that such imports cannot be financed by current export earnings. A shortage of external financing may therefore hamper policies aimed at supporting GDP growth, investment and diversification. On the other hand, an overabundance of foreign capital inflows usually generates financial bubbles, currency appreciation, current account deficits and rising indebtedness of domestic agents. These developments also affect policy space, as they weaken the likely impact of monetary and credit policies and the regulation of key macroeconomic prices. In the absence of capital account management, the situation in developing and transition economies that have access to international financial markets (and are thus also exposed to the vagaries of those markets) tends to oscillate from one extreme to the other: overabundance leads to the accumulation of external liabilities, followed by sudden stops or even reversals of capital inflows, possibly precipitating a financial crisis, which in turn is followed by a period of capital scarcity.

Economies are particularly vulnerable to financial instability when international capital flows are mainly of a short-term nature. Unlike the foreign capital that is used in fixed capital formation,[1] short-term flows are normally used for the acquisition of financial assets, real estate investments or consumption credit, directly or through the intermediation of domestic financial systems. Such flows are particularly prone to boom-and-bust cycles, depending mainly on events in the more developed economies. They exacerbate the fragility and vulnerability of domestic financial systems and lead to unsustainable current account deficits.

Indeed, excessive exposure to external capital flows and the fact that in large part they were not oriented to productive uses were major factors in the build-up of economic crises in developing and emerging economies in the past few decades, beginning with the Latin American debt crises in the 1980s. These were not only balance-of-payments and banking crises; they were also fiscal crises, as governments themselves resorted to external borrowing and, in addition, felt compelled to bail out private debtors and socialize their losses (Díaz-Alejandro, 1985). As a result, their fiscal policy space shrank dramatically as governments had to service their external debt while economic recession depressed fiscal revenues and access to private credit dried out. In such a situation, the only remaining sources of credit supply were official institutions (mainly the Bretton Woods institutions), which imposed policy conditionalities on their lending that placed the whole burden of adjustment on what then became debtor countries, and further altered these countries' policy space. This experience has been recently replicated by some developed countries that were severely hit by the global financial crisis that started in 2007-2008.

Partly as a reaction to these negative experiences, authorities in a number of developing countries have tried to reduce their dependence on foreign capital. They have sought to avoid current account deficits and reduce their external debts, and many of them have significantly increased their international reserves in order to lessen their external vulnerability. Some of them have been particularly reluctant to return to IMF-led adjustment programmes.

Therefore, there is a strong case for governments to manage capital flows by seeking to influence not only the amount of foreign capital movements, but also their composition and use. Such a pragmatic and selective approach to capital flows, rather than unrestricted openness or a complete ban, could help maximize policy space within a given development strategy and given existing international institutional arrangements. This chapter examines possible ways for applying needed policies in the context of financial globalization, as well as various obstacles to such policies (see also chapter V).[2]

Constraints on the ability of governments to introduce proactive policies can be either de facto or de jure. De facto restrictions on capital management refer to pressures from existing and potential lenders and investors. They may deem a country's capital control measures as detrimental to the "business climate", and may therefore reduce or threaten to withdraw capital flows to that destination. The risk of this happening may deter governments from applying capital management measures, but this could increase the symmetric risk of excessive short-term capital inflows as well as sudden outflows.

De jure obstacles stem from multilaterally or bilaterally agreed rules that forbid or limit a resort to capital management measures. For instance, countries joining the OECD or the EU commit to maintaining open capital accounts to other members, and within various regional trade agreements countries often pledge to liberalize trade in financial services.

Over the past 25 years, a large number of countries have signed international investment agreements (IIAs), either in the form of bilateral investment treaties (BITs) or as an "investment chapter" of an RTA. Such agreements provide for special treatment of foreign investors, which tends to reduce the policy space of the participating governments. A key component of those agreements is the "investor-State dispute settlement" (ISDS) mechanism, whereby national governments accept the jurisdiction of foreign arbitration centres on issues that might directly or indirectly affect the profitability of foreign investments and the rights of foreign investors under provisions of the IIAs. Such mechanisms have allowed international investors to sue governments and obtain monetary compensation for policy measures that, in one way or another, allegedly affected the profitability of those firms. Some of these measures consist of regulations directly related to the public interest or to development choices, such as public health, environmental protection and the kinds of energy sources a country opts to exploit. Others are related to macroeconomic management, including exchange rate management and restructuring of the banking system in times of crisis.

This chapter is organized as follows. Section B discusses the need for capital management and other prudential measures to enable governments to preserve their policy space for conducting macroeconomic policies and pursuing their national development strategies. It reviews the experiences of developing countries that were affected by volatile capital flows before and after the global financial crisis. It then analyses the obstacles to capital management policies and examines which policies countries can still apply – and in some cases are implementing – in order to avoid the potentially disruptive macroeconomic impact of capital flows and better channel them to finance investment and development goals. Section C addresses the challenges IIAs pose to governments, which face a trade-off between what they believe is a way of encouraging inward foreign investment while preserving their sovereignty in a

number of strategic areas. It examines in what ways and to what extent these agreements have reduced the policy space of governments seeking to implement proactive industrial policies, and thus possibly undermining the development contribution of foreign investment flows. Finally, it considers some of the alternative approaches currently being discussed by policymakers in developing countries to address the serious shortcomings of IIAs.

B. Capital management in an era of globalized finance

1. Capital flows and their impact on macroeconomic policy space

The traditional view on how openness to capital flows affects macroeconomic management has been termed the "impossible trinity" or "trilemma", following Robert Mundell, according to which a country cannot have an open capital account, a fixed exchange rate and monetary sovereignty at the same time. For instance, with capital account openness and a fixed exchange rate, the central bank would lose its ability to determine the money supply, because an expansionary monetary policy would tend to lower interest rates. This would cause capital outflows, and therefore reduce international reserves and the monetary base, hence cancelling the initial monetary expansion. The same mechanisms would work the other way to compensate for a contractionary monetary policy.

However, the reality is often more shaded, as countries do not opt for either complete capital openness or a totally fixed exchange rate, nor do central banks aim at full autonomy, and there cannot be completely closed capital accounts in the era of globalization. Hence, the real challenge seems to be how to flexibly manage the capital account and other policy variables in order to generate a favourable macroeconomic framework for growth and structural change at a time when the volume and pattern of

international capital flows exceeds the capacity of most countries to absorb them productively.

This section examines how the rapid opening up of developing countries to international capital flows since the late 1970s has affected their ability to conduct their macroeconomic policies in two major ways. One channel consists of the direct impact that capital movements have on key macroeconomic variables, such as exchange rates, monetary aggregates and interest rates, which in turn affect the availability and cost of domestic credit, asset prices, and consumption and investment decisions. The other has to do with the greater leverage of the main international financial agents on economic policy decisions. This is because policymakers frequently have to take into consideration the agenda, perceptions and interests of foreign investors in the formulation of their macroeconomic policies, since the portfolio decisions of those investors may have a significant impact on economic growth and the stability of domestic financial systems.

(a) Impact of capital flows on macroeconomic variables

Given the size of accumulated global financial assets, the impact on a country's macroeconomic stability of even marginal changes in its international

Chart 6.1

CAPITAL INFLOWS, 2007 Q1–2013 Q3

(Billions of current dollars)

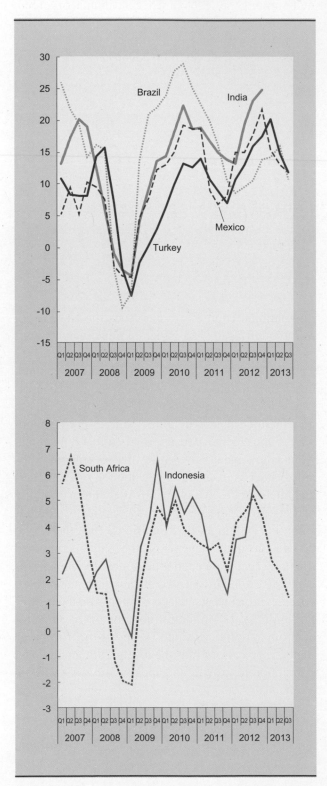

Source: UNCTAD secretariat calculations, based on IMF, *Balance of Payments Statistics* database.
Note: Capital inflows refer to portfolio and "other investment" flows (3-quarter moving average).

capital flows can be huge (Haldane, 2011). These flows tend to follow a global financial cycle, in which "push factors" in the developed economies where the main suppliers of international credit are based have more influence than country-specific "pull factors" (i.e. countries' demand for credit) (Rey, 2013).[3] Indeed, almost all the major "waves" of capital inflows received by developing countries since the late 1970s were triggered by expansionary monetary policies in developed countries (Akyüz, 2012), and were amplified by the leverage cycles of global banks (Bruno and Shin, 2013). But they were also influenced by risk perceptions in the developed countries' financial markets. Those waves usually came to an end with monetary tightening in the reserve currency countries. This pattern was repeated following the global financial crisis. Moreover, the capital inflows received by developing and emerging economies have remained synchronized since that crisis (chart 6.1). After the sharp flight-to-safety of capital in late 2008, resulting in a significant withdrawal of foreign portfolio and "other" investments from developing countries, capital flows to these countries recovered – or even surpassed – pre-crisis levels. This was at a time when developed countries followed very expansionary monetary policies and developing countries seemed to have successfully recovered from the global crisis. Alternating episodes of financial strain and restored confidence in developed countries, despite continued monetary easing, may explain the fall in capital flows to developing countries in mid-2011 and their subsequent recovery one year later. Risk perceptions also changed significantly, due to anticipated changes in United States monetary policy, as reflected in new volatility of capital flows to developing countries.

Since the global financial cycle is driven mainly by developed countries' economic conditions and decisions, there is no reason for it to be aligned with developing or transition economies' macroeconomic conditions and financial needs. Even though the major developed countries that issue reserve currencies have committed themselves to taking into account any possible repercussions of their policy actions for other countries, their monetary authorities are essentially guided by the needs of their own domestic economies. This can lead to inconsistencies between their goals and those of other countries. For instance, since the 2008 financial crisis, the United States Federal Reserve has been pursuing an extremely expansionary monetary policy to support domestic activity. This policy has effectively led to large capital flows to a number of emerging economies, as a result of which they have experienced a domestic credit boom and an unwanted currency appreciation. Conversely, the progressive reduction of monetary support in the United States may lead to a financial shock in emerging economies resulting from a reversal of capital flows, higher interest rates and credit attrition.

International capital flows generally generate a financial cycle in the receiving countries. Capital inflows tend to result in an increase in domestic banks' credit supply, a fall in interest rate spreads and an appreciation of domestic assets and the exchange rate. This provides a new stimulus for increasing domestic credit, as the economy tends to grow faster and higher asset prices improve the (apparent) solvency of borrowers. On the other hand, it also stimulates new capital inflows, including in the form of carry trade.[4] But these effects of capital inflows greatly increase financial fragility, as growing indebtedness and deteriorating current accounts eventually lead to a reversal of those flows and, possibly, a financial crisis.

In order to be able to create and maintain domestic macroeconomic and financial conditions that are supportive to growth and structural transformation, governments must have at their disposal suitable policy instruments to prevent or cope with these recurrent shocks. They must be able to follow countercyclical fiscal and financial policies, including through discretionary fiscal spending and adapting bank leverage to moderate credit during economic booms while preventing deleveraging during depressions. They must also be able to maintain key financial prices, such as interest rates and the real exchange rate, at levels that promote productive investment, expand domestic incomes and demand, and increase external competitiveness. This may require active intervention by central banks as well as complementary macroeconomic measures, such as an incomes policy.

A combination of macroeconomic and financial policies can form a coherent framework for a catch-up growth strategy and structural transformation. Such policies would include low interest rates, exchange rate management aimed at fostering a competitive economy, investment-oriented fiscal and financial policies, and an incomes policy aimed at boosting domestic demand. These would need to be accompanied by prudential policies that can regulate capital movements in order to limit any undesired impacts they may have on macroeconomic variables, such as those discussed above. But such policies face resistance by those who argue that financial liberalization contributes to the optimization of factor allocation. They stress that, in order to prevent negative financial shocks and make finance work for development, the key is to gain and retain the confidence of financial markets.

> The global financial cycle is driven mainly by developed countries' policy decisions guided by the needs of their own domestic economies …

> … thus, such a cycle is not necessarily aligned with developing or transition economies' financial needs.

(b) The confidence game

Following capital account liberalization and a succession of international financial shocks since the 1980s, developing countries were under strong pressure from international financial institutions to adopt confidence-building policies and structural reforms. They believed that such measures would contribute to economic stability and help reduce the likelihood of economic crises caused by volatile flows. Recommended policies included fiscal austerity and the adoption of corner solutions for their exchange rate regimes (i.e. either fully fixed or fully flexible exchange rates), which, supposedly, could withstand speculative attacks against a country's currency. Accompanying economic reforms were expected to include liberalization of markets and privatization of both State assets and delivery of essential services.

These recommendations, particularly influential during the 1990s, were closely linked to a broader set of adjustment measures that international financial institutions had been recommending since the external debt crisis of the 1980s (*TDR 2006*, chap. II). The proposed policies and reforms were based on an understanding that free markets ensure an efficient allocation of resources, thereby leading to both stability and growth. Therefore, it was suggested that countries should implement measures which would demonstrate to financial markets that they were opting for "credible" policies. Such confidence-building with those markets would attract continuous capital inflows and help prevent a full-blown economic crisis. Playing this "confidence game" (Krugman, 1998) forced policymakers into guessing which policies financial market agents would judge to be good for addressing specific economic conditions, even if these may not be considered the most suitable by the policymakers themselves and by a non-negligible number of economists.

A major problem in playing this game is that market actors' perceptions of a developing country's policies and economic conditions, and assessments of their sustainability, are frequently influenced by their ideological belief in self-correcting financial markets and their disapproval of public intervention, such as regulation of the financial system and countercyclical policy measures. In addition, their perceptions can change very rapidly, even if no change in such policies and conditions has actually taken place.[5] The result of these changing perceptions has been that, in times of economic turbulence in international financial markets, countries face a great deal of uncertainty as to whether adoption of "credible" policy choices would be effective or not in mitigating major turbulence effects on their economies and, ultimately, in avoiding an economic crisis. At the same time, given the close alignment between the markets' understanding of confidence-building policies and mainstream economic reasoning, governments have few possibilities to adopt alternative macroeconomic policies, even if they consider these to be more appropriate for tackling their economic difficulties.[6]

In particular, fiscal responsibility has been an important element in arguments for a confidence-building strategy on the grounds that market operators and rating agencies usually attach great importance to fiscal balances when they assess credit risk, not only the risk on sovereign bonds but also on debt issued by the domestic private sector. Indeed, this drives the view that integration into global capital markets has a positive impact on fiscal discipline, and therefore on macroeconomic stability.[7]

However, this view overlooks the fact that, in many cases, economic imbalances and related instability are caused by private excessive borrowing and spending, encouraged by easy access to external financing. This was amply demonstrated during periods of abundant capital inflows, which corresponded to periods of expansionary monetary stances in developed countries (such as 1976–1981, 1991–1997 and 2001–2007), when fiscal policy played a minor role in the rapid increase of domestic demand, rising private debt and deteriorating external balances. Conversely, when capital flows decreased or reversed, in many cases triggering a financial crisis, fiscal austerity – when applied – was unable to restore the confidence of financial markets and cause a resumption of private capital inflows. On the contrary, by further cutting domestic demand, fiscal retrenchment accentuated economic depression, and consequently, increased the perceived credit risk.

To the extent that they give rise to boom-and-bust episodes, large and unstable capital movements affect fiscal policy and fiscal space. This is not because they favour balanced fiscal accounts and low debt ratios, but rather because the financial crises they cause entail large fiscal costs, due to both costly bailouts of private banks and non-financial debtors and to public revenue losses resulting from shrinking taxable incomes. Thus, fiscal expenditure does not always decrease after crises, but its composition changes, with higher payments on debt servicing and lower expenditures on investment, social transfers and public services.

In the context of strong capital flows, countries have been advised to adopt either a totally fixed or a fully flexible exchange rate regime – the so-called "corner solutions" (Eichengreen, 1994; Obstfeld and Rogoff, 1995). They have been told that, by moving to one or the other of the corners, they would be better able to withstand an external shock, and thereby avoid a currency crisis, which could rapidly develop into a generalized economic crisis. Outcomes in the 1990s, however, have provided little support for this advice. Neither full exchange rate flexibility nor

> International capital flows generally generate a financial cycle in the receiving countries and increase their financial fragility, which can eventually lead to a financial crisis.

"hard pegs" brought about economic stability. On the contrary, they tended to exacerbate the impact of volatile capital flows. In times of monetary expansion in developed economies and growing risk appetite by international investors, developing countries lacked the macroeconomic policy tools to be able to absorb the resulting capital inflows productively and avoid major internal macroeconomic imbalances. Under a free-floating exchange rate regime, inflows led to strong nominal exchange rate appreciation, thereby weakening the international competitiveness of import-competing industries and exports. On the other hand, under a "super-fixed" exchange rate regime, inflows led to domestic credit expansion, asset price bubbles and an appreciation of the real exchange rate. In both cases, the result was almost invariably the emergence or deepening of current account deficits, making those economies overly dependent on continuous capital inflows. When these flows tapered off or reversed into capital outflows, policymakers typically responded by sharply increasing short-term interest rates and using a contractionary fiscal policy to maintain the confidence of international investors, thereby reinforcing the recessionary effects of the outflows.[8] They could not generally prevent a steep currency depreciation, its pass-through to inflation and a rapid deterioration of the balance sheets of those agents − including the public sector − that had net debts in foreign currency.

Following the crises of the late 1990s and early 2000s, most developing and emerging market economies had less confidence in the ability of market mechanisms to handle large and volatile capital movements. When a new wave of capital inflows took place between 2003 and 2008, most of these countries adopted a more hands-on approach to their exchange rate systems, generally implementing a "managed floating" regime in order to prevent excessive volatility and mispricing. They preferred to accumulate international reserves rather than passively accept strong currency appreciation.[9] In addition, adoption of capital controls in some countries and more prudent banking policies prevented the generation of new credit bubbles. As a consequence, most developing and emerging countries were able to apply counter-cyclical policies and avoid financial distress during the 2008-2009 global financial shock. However, this did not mark the end of the "confidence game". In the years following the eruption of the crisis, pressure by financial market agents in favour of fiscal austerity and against public intervention in financial markets

resumed. Fiscal austerity policies − particularly in developed economies − were deemed essential for "ensuring that doubts about fiscal solvency do not become the cause of a new loss of confidence" in financial markets, which could trigger a new crisis (IMF, 2010: 28). In developing countries, as explained in chapter II, renewed instability in the financial account of the balance of payments reinforced the influence of actors that asked for a more "market-based" approach in exchange rate and capital management policies.

2. The need for policy space for capital controls

The global financial crisis showed, once again, that finance should be regulated. At present, there is broad consensus on the need for better regulation of domestic financial systems. Efforts to contain bank leverage, shadow banking and toxic assets have advanced at the international level (e.g. in the Basel Committee on Banking Supervision and the Financial Stability Board) and the national level (e.g. the Dodd-Frank Bill in the United States and the proposed ring-fencing of deposit-taking institutions from investment bank activities in the United Kingdom).[10] Moreover, macroprudential regulations that aim to avoid endogenous risk and contagion within the financial sector, as well as negative spillovers from the financial sphere to the rest of the economy, are under discussion (Galati and Moessner, 2011; Moreno, 2011; IMF, 2013; Tarullo, 2013; Esen and Binatli, 2013). However, these efforts remain tentative and face strong obstacles on several fronts.

First, since domestic and international financial markets are closely intertwined, it seems impossible to regulate the first if the latter are totally liberalized. Indeed, foreign capital flows to countries have caused financial fragility when they have been too abundant and volatile, not only because they have afforded easy access to credit that encourages excessive risk-taking at the micro level, but also because they generate macroeconomic distortions leading to systemic risks. A more selective approach to capital inflows is therefore indispensable if those flows are to be maintained at manageable levels and directed towards productive uses. At the same time, supervisory authorities in the countries from where those flows originate cannot disregard the potentially negative impact resulting from the possible accumulation of non-performing credits in the balance sheets of their financial institutions, which would eventually weaken their own financial systems.

Second, large private financial actors continue to resort to de facto pressures and persuasion to discourage policymakers from applying regulatory measures, particularly capital controls. But while it is understandable that major banks and other financial institutions with direct interest in international transactions would argue against regulatory restraints by claiming that their profit-making activities are in the general interest, this is deeply misleading. Similarly misleading is equating trading in financial assets and liabilities with trading in any other goods or services, implying that no special regulation is therefore justified (see, for example, Fama, 1980).

Third, policymakers and international institutions have been reluctant to regulate capital flows. Indeed, there is widespread belief that, with sound domestic regulation, financial deepening and strong macroeconomic fundamentals, any economy can benefit from free capital movements, as such a framework would minimize the economic instability they might generate and maximize their positive impact on growth. According to this view, even if some kind of capital management may be necessary in exceptional circumstances, such as a balance-of-payments crisis, it should be the exception, not the rule. It further posits that in normal times countries should refrain from using capital controls as an easy but precarious solution, and instead address the structural or macroeconomic shortcomings that are the true reasons for financial fragility. With some nuances, this has been the position of the IMF and the OECD and, to some extent, it has been translated into the formal rules set by these institutions as de jure obstacles to capital controls. This last constraint on policy space merits closer attention.

Even though the IMF's Articles of Agreement explicitly authorize the use of capital controls, the IMF discouraged them for many years. In 1997, at the Ministerial Meeting in Hong Kong (SAR China),

> A selective approach to capital inflows is indispensable if those flows are to be maintained at manageable levels and directed towards productive uses.

its Managing Director even proposed incorporating free capital movement in the IMF members' commitments. However, the succession of financial crises that erupted immediately after the meeting, and the fact that capital movements were identified as a major cause of such crises, undermined support for fully open capital accounts.

It was only in 2012 that the IMF provided an "institutional view" on this issue (IMF, 2012). It proposed a planned and sequenced process of liberalization that would maximize the benefits that countries could obtain from foreign capital and minimize the costs of "large and volatile capital flows". Proposed policies would include a range of progressively deeper and broader supporting reforms, including reform of the legal framework, prudential regulation and supervision, and development of capital markets (including a deepening of domestic bond and equity markets and pension funds). The IMF conceded that "temporary re-imposition of capital flow management under certain circumstances is consistent with an overall strategy of capital flow liberalization" (IMF, 2012: 15), and can therefore be used to prevent risks to stability, together with macroeconomic adjustment and macroprudential measures. However, not all the tools were accorded the same status. It suggested that capital flow management (CFM) measures may be useful under certain circumstances for supporting (never for substituting) macroeconomic adjustment, but macroeconomic, structural and financial policies remained the primary tools for handling destabilizing capital flows. In addition, as CFMs involve some costs and distortions, they "should be targeted, transparent and generally temporary" and therefore lifted once the disruptive capital inflows or outflows had abated (IMF, 2012: 36). For the IMF, liberalization remains the rule, and capital controls a temporary exception subject to obligations set in its Articles of Agreement. In particular, the legality of capital controls would depend on their objective: a country would not be allowed to restrain capital inflows in order to artificially keep its currency undervalued, but would be entitled to do so for macroprudential reasons, or for avoiding excessive currency depreciation or appreciation caused by financial speculation (IMF, 2012).

Some countries have made specific commitments to opening their capital account. Accession to the EU, in particular, is conditional on full capital account liberalization.[11] Similarly, the 34 OECD members adopted the Code of Liberalisation of Capital Movements, which obliges them to "progressively abolish, between one another... restrictions on movements in capital to the extent necessary for effective economic co-operation". In addition, "members shall endeavour to extend the measures of liberalisation to all members of the International Monetary Fund" (OECD, 2013: 9). Each country may make reservations to free capital flows,[12] and the Code states that it cannot prevent a member from taking action for the maintenance of public order and essential security interests. Furthermore, some measures of liberalization can be withdrawn by a country if they result in serious economic and financial disturbance, or temporarily suspended in case of serious difficulties with its balance of payments. But again, such actions are supposed to be exceptional.

> In the increasingly globalized economy, it is impossible to regulate domestic finance when international financial markets are totally liberalized.

The rather stringent capital liberalization rules of the EU and OECD apply mainly to developed countries, although they also involve a number of developing countries, such as Chile, Mexico and Turkey, as well as several former transition economies that have joined the EU. However, the main de jure restrictions on developing and emerging economies in managing their capital accounts are imposed by international trade agreements. Indeed, as already discussed in chapter V of this *Report*, those agreements do not deal only (or mainly) with merchandise trade issues; they also incorporate a large number of provisions related to other areas, including capital movements. The most relevant of such agreements at the multilateral level is the GATS.[13]

> Capital management measures should be applied in a preventive way as a normal instrument in the policymakers' toolkit, and not as an exceptional and temporary device for use in critical times.

Since the 1990s, over a hundred countries have committed to obligations to apply a whole series of measures for financial sector liberalization as covered by the GATS and its Annex on Financial Services.

Those obligations responded not only to some private sector interests, but also to the general conviction of that time, that markets – including financial markets – could take care of themselves without jeopardizing the functioning of the rest of the economy. Events of the past few years have shown the dangers of such logic, and have spawned efforts to re-regulate finance.

But such efforts at financial regulation – even those agreed at international institutions such as the Basel Committee and the Financial Stability Board – may not be fully compatible with commitments on financial services under the GATS (see *TDR 2011*). Consequently, they could lead to litigation under the procedures established by the GATS which could affect access to markets for other goods and services. Moreover, because of the imprecise language of the GATS – and its Annex on Financial Services – the areas of potential conflict are vaguely defined (for a detailed analysis, see Tucker and Ghosh, 2011). As in other matters related to the WTO, when some regulation is challenged by a third party, WTO dispute panels and the Appellate Body should clarify the meaning of such terms as "restrictions", "regulations" and "prudential".

It is precisely because of the potential for conflict, that some contracting parties have tried to take preventive action by reaching agreement on the interpretation of some terms.[14] On the one hand, under article XI (Payments and Transfers) no restrictions on international transfers and payments on the current account (section 1) or on the capital account (section 2) may be applied if "inconsistent" with specific commitments. This means that capital controls could be challenged under this article.[15] Furthermore, under paragraph 2 of article XVI (Market Access), once commitments about market access have been entered, it is no longer possible to set limits on such aspects as the size of the service, number of branches, types of products offered, legal character, and foreign capital participation. Most of these considerations could clash with attempts, for instance, to prevent banks from becoming "too-big-to-fail", to impose "ring-fencing" between deposit-taking and investment banking activities, or to function as a locally incorporated firm – with its own capital – rather than as a branch of a foreign institution. These are all areas of financial regulation currently being debated, and in some countries already being implemented.

On the other hand, the GATS does contain provisions that reaffirm the right of countries to apply regulations. The fourth paragraph of the Preamble to the GATS reads: "Recognizing the right of members to regulate, and to introduce new regulations, on the supply of services within their territories in order to meet national policy objectives and, given asymmetries existing with respect to the degree of development of services regulations in different countries, the particular need of developing countries to exercise this right...". More specifically, in the Annex on Financial Services, art. 2 on Domestic Regulation contains a general reservation that allows countries not to comply, for some specific reasons, with their commitments on services liberalization, particularly that of financial services: "(a) Notwithstanding any other provisions of the Agreement, a Member shall not be prevented from taking measures for prudential reasons, including the protection of investors, depositors, policy holders or persons to whom a fiduciary duty is owed by a financial service supplier, or to ensure the integrity of the financial system. Where such measures do not conform with the provisions of the Agreement, they shall not be used as a means of avoiding the Member's commitments or obligations under the Agreement".[16]

Despite the ambiguity of the last sentence, this "prudential carve-out" clause gives a legal basis for governments to undertake capital management measures in a preventive way; in other words, *before* undesired capital flows generate macroeconomic disturbances. Capital controls would therefore be a normal instrument in the policymakers' toolkit, not an exceptional and temporary device for critical times.

More generally, beyond GATS interpretations, governments willing to re-regulate finance should

> When negotiating trade and investment agreements, governments wishing to re-regulate their financial systems should reject clauses requiring full capital flow liberalization and deregulation of financial services.

abide by that goal when they negotiate new trade and investment agreements. In many cases, they introduce clauses calling for full liberalization of capital flows and deregulation of financial services, in direct contradiction to the policies they apply or intend to apply in their own financial systems. In addition, as hinted above, the term "international investment" is sometimes broadened to include all sorts of capital flows, so that commitments not to restrict such flows would be much more stringent than what may have been initially intended. In such cases, legitimate efforts at capital management risk accusations of "murky investment protectionism".

3. Macroprudential regulation and capital management

(a) The need for capital management

In conditions of growing macroeconomic volatility caused by international capital movements, and given the relative inability of so-called "market confidence-enhancing policies" to bring about stability and long-term growth, developing-country policymakers resorted to managed exchange rates, lower interest rates and countercyclical fiscal policy. Since the global financial crisis, these growth-supporting measures started to find increasing acceptance in international policy circles, including among the international financial institutions.[17]

A number of countries managed to gain some room for manoeuvre in policymaking as a result of their accumulation of international reserves, reduction of external public debt and creation of fiscal buffers, made possible by a benign international economic environment in the 2000s. They responded to the global financial crisis by adopting a countercyclical fiscal policy and liquidity expansion, which helped stimulate their economies and support sectors that were more exposed to the external shock. They were able to use their international reserves to prevent excessive currency depreciation, thus helping to reduce inflationary pressures and protect sectors from currency mismatches in their balance sheets. They could also use those reserves to finance the larger current account deficits arising from expansionary policies and to counter any sudden contraction of external demand.

However, even these developing countries, along with their less fortunate counterparts who did not have the buffers described above, still face serious obstacles to more active macroeconomic policies in support of catch-up growth and structural transformation. An open capital account can present a severe constraint on autonomous monetary policy, which, for instance, could be used countercyclically when the economy is booming as a result of capital inflows, even when a floating exchange rate regime is in place.[18] Under these booming conditions, the alternative, as recommended by institutions such as the IMF, and supposedly favoured by financial markets, is to adopt a tight fiscal policy to manage aggregate demand. However, this policy choice can be problematic, since it implies spending cuts, generally in public investment. Yet, such spending is necessary to support sectors of the economy that are important for catch-up growth, structural transformation and social inclusion.

The pursuit of the policy goal of a competitive exchange rate is equally difficult. When a large volume of capital is flowing in, the central bank might have to intervene in the foreign exchange market to prevent currency appreciation by accumulating international reserves and undertaking sterilization operations to avoid an excessive increase in liquidity. However, these operations may be fiscally costly if domestic interest rates paid on issued bonds are much higher than those obtained on reserves.

These macroeconomic management difficulties suggest that a more effective approach to the management of capital flows would be to target them directly and up front, rather than just trying to mitigate their effects. For sure, it would be unrealistic to seek a complete delinking from the global financial cycle, and anticyclical and pro-growth policies in both the fiscal and credit spheres will remain of the utmost importance. However, reducing the volume and negative impact of unwanted capital flows would improve macroeconomic management and create the requisite space for pro-growth policies. Therefore, proper consideration should be given to establishing a framework for effective capital account management.

(b) Recent experiences with capital account management

Developing countries' experience with capital account management is nothing new, dating as it does back to the nineteenth century. Only a few months after many countries in Latin America had accumulated massive arrears on their debt service, and with some of them not being party to the Brady Plan – and running serious macroeconomic imbalances – a new cycle of massive private capital flows started. This was a result of the United States Federal Reserve's policy of near-zero interest rates as a solution to the fragile situation in this country's banking system. Many developing countries, not learning from their previous experience, again reacted to the easy supply of funds by introducing financial liberalization measures in the late 1980s and early 1990s. A few countries, however, created a specific mechanism of capital management to regulate the volume of capital inflows and their maturity. The ultimate goal of these controls was to mitigate the negative macroeconomic effects of inflows, such as exchange rate appreciation and the need for sterilization to address excess liquidity, which carried fiscal costs (Massad, 1998). Chile's experience with unremunerated reserve requirements (URR) is well known and has been widely discussed in the literature and in policy circles, but other countries also experimented with different sorts of controls during the 1990s. For instance, Colombia employed similar tools as Chile, and in Brazil controls took the form of an entrance tax on certain capital transactions, together with other restrictions, mainly on short-term fixed-income securities (Prates, 1998; Epstein et al., 2004).

Overall, controls on capital inflows proved successful in helping countries regain a certain level of monetary and fiscal policy autonomy, reduce exchange rate pressures and lengthen the maturity of flows. However, most of these controls were removed in the late 1990s, when capital became scarce with the onset of the East Asian crisis in the second half of 1997.[19]

When a new cycle of capital inflows started in 2002-2003, developing countries again had to find ways to manage them. Many countries responded by intervening heavily in their foreign exchange markets to avoid excessive currency appreciation and by building foreign reserves as a self-insurance mechanism. Other countries, such as India, never entirely removed their controls, maintaining restrictions such as ceilings on external borrowing abroad. The 2008 global financial crisis caused a sudden reversal of capital out of these developing countries, but it was short-lived as it was succeeded by a new cycle of large capital inflows, even exceeding pre-crisis levels in countries such as Brazil, Indonesia, the Republic of Korea and Thailand (IMF, 2011). As these flows again started to exert upward pressure on their currencies, in addition to creating excess liquidity, rapid credit growth and asset bubbles, several developing countries imposed new capital controls. Although varying in form and intensity across countries, these controls had the common purpose of taming the inflows in order to mitigate their negative macroeconomic effects.[20]

The measures adopted were related both to prices and quantities, including taxes on certain forms of capital flows, unremunerated reserve requirements, ceilings on different types of capital flows and derivative operations, and minimum stay periods (Ocampo, 2012). Brazil introduced taxes on portfolio inflows and later on derivatives; Peru increased its fee on the purchase of central bank paper by non-residents; the Republic of Korea reintroduced a withholding tax on foreign purchases of treasury and central bank bonds; Indonesia adopted a minimum holding period for central bank paper and a limit on short-term borrowing by banks; Thailand adopted a withholding tax on foreign investors in State bonds; and Turkey changed its withholding tax rate on bonds issued by Turkish corporations abroad, with lower rates for longer maturities. These countries also used macroprudential domestic financial regulations to influence capital flows, including reserve requirements on banks' short foreign exchange positions (Brazil), additional capital requirements for foreign exchange credit exposure (Peru), higher reserve requirements on foreign currency deposits (Indonesia), and ceilings on their banks' foreign exchange positions (the Republic of Korea).[21]

During the period 2009–2010, these measures helped countries moderate capital inflows, at least for some time. In addition, continued interventions in the foreign exchange markets reduced upward pressures on their exchange rates. More broadly, the measures provided greater possibilities for macroeconomic policy management in line with countries' policy objectives of macroeconomic stability and sustained growth. For instance, a few countries, such as Indonesia, kept their interest rates unchanged despite strong capital inflows and possible overheating, and South Africa and Turkey even lowered their rates, although this was intended to deter even more flows rather than to maintain a pro-growth policy stance. In the fiscal area, Brazil and Turkey continued their expansionary fiscal policy, while Indonesia, the Republic of Korea and Thailand abstained from pursuing a more proactive fiscal policy to curb the inflationary effects of the inflows (IMF, 2011).

However, this new cycle of capital flows is proving shorter than previous ones. Between May 2013 and February 2014, turbulence in the international financial markets hit developing countries twice as a result of announcements of (and later initial steps towards) changes in United States monetary policy. These recent shocks have shown that developing countries remain vulnerable to sudden reversals of capital flows. This is despite capital account management and other precautionary measures that many of them undertook during the 2000s to restrain speculative capital inflows and reduce possible fallouts from their subsequent reversal. Those precautionary measures included the accumulation of international reserves, a reduction of the external public debt as a proportion of GDP, a lengthening of debt maturity and larger local-currency-denominated debt, as well as more stringent macroprudential regulation targeting currency mismatches in the domestic financial system (UNCTAD, 2014).

During these latest financial shocks, some developing countries have been using their reserves to try to neutralize their impact on the exchange rates, but others, lacking or not willing to use their reserves, have been adopting standard policy responses such as sharp increases in interest rates in order to halt currency depreciation and contain inflationary pressures, as well as fiscal tightening to restore or maintain market

> Capital management measures recently applied by developing countries provided greater scope for countercyclical policies in line with macroeconomic stability and sustained growth objectives.

confidence. These policy responses demonstrate, once again, that implementation and maintenance of pro-growth policies are extremely challenging in the current international environment. This difficulty is aggravated by the frequency of financial shocks, which has limited the ability of affected countries to fully recover from previous shocks and rebuild their foreign currency buffers.[22]

This latest cycle of capital flows indicates that developing countries still have a way to go before they have fully effective capital account management. Indonesia's minimum holding period for central bank paper led non-resident investors to increase their holdings of government bonds, since the latter were not subject to the same holding requirement restriction. Brazil increased its tax on portfolio inflows twice, and extended its coverage to derivative transactions; it also introduced reserve requirements on resident banks' foreign exchange short positions to increase the effectiveness of controls (IMF, 2011) Indonesia's experience shows the difficulties that arise when controls are not extensive enough to contain inflows. Similarly, Brazil was initially timid and slow in introducing controls, and it was only after its policymakers adopted a wider range of controls that they succeeded in curbing inflows. However, the delay in strengthening controls meant that, by the time they gained teeth, substantial capital had already entered the country, so that it remained vulnerable to sudden outflows.

The lessons to be learned from these country experiences are that capital account management should be strong, comprehensive and dynamic enough to cover possible loopholes that investors quickly exploit to their advantage. Moreover, capital account management measures should be supported by an administration that has the power and capacity to implement them effectively. Indeed, based on recent empirical analysis, Eichengreen and Rose (2014) argue that adjusting controls in response to cyclical needs is easier if the countries already have controls and the necessary associated bureaucratic apparatus. Furthermore, controls should apply to both inflows and outflows, and discriminate between different groups of financial actors, so that they target specific investors as well as specific types of flows in order to be effective (Gallagher et al., 2012).

> Capital account management should be strong, comprehensive and dynamic enough to plug possible loopholes that investors could exploit to their advantage.

These recommendations for capital management go beyond those made by the IMF (2012). This is because capital account management is not just a means of crisis management; it also has a fundamental macroprudential, and thus preventive, role to play. This is particularly true in view of the limited effectiveness of more conventional policy tools, such as flexible exchange rates and austere fiscal policy, to prevent growing macroeconomic imbalances resulting from capital flows.

Thus, in the current international economic environment, the short-term challenge for countries is to develop a macroeconomic management framework that is sufficiently strong and effective to deal with volatile private capital flows. The long-term challenge is for them to develop the capacity to deploy a wider range of instruments to ensure not just reduced volatility, but also sustained catch-up growth. In addition to a coherent macroeconomic framework, development and industrial policies need to use other instruments and mechanisms of capital management policies.

(c) Channelling capital to productive uses

Reducing instability arising from volatile capital flows may improve the capacity to use macroeconomic tools for growth-oriented policies and social inclusion; however, it does not guarantee that inflows will be used productively. To ensure their productive deployment, this has to be made an explicit policy objective. Capital account management should be used to try to influence the composition and maturity of flows. Thus long-term flows should be sought, and those of a speculative nature discouraged. Similarly, efforts should be made to attract flows that are more likely to finance investment rather than consumption. Several instruments are available to policymakers for managing the capital account for this purpose, including unremunerated reserve requirements and minimum stay periods aimed at lengthening the maturity of flows, or forbidding certain types of flows, such as investments in derivatives markets. Domestic banking regulations can also be used for encouraging or discouraging different kinds of foreign borrowing.

Still, although such capital account measures may indeed yield positive results, their power to influence the end use of external capital probably is somewhat limited. Due to the growing complexity of financial markets, it has become difficult to establish, *ex ante,* which flows are short- or long-term, and which will be used productively. This difficulty applies to all sorts of capital, including FDI, which is commonly viewed as more long term and often perceived exclusively as greenfield investment. However, FDI may also involve short-term bank loans as well as potentially destabilizing hedging operations, and it may be associated with mergers and acquisitions rather than with greenfield projects.

Apart from uncertainty about the nature of capital flows, capital account management has only a limited capacity to direct capital towards productive ends because, above all, the ways capital feeds into an economy and how it is ultimately employed largely depend on how a country's financial system is structured and regulated. After all, most of the capital that enters a country is mediated by the domestic financial system at some point or another.

Economic liberalization and reforms, which the majority of developing countries have undertaken during the past 35 years, have consisted mainly of deregulation of markets and privatization. These, have deprived their governments not only of macroeconomic policy tools, but also of financial resources and other policy instruments and levers necessary for growth and development. In the financial sector, deregulation of financial markets and, in many countries, privatization of State-owned banks have substantially reduced the number of instruments of industrial, financial and social policies. Productive investment has been particularly affected by these changes.

The hope was that privatization of financial activity would spur productive investment, structural change and growth through a more efficient allocation of capital, that is, by channelling capital to the most productive uses. But this has not happened: the private financial sector emerging from these reforms has not, by and large, filled the gap left by the withdrawal of the public sector from this area. Indeed, generally, the outcome has been just the opposite. Banks and other financial institutions have increasingly focused their activities on the provision of mainly short-term finance – largely consumption lending – instead of the long-term finance needed for infrastructural and industrial projects.

Thus, given how financial systems distribute domestic credit it cannot be expected that external capital channelled through them will be deployed for productive purposes either. It would therefore be necessary to reform national financial systems and policies in order to restore a country's capacity to provide finance for productive activities (*TDR 2013*, chap. III). These should include the following: measures by central banks and governments aimed at encouraging maturity transformation operations by commercial banks so that they provide more long-term credit; credit allocation policies in the banking system to support specific productive sectors or areas that are vital for development, such as basic infrastructure and research; and establishing institutions, particularly development banks, specialized in the provision of long-term finance. Development banks are critical institutions for developing countries because they provide long-term financing not offered by private banks, mainly for projects that are development oriented and generate positive economic and social externalities. Since they have clear mandates to fulfil this role, their capital and funding structure is designed to enable them to meet these expectations effectively.

Brazil is among the few developing countries with a strong network of development banks. At the centre of this network is the Banco Nacional de Desenvolvimento Econômico e Social (BNDES), which provides loans and invests in firms' equity, as well as engaging in on-lending to other development banks. Funding for these loans and investments comes in different forms, including compulsory savings from Brazilian workers,[23] transfers from the treasury, government deposits derived from funds from privatization, bond issues and resources from multilateral organizations. Loans and investments are made in support of a wide range of industrial sectors (Chandrasekhar, 2014).

Like Brazil, the Republic of Korea counts on a number of development-oriented financial institutions, including the Korean Development Bank, which provides long-term credit for industrial activities drawing on funds derived from borrowing from the government, international financial institutions and foreign banks, as well as by issuing bonds. In Turkey, the Turkish Industrial Development Bank

(TSKB) is among the country's main development finance institutions. It is privately owned, as its equity capital base comes from the country's private financial institutions, but other sources of its funding also include the government and international financial institutions, such as the World Bank, the European Investment Bank and the International Finance Corporation. The TSKB is thus able to make loans and equity investments across a wide range of sectors of the Turkish economy. It also supports access by Turkish companies to credit from both domestic and foreign banks (Chandrasekhar, 2014).[24]

Examples of national development banks can also be found in some LDCs. Ethiopia, for instance, has three State-owned banks. One of them, the Development Bank of Ethiopia (DBE), provides long-term finance to priority sectors, as identified by the Government, such as commercial agriculture, agro-processing activities and manufacturing. Its funding base includes loans from the Commercial Bank of Ethiopia (another State-owned bank),

concessional loans from donors and funds from the central bank, the National Bank of Ethiopia (NBE), which are raised through bond issues. The NBE, in turn, derives its resources from bills issued by it for purchase by the private banking system on a compulsory basis (Alemu, 2014).

These are examples of national development banks that have a funding base that carries long-term liabilities, or that are supported by government guarantees, which then permit these banks to finance long-term projects. A World Bank survey covering 90 development banks from around the world found that 64 per cent of those banks benefit from government guarantees for their debts and other liabilities, allowing them to borrow at lower costs and transfer this lower cost to their own borrowers (Luna-Martínez and Vicente, 2012). Moreover, these institutions have the ability to borrow abroad and then channel the resources to productive activities, or, like the Turkish development bank, they can help firms obtain resources abroad to finance real sector activities.

C. Policy space with regard to foreign investment

Attracting foreign capital is not a goal in itself. As discussed above, it may have positive or negative effects on both macroeconomic stability and economic development depending on its volume, its nature and its use. It is not surprising, then, that different authors have not found any positive relationship between capital inflows and growth (Bhagwati, 1998; Prasad et al., 2003; Stigltiz, 2004; Prasad et al., 2007), or, for that matter, a negative relationship (Aizenman, 2005). It is therefore clearly essential to have national policies for managing these flows, not only portfolio and short-term flows, but also longer term capital, including FDI. How

> The contribution of TNCs to economic dynamism and diversification depends critically on the macroeconomic and regulatory framework in the different locations in which they operate.

much (or how little) TNCs contribute to economic dynamism and diversification, environmental conservation, technology transfer, tax revenues and a healthy trade balance depends critically on the macroeconomic and regulatory framework in the different locations in which they operate. Influencing their performance in some of those aspects has been a key ingredient of industrial policies, as observed in chapter V and previous UNCTAD research (see, for instance, UNCTAD, 2003 and 2012).[25] However, these tools have been progressively limited by the URAs, as well as by a large number of bilateral and plurilateral trade and investment agreements.

This section examines how policy space is being restricted by those agreements, and explores some possible ways to help overcome such restrictions.

1. Investment protection rules

(a) Rules governing investor-State relations

Traditionally, the main legal framework for foreign investment in every country has been provided by domestic law, which specifies the permissible investments by foreign companies, the procedures for their admission and implementation, and the obligations of investors. Domestic law also governs contractual relations between foreign investors and host countries. It normally guarantees to foreign investors settled in the country the same treatment by public authorities and legal guarantees as those accorded to domestic investors. In addition, several developing countries that give high priority to increasing inward FDI have passed specific investment promotion laws which provide various incentives to foreign investors, particularly tax incentives. In so doing, States are able to determine the content of their domestic laws governing investor-State relations and to resist, to a large extent, the jurisdiction of foreign courts (according to the principle of State immunity). In case of a legal dispute, foreign firms can resort to domestic courts, just like domestic firms (principle of national treatment).

This legal framework has seemed insufficient to potential foreign investors. Consequently, they have pushed for investment liberalization and supplementary guarantees for their property rights and expected profits. With the increase in FDI flows to developing countries and to several newly independent countries in the 1960s, international investors (almost exclusively from developed economies) sought the creation of a judicial body that would supplement or replace domestic laws and national courts in developing countries, which, in their view, did not meet high standards of independence and impartiality. The resulting North-South debate saw developing countries subscribing to the Calvo Doctrine that advocated the principle of national treatment, and the United States and European countries supporting the doctrine of an "international minimum standard" that required the protection of foreign investors under international law (independent from national laws).[26]

While the OECD conducted long discussions which eventually failed to create a judicial body that would supplement or replace domestic laws and national courts in developing countries,[27] the Convention on the Settlement of Investment Disputes between States and Nationals of Other States, negotiated in parallel under World Bank auspices, was adopted in 1965. This Convention still governs investment protection today. It does not contain substantive provisions in this regard, but provides procedural rules for the settlement of disputes through arbitration. To that end, it created the International Centre for Settlement of Investment Disputes (ICSID), which is one of the five institutions constituting the World Bank Group.

The lack of agreement on a common international legal framework for foreign investment despite several attempts since the 1960s has meant that there is no uniform regime governing investor-State relations. Different legal rules are found in a variety of bilateral and multilateral agreements concerning investment liberalization and investment protection (Schill, 2014).

Some rules on investment liberalization (e.g. rules reducing barriers to market access for foreign investors) can be found in international trade law. The TRIMs Agreement and the GATS contain investment-related regulations, as discussed in chapter V of this *Report* and in section B of this chapter. Provisions on investment liberalization, namely the right of establishment and free movement of capital, can also be found in EU law. Likewise, the OECD Codes of Liberalisation of Capital Movements and Current Invisible Operations contain non-discrimination commitments by OECD member States, and thereby aim at investment liberalization in specific sectors.

However, most of the new international rules are embedded in bilateral agreements among States,

> A key ingredient of industrial policy has been to influence TNCs performance, but it has been progressively limited by the URAs and many other trade and investment agreements.

which incorporate mechanisms for investment protection. By the end of 2012 there were 2,857 BITs and more than 339 investment chapters in free trade agreements (FTAs) (UNCTAD, 2013a). These agreements are based on similar general substantive principles, such as property protection and the rule of law, and generally include investor-State dispute settlement mechanisms (ISDS), which enable investors of signatory countries to demand the enforcement of the rights granted under the agreements by host countries. The above-mentioned ICSID and the United Nations Commission on International Trade Law (UNCITRAL) are the two most active arbitration centres. (When more than one possibility is allowed in the bilateral treaty, the choice is generally made by the investor.)

> Since the 1960s, international investors have sought the creation of a judicial body to replace domestic laws and national courts in developing countries and obtain supplementary legal guarantees.

(b) Growing restrictions on policy space

By creating a dispute settlement mechanism in the absence of a comprehensive body of law, investment tribunals have gained a singularly important role: instead of applying pre-existing rules to the facts of individual cases they have generated the rules themselves.[28] This strategy has given an extraordinary power to arbitrators, especially because the terms of bilateral agreements protecting investments are generally vague and the legal framework in which they operate are extremely loose.

Indeed, few standards of protection in international investment treaties are crafted as specific rules that have a clear scope of application and target specific behaviour. Instead, they are crafted as loose and open-ended standards. The concept of "indirect expropriation", and the standards of fair and equitable treatment, national treatment, most-favoured-nation treatment, full protection and security, and free capital transfer are all formulated in a manner that leaves considerable scope for discretion by arbitral tribunals. Case law has shown that they can also be applied to measures taken by a host government, even when those measures are in the public interest, including implementation of a national development strategy. In fact, States may find that they are subject

to commitments they never thought they were making when signing those treaties.

To begin with, the very definition of "investment" is not unequivocally made explicit in many treaties. What exactly is protected is therefore left to the judgement of arbitrators. A government may think it is giving special guarantees only to FDI, only to find out that other kinds of capital movements, in particular portfolio investments and sovereign debt, are also covered by a BIT. Therefore, in case it needs to restructure a foreign debt, holders of debt instruments (including vulture funds) may resort to ISDS to request the entire face value of the original debt instead of participating in the restructuring process (UNCTAD, 2011).[29]

Furthermore, the vagueness of investment treaty standards can unduly restrict the freedom of host governments to regulate in the public interest, and gives considerable power to tribunals. For example it is up to tribunals to determine what constitutes compensable indirect expropriation and non-compensable general regulation, the scope of national treatment, the content of fair and equitable treatment (FET), and the amount of flexibility it grants to government decision-making. In the latter case, the accepted interpretation of FET under customary international law (CIL) provides for compensation for denials of justice, understood as "denial of due process in court or administrative proceedings or denial of police protection". However, arbitrators have frequently adopted a broader interpretation of FET to include the right to a "stable and predictable regulatory environment", and therefore consider any changes in regulatory or tax policies as violating IIA provisions.[30] As a result, governments might find their normal functions circumscribed by the threat of having to compensate foreign investors if they introduce policy measures designed to respond to changing circumstances (such as financial crises[31] or new scientific findings) or to public demand with laws of general application (Wallach, 2012). The sole possibility of breaching an investment treaty can be sufficient to deter a State from taking any measure that might alter the business environment, even if this is necessary for economic, social or environmental reasons (so-called "regulatory chill").

A number of cases can be cited in this context, such as arbitrations in connection with Argentina's economic crisis in 2001-2002, water concessions in Bolivia, Argentina and the United Republic of Tanzania, an affirmative action programme aimed at remedying injustices remaining from the apartheid system in South Africa, banning of harmful chemicals in Canada and the United States, protection of the environment in Canada, Germany and Mexico, anti-tobacco legislation in Uruguay and Australia, and Germany's nuclear energy phase-out.[32] In these cases, the many vague legal terms used in BITs raise concern that arbitration tribunals may use them to curtail government measures aimed at protection of the environment, human rights and labour and social standards, or when dealing with financial crises, for the sake of investor protection, without considering the public interests involved.

The general idea behind the establishment of ISDS was to put "procedure before substance" with the expectation that this process would generate an accepted legal framework for international investment. However, this "procedure" has not been transparent and balanced enough for generating an accepted body of law. To begin with, this principle in itself transfers enormous power to a body of non-democratically elected arbitrators whose ruling often has been criticized (Eberhardt and Buxton, 2012).

Investor rights, such as receiving fair and equitable treatment, full protection and security of their investment, national treatment or protection from indirect expropriation, leave a wide margin of discretion to tribunals in determining the normative content of those principles and in applying them to the specific facts of a case. In fact, the principles of international investment protection are often so broad that it is appropriate to compare them with "general clauses" in civil codes that delegate substantial rule-making powers to dispute settlement bodies. Consequently, arbitral tribunals emerge as important lawmakers in international investment law when transforming the broad principles of investment protection into more precise rules which govern the way the executive, legislature and judiciary of a host

> **Critiques of the investor-State arbitration mechanism focus on its consistency, transparency and pro-investor bias, and on its adequacy to address matters of public policy.**

State must conduct activities affecting foreign investors (Sornarajah, 2008). They are often able to do so, not primarily by applying the principles of treaty interpretation as enshrined in the Vienna Convention on the Law of Treaties (VCLT) or by having recourse to customary international law, but rather by turning to and relying on arbitral precedent.

Such law-making through precedent raises concern because it enables investment treaty tribunals to take over a function that, in international law, is usually allocated to States, and that normally takes place through the conclusion of international treaties or the decision-making processes of international organizations. It is also problematic because there are usually only a few control mechanisms States can use to undo the decisions of the tribunals with which they do not agree and restrict the effect of those decisions as precedents for future cases. Sometimes, investment treaties provide for institutional mechanisms through which contracting parties to IIAs can issue joint interpretations of the underlying agreements that have binding effect on future arbitrations, but such mechanisms are still the exception. What is more, there is an imbalance between the potential system-wide effect of arbitral decisions as precedent and the bilateral structure of investment treaties in which States cannot generally be expected to monitor arbitrations to which they are not parties, or that take place under treaties to which they are equally not parties. This structure favours the interpretative power of arbitral tribunals to the detriment of the interpretative powers of States under international law. As these tribunals tend to treat the cases from the point of view of commercial arbitration, they cannot be expected to take into account the public law aspects of those disputes related to the scope of the host State's regulatory powers, including, for example, disputes concerning limits of emergency powers, regulatory oversight over public utility companies and the tariffs they charge, control or banning of harmful substances, the protection of cultural property or the implementation of non-discrimination policies. Therefore, they can hardly be expected to consider the interests of an economy as a whole and aspects of an overall development strategy.

(c) Increasing criticism of current arbitration procedures

Problems relating to arbitration procedure became more visible as more countries adhered to the system and more cases were brought by investors (Schill, 2011). Between 1965 and 2000, ISDS arbitrage centres registered only 50 cases (less than 1.5 cases per year on average), whereas by the end of 2013, the cumulative number of known cases had climbed to 568 (almost 40 cases per year on average since 2000) (UNCTAD, 2014). The most frequent critiques of ISDS procedure focus on its consistency, transparency and pro-investor bias; more generally, its legitimacy and adequacy to address matters involving public policies are increasingly challenged (see for instance Franck, 2005; Van Harten, 2007; and Van Harten et al., 2010).

The core of the criticism is that, while investment treaty disputes often involve matters of public policy and public law, the dispute settlement mechanism, namely investor-State arbitration, follows a model that has been developed for the resolution of disputes between private commercial actors.[33]

Such rules do not take into consideration the public interests that may be affected in investment treaty arbitration (Kingsbury and Schill, 2009). One procedural maxim is the confidentiality in investment treaty arbitration.[34] Confidentiality is a problem because those affected by arbitrations, in particular the population of the host State – including citizens and competitors of TNCs – cannot receive information about proceedings that impact their interests and their government's conduct.[35] Moreover, confidentiality restricts the possibility for domestic democratic processes to monitor arbitration proceedings and to assess whether they deliver a balanced and fair decision in foreign investment disputes. Confidentiality is also contrary to how disputes involving the government are usually settled in domestic courts, namely through open and accessible proceedings.

Closely related to the lack of transparency, is the issue of access of non-parties to arbitration, in particular those that intend to voice a specific interest relevant to the dispute. While such *amicus curiae* submissions are occasionally accepted by arbitral tribunals, the idea that arbitration is a party-owned process is at odds with opening up the proceedings to outsiders. This issue is increasingly often addressed in newer investment treaties and also in the 2014 UNCITRAL Rules on Transparency in Treaty-based Investor-State Arbitration, but it remains problematic in a great number of cases.

Another major area of criticism by several governments, academics and civil society organizations concerns the standards of independence and impartiality of investment arbitrators and their professional ethics. In this context, a problem is that there are no rules that strictly separate the roles of arbitrator and counsel within investment dispute settlement system. Thus, except in cases of so-called issue conflicts, serving as arbitrators in one case, and as counsel in another is largely accepted in the practice of investment arbitration. Similarly, the ethical standards applicable to arbitrators and counsel are often rather open-ended and vague, leading to standards of independence and impartiality that are well below those applicable in domestic court proceedings. A recent study showed that the most prominent arbitrators had accumulated several roles, simultaneously or successively, including those of counsel, academic, government representative, expert witness and senior corporate positions. From their different positions, they have been able to promote a system from which they benefit (Eberhardt and Buxton, 2012). Moreover, arbitrators have pecuniary and career interests in accepting cases on behalf of investors, and therefore in making an expansive interpretation of investment rules, which leads to more cases. An empirical study by Van Harten (2012) analysed how investment arbitrators resolved the admissibility of claims in cases on which an investment treaty is ambiguous or silent. He found that, in the resolution of contested issues, they tended to favour claimants by a broad interpretation of the investment treaty and by allowing more claims to proceed.[36]

The ease of suing a State before the ISDS gives the investor strong leverage against the host State. Even if it does not result in a final resolution, the mere

> Arbitration tribunals follow a model developed for resolving disputes between private commercial actors, and thus have no reason to consider the broader interests of a host country and its development strategy.

possibility of a case being taken to the ISDS alters the terms of any negotiated settlement. In several instances, settlements have included some payments or commercial advantages given to investors in exchange for their withdrawal of the claim which the host government would probably not have granted without the threat of an onerous fine.

The pro-investor bias of ISDS schemes can be partly explained by the incentives structure for arbitrators, but, more generally, it may also result from the very nature of the ISDS: it has been designed for providing supplementary guarantees to investors; not for making them respect host-country laws and regulations. Investors, not States, are the ones that can therefore initiate a case, and can even choose the arbitration centre. Therefore, TNCs with a presence in several countries can also choose the treaty they will invoke by establishing their residence accordingly.

Hence, international investment law does not include any enforceable obligations on the part of the investor with respect to, for instance labour standards, human rights or environmental protection. Rather, obligations that directly bind foreign investors are mainly contained in the domestic law of the host State. However, it is not always easy for a State to obtain reparation from a foreign investor due, for instance, to tax avoidance (case of Mali against Randgold; see chapter VII, section D) or to environmental damage (e.g. the case of Ecuador against Chevron). Indeed, sometimes ISDS mechanisms have been used by TNCs to retaliate against prosecution for their alleged wrongdoing.

This shows an asymmetry of governance in international relations: while investment protection is deeply enshrined in the current investment framework based on IIAs, competing interests, both public and private, rights of States and obligations of foreign investors are not enforced at the international level through comparable institutions. Moreover, while human rights are protected under human rights treaties and environmental concerns are protected under international environmental law, these international regimes have much weaker dispute settlement and implementation mechanisms than the investment treaty framework.[37] This also has a direct implication for policy space: governments that attempt to introduce policies in the direction of a progressive realization of the various human rights of their citizens, including the right to development, or to prevent their rights from being violated by the actions of international investors, may face problems related to the stipulations of investor protection in various trade and investment treaties.

Only a few years after the first investment treaty arbitrations started, the problem of inconsistent decisions and parallel proceedings became apparent. It arose after two arbitral tribunals constituted under two separate BITs heard different disputes related to the same facts, and arrived at opposite judgements.[38] Similar inconsistencies in arbitral jurisprudence also arise in relation to interpretations of identical, or essentially comparable, clauses in different BITs or to the same rule of customary international law by different tribunals. Notorious examples are the inconsistent interpretations of most-favoured-nation clauses − in particular arising from arbitral procedure and arbitral jurisdiction − the interpretation of umbrella clauses, the application of the defence of necessity and non-precluded-measure clauses in IIAs, as well as the treatment of procedural access to arbitration requirements.

The lack of consistency is an obvious obstacle to the strategy of generating the "substance" of international investment law through convergence in the jurisprudence of arbitral tribunals. Nevertheless, it seems that precedent is increasingly used by arbitral tribunals in different ways, such as adopting relatively cautious approaches, where precedent serves as an indication of the ordinary meaning of a treaty provision[39] or as a "source of inspiration"[40] for interpretation; or for more imposing uses, whereby precedent becomes a standard-setting device or even an instrument of system-wide law-making.[41] Nonetheless, the danger of inconsistent decisions persists because of the applicable law enshrined in bilateral treaties being couched in vague terms, whose interpretation is left to one-off arbitral tribunals rather than to a permanent and centralized judicial system.[42] More fundamentally, following precedents does not mean improving the fairness and rationality of the system if some past rulings were themselves flawed, and were neither annulled nor corrected by the ICSID annulment committee even after having identified "manifest errors of law" (UNCTAD, 2014: 3).[43]

2. The current debate on investment protection rules and policy proposals

(a) The need for change

As already mentioned, during the 1990s, there was a proliferation of investment treaties, including the ISDS, at a time when FDI was seen as the key to unlocking a country's development potential, and indeed was viewed almost as a goal in itself. At that time, the dominant economic thinking opposed active intervention by the State in the economy. In that context, it was believed that losing policy space was not a high price to pay for an expected increase in direct investment inflows.

This perception began to change in the 2000s. In particular, the impact of FDI on economic performance – including fixed investment, technology transfer, provision of public utilities, fiscal revenues, employment, exports and balance of payments – proved to be less significant and more contingent than expected in countries where it was not accompanied by strong industrial policies. However, it also became apparent that investment-related rules could obstruct the policies aimed at improving the impact of FDI on the economy. This was reflected in the sharp rise in the number of cases brought to arbitration mechanisms as a response to government policies in a number of countries. At the same time, econometric studies on the impact of BITs on FDI flows reached ambiguous results,[44] with several studies finding that the existence of BITs or other arrangements that incorporated investment protection had a minor influence – if any at all – on bilateral FDI inflows from developed to developing countries (see annex to this chapter).

While benefits from BITs became less evident, the financial costs they could involve clearly appeared, and they were sometimes exorbitant and difficult to justify.[45] From governments' point of view, the perceived cost-benefit equation of IIAs, involving the loss of policy space on the one hand and encouraging FDI flows on the other, began to change, prompting a general re-examination of such agreements – particularly of their main juridical instrument, ISDS mechanisms.

Somewhat paradoxically, new negotiations of investment treaties which mostly replicate the features of the old ones are under way at the same time as vigorous discussions are taking place about the net usefulness of such treaties, the serious problems they present for contracting governments, and the fact that they may not comply with some basic principles of international law. Those principles can be found in United Nations constitutional law and in comparable domestic constitutional laws. One basic principle is the protection of *self-determination* which reflects the right of host governments to set their development strategies independently and implement them accordingly.[46] The principle of self-determination therefore provides the basis for a claim for sufficient policy space and for allowing host governments to control and regulate foreign investors in the public interest and in line with overall economic policy and longer term development strategies.

The principle of *sovereign equality* requires that investment rules should not be asymmetrical or one-sided to the detriment of certain States.[47] This not only excludes treaties that impose obligations on just one class of contracting parties (i.e. capital-importing developing countries); it also excludes treaties that one-sidedly benefit one class of contracting parties and their investors, namely capital-exporting countries, without recognizing at the same time the duties of investors and their home States to ensure that both capital-importing and capital-exporting countries should be able to benefit from their sovereignty by being allowed to introduce regulations in the public interest.

The protection of *human rights* is a further principle of United Nations constitutional law that should inform international investment relations.[48] Together with the protection of property, due process and access to justice to all investors, national or foreign, this principle stresses the responsibility of host States to regulate foreign investors effectively in order to protect the human rights of their populations, including for instance, the right to a safe environment, drinking water and public health. This responsibility should also be extended to the macroeconomic and industrial policies needed for *development*, which is another essential objective of United Nations constitutional law.[49]

While problems arising from the current international investment framework based on IIAs are increasingly recognized (even by actors that previously championed those agreements), there is less consensus on how to resolve them. Some observers who believe the system should be substantially reformed propose a variety of changes, and methods to implement them; others believe that countries should avoid even entering into such treaties, and indeed should consider exiting from those they may have already signed, as discussed below.

(b) Reforming international investment rules, an arduous task

An essential characteristic of a good legal system is that it can be amended to correct its shortcomings or to be adapted to the changing preferences in the community it applies to. This points to another problem of the present investment law system: it is difficult to reform.

In the last few years, there have been a number of initiatives and proposals for reforming the current rules on international investment to better safeguard policy space for host States (see in particular UNCTAD, 2013b). Proposed reforms suggest that substantive standards in future treaties be clarified and improved, and the procedures relating to investor-State arbitration changed to ensure that investment treaties are interpreted in a way that is acceptable to all stakeholders involved.

> Recognizing the problems arising from the current international investment framework based on IIAs, some observers believe the system should be substantially reformed…

Regarding the first issue, clarifications of investment protection rules could include considering the breadth of what kinds of investment are protected under the treaties and who is protected as an investor.[50] Changes could specify whether sovereign debt should be protected as direct investment, or whether there should be special rules with regard to debt, as is the case in some more recent investment treaties.[51] Treaties could also reaffirm States' right to regulate in order to protect the environment, public health and safety, social concerns and cultural diversity, and clarifications to this effect could be introduced in the key provisions on indirect expropriation, and FET. These considerations were incorporated, for instance, in the investment chapter of the Canada-EU Comprehensive Economic and Trade Agreement, which stressed the intention of both contracting

parties to conclude a treaty that respects the parties' right to regulate.

Regarding dispute settlement, the Canada-EU treaty, as well as the EU's investment policy more generally, includes investment treaty provisions that prevent investors from filing multiple claims at the international and national levels, and rules that allow arbitral tribunals to filter out spurious or frivolous claims at an early stage of arbitral proceedings, thus avoiding high costs of a full hearing. Furthermore, transparency of arbitration proceedings is strengthened through reference to the new UNCITRAL Rules on Transparency in Treaty-based Investor-State Arbitration that became effective on 1 April 2014. Additionally, stricter rules on professional ethics for investment arbitrators are to be included in future EU investment agreements. In the Canada-EU treaty, the contracting parties have also agreed to a roster of arbitrators, thereby restricting who can act as arbitrator in the disputes under the agreement. This is a key issue, as one of the basic principles in international law is that arbitrators must be explicitly approved by all litigating parties, a principle that procedures in ICSID do not respect.[52] The treaty also states that the contracting parties have agreed to consider creating an appellate mechanism for arbitral awards in the future in order to ensure consistency and increase the legitimacy of the system. Finally, mechanisms for joint interpretation of the governing agreement are included, as are mechanisms for the contracting parties to jointly filter out arbitral proceedings in the financial sector.

This approach faces several limitations. First, even if definitions in new treaties are drafted more clearly and precisely, there is no guarantee that this will translate into actual rulings, as shown in the case of Railroad Development Corporation (RDC) against Guatemala. In that ISDS case involving the Dominican Republic-Central America-United States Free Trade Agreement (CAFTA-DR), the Government of the United States attempted to restrict the possibility of interpretation of "fair and equal treatment" by means of a customary international law annex, but the tribunal ignored the annex, still interpreted the FET broadly and found the Guatemalan Government guilty.[53]

Second, changes would only apply to new agreements, leaving all the previously agreed unchanged – unless they are renegotiated, which would require the agreement of all the governments involved. As the treaties will remain bilateral in form, any improvement will only have effect for the bilateral agreement in question. In this framework, restrictions of the scope of investment protected in some treaties may be circumvented by foreign investors by invoking most-favoured-nation clauses or by structuring their investments to come under a different treaty that provides more favourable provisions on investment protection.

To face the problems of such "piecemeal approach", other proposals aim at reforming the arbitration system all IIAs would refer to. Functioning of arbitration centres can be modified. For instance, a reform to ICSID Convention could ask contracting States to pre-approve a number of potential arbitrators from the Panel of Arbitrators established in section 4 of the Convention, limiting the discretionary power the President of the World Bank currently exercises.[54] More ambitious proposals suggest creating an appeals facility, or replacing ad hoc arbitration tribunals with an international investment court, with judges appointed by States on a permanent basis (Van Harten, 2008). Such institutions, it is argued, would give more coherence to international investment law: although they should still interpret hundreds of potentially dissimilar treaties, at least the interpretations would be more coherent than that provided by numerous ad hoc tribunals (UNCTAD, 2013b). But these institutions, while potentially leading to more convergence in international investment law, could also develop the law in directions that states did not foresee and may not control. Centralisation may lead to more coherence, not necessarily to more fairness.

Changes to the current system cannot be limited to processes. As discussed earlier, one of the roots of the present flaws of ISDS was procedure coming before substance. This put in the hands of a reduced number of non-democratically elected arbitrators, working without control, coherence or transparency, the role of generating a corps of law on international

> ... while others believe that countries should avoid even entering into such treaties, and indeed should consider exiting from those they may have already signed.

investment. It is not only the procedure for dispute settlement that must be improved, it is the whole logic that must be changed: substance must be redefined, in a way that respects the constitutional basis and principles presented in subsection (a) above. It must also recognise that the issues involving governments and a country's policy space are consubstantial to public, not to private law. Public and private laws do not only differ because they apply to different subjects of law, but also because of deep differences in their respective content and inspiration. Private law applies to private individuals that are considered equal before the law, while in public law, what is relevant is the general interest which is pursued by public persons. This is why different solutions are given to problems that in themselves might appear comparable or even identical (de Laubadère and Devolvé, 1986). In a nutshell, general interest prevails in public law interpretations, and private interests in those of private law. Re-examination of the legal principles should lead to a radical reorientation of how these disputes are handled: in particular, "a private model of adjudication (i.e. arbitration) is inappropriate for matters that deal with public law" (UNCTAD, 2013a: 116; see also Van Harten, 2008).

Can a multilateral institution provide an alternative framework based on public law? An answer to this question should examine several unsolved issues, addressing in particular that of the one-sided logic in which investors are always the claimants and governments the respondents. More generally, it should discuss whether it will remain a mechanism for solving disputes between states and private investors, or will need to provide a state-to-state dispute solving mechanism as does, for instance, the WTO. Furthermore, countries may want to preserve their own interpretation of public law, reflecting national values and choices, rather than accepting a uniform corps of law in which definition they may have little say. This has been a key concern, which explains the reluctance of most developing and also some developed countries to accept initiatives like the Multilateral Agreement on Investment (MAI), negotiated in the OECD between 1995 and 1998.

(c) Terminating treaties and reverting to national law

Strictly speaking, ISDS mechanisms do not address the problem that justified their establishment. If the judicial system of a country does not provide independent justice or enforce the rule of law (including the protection of private property), the appropriate response should be to fix those shortcomings, rather than allow a select group of agents (i.e. foreign investors) to seek justice elsewhere. This would tackle the root of the problem without renouncing important aspects of national sovereignty, and without breaching the principle of equality before the law by giving foreign firms an advantage over domestic firms.

For sure, improving the domestic judicial system may be difficult and may take time, but relying on a system based on BITs and other IIAs cannot be considered an alternative to such reforms, because such a system has serious legal flaws, sacrifices national legal sovereignty and can obstruct the pursuit of national policy objectives. Where necessary, filling gaps in the domestic legal system should be given priority over allocating scarce juridical and administrative resources to negotiation of such international treaties and defending the State from subsequent cases presented to ISDS tribunals. In addition, even if policymakers give high priority to attracting FDI, there is no solid evidence that these treaties increase such investment significantly (see the annex to this chapter). And even if entering in IIAs may increase the attractiveness of developing countries for TNCs, it would only complement other more fundamental motivations for FDI, in particular the general performance of the host economy (UNCTAD, 2009). Hence, if the loss of policy space and the financial charge those agreements may involve to governments affect negatively the economic growth, it would not only lessen FDI inflows, but also weaken their potential contribution to faster growth and structural transformation. From the host governments' point of view, they would pay a high price in terms of lost policy space and potential fines in return for few, if any, gains.

On these grounds, it might be sensible not to sign such treaties, a decision already taken by a number of developing countries. But what if a country has already signed? Renegotiating existing agreements may be an alternative, but it presents many difficulties, as already discussed. Most of all, it does not address the "original sin" of IIAs, which is reducing governments policy space by applying private commercial law to public matters (and, in addition, in an unbalanced way, since the claimant can only be the investor). The question would not be, then, just to obtain more "balanced" IIAs, but to revolve to public law, which privileges general interests over private ones. Another strategy pursued by some countries is to terminate their investment treaties and/or withdraw from the ICSID Convention. For example, Bolivia, Ecuador, and the Bolivarian Republic of Venezuela have withdrawn from the ICSID Convention; some countries, including the Czech Republic, Ecuador, Indonesia, South Africa and the Bolivarian Republic of Venezuela, have already terminated investment treaties or have announced the widespread termination of their treaty programmes.

The rationale behind such action is to once again have investor-State relations governed by domestic law and domestic courts only. For example, in South Africa protection under investment treaties is intended to be replaced by a Promotion and Protection of Investment Bill. In some countries this does not necessarily eliminate arbitration in forums other than ICSID and the problem of following different legal standards. Ecuador has proposed the creation of a mechanism within the Union of South American Nations (Union de Naciones Suramericanas – UNASUR) that would apply different legal standards.[55] Other countries, such as the Czech Republic and Indonesia, have chosen to retain some investment protection under other international legal agreements (e.g. ASEAN and the EU, respectively).

Terminating investment treaties and/or withdrawing from the ICSID Convention involve various preconditions and limitations (UNCTAD, 2010 and 2013a). First, in order to be effective, a host State has to withdraw from all of its investment treaties; otherwise, investors will be able to structure or restructure their investments so that they come under the scope of protection of one of the remaining investment treaties. Second, the termination of investment treaties affects new investments but does not usually immediately end the protection of existing investments, since most investment treaties have survival or sunset clauses that extend such protection to between 10 and 15 years. In order to circumvent the survival clauses in investment treaties, the Czech Republic has chosen a somewhat different approach to terminating investment treaties with the consent of some of its investment treaty partners. In a first step, its treaty partners have agreed to amend the survival clauses to state that they no longer apply; in a second step, the treaty partners have agreed to jointly terminate the investment treaty with immediate effect. Finally, concerning withdrawal from the ICSID Convention, most investment treaties contain the host State's consent to various arbitral forums, including arbitration under the UNCITRAL rules, or ad hoc arbitration. Withdrawing from the ICSID Convention only will therefore not signify a complete exit from the investment treaty and from the investor-State arbitration

system, although it may reduce an investor's choice by eliminating the institution that has been criticized the most with regard to transparency and fairness.[56]

In any event, retreating from an investment treaty remains an option that a sovereign country may take without depending on the approval of other actors, and it has an immediate impact on all new foreign investments. In addition, terminating a treaty could also be a negotiating strategy for reforming existing ones, pushing for a complete revision of the present system and recovering some policy space in the process.

D. Summary and conclusions

Foreign capital flows to developing and transition economies may support investment, economic diversification and growth, or generate macroeconomic instability, external imbalances and boom-and-bust credit episodes. The effects are highly dependent on their amount, composition and use. Governments need to apply capital management policies in order to establish a suitable macroeconomic framework for investment and growth, influence the amount and type of capital inflows and channel them to productive uses. This is also true for FDI, as its contribution to structural change, technological upgrading, access to world markets, employment generation and output growth depends critically on the regulatory and policy framework in the host country. However, different trade and investment agreements may reduce the scope for host-country governments to regulate capital movements and curtail their ability to influence the behaviour of investors to ensure that FDI supports their development strategy.

This chapter has looked at the ways in which developing and transition economies are affected by a global financial cycle that is mainly driven by developed countries' economic conditions and monetary

policy decisions. The resulting capital movements do not necessarily coincide with the needs of developing countries. Besides, given their magnitude and volatility, they tend to generate disruptive macroeconomic and financial effects. Indeed, international capital flows generally create a financial cycle in the receiving countries. Capital inflows tend to result in an increase in domestic banks' credit supply, and an appreciation of domestic assets and the exchange rate. These effects, in turn, tend to increase financial fragility, as growing indebtedness and deteriorating current accounts eventually lead to a reversal of those flows and, possibly, a financial crisis.

For macroprudential and developmental reasons, governments need sufficient policy space to be able to manage foreign capital flows, influence their amount and composition, and channel them to productive uses. In order to create and maintain domestic macroeconomic and financial conditions that support growth and structural transformation, governments should have at their disposal suitable policy instruments for managing capital flows and for preventing or coping with the recurrent shocks they could provoke. This requires the preventive use of capital management measures as a normal instrument in policymakers' toolkit, rather than as an exceptional and temporary device to be employed only in critical times. Several developing countries have recently applied capital account management measures that, despite some shortcomings, can be credited with reducing their financial vulnerability and increasing their resilience when the global financial crisis started.

There may be de facto and de jure obstacles to the implementation of capital management policies. The first is related to the action of financial agents and the second to formal commitments taken in favour of capital liberalization. On the latter, despite some diverging views, it seems that multilateral rules in the IMF's Articles of Agreement and in the WTO's GATS enable governments to manage their capital accounts for prudential reasons, including through capital controls. However, some new bilateral and/ or plurilateral agreements that have been signed or are being negotiated introduce more stringent commitments with respect to financial liberalization that might greatly reduce policy space in this context. Therefore, governments that aim to maintain macroeconomic stability and wish to re-regulate their financial systems should carefully consider the risks of taking such commitments.

This chapter also analyses how the rules embedded in IIAs could restrict governments' policy space and how these restrictions may impact on their development possibilities. Such agreements can help policymakers to focus on how best to attract FDI. But taking a historical perspective, it shows the changing perception of these agreements. When most of the IIAs were signed in the 1990s, it was believed that any likely loss of policy space resulting from those agreements was a small price to pay for an expected increase in FDI inflows. This perception began to change in the early 2000s with growing concerns that investment rules could obstruct policies aimed at improving the impact of FDI on the economy. This is reflected in the sharp rise in the number of cases that investors have brought to arbitration as a response to government policies, sometimes entailing high financial costs to States. Moreover, after several decades of operating IIAs, there is no strong empirical evidence that they significantly increase FDI inflows, which has been their main *raison d'être*.

The most controversial aspect relating to IIAs' impacts on governments' policy space is the ISDS, which takes the form of arbitration tribunals aimed at enforcing the general rules stated in those agreements. As those rules are frequently crafted as loose and open-ended standards, the tribunals have a wide margin of discretion in determining their normative content. Consequently, arbitration tribunals have become important lawmakers in international investment law, assuming a function that is usually allocated to States. In addition, the lack of transparency and coherence often observed in the operations of those ad hoc tribunals, and their apparent pro-investor bias, have given rise to concerns about the entire dispute settlement mechanism. This has led to different initiatives related to ISDS with the aim of recovering the space for national development policies. These include: (i) progressive and "piecemeal" reforms, including adding new principles for drafting sustainable development-friendly agreements and renegotiating bilateral treaties one at a time (UNCTAD, 2013b); (ii) the creation of a centralized, permanent international investment tribunal; and (iii) retreating from investment treaties and reverting to national law.

If the reason for establishing ISDS is to respond to failures in national judicial systems that do not provide independent justice or enforce the protection of private property, the appropriate response should be to fix those shortcomings, rather than allowing foreign investors to seek justice elsewhere. The legal framework for international investment based on IIAs and on ad hoc arbitration tribunals has failed so far to provide a legitimate alternative to national courts. As investment disputes often involve matters of public policy and public law, the dispute settlement mechanism can no longer follow a model that was developed for the resolution of disputes between private commercial actors. Instead, it should take into consideration the public interests that may be affected in investment treaty arbitration. ■

Notes

1 Long-term capital flows that finance capital formation may include greenfield investments and some long-term credit or portfolio investments. However not all FDI flows (e.g. mergers and acquisitions) expand productive capacity, and neither are they all long-term capital flows (e.g. intra-TNC short-term credits).

2 For an earlier discussion of related issues, see *TDR 2006*, chaps. IV and V.

3 Rey (2013) highlights the interdependence between risk perceptions, leverage and global capital flows, evidenced by the fact that receiving countries and regions borrow them at the same time. As noted by Rey, "There is a global financial cycle in capital flows, asset prices and credit growth. This cycle co-moves with the VIX, a measure of uncertainty and risk aversion of the markets." She further observes, "…one important determinant of the global financial cycle is monetary policy in the centre country, which affects leverage of global banks, credit flows and credit growth in the international financial system" (Rey, 2013: 17). Therefore, the volume of cross-border lending/borrowing is determined by events in countries where the big financial institutions channelling the lending are based.

4 Carry trade refers to capital flows motivated by the opportunity for arbitrage profits that can be had from differentials in nominal interest rates in different countries, and by the expectation of exchange rate appreciation in the destination country (see *TDR 2011*, chap. VI).

5 In discussing the interactions between politics, credibility and confidence, Martínez and Santiso (2003) show, for example, how perceptions of Wall Street investors about the sustainability of Brazil's national debt suddenly changed in a matter of days during that country's presidential elections of 2002.

6 See Grabel (2000) for an extensive discussion of the relationship between policy credibility and confidence-building in emerging markets.

7 A good example of this view is that of Domingo Cavallo, Minister of Economy in Argentina in April 1995, at the time of the "tequila" crisis: "Few would dispute that capital inflows of the early 1990s helped the Argentine economy. But I would argue, more controversially, that the capital outflows that Argentina has experienced more recently have helped, too. They helped because, in spite of the Argentine economy's impressive progress toward transparency during the last few years, some politicians still did not get the message (i.e. that fiscal discipline was necessary). (…) Thanks to the pressures exerted by the recent outflows, several important reforms that the executive branch had proposed to the Congress year after year without success have at last been approved" (Cavallo, 1996: 47).

8 For an early account of country experiences with capital inflows and outflows since the early 1990s, see Gavin et al., 1995; for a more recent analysis, see Akyüz, 2013. On the role of confidence-building policies in explaining macroeconomic outcomes, see Bresser-Pereira, 2001.

9 International reserves held by developing countries increased from $1,350 billion to $4,257 billion between the end of 2002 and the end of 2007 (IMF, *International Financial Statistics* database).

10 Developing countries have also adopted new regulatory measures in their banking systems, including supervisory rules and credit orientation. In Argentina, for example, the reform of its Central Bank Charter in 2012 gave that bank the authority to direct bank credit on various grounds.

11 Directive 88/361/EEC, June 24, 1988, art. 63 of the Consolidated Version of the Treaty on the Functioning of the European Union.

12 The most frequent reservations apply to FDI in banking, broadcasting, energy, primary sectors, telecommunications and transportation. Reservations are regularly examined by the OECD with the aim of assisting members to eventually withdraw their reservations.

13 The GATS is a positive-list agreement (i.e. countries list their commitments in terms of mode and the specific services they will liberalize, but retain autonomy over all other sectors (see also chapter V, section B.1)). It defines four different modes of supply for delivery of services: Mode 1 refers to cross-border trade, Mode 2 refers to consumption abroad, Mode 3 refers to the commercial presence in

the territory of another member (FDI), and Mode 4 refers to the presence of the service supplier in the territory of another member.

14 In particular, in 2009 and 2011, the Republic of Ecuador, at the Committee of Trade in Financial Services of WTO, argued for the need to clarify the wording of some articles of GATS and the Annex on Financial Services relating to macroprudential measures and, most specifically, capital flows management. The issue was far from settled but remained on the agenda of the Committee. Subsequently, at its meeting in March 2013, various countries made presentations on their macroprudential framework, but no consensus was reached as to whether their framework was compatible with the relevant GATS provisions.

15 Also, under art. XVI (Market Access), part III, if a Member has granted access to a service provided from the territory of another Member, it must allow the capital movements which are "essentially part" or "related" to the provision of such a service.

16 At first glance, the second sentence seems to cancel the first one, that is, there would be no room to regulate anything going against a commitment previously entered into. But it has been argued that, first, the statement, "notwithstanding any other provisions of the Agreement…", provides an exception for measures taken for prudential reasons, which could mean that even if inconsistent with a member's general obligations and specific commitments, they would still be legally allowed. Second, the list of prudential measures is merely indicative, as revealed by the word, "including". Therefore, any other measure taken for "prudential reasons" could be acceptable. Moreover the measure may not even have to be "prudential", but simply taken for "prudential reasons". Third, as to the second sentence, it has been argued that it only imposes an obligation of good faith in adopting those "measures for prudential reasons", implying that they cannot be ad hoc in order to avoid obligations entered into (see Leroux, 2002; Von Bogdandy and Windsor, 2008).

17 However, this acceptance is not uniform, as mentioned above when discussing the IMF's ambiguous position vis-à-vis such policies.

18 See, for example, Rey (2013), who argues that, in international macroeconomics, countries do not face a "trilemma" but a "dilemma"; that is to say, that "independent monetary policies are possible if, and only if, the capital account is managed".

19 In Chile, capital controls implemented in the early 1990s enlarged not only monetary policy space, but fiscal space as well. As the new elected government intended to expand public expenditure and social transfers, it sought to control aggregate demand and inflation by raising interest rates, and the only way to prevent this from leading to excessive capital inflows that would have affected monetary policy was by means of capital controls on inward FDI. In 1998, Malaysia responded to the crisis in the region by adopting controls on capital outflows − rather than on inflows as other countries had done in the early 1990s − in order to stem these outflows and regain control over macroeconomic policy (Ariyoshi et al., 2000).

20 See, for example, Eichengreen and Rose (2014), who discuss the rationale underlying the adoption of these controls by countries like Brazil, Indonesia, Thailand and the Republic of Korea.

21 Although the focus was on restraining inflows, some countries, such as Peru, the Republic of Korea and South Africa, also changed their regulations aimed at encouraging more capital outflows (IMF, 2011: 30–34).

22 See, for example, IADB (2014), which notes that in Latin America, for instance, both actual and structural fiscal balances have deteriorated alongside the increase in public debt ratios since the 2008 global crisis. This emphasizes the need to rebuild buffers in the region to give countries sufficient fiscal capacity to respond to future shocks.

23 In Brazil, the Fundo de Garantia de Tempo de Serviço (FGTS) is a severance indemnity fund for workers, generated by mandatory contributions by employers of up to 8 per cent of wages, which are deposited in a public development bank, the Caixa Econômica Federal.

24 See also: IDFC, 2014, at: http://www.idfc.org/Members/tskb.aspx (accessed 21 March 2014).

25 According to UNCTAD (2003: 87), "Attracting FDI may not be enough to ensure that a host country derives its full economic benefits. Free markets may not lead foreign investors to transfer enough new technology or to transfer it effectively and at the depth desired by a host country. But policies can induce investors to act in ways that enhance the development impact—by building local capabilities, using local suppliers and upgrading local skills, technological capabilities and infrastructure." More recently, UNCTAD (2012: 102) included among the "key investment policy challenges" the need to "connect the investment policy framework to an overall development strategy or industrial development policy that works in the context of national economies, and to ensure coherence with other policy areas, including overall private sector or enterprise development, and policies in support of technological advancement, international trade and job creation. 'New generation' investment policies increasingly incorporate targeted objectives to channel investment to areas key for economic or industrial development and for the build-up, maintenance and improvement of productive capacity and international competitiveness."

26 The UN Resolution 1803 of the General Assembly of 1962 on Permanent Sovereignty over Natural Resources, UN Doc A/RES/1803(XVII), 2 I.L.M. 223 (1963) represents a compromise on this issue, although it clearly recognizes the ownership of natural resources by the people of the producing countries.

27 Draft Convention on the Protection of Foreign Property and Resolution of the Council of the OECD on the Draft Convention, 7 I.L.M. 117 (1968).

28 When creating the ICSID in the mid-1960s, Aron Broches, then General Counsel of the World Bank, championed the formula, "putting the procedure before substance". In order to overcome the impasse in finding a global consensus on rules of property protection during the times of decolonization and the Cold War, he advocated setting up a framework for resolving investor-State disputes that could work out substantive rules on the go.

29 Three cases against Argentina have been accepted by ICSID, under the Argentina-Italy BIT.

30 Some treaties include partial exceptions for taxation measures, stating that if both home and host governments agree within the specified period that a tax measure is not expropriation, then the investor cannot challenge that tax measure under the ISDS.

31 For instance, Argentina was forced to sharply devalue its currency in early 2002, which resulted in a large number of claims against the country. Similarly, a claim was opened against Cyprus for taking over a bank in 2012 to avoid the implosion of its banking system, and another against Greece due to its renegotiation of sovereign bonds.

32 See respectively: 1) CMS Gas Transmission Co v. Argentine Republic, ICSID Case No. ARB/01/8, Award, 12 May 2005; LG&E Energy Corp, LG&E Capital Corp, LG&E International Inc v. Argentine Republic, ICSID Case No. ARB/02/1, Decision on Liability, 3 October 2006; BG Group plc v. Republic of Argentina, UNCITRAL, Final Award, 24 December 2007; Continental Casualty Co v. Argentine Republic, ICSID Case No. ARB/03/9, Award, 5 September 2008; National Grid plc v. Argentine Republic, UNCITRAL, Award, 3 November 2008; 2) Aguas del Tunari SA v. Republic of Bolivia ICSID Case No. ARB/02/3, Decision on Respondent's Objections to Jurisdiction, 21 October 2005; Suez, Sociedad General de Aguas de Barcelona SA, and Vivendi Universal SA v. Argentine Republic, ICSID Case No ARB/03/19 and AWG Group v. Argentine Republic, Decision on Liability, 30 July 2010; Biwater Gauff (Tanzania) Ltd v. United Republic of Tanzania, ICSID Case No. ARB/05/22, Award, 24 July 2008; 3) Piero Foresti, Ida Laura de Carli and ors v. Republic of South Africa, ICSID Case No. ARB(AF)/07/1, Award, 4 August 2010; 4) Methanex Corp v. US, UNCITRAL/NAFTA, Final Award of the Tribunal on Jurisdiction

and Merits, 3 August 2005; Chemtura Corp (formely Crompton Corp) v. Canada, UNCITRAL/NAFTA, Award, 2 August 2010; 5) Vattenfall AB, Vattenfall Europe AG, Vattenfall Europe Generation AG & Co KG v. Federal Republic of Germany, ICSID Case No. ARB/09/6, Request for Arbitration, 30 March 2009; Metalclad Corporation v. The United Mexican States, ICSID Case No. ARB(AF)/97/1 (NAFTA), Award, 30 August 2000; SD Myers, Inc v. Canada, UNCITRAL (NAFTA), Partial Award, 13 November 2000; 6) FTR Holding SA, Philip Morris Products S.A. and Abal Hermanos SA v. Oriental Republic of Uruguay, ICSID Case No. ARB/10/7, Notice of Arbitration, 19 February 2010 (pending); Philip Morris Asia Limited v. Australia, UNCITRAL, Notice of Arbitration, 21 November 2011 (pending); and 7) Vattenfall AB and others v. Federal Republic of Germany, ICSID Case No. ARB/12/12, registered 31 May 2012 (pending).

33 In fact, many investment disputes rely on the same dispute settlement rules as those applicable in private-private arbitration, such as the rules of the Arbitration Institute of the Stockholm Chamber of Commerce, or in some cases those of the International Chamber of Commerce, or are modelled on such rules, such as the UNCITRAL Arbitration Rules.

34 Recently, some positive developments have taken place towards more transparency, inter alia in NAFTA and in other more recent investment treaties, in the revisions in 2006 of the ICSID Arbitration Rules and under the new 2014 UNCITRAL Rules on Transparency in Treaty-based Investor-State Arbitration.

35 The arbitration concerning Germany's nuclear power phase-out, for instance, remains confidential; only the registration of the case and some procedural details about it are known and available on the ICSID website.

36 Van Harten (2012) examined the frequency of expansive and restrictive interpretation of rules on issues on which the text of an investment treaty is ambiguous or silent. Resolutions of an issue from an expansive interpretation tend to favour claimants and allow more claims to proceed. The study found "tentative evidence of systemic bias" resulting from expansive interpretations of the treaties, based on the resolution of four issues: the concept (large or strict) of investment, the acceptability of claims presented by minority shareholders, the acceptability of claims by corporations when the ownership of the investment extends through a chain of companies running from the host to the home State via a third State; and the acceptability of parallel claims. That bias was even greater when the claimant was from a Western capital-exporting State.

37 For instance, human rights complaints, whether before one of the regional human rights courts or

before the committees in the universal regime, are only accessible regularly after the exhaustion of local remedies; in international environmental law, individual access is even more limited. This leads to an asymmetric enforcement of international norms on investment protection to the detriment of other international legal regimes.

38 The case referred to an investment in the telecommunications sector in the Czech Republic. One proceeding was brought by the investor itself, and the other by its shareholders. Even though the applicable BITs were virtually identical, one tribunal held the respondent State liable for approximately $270 million in damages, while the other found no compensable wrongdoing. Compare CME Czech Republic B.V. v. The Czech Republic, UNCITRAL, Partial Award, 13. 13 Sept. 2001, Final Award, 14 March 2003, with Ronald S. Lauder v. The Czech Republic, UNCITRAL, Final Award, 3 Sept. 2001.

39 See, for example, Azurix Corp. V. Argentine Republic, ICSID Case No. ARB/01/12, Award, 14 July 2006, para. 391.

40 AES Corp. V. Argentina, ICSID Case No. Arb/02/17, Decision on Jurisdiction, 26 April 2005, para. 31. A similar approach may be found in Gas Natural v. Argentina, ICSID Case No. ARB/03/10, Decision on Jurisdiction, 17 July 2005, para. 36. Similarly, Romak S.A. v. Republic of Uzbekistan, UNCITRAL, PCA Case No. AA280, Award, 26 November 2009, para. 170; Chevron Corp. and Texaco Petroleum Co. V. Republic of Ecuador, UNCITRAL, PCA Case No. 34877, Partial Award on the Merits, 30 March 2010, para. 164.

41 On the different uses of precedent in international law, see Jacob, 2011.

42 UNCTAD (2014) presents a number of decisions taken in 2013 as examples of contradictory interpretations.

43 See CMS Gas Transmission Company v. the Republic of Argentina, ICSID Case No ARB/01/8, Decision of the ad hoc Committee on the application of the annulment, 25 September 2007.

44 See UNCTAD (2009), Annex: A summary of econometric studies on the impact of BITs on FDI.

45 Up to now, the highest award was ruled against Ecuador, which was sentenced to pay $1.8 billion because it terminated the contract with an oil company that had failed to comply with its conditions. See *Occidental Petroleum Corporation and Occidental Exploration and Production Company v. The Republic of Ecuador* (ICSID Case No. ARB/06/11), Award 5 October 2012.

46 See United Nations Charter Art. 1(2), and Art. 2(7) (regarding non-interference in matters of domestic jurisdiction).

47 UN Charter, Art. 2(1).

48 UN Charter, Preamble, Recital 2, Art. 55(c).

49 UN Charter, Preamble, Recital 3 ("social progress"), Art. 55 ff.

50 To help design investment treaties that strengthen the development dimension, rebalance rights and obligations of States and investors, and that manage the systemic complexity of the IIA regime, UNCTAD (2012) presents a detailed list of alternative model clauses on every issue usually included in an investment treaty, starting with definitions of investment and investor, and including substantive standards, such as indirect expropriation and fair and equitable treatment, and provisions relating to investor-State dispute settlement.

51 For example, the Peru-Republic of Korea Free Trade Agreement which entered into force on 1 August 2011, states (in annex 9d): "The Parties recognize that the purchase of debt issued by a Party entails commercial risk. For greater certainty, no award may be made in favor of a disputing investor for a claim with respect to default or non-payment of debt issued by a Party unless the disputing investor meets its burden of proving that such default or non-payment constitutes an uncompensated expropriation [...] or a breach of any other obligation under this Chapter." And: "No claim that a restructuring of debt issued by a Party breaches an obligation under this Chapter may be submitted to, or if already submitted continue in, arbitration under this Chapter if the restructuring is a negotiated restructuring at the time of submission, or becomes a negotiated restructuring as per such submission, except for a claim that the restructuring violates Article 9.3 or 9.4 [i.e. national treatment or MFN treatment]."

52 Article 37.2 (b) states: "Where the parties do not agree upon the number arbitrators and the method of their appointment, the Tribunal shall consist of three arbitrators, one arbitrator appointed by each party and the third, who shall be the president of the Tribunal, appointed by agreement of the parties." Article 38 states: "If the Tribunal shall not have been constituted within 90 days after notice of registration of the request has been dispatched by the Secretary-General in accordance with paragraph (3) of Article 36, or such other period as the parties may agree, the Chairman shall, at the request of either party and after consulting both parties as far as possible, appoint the arbitrator or arbitrators not yet appointed." Article 5 specifies that "The President of the Bank shall be ex officio Chairman of the Administrative Council (hereinafter called the Chairman)." A reform to ICSID Convention could ask contracting States to pre-approve a number of potential arbitrators from the Panel of Arbitrators established in section 4 of the Convention.

53 See: http://www.citizen.org/documents/RDCvs-Guatemala-Memo.pdf. Various attempts to narrow FET have all been ignored by ISDS tribunals, such

that some investment law experts are beginning to think that no precise wording of FET is possible.

54 See Articles 5, 13.2, 14.2 and 38 of the Convention on the Settlement of Investment Disputes Between States and Nationals of other States, available at: https://icsid.worldbank.org/ICSID/StaticFiles/basic-doc/CRR_English-final.pdf.

55 The main difference between ICSID arbitration and alternative options is the greater control domestic courts can exercise in overseeing non-ICSID arbitrations and in enforcing non-ICSID awards under the New York Convention for the Recognition and Enforcement of Foreign Arbitral Awards, which contains, inter alia, a public policy exception for recognition and enforcement.

56 In addition, art. 72 of the Convention provides that withdrawal from the Convention "shall not affect the rights or obligations under this Convention of that State or of any of its constituent subdivisions or agencies or of any national of that State arising out of consent to the jurisdiction of the Centre given by one of them before such notice was received by the depositary." How this provision is to be interpreted, and whether it only covers the effect of arbitral proceedings that have been initiated by foreign investors before the effects of denunciation of the Convention take place or whether it ensures the survival of all consents to ICSID arbitration contained in any prior investment treaty is a heavily contested and, so far, unresolved issue.

References

Aizenman J (2005). Financial liberalization in Latin-America in the 1990s: A reassessment. NBER Working Paper No. 11145, February.

Akyüz Y (2012). The boom in capital flows to developing countries: Will it go bust again? *Eckonomi-tek*, 1: 63–96.

Akyüz Y (2013). Waving or drowning: Developing countries after the financial crisis. Research Paper 48, South Centre, Geneva.

Alemu G (2014). Financial regulation and inclusive growth in Ethiopia. Paper prepared under the UK DFID-ESRC project, Financial Regulation in Low-Income Countries: Balancing Inclusive Growth with Financial Stability. Addis Ababa, Addis Ababa University.

Ariyoshi A, Habermeier K, Laurens B, Ötker-Robe I, Canales-Kriljenko J and Kirilenko A (2000). Capital controls: Country experiences with their use and liberalization. IMF Occasional Paper No 190, IMF, Washington, DC.

Bhagwati J (1998). The capital myth: The difference between trade in widgets and dollars. *Foreign Affairs*, May/June: 7–12.

Bresser-Pereira LC (2001). Incompetência e confidence building por trás de 20 anos de quase estagnação da América Latina. *Revista de Economia Política*, 21(1): 141–166.

Bruno V and Shin HS (2013). Capital flows, cross-border banking and global liquidity. Griswold Center for Economic Policy Studies. Working paper No. 237a, June.

Cavallo D (1996). Commentary to Gavin M, Hausmann R and Leiderman L, The macroeconomics of capital flows to Latin America: experience and policy issues In: Hausmann R and Rojas-Suarez, eds. *Volatile Capital Flows. Taming their impact on Latin America*. Washington, DC, Inter-American Development Bank.

Chandrasekhar CP (2014). National development banks in a comparative perspective. New Delhi, Jawaharlal Nehru University.

de Laubadère A and Delvolvé P (1986). *Droit Public Économique*, Paris, Dalloz.

Diaz-Alejandro C (1985). Good-bye financial repression, hello financial crash. *Journal of Development Economics*, 19: 1–24. North-Holland.

Eberhart P, Olivet C, Amos T and Buxton N (2012). Profiting from injustice. How law firms, arbitrators and financiers are fuelling an investment arbitration boom. Corporate Europe Observatory and the Transnational Institute, Brussels and Amsterdam, November; available at: http://www.tni.org/sites/www.tni.org/files/download/profitingfrominjustice.pdf.

Eichengreen B (1994). International Monetary Arrangements for the 21st Century. Washington, DC, Brookings Institution.

Eichengreen B and Rose AK (2014). Capital controls in the 21st century. VOX; available at: http://www.voxeu.org/article/capital-controls-21st-century.

Epstein G, Grabel I and Jomo KS (2004). Capital Management Techniques in Developing Countries: An Assessment of Experiences from the 1990s and

Lessons for the Future. G-24 Discussion Paper Series No. 27, March.

Esen O and Binatli AO (2013). The Minsky Perspective on Macroprudential Policy, PERI Working Paper Series, No. 308, University of Massachusetts, Amherst, MA.

Fama E (1980). Banking in the theory of finance. *Journal of Monetary Economics*, 6: 39−57.

Franck S (2005). The legitimacy crisis in investment treaty arbitration: Privatizing public international law through inconsistent decisions, 73 *Fordham Law Review*, 1521.

Galati G and Moessner R (2011). Macroprudential policy – a literature review. BIS Working Papers No. 337, Bank for International Settlements, Basel.

Gallagher KP, Griffith-Jones S and Ocampo JA (2012). Capital account regulations for stability and development: A new approach. In: Gallagher KP, Griffith-Jones S and Ocampo JA, eds. *Regulating Global Capital Flows for Long-Run Development*. Pardee Center Task Force Report, Boston University, Boston, MA.

Gavin M, Hausmann R and Leiderman L (1995). The macroeconomics of capital flows to Latin America: Experience and policy issues. Revised version of a background paper prepared for a seminar on International Capital Flows: Prospects and Policy Issues at the Annual Meetings of the Inter-American Development Bank in Jerusalem, 3 April.

Grabel I (2000). The political economy of 'policy credibility': The new-classical macroeconomics and the remaking of emerging economies. *Cambridge Journal of Economics*, 24(1): 1−19.

Haldane AG (2011). The big fish, small pond problem. Speech delivered at the Annual Conference of the Institute for New Economic Thinking, Bretton Woods, New Hampshire, 9 April 2011.

Hallward-Driemeier M (2003). Do Bilateral Investment Treaties Attract FDI? Only a bit…and they could bite. World Bank Development Research Group (DECRG), July.

IADB (2014). *Global Recovery and Monetary Normalization: Escaping a Chronicle Foretold?* Latin American and Caribbean Macroeconomic Report, 2014. Washington, DC, Inter-American Development Bank.

IEO (2007a). The IMF and aid to sub-Saharan Africa. Washington, DC, Independent Evaluation Office, IMF.

IEO (2007b). Structural condionality in IMF-supported programs. Washington, DC, Independent Evaluation Office, IMF.

IMF (2010). *Fiscal Monitor*. Washington, DC, May.

IMF (2011). Recent experiences in managing capital inflows − Cross-cutting themes and possible policy framework. Prepared by the Strategy, Policy, and Review Department. Washington, DC, February.

IMF (2012). The liberalization and management of capital flows: An institutional view. Washington, DC, November.

IMF (2013). Key aspects of macroprudential policy. Background paper, June.

Jacob M (2011). Precedents: Lawmaking through international adjudication. 12 *German Law Journal*: 1005−1032.

Kingsbury B and Schill S (2009). Investor-State arbitration as governance: Fair and equitable treatment, proportionality, and the emerging global administrative law. In: Van den Berg AJ, ed. *50 Years of the New York Convention*, ICCA Congress Series, 14: 5−68. London, Kluwer Law International.

Krugman P (1998). The confidence game: How Washington worsened Asia's crash; available at: www.pkarchive. org/crises/krugman1.html.

Leroux E (2002). Trade in financial services under the World Trade Organization. *Journal of World Trade*, 36(3): 413−442.

Luna-Martinez J and Vicente CL (2012). Global survey of development banks. Policy Research Working Paper 5969, World Bank, Washington, DC.

Martinez J and Santiso J (2003). Financial markets and politics: The confidence game in Latin American emerging economies. *International Political Science Review*, 24(3): 263−395.

Massad C (1998). The liberalisation of the capital account: Chile in the 1990s. In: Fischer S, ed. Should the IMF Pursue Capital-Account Convertibility? *Essays in International Finance*, No. 207: 34−46. Princeton, NJ, Princeton University.

Moreno R (2011). Policymaking from a "macroprudential" perspective in emerging market economies. BIS WP No.336, Bank for International Settlements, Basel.

Obstfeld M and Rogoff K (1995). The mirage of fixed exchange rates. *Journal of Economic Perspectives*, 9(4): 73−96.

Ocampo JA (2012). The case for and experience with capital account regulations. In: Gallagher KP, Griffith-Jones S and Ocampo JA, eds. *Regulating Global Capital Flows for Long-Run Development*. Pardee Center Task Force Report, Boston University, Boston, MA.

OECD (2013). OECD Code of liberalization of capital movements; available at: http://www.oecd.org/daf/inv/investment-policy/CapitalMovements_WebEnglish.pdf.

Prasad E, Rajan R and Subramanian A (2007). Foreign capital and economic growth. *Brookings Papers on Economic Activity*, (1): 153−209.

Prasad E, Rogoff K, Shang-Jin W and Kose MA (2003). The effects of financial globalization on developing countries: Some empirical evidence. IMF Occasional Paper 220, Washington, DC.

Prates D (1998). Investimentos de portfolio no mercado financeiro domestico. *Abertura Externa e Sistema Financeiro*. Final report, chapter 1, São Paulo, Fundacion para el Desarrollo.

Rey H (2013). The Global Financial Cycle and Monetary Policy Independence. London, London Business School, CEPR.

Schill S (2011). Enhancing International Investment Law's Legitimacy: Conceptual and methodological foundations of a new public law approach. *Virginia Journal of International Law*, 52 (1): 57–102.

Schill S (2014). International investment law as international development law. *Yearbook on International Investment Law and Policy*. New York, NY, Oxford University Press.

Sornarajah M (2008). A coming crisis: Expansionary trends in investment treaty arbitration. In: Sauvant K, ed. *Appeals Mechanism in International Investment Disputes*. New York, NY, Oxford University Press: 39–80.

Stiglitz J (2004). Capital-market liberalization, globalization and the IMF. *Oxford Review of Economic Policy*, 20(1): 57–71.

Tarullo DK (2013). Macroprudential Regulation. Speech at the Yale Law School Conference on Challenges in Global Financial Services, New Haven, CT, September.

Tucker T and Ghosh J (2011). WTO conflict with financial re-regulation. *Economic and Political Weekly*, XLVI(51): 75–79.

Turner P (2014). The global long-term interest rate, financial risks and policy choices in EMEs. BIS Working Papers No 441, Bank for International Settlements, Basel.

UNCTAD (2003). *World Investment Report 2003 – FDI Policies for Development: National and International Perspectives*. United Nations publication, sales no. E.03.II.D.8, New York and Geneva.

UNCTAD (2009). The role of international trade agreements in attracting foreign direct investment to developing countries. UNCTAD Series in International Investment Policies for Development, Geneva.

UNCTAD (2010). Denunciation of the ICSID Convention and BITs: Impact on investor-State claims. IIA Issues Note No. 2. Geneva, December.

UNCTAD (2011). Sovereign debt restructuring and international investment agreements. IIA Issues Note No. 2. Geneva, July.

UNCTAD (2012). *World Investment Report 2012 – Towards a New Generation of Investment Policies*. United Nations publication, sales no. E.12.II.D.3, New York and Geneva.

UNCTAD (2013a). *World Investment Report 2013 – Global Value Chains: Investment and Trade for Development*. United Nations publication, sales no. E.13.II.D.5, New York and Geneva.

UNCTAD (2013b).Reform of investor-State dispute settlement: in search of a roadmap. IIA Issue Note No. 2. Geneva, June.

UNCTAD (2014). The recent turmoil in emerging economies. Policy Brief No. 29, Geneva, March.

UNCTAD (*TDR 2006*). *Trade and Development Report, 2006. Global Partnership and National Policies for Development*. United Nations publication, sales no. E.06.II.D.6, New York and Geneva.

UNCTAD (*TDR 2011*). *Trade and Development Report, 2011. Post-crisis Policy Challenges in the World Economy*. United Nations publication, sales no. E.11.II.D.3, New York and Geneva.

UNCTAD (*TDR 2013*). *Trade and Development Report, 2013. Adjusting to the changing dynamics of the world economy*. United Nations publication, sales no. E.13.II.D.3, New York and Geneva.

Van Harten G (2007). Investment Treaty Arbitration and Public Law. New York, NY, Oxford University Press.

Van Harten G (2008). *A Case for an International Investment Court*. Inaugural Conference of the Society for International Economic Law, 16 July; available at: http://papers.ssrn.com/sol3/papers.cfm?abstract_id=1153424.

Van Harten G (2012). Arbitrator behaviour in asymmetrical adjudication: An empirical study of investment treaty arbitration. *Osgoode Hall Law Journal* 501(1): 211–268; available at: http://digitalcommons.osgoode.yorku.ca/ohlj/vol50/iss1/6/.

Van Harten G et al. (2010). Public statement on the international investment regime, 31 August; available at: http://www.osgoode.yorku.ca/public_statement.

Von Bogdandy A and Windsor J (2008). Annex on financial services. In: Wolfrum R, Stoll P-T and Feinäugle C, eds. *Max Plank Commentaries on World Trade Law, Vol. VI: WTO – Trade in Services*. Leiden/Boston, Martinus Nijhoff Publishers: 640–666.

Wallach L (2012). 'Fair and equitable treatment' and investor's reasonable expectations: Rulings in the US FTAs & BITs demonstrate FET definition must be narrowed. Washington DC, Public Citizen, 5 September.

DO BILATERAL INVESTMENT TREATIES ATTRACT FDI FLOWS TO DEVELOPING ECONOMIES?

This annex presents an econometric exercise aimed at testing whether bilateral investment treaties (BITs) fostered bilateral foreign direct investment (FDI) flows from developed to developing economies between 1985 and 2012.

Model and data sources

This exercise relies on the standard gravity panel data model, which predicts that FDI between home and host countries is proportional to their market size and inversely proportional to the geographic distance between them:

- The explained variable is FDI as measured by the net bilateral FDI outflows from developed (home) to developing countries (host), in millions of dollars. The main source for bilateral FDI outflows was the OECD *International Direct Investment Database*. Series were completed with data from the United States Bureau of Economic Analysis and from UNCTAD databases.

- Market size was measured by real GDP of the home and host countries in constant 2005 dollars, using United Nations *National Accounts Main Aggregates* database and national sources. A positive sign was expected for the coefficients of both GDPs. The larger the size of the home

country, the more FDI should flow from that country; and the larger the size of the host country the greater should be the potential demand for the output of foreign investors.

- Geographical distance between the capital cities of the home and host countries was obtained from the *CEPII GeoDist database* (Mayer and Zignago, 2011). It is used as a proxy for transaction and transportation costs as well as for the institutional and cultural distances between two countries. The sign of the coefficient is indicative of the prevailing kind of FDI. A positive sign would suggest exports and FDI are substitutes, because enterprises will serve customers by investing in the host country rather than by exporting from the home country. A negative sign would indicate complementarity between FDI and bilateral trade, typically in investments related to an international production network involving the home and host countries.

A set of dummies representing time-invariant variables taken from *CEPII GeoDist* data were included. They capture geographical, cultural and historical similarities of country pairs, which increase economic ties or reduce transaction costs. Corresponding dummies are equal to one when both countries share a common land border, language or colonial history. A positive sign was expected for the coefficients of these variables.

The standard gravity model was modified to introduce the variables related to BITs and other determinants of FDI to complete the estimable equation:

- A dummy variable equals one after the country pair has signed a BIT, as reported by UNCTAD. Given than BITs are supposed to reduce investment risks, they can be viewed as providing an incentive to investors, therefore the expected sign is positive. Three alternative variables representing BITs were used in the estimations: two dummy variables (a signed BIT and the entry into force of a BIT) and one variable which measured the number of years that had passed since the signing of the BIT.

- Labour skill was measured by the average years of secondary schooling in the adult population (over 25 years of age) of host countries. Data were taken from Barro and Lee (2010), which provide the educational attainment data at five-year intervals from 1950 to 2010. A linear interpolation was used to obtain data by year. A positive sign was expected for this coefficient.

- The difference in average years of schooling was used as a proxy for the absolute skill difference between the home and host country.[1] If FDI is motivated by market access, a negative sign should be expected, as "absolute skill differences reduce affiliate sales" (see Blonigen et al., 2002); however, if FDI is motivated by lower wage costs in the host country, a positive sign was expected.

- Openness was measured by the ratio of imports to GDP. Data were extracted from UNCTAD databases and national sources. A positive relationship was expected, as it could be interpreted as a measure of overall openness.

- Regional trade agreements (RTA) was a dummy variable equal to one after both countries had signed a bilateral free trade agreement or a regional trade agreement. Data were derived from a database in de Sousa (2012). A positive relationship was expected, given that RTAs lower trade barriers and facilitate the movement of intermediate and final goods between firms in home countries and foreign affiliates in host countries. Moreover some RTAs include other conditions such as investment regulations that facilitate the mobility of funds and capital flows. Since some RTAs include FDI-related clauses, RTAs were excluded from the estimable equations to isolate the impact of BITs. In that case, the coefficient of the BIT variables was expected to be biased upwards.

Estimation methods and results

A large panel data of bilateral FDI outflows to 119 developing economies from 27 developed economies over the period 1985–2012 was used to examine the effect of BITs on FDI to developing economies. The modified gravity equation was estimated based on two estimation methods: ordinary least squares (OLS) and Poisson pseudo-maximum likelihood (PPML). All time-variant explanatory variables were lagged by one period to reduce endogeneity problems.

Ordinary least squares (OLS)

- Given the multiplicative form of the gravity equation, the usual method is to take the natural logarithms of the explained and explanatory variables (excluding dummies) and apply ordinary least squares to the resulting log-linear equation.[2]

- To control for omitted variable bias, home and host fixed effects were included through dummy variables which control for all time-invariant home or host country characteristics.[3] Also included were time fixed effects to account for any shocks that affect all countries.

- Columns 1 to 5 of the table 6.A.1 present the results of the estimations obtained by OLS, along with robust standard errors and three types of fixed effects (year, host country and home country). Overall, this specification explains about 50 per cent of the variation of bilateral FDI outflows. Results show that except for openness and common border, coefficients are all statistically significant. In particular, "geographical distance" has a strong effect: its negative sign indicates either that FDI is related to bilateral trade or high operating costs due to geographical distance, and cultural and institutional differences. The coefficient of "labour skill" in host countries has a positive sign, suggesting a more important role of domestic markets. All other variables have the expected sign. In this specification BITs coefficients are significant and positive. However, the proportion of FDI that can be attributed to BITs is very low, as reflected in negligible change in R-squared when including a BIT variable.

Poisson pseudo-maximum likelihood (PPML)

- Santos Silva and Tenreyro (2006) showed that due to Jensen's inequality[4] the use of log-linearized gravity models by OLS can generate biased[5] estimations and produce misleading conclusions. They suggested that the coefficients in the gravity equation should be estimated in its multiplicative form, and proposed using the Poisson pseudo-maximum-likelihood (PPML) estimation method. PPML is consistent in the presence of heteroskedasticity, and provides a way to deal with zero values (unlike logarithm specifications).

- Columns 6 to 10 show results obtained by PPML, along with robust standard errors and three fixed effects. The coefficient of skill difference is statistically significant, and its positive sign provides support for FDI that is motivated by lower wage costs in the host country. Market size, labour skill, openness and RTA are all statistically significant and have the expected sign, whereas coefficients of BIT variables are not significant. The coefficients of the four time-invariant variables – geographic distance, common border, common language and colony – are all statistically significant.

- Ruiz and Vilarrubia (2007) argue that because cultural and historical factors are difficult to measure, gravity models should be estimated by using time and country-pair[6] fixed effects. Columns 11 to 15 show the results of the estimations by PPML, with year and country-pair treated as fixed effects. Except for BIT variables, all time-variant coefficients are statistically significant. Sizes of coefficients are, in general, higher than those obtained by PPML with year, home and host country fixed effects.

- When comparing results with those obtained using the OLS specification, OLS estimates tend to be much larger than those estimated by PPML. This shows that results are quite sensitive to the specification. For this reason, the results of previous studies using OLS should be interpreted with caution.

- To check for robustness, the gravity equations were also estimated by including alternatives definitions of variables such as openness (i.e. total trade over GDP), skill difference (i.e. absolute value, positive and negative values), and BIT (i.e. number of years since ratification of a BIT). Moreover, various transformations of the FDI variables were tried.[7] In all these specifications the PPML estimates of the coefficients of BIT remained statistically insignificant.

Table 6.A.1

REGRESSION RESULTS, 1985–2012

(Bilateral FDI, millions of dollars)

Explanatory variable	OLS: ln FDI					Poisson-Pseudo-Maximum Likelihood (PPML): FDI									
	1	2	3	4	5	6	7	8	9	10	11	12	13	14	15
ln GDP - host	0.93***	0.96***	0.90***	0.88***	0.94***	1.16***	1.19***	1.16***	1.15***	1.16***	1.22***	1.23***	1.22***	1.21***	1.22***
ln GDP - home	2.40**	2.33**	2.42**	2.41**	2.40**	0.97**	0.93**	0.97**	0.98**	0.97**	1.40**	1.40**	1.41**	1.40**	1.40**
ln labour skills - host	3.94***	3.89***	3.90***	3.87***	3.95***	1.58***	1.48***	1.60***	1.57***	1.58***	1.93***	1.91***	1.88***	1.88***	1.93***
ln skill difference	2.57***	2.58***	2.48***	2.39***	2.59***	0.95**	0.96**	0.98***	0.90**	0.94***	1.44***	1.46***	1.36***	1.32***	1.40***
ln openness	-0.10	-0.11	-0.13	-0.14	-0.10	0.36**	0.40**	0.36**	0.35**	0.36**	0.45***	0.47***	0.44***	0.43***	0.43***
Regional trade agreement		0.35**					0.42***					0.20**			
BIT - signature			0.25**					-0.04					0.09		
BIT - entry				0.44***					0.06					0.14	
BIT - years since signature					0.00					0.00					0.01
Time-invariant variables															
ln distance	-2.61***	-2.57***	-2.59***	-2.58***	-2.62***	-0.73***	-0.68***	-0.73***	-0.73***	-0.73***					
Common border	-0.06	-0.10	-0.00	0.00	-0.06	0.53**	0.47**	0.52**	0.54**	0.52**					
Common official language	2.54***	2.54***	2.56***	2.56***	2.53***	0.92***	0.88***	0.92***	0.94***	0.93***					
Colony	1.51***	1.51***	1.48***	1.46***	1.51***	0.26**	0.31***	0.27**	0.24**	0.25**					
Number of observations	12 573	12 573	12 573	12 573	12 573	12 573	12 573	12 573	12 573	12 573	12 573	12 573	12 573	12 573	12 573
R-squared[a]	0.500	0.500	0.500	0.500	0.500	0.734	0.737	0.734	0.734	0.734	0.825	0.826	0.825	0.825	0.825
Fixed effects															
Year	Yes	Yes	Yes	Yes	Yes	Yes	Yes	Yes	Yes	Yes	Yes	Yes	Yes	Yes	Yes
Host country	Yes	Yes	Yes	Yes	Yes	Yes	Yes	Yes	Yes	Yes					
Home country	Yes	Yes	Yes	Yes	Yes	Yes	Yes	Yes	Yes	Yes					
Country pair	Yes	Yes	Yes	Yes	Yes						Yes	Yes	Yes	Yes	Yes

Note: *** Significant at 1 per cent. ** Significant at 5 per cent. * Significant at 10 per cent.
      Home: developed economies. Host: developing economies.
     a   Pseudo R-squared is reported for PPML.

Concluding remarks

This econometric analysis shows that standard gravity models permit a meaningful explanation of FDI bilateral flows from developed to developing countries. However, when the BITs variable is included, the results are ambivalent. Using one methodology (OLS estimation of log-linear regression), results indicate that BITs have a positive impact on bilateral FDI, although the estimated magnitude of this impact is small. Since, according to recent literature, this methodology produces biased estimates, an alternative method (PPML) was also used. This method showed that BITs appear to have no effect on bilateral North-South FDI flows: the magnitude of the estimated coefficients is close to zero. Moreover, the BIT coefficients are not statistically significant; in other words, results do not support the hypothesis that BITs foster bilateral FDI.

These results are consistent with the existing literature, which observes that the current state of the research is unable to fully explain the determinants of FDI, and, in particular, the effects of BITs on FDI. Thus developing-country policymakers should not assume that signing up to BITs will boost FDI. Indeed, they should remain cautious about any kind of recommendation to actively pursue BITs. ∎

Notes

1 Skill difference is measured as the logarithm of the ratio of the highest to the lowest average years of schooling in the two countries.

2 The FDI data used here contain 15,983 observations of which 2,844 are zero and 3,410 are negative. As it is usual in the literature to avoid deleting observations when applying logarithms, the value of FDI was increased in 1 dollar and negative values were deleted.

3 In panel data estimations, coefficients may be subject to omitted variable bias; that is, the estimated coefficient of an explanatory variable is biased when important variables that are unknown or difficult to measure are not included in the equation and are correlated with the above explanatory variable. See Anderson and van Wincoop (2003) for a discussion of omitted variables bias in the trade gravity literature.

4 According to Jensen's inequality, the mean value of a logarithm is different from the logarithm of a mean value.

5 They showed that in a gravity model, even controlling for fixed effects, the presence of heteroskedasticity can affect the consistency of estimators. This is because, due to Jensen's inequality, the log of the explained variable changes the properties of the error term in a way that renders the coefficients biased.

6 Country-pair dummies absorb the effects of all omitted variables that are specific to the country pairs but remain constant over time, including the standard gravity variables (geographical distance, common border, common language and colony).

7 The first robustness check considered only a strictly positive value for FDI. The second included the negative value by applying the Levy-Yeyati et al. (2007) transformation, i.e. replacing the original FDI variable by sign (FDI)*log(abs(FDI)+1). Finally, nominal FDI values were deflated by the GDP United States deflator.

References

Anderson JE and van Wincoop E (2003). Gravity with gravitas: A solution to the border puzzle. *American Economic Review*, 93(1): 170–192.

Barro RJ and Lee JW (2010). A new data set of educational attainment in the world, 1950–2010. NBER Working Paper 15902, National Bureau of Economic Research, Cambridge, MA.

Blonigen BA, Davies RB and Head K (2002)..Estimating the Knowledge-Capital Model of the Multinational Enterprise: Comment. NBER Working Paper No. 8929, NBER, Cambridge, MA.

de Sousa J (2012). The currency union effect on trade is decreasing over time. *Economics Letters*, 117(3): 917–920.

Levy-Yeyati E, Panizza U and Stein E (2007). The cyclical nature of North-South FDI flows. *Journal of International Money and Finance*, 26(1): 104–130.

Mayer T and Zignago S (2011). Notes on CEPII's distances measures (GeoDist). CEPII Working Paper No. 2011-25, Paris.

Ruiz JM and Vilarrubia JM (2007). The wise use of dummies in gravity models: Export potentials in the EuroMed region. Research Paper No. WP-0720, Bank of Spain, Madrid.

Santos Silva JMC and Tenreyro S (2006). The log of gravity. *The Review of Economics and Statistics*, 88(4): 641–658.

Chapter VII

FISCAL SPACE FOR STABILITY AND DEVELOPMENT: CONTEMPORARY CHALLENGES

A. Introduction

An appropriate macroeconomic environment and industrial policies aimed at production upgrading and diversification need to be permanent elements of a long-term national development strategy, but they have become even more critical as economies are forced to adapt to the new economic landscape emerging from the global financial crisis (*TDR 2013*). Previous chapters of this *Report* have shown how current international arrangements in trade and capital flows can inhibit the national policy space needed for countries to adapt; they have also suggested ways for encouraging different patterns of economic integration that would open up new opportunities both for developing countries and their trading partners. Yet this is only one part of the story: even if governments were allowed, within the framework of multilateral, regional and bilateral agreements, to pursue their desired development strategy, they would still need to finance it. In the context of preserving policy space, strengthening fiscal revenues is key, as these are not only more sustainable than other sources of long-term finance, but also less constrained by restrictions and conditions that impose limits on policy space.

As noted in previous UNCTAD reports, strategies for boosting public finances have been essential underpinnings of developmental States, and are also critical for macroeconomic stability (UNCTAD, 2009). However, the globalized economy poses serious challenges to increasing fiscal revenues. This chapter examines how fiscal space has been affected by tax competition among countries and by tax avoidance by international firms and wealthy households, as well as by the specific challenges facing countries that are heavily dependent on natural-resource rent. It explores some ways of addressing these problems concentrating on issues related to the domestic collection of taxes and other current public revenues. Development assistance and debt financing can provide alternative sources of revenue and are of particular significance to some developing countries. The different challenges these flows pose for fiscal and policy space have been discussed in greater detail in *TDRs 2008, 2010, 2011* and *2013*, and therefore are not discussed at length in this *Report*.

Fiscal space refers to the ability of a government to use fiscal instruments to pursue various economic, development and social policy objectives. An increase in public revenues can enhance the possibilities of using particular instruments, such as differential tax rates, subsidies and social transfers, to meet social and developmental goals. Fiscal space has a quantitative or budgetary dimension, which can be roughly approximated by measuring the share of public revenue in GDP. But the notion of fiscal space should not be restricted to current levels of public revenue. In particular, it should not be seen as being equivalent to fiscal balance; a government may be in deficit, and yet be able to finance additional desired expenditures if these generate growth, or it may incur debt if this does not threaten stability and other policy goals. Fiscal space also refers to the potential for increasing public expenditure, including for measures in support of structural transformation, and for variations in that expenditure as an instrument of demand management.

Fiscal space also has a qualitative dimension, related to the level and compositions of public revenues and expenditures. Decision-making on this can be constrained, de jure, by international arrangements and agreements, by externally imposed conditionalities and by legal rules such as those relating to deficit ceilings; but it can also be constrained de facto, for example by the perceived requirements of global investors and financial markets, or by the power of domestic interest groups.

Fiscal space is a dynamic concept, since changes in public spending have an impact on the economy, and consequently on government revenues. In the short run, it can be expanded through the multiplicative effects of pro-growth policies. In particular, in a recessionary setting, when countercyclical stimulus may be required, fiscal space can be created by augmenting revenues through various short-term measures, in addition to increasing public borrowing (*TDR 2011*). However, from a longer term, development perspective, fiscal space means having the capacity to finance spending requirements that increase and change over time. Indeed, during the process of development, public spending as a share of GDP grows, particularly for financing infrastructure, social transfers and basic services, and in parallel, so do the revenues to finance it. Fiscal space

> Fiscal space is an essential element of the policy space needed for development, and at the same time fiscal space increases with development.

is an essential element of the policy space needed for development, and at the same time fiscal space increases with development.

Section B of this chapter examines current trends in the fiscal revenues of different groups of countries, and the challenges faced by governments that are seeking to improve the volume and composition of those revenues. It presents the long-term trends of fiscal space, and shows that it is a constitutive part of the development process. It also discusses how globalization and related policy choices have been altering the composition of fiscal revenues.

The subsequent sections focus on the ways in which global governance and international actors greatly affect the fiscal space of developing and developed countries alike. Section C examines how tax havens, secrecy jurisdictions and illicit financial flows erode the tax base, undermine the fairness of the tax system, and distort trade and investment patterns. It evaluates the amount of tax leakages caused by those mechanisms, and describes some national and multilateral initiatives taken to tackle this problem. Section D analyses issues relating to the extractive industries that are of particular relevance for many developing countries. Given the boom in commodity prices, these industries offer huge potential to boost fiscal revenues. However, this potential is not always well exploited due to inadequate tax rules or to difficulties in enforcing them, since TNCs in these industries frequently resort to tax avoidance techniques. The section also analyses how the rent from natural resources is distributed in selected countries, and explains how the rules affecting this distribution have been changing in recent years. Finally, section E summarizes the main findings and presents some policy orientations aimed at improving the fiscal space for development strategies.

B. Developmental States and their fiscal space

1. Developmental States

Successful developmental States have had the foresight and capacity to encourage private sector development, including by increasing profits and investment above the level likely to have been possible by relying on market forces alone. They have also been able to design effective mechanisms to discipline private investors and direct their resources to areas where the economic and social returns might be particularly high (*TDRs 1996, 1997, 2003* and *2009*). From this perspective, Adelman (2000) has identified essential elements for a successful developmental State. These include a substantial degree of autonomy, capacity and credibility to set policies in the national interest, leadership commitment to economic development, good economic policies, and a necessary degree of economic autonomy with respect to the international environment.

Previous chapters have focused, in particular, on the last of these elements in securing the requisite degree of policy space. But developmental States are also in the business of mobilizing and allocating resources, which are likely to be key to their success in the long term. These are needed to support infrastructure development by investing in both physical and human capital, where the private sector, particularly in developing countries, is likely to be weak, or absent, and dependent on good infrastructure for its own profit-making activities. However, the basic bargain between the State and business goes well beyond providing only good infrastructure; at various times and to varying degrees, it also requires the State to assume other functions as well, such as increasing the supply of investable resources, socializing long-term investment risks, and providing support services in such areas as technology, training and exporting. State-sponsored accumulation and

technological progress is likely to involve, variously, the transfer of assets from less to more productive sectors, control of the financial system, the obtaining of foreign technologies and their adaptation to local conditions, and direct public investments in some activities along with selected priority investments to encourage diversification and upgrading.

These activities can only be pursued within an integrated strategy based on a shared vision of a country's development, and they depend on building broad social consent, supported by institutional arrangements for continuous dialogue and coordination with key stakeholders. Public finance, including the mobilization of tax revenues, is a key component in legitimizing the role of the State and establishing the areas of government responsibility in the economic and social spheres. Ocampo (2007) identifies five components of this "fiscal covenant" that are essential for effective State mobilization of resources: clear rules of fiscal discipline, accompanied by adequate tax revenues to finance the functions that society assigns to the State; transparency of public expenditure; the design of efficiency criteria for the management of State resources; acknowledgement of the central role of the public budget in the provision of "goods of social value", and, more generally, in the distribution of income; and the design of balanced and democratic fiscal institutions which are open to citizens' participation.

The challenge is particularly demanding at lower levels of income and development when the potential sources of revenue are limited, and even more so for countries that are heavily dependent on natural resources for their initial development drive. Most extractive industries have a limited local market and seek to maximize their revenues from exports. This can generate significant profits and valuable foreign-exchange earnings, which, if properly managed, can ease a number of constraints on faster growth. However, this is easier said than done: the problem of "Dutch disease", whereby an expanding mining sector triggers a real currency appreciation and a fall in output and employment in other tradable sectors, can introduce serious macroeconomic imbalances and increase exchange rate volatility and economic vulnerability. However, a large body of evidence suggests that this is manageable provided policymakers have the requisite policy space (IMF, 2003; UNCTAD, 2005).

More damaging to long-term prospects is when this kind of expansion generates a pattern of lopsided internal integration through the creation of enclave economies. The structure of international commodity markets is such that when policymakers invite TNCs to develop this sector, they find themselves in a weak negotiating position, as these very large firms have at their disposal better information than their hosts as well as greater financial, technological and market strengths, including the threat of capital flight. Moreover, unpredictable rents associated with price volatility can seriously distort the wider incentive structure, adding a speculative dimension to investment planning in both the private and public sectors. The solution is not one of either State or foreign ownership of natural resources; it has to do with how best to manage resource rents with long-term development goals in mind. In recent years, as discussed in previous chapters, the pendulum has swung towards trying to attract FDI to this sector, with insufficient attention given to strengthening the bargaining position of host governments to obtain better returns from their natural-resource base and stimulate the upgrading and diversification of national output. Refocusing on long-term development will require changes in existing fiscal and legislative arrangements in order to increase revenues and ensure that a greater proportion of value added remains in the host economy, as discussed further below.

2. Long-term fiscal trends

In general, developed countries tend to have greater fiscal space than developing countries, as they collect larger revenues as a share of GDP. This is the result of a long historical process: in the early 1900s, revenues collected by the Government in the United Kingdom amounted to 15 per cent of GDP, compared with 40 per cent one century later (Clark and Dilnot, 2002); in the United States, government revenues rose from below 10 per cent of GDP to 30 per cent during the same period (Maddison, 2001). This enlargement of the tax base was the result not only of the growth of the modern (and formal) sector of the economy, but also of adjustments in legislation, the introduction of new taxes and other fiscal charges, and their variation over time, as well as considerable efforts to strengthen tax administration and enforcement (Besley and Persson, 2013). Greater revenue collection capacity, in turn, provided the means for meeting the demands of citizens for publicly provided goods and services based on the concept of a welfare State. More generally, it permitted financing higher growth-enhancing public spending, which generated a positive interrelationship between development and fiscal space. In the period 2011–2012, developed countries, on average, collected public revenues totalling 41.5 per cent of GDP, with tax revenues alone amounting to 25.5 per cent. In contrast, during that period the total revenues and tax revenues of general government in LDCs amounted to 23 per cent and 14.5 per cent of GDP, respectively.

Despite this broad association between levels of income and fiscal revenues, there is no benchmark for the ratio of public revenue to GDP. The latter depends as much on an economy's capacity to furnish public revenues − and the administrative capability to collect them − as on political choice. There are significant differences in this ratio across countries at similar levels of per capita income, reflecting historical circumstances, dissimilar revenue-generating capacities and socially accepted policy choices about the role of the State. Those policy choices concern its redistributive role and the extent to which both socially important services should be delivered by the public sector, and instruments of public finance are used for macroeconomic management and to support policies for structural transformation.

There is a positive relationship between government revenues as a share of GDP and per capita GDP across a wide range of developed, developing and transition economies, but also a significant dispersion within these groups (chart 7.1). For example, government revenues in most high-income European countries, including (in decreasing order) Norway, Denmark, Finland, Sweden, France, Belgium, Austria, Italy, the Netherlands and Germany, are above or

Chart 7.1

RELATIONSHIP BETWEEN GOVERNMENT REVENUES AND PER CAPITA GDP, 2012

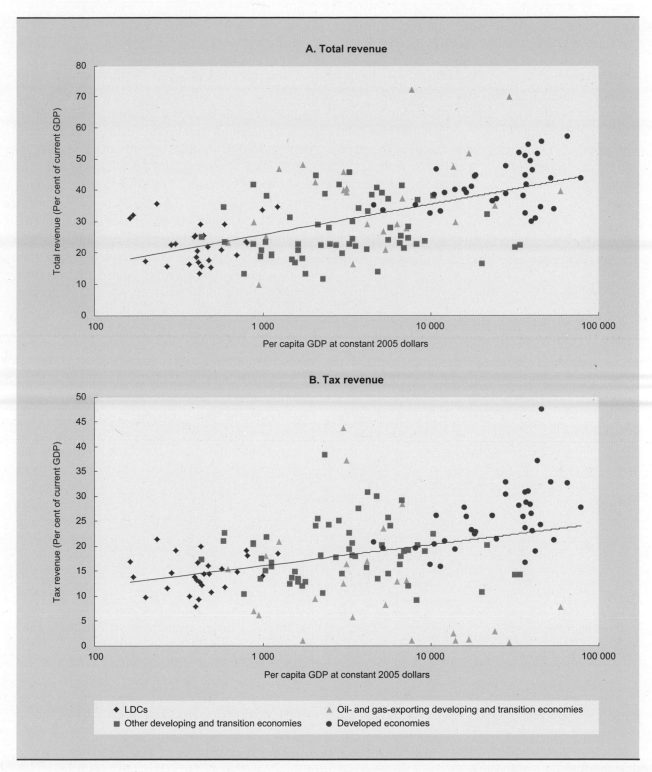

Source: UNCTAD secretariat calculations, based on ECLAC, *CEPALSTAT*; Eurostat, *Statistics Database*; *OECD.StatExtracts* database; European Commission, *Annual macro-economic* database (*EC-AMECO*); and IMF, *World Economic Outlook* and *Government Finance Statistics* databases.

Note: Data refer to 2012 or latest year available. Revenue data refer to general government revenue, except for Argentina, the Plurinational State of Bolivia, Colombia, Ecuador, El Salvador, Mexico, Panama, Paraguay, Uruguay and the Bolivarian Republic of Venezuela, for which data refer to the non-financial public sector. Per capita GDP data are shown in logarithmic scale.

close to 50 per cent of GDP; while in Japan, the United States and Australia, government revenues are around 30 per cent of GDP. This difference illustrates diverse models of social coverage and the welfare State. At the other end of the income hierarchy, LDCs also show some heterogeneity, with government incomes ranging from around 15 per cent of GDP (in ascending order) in Haiti, Sierra Leone, Uganda, Ethiopia, Guinea-Bissau and the Central African Republic, to close to 30 per cent in Malawi, Burundi, the Democratic Republic of the Congo and Mozambique. The latter two countries are exporters of mineral ores and metals, which provide revenues to their governments independently of the average income of the population.

The capacity for raising public revenue from the extractive industries, largely unrelated to per capita income, is clearly apparent in oil- and gas-exporting developing countries and transition economies. Whereas in most other countries, income tax collection contributes around two thirds of government revenues, in oil-exporting countries that share is close to only one third (compare charts 7.1A and 7.1B). Government revenues of Angola, the Plurinational State of Bolivia, Iraq, Kuwait, Libya, Oman and Saudi Arabia are close to or over 50 per cent of GDP, despite the fact that these countries range from lower-middle-income to high income levels. Most of their government revenues come directly from dividends of State-owned extractive firms, royalties or production-sharing agreements, while income tax contributes a lower share. However, exporting minerals or hydrocarbons does not guarantee high levels of government income, as indicated by the data from Peru, Turkmenistan and Zambia. It depends largely on domestic policies related to the distribution of the rents from natural resources, as discussed in section D of this chapter.

Non-oil-exporting developing and transition economies, mostly middle-income countries, have an intermediate level of public revenues, with a non-weighted average of 26.8 per cent of GDP. In this heterogeneous group, transition economies have clearly above-average public revenue levels (most notably Bosnia and Herzegovina, Serbia, Ukraine and Uzbekistan), partly due to the significance of social contributions. This is also the case for a number of Latin American countries with strong redistributive policies, and where the social security and pension system have remained the State's responsibility

(e.g. Argentina, Brazil and Cuba). By contrast, public revenue levels are comparatively low in several Central American countries (e.g. Guatemala and Honduras) and South Asia (e.g. Pakistan and Sri Lanka).

The gap between a number of developing and developed countries in terms of public revenue shares in GDP has narrowed over the past two decades, as a result of growing domestic resource mobilization in most developing and transition economies. In Latin America and Africa, total tax revenues as a percentage of GDP rose significantly, bolstered by stronger economic growth and a broadly favourable macro-economic environment (chart 7.2).[1] Increased public earnings from commodity exports also contributed, reflecting higher commodity prices, and in some cases, changes in the terms of contracts agreed with oil and mining corporations. In Latin America, lower unemployment, higher real wages and a larger share of formal jobs also raised social contribution levels. The resulting progressive reduction of inequality was accompanied by a rise in consumption and indirect taxes. Furthermore, revenues benefited from the introduction of new taxes alongside advances in tax administration (ECLAC, 2014a). In Africa, overall growth of public revenues was smaller, in part due to the lower contribution of border taxes, which remain an important component of total tax revenues. Total government revenues also increased significantly in West Asia and in the transition economies, largely due to gains from rising oil prices. In general, in all developing regions and transition economies the share of government revenue in GDP increased, with the exception of East, South and South-East Asia. The low rates of growth of taxes relative to GDP in parts of Asia and the Pacific, despite years of rapid economic growth, has been attributed to the region's low levels of personal income tax and heavy reliance on value added tax (VAT) (ESCAP, 2013). On the other hand, in developed countries, the share of government revenues in GDP declined slightly, from an average of 43 per cent in the period 1991–1995 to 41.5 per cent in 2011–2012.

Output growth has broadly positive effects on fiscal space. In most developing and transition economies, government revenues have tended to increase faster than GDP, especially in middle-income countries. A study of 17 Latin American and 6 South-East Asian countries suggests that during the period 1990–2012, a 1 per cent rise in

Chart 7.2

GOVERNMENT REVENUES BY SOURCE, SELECTED COUNTRY GROUPS, 1991–2012

(Per cent of GDP)

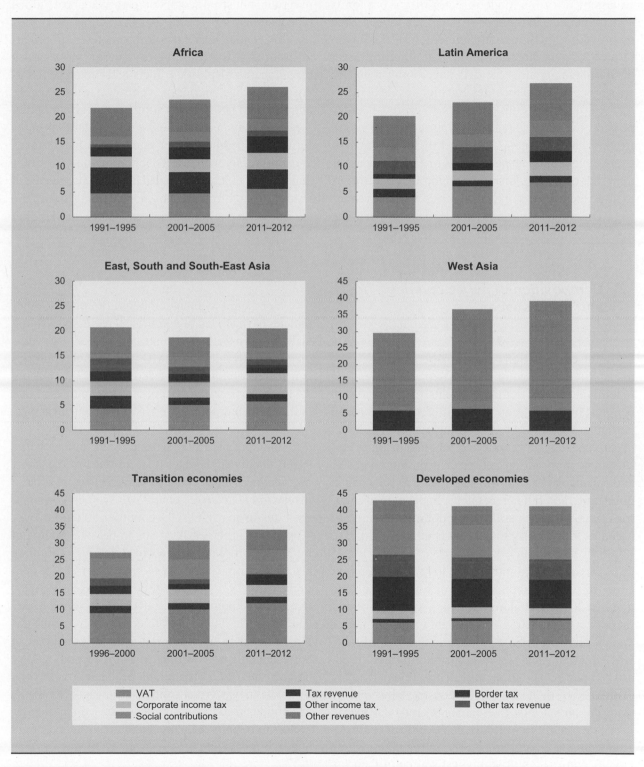

Source: UNCTAD secretariat calculations, based on ECLAC, *CEPALSTAT*; IMF, *World Economic Outlook* and *Government Finance Statistics* databases; Eurostat, *Statistics Database*; *OECD.StatExtracts* database; and *EC-AMECO* database.

Note: Data refer to the five-year average of the mean observation of general government revenue, except for Argentina, the Plurinational State of Bolivia, Colombia, Ecuador, El Salvador, Mexico, Panama, Paraguay, Uruguay and the Bolivarian Republic of Venezuela, for which data refer to the non-financial public sector. Data for China refer to budget revenue only; they do not include extra-budgetary funds or social security funds. Other revenues include capital revenues.

GDP caused a 1.15 per cent increase in government revenues (Weeks, 2014). This can partly be explained by structural transformations taking place in parallel with output growth, mainly resulting from the enlargement of the modern sector of the economy, and an increase in the proportion of the labour force employed in medium and large enterprises. This in turn provides a larger tax base, including for direct taxation. On the other hand, in developing countries with low per capita incomes and high levels of informal employment, governments have fewer entry possibilities through which to capture more revenues from private incomes. Consequently their growth of fiscal revenues as a percentage of GDP is weaker than that of middle-income developing countries. A major exception may be in countries where revenues are augmented by various taxes on large firms in the extractive industries, as discussed in section D.

3. Composition of public revenue and fiscal space

The composition of taxes matters because of its distributive implications and its role in generating incentives for particular elements of demand and supply. For example, applying differential tax rates to particular sectors is a form of industrial policy. Direct taxes, especially corporate and personal incomes taxes, can be tailored for income distribution purposes, and can also act as built-in stabilizers, as they rise in good times and fall in recessions. In developed countries, income tax is still the predominant source of revenue, followed by social contributions (chart 7.2).

Developing countries tend to rely more on revenues raised from indirect taxes on consumption and trade. In 2012, VAT alone accounted for 22 per cent of total revenues in Africa, 26 per cent in Latin America and 29 per cent in East, South and South-East Asia. Only in West Asia was its contribution rather modest (12 per cent), since most of the revenues there originated from the extractive industries. In addition, since the early 1990s, the share of VAT in GDP rose in every region of the world. Even developed countries are increasingly applying consumption taxes, which have become the second highest source of their tax revenues after income taxes.

This trend has a negative distributional impact, as VAT and other indirect taxes are regressive compared

with income taxes. Some countries have tried to reduce their regressive nature through exemptions and differential treatment. In Latin America, some products are zero-rated and exemptions are offered in certain industrial sectors or to particular categories of consumers (ECLAC, 2014a).[2] Other countries use differential VAT rates to promote environmental priorities, for example, by setting higher rates on purchases of plastics, fuels and motor vehicles. Also in Latin America, several countries recently adopted dual tax systems similar to those applied in the Scandinavian countries, with standard tax rates for capital income, higher rates for corporate taxes and progressive rates on labour income. In other countries of that region, fiscal instruments have been used to boost formal employment, helping to shift the tax burden from companies in sectors that employ more formal workers towards those, such as extractive industry TNCs that are more capital-intensive (ECLAC, 2014a).

Compared to such compensatory efforts, other policies have tended towards fiscal regressivity. Ortiz and Cummins (2013) found that some 94 governments in 63 developing and 31 high-income countries considered options to boost revenue by increasing VAT or sales tax rates or removing exemptions as one of the most common post-crisis adjustment measures.

In addition, a major trend in all regions is the steady decline in the rates of corporate income taxes, as governments compete to attract or retain mobile investors (*TDR 2012*, chap. V). Average corporate tax rates in many OECD countries fell from over 45 per cent in the early 1980s to below 25 per cent by 2012. Corporate tax rates in developing countries also fell significantly, on average from 38 per cent in the early 1990s to 32 per cent by the early 2000s (Keen and Simone, 2004), and again to around 27 per cent in 2012.[3] These cuts in corporate tax rates did not necessarily lead to proportional reductions in corresponding tax revenues. In some cases they were compensated by a broadening of the tax base, while in others they were amplified by measures such as tax holidays, reduced statutory rates for particular sectors or regions, and direct tax breaks for exporters and free-trade zones.

Reducing corporate tax rates in developing countries seems to go against the usual advice to broaden their tax revenues: if those countries have huge public revenue requirements to finance investment and limited capacity to raise revenues by other means, why would they reduce tax rates for the economic agents most easily taxable (at least technically)? One possible reason is that "perhaps their political and institutional structures are more vulnerable to the exercise of influence by interest groups, including foreign multinationals" (Keen and Simone, 2004: 1321). Such a tendency may also be a response to greater competition to attract global investors, although tax differentials do not seem to be the most important determinant of FDI. This is evidenced in developed economies, where tax incentives to corporations have not led to rising productive investment. Despite the steady fall in the rate of statutory corporate income taxes since the early 1980s, and other tax incentives designed to encourage investors, gross fixed capital formation declined in a large number of developed countries, even before the global crisis (*TDR 2012*, chap. V, section C).

In 2011–2012, the share of government revenues from corporate taxes in GDP increased, despite the continued downward trend of corporate tax rates, mainly because the share of profits in GDP increased in most countries. Public revenues from corporate taxes rose significantly in most regions of the developing world, as company profits benefited from economic growth and the rise in international trade. However, the extent to which corporate taxes contributed to total revenues has varied, and in general it has not kept pace with the increase in profits during these years (UN-DESA, 2013).

Another major change in fiscal composition that reflects global influences concerns border and trade taxes. Revenues from import tariffs typically accounted for a large proportion of public revenues in developing countries, and especially in LDCs. This was mainly because they are fairly easy to implement, requiring only a relatively simple institution such as a customs authority at the border, compared with other taxes, such as VAT or income and corporate taxes. However, trade liberalization agreements and progressive tariff reductions have had a major impact on what was once one of the most important sources of revenue for many developing-country governments.[4] By 2012, almost 40 per cent of international trade was

> The composition of taxes matters because of its distributive implications and its role in generating incentives for particular elements of demand and supply.

duty-free under MFN terms, and an additional 35 per cent was duty-free under bilateral or regional preferential terms. In addition, given the many ongoing negotiations for bilateral and plurilateral economic partnership agreements, the contribution of import duties to public revenues will likely continue to erode in the years to come.

Such a trend would have significant adverse effects on fiscal revenues in a number of low-income countries. In Africa, border taxes accounted for 15 per cent of government revenues in 2011–2012. Those revenues remain particularly significant for LDCs; indeed, they have become even more important in recent years, partly owing to these countries' increasing participation in international trade (both in imports and exports), and partly because their tariff rates remain higher than those of other countries (UNCTAD, 2014). The total imports of sub-Saharan African countries, for instance, increased by over 70 per cent between 2006 and 2011. Import tariff revenues accounted for 5 per cent of GDP on average in LDCs, compared with just 0.5 per cent in developed countries (chart 7.2).

Export taxes can also be applied, and are imposed most frequently on exports of metals, including waste and scrap, minerals and agricultural commodities. Those tax rates can be relatively high, at around 20 per cent on unprocessed commodities and 13–17 per cent on semi-processed or finished goods (UNCTAD, 2014). Apart from augmenting revenues, export taxes are imposed by governments for a number of other reasons as well, including for conserving natural resources, protecting health and the environment, encouraging domestic value-added activities in processing primary commodities, and also for "sterilizing" windfall profits from price increases. However, many of the ongoing trade negotiations at multilateral and bilateral levels include reducing or eliminating these taxes, which means their use may diminish in the future. Given the multiple purposes served by export taxes, such restrictions may have negative impacts, and not only on fiscal revenues.

Many governments have turned their attention to new sources of tax revenue relating to the financial sector and financial transactions, including proposing levies on trading in stocks, bonds and derivatives (in the EU), or taxes on the repatriation of overseas earnings (in the United States). If these were to materialize, they could create a significant change in tax structures. The proposed financial transactions tax (FTT) could be considered a globalized version of stamp duty, which is one of the oldest taxes in existence. The latter was introduced in the United Kingdom more than 300 years ago, and has long been applied to purchases of shares, as well as property, in many other countries as well. Like many fiscal charges, they are promoted for multiple purposes. The FTT is proposed not only for its capacity to earn substantial revenues, but also as an instrument to influence the behaviour of economic agents. It may dampen speculative activities that can be damaging for the rest of the economy, and ensure a more equitable treatment of the financial sector vis-à-vis other sectors.

It seems, therefore, that different forces are influencing the composition and level of fiscal revenues, sometimes in opposite directions. These are not purely technical matters, since the enlargement or retrenchment of fiscal space is key to the implementation of different development strategies. Furthermore, they involve a distribution of the tax burden, which has distributional and economic impacts, benefiting (or affecting) some agents more than others.

In this context, it is worth mentioning the de facto pervasive influence of sophisticated lobbyists and interest groups on national and international policymaking, which is often insufficiently recognized. While lobbying has been a long-standing and accepted feature in the United States, it is gaining in importance in other developed and developing countries as well. Lobbyists can benefit society as a whole by conveying complex information from experts to legislators and bureaucrats, but they can also lead to the generation and private appropriation of rents that are detrimental to society. Lobbying is costly, and collective action problems mean that households, consumers and industry groups with many small actors and disparate interests are unlikely to be adequately represented. The financial sector, for example, is well organized and has a high level of "firepower" aimed at fiscal policymaking far beyond the scope of the households who use or are affected by financial services.[5] Its influence on fiscal space can be direct; for example, more than 900 of the 1,700 amendments that were tabled by EU parliamentarians to legislate on the activities of hedge funds and private equity firms had been authored by financial industry lobby groups, and there was evidence of large-scale "copy and paste" of texts given by the lobbyists (Corporate Europe Observatory et al., 2014). Similarly, in the United States it has been found that firms that increased their lobbying expenditures by 1 per cent in one year reduced their effective tax rates in the range of 0.5 to 1.6 percentage points the following year (Richter et al., 2009). The suggestion that strategic lobbying yields quantifiable benefits for particular groups is supported by the scale of recent efforts on the part of corporations to promote a package of tax breaks estimated to cost $46 billion in 2014 and about $700 billion over 10 years, according to data from the Congressional Budget Office reported in a recent survey.[6] Particularly when combined with the "revolving door" that often allows lawmakers, bureaucrats and lobbyists to change places, these practices directly and indirectly affect fiscal policies. The recent proliferation of such practices in several developing countries is another factor affecting fiscal space.

C. Tax leakage and international governance of taxation

Until the twentieth century, tax collection and enforcement were primarily a domestic concern, with little spillover to tax systems in other countries. Today, although tax collection remains mostly a national concern, with the process of globalization tax systems in some countries can affect public revenue collection in other countries. This has had the negative effect of creating new channels through which some taxpayers – particularly high-net-worth individuals (HNWIs) and TNCs – can reduce or even avoid paying taxes. HNWIs avoid paying wealth and inheritance taxes, as well as taxes on income from these assets, mainly by placing their financial assets in tax havens. In addition, part of their income is sometimes routed through these jurisdictions to hide it from the tax authorities. As for TNCs, tax avoidance mainly takes the form of "creative accounting" practices, although they may also hold financial assets or register non-financial assets in tax havens.

Three points are important when looking at the international dimension of tax leakages. First, such practices result in massive losses of public revenues. Second, a large proportion of the financial flows resulting from such creative accounting goes through offshore financial centres (OFCs) based in tax havens, or more precisely, in secrecy jurisdictions. Third, many flaws remain in the international taxation architecture, which has failed to properly adapt to the current reality.

1. *Key concepts*

(a) *Tax havens, secrecy jurisdictions and offshore financial centres*

Tax havens, secrecy jurisdictions and OFCs are often considered synonymous. However, the three terms refer to distinct aspects of the same problem. Tax havens are political jurisdictions – not all of them identical to sovereign States – which have sufficient autonomy to write their own tax, finance, and other laws and regulations in order to create a legislative framework designed to assist non-resident persons or corporations in avoiding regulatory obligations imposed on them in the places where they undertake the substance of their economic transactions (Palan et al., 2010). They provide a place to record, for accounting and tax purposes, transactions that have impacts elsewhere (Tax Justice Network, 2012). Such places offer an escape not just from taxes, but also from many other rules and regulations, because the structures created under their local laws can be used either completely anonymously, or largely so (Shaxson, 2011). In addition, prosecution of economic and financial crimes and judicial cooperation with other countries are often extremely limited. For these reasons, these places are also widely referred to as "secrecy jurisdictions" because they provide secrecy to OFC commercial operators and their clients, thereby facilitating various kinds of illicit financial flows (IFFs).

In many respects OFCs are fictional spaces. The term refers more to a set of activities than to a geographical setting.[7] The term offshore derives from the fact that the transactions recorded in the secrecy jurisdictions actually take place in other locations. A subtle distinction is sometimes made between tax havens and secrecy jurisdictions, on the one hand, and OFCs on the other. The latter comprise accountants, lawyers and bankers, plus their associated trust companies and financial intermediaries, who sell services to the residents of other territories or jurisdictions wishing to exploit the mechanisms created by legislation in the tax havens or secrecy jurisdictions. In practice, these operators can easily move their operations to wherever they want at any time; indeed, they have sometimes used this power to threaten to leave a jurisdiction that does not secure the legislation they desire (Murphy, 2008).

The OECD has taken the lead at the international level to address the problem of tax havens, using several criteria on the size and transparency of fiscal rules to identify such locations (OECD, 1998).[8] Based on these criteria, the OECD identified 35 jurisdictions as tax havens in 2000, but this list was criticized by a number of researchers because it omitted many jurisdictions that displayed the characteristics of tax havens.[9] Between 2000 and April 2002, the majority of these listed tax havens made formal commitments to implement the OECD's standards of transparency and exchange of information and were subsequently taken off this list; only seven jurisdictions that did not make commitments to the OECD's standards were identified as "unco-operative tax havens", but subsequently, following various commitments by them, they were removed from the list between 2003 and 2009. As a result, no jurisdiction remains currently listed as an "unco-operative tax haven" by the OECD, though new lists have recently appeared under the umbrella of the Global Forum (see below subsection 4 (a)).

The 2013 Financial Secrecy Index (FSI) developed by the Tax Justice Network (TJN) offers an alternative to the OECD approach (TJN, 2013). It establishes a ranking of 82 jurisdictions that provide financial secrecy according to both their degree of secrecy and their relative importance in global finance. The focus shifts, therefore, from governance issues within countries to the jurisdictions' responsibility for offering financial secrecy at the global level. Instead of relying on a binary indicator, which is often prone to political negotiations, the FSI is based on a secrecy score constructed from 15 indicators, which ranges from zero (total financial transparency) to 100 (total financial secrecy).[10] None of the analysed jurisdictions has scored less than 30, suggesting that there is no clear dividing line between "secrecy jurisdictions" (or tax havens) and others, and that there is a wide spectrum of secrecy.

From this perspective, some of the world's leading providers of financial secrecy are among the world's largest and wealthiest countries. This contrasts with the widespread perception that tax havens are small (often tropical) islands or micro-States.[11] Indeed, tax havens are not working on the

margins of the world economy, but rather as an integral part of modern business practices. According to one estimate, two million international business companies and thousands (if not millions) of trusts, mutual funds, hedge funds and captive insurance companies are located in the 56 countries that could be considered tax havens in 2009. About 50 per cent of all international bank lending is routed through these jurisdictions and 30–40 per cent of the world's stock of FDI is accounted as assets of firms registered there (Palan et al., 2010).

It has been pointed out that a number of developed countries, and even locations within these countries,[12] have some key features in common with more traditional tax havens. *The Economist* has recently shared this view by noting that "some of the biggest tax havens are in fact OECD economies". Moreover, it draws attention to the fact that "[these economies] provide something the offshore islands cannot: a destination for money rather than a mere conduit".[13] They also benefit from the perception that, overall, they are politically stable and that there are strong lobbies that support their tax haven status. Thus, OFCs, and the secrecy jurisdictions that host them, are not part of a parallel economic system; they are fully integrated into the global financial system and exist not necessarily in opposition to the State, but often with its accord. Moreover, as further discussed in subsection 2, many well-established taxpayers, both individuals and corporations, turn to them with a certain degree of impunity and (at least alleged) innocence. In the view of TJN,[14] the implications for global power politics are significant, and could help explain why international efforts to crack down on tax havens, OFCs and financial secrecy have so far been rather ineffective, despite recurrent announcements by the G20 and OECD countries for the need to address these issues. Indeed, some of the economically powerful residents of these economies are the primary beneficiaries of the so-called "illicit financial flows" and are able to influence the rules of the game (Rodrik, 2014).

(b) Illicit financial flows

One of the major roles of secret jurisdictions is the facilitation of illicit financial flows. There are two definitions of IFFs. In a narrow sense, they refer to

> Tax havens are not working on the margins of the world economy, but rather as an integral part of modern business practices.

all unrecorded private financial outflows involving capital that is illegally earned, transferred, or utilized. In this regard, they are generally used by residents to accumulate foreign assets in contravention of applicable domestic regulatory frameworks. Thus, even if the funds originate from legitimate business activities, their transfer abroad in violation of local law, such as exchange control regulations or tax regulations, would render the capital illicit. In a broader sense, IFFs also encompass all kinds of artificial arrangements that have been put in place for the essential purpose of circumventing the law or its spirit. Thus, illicit might not necessarily mean contravening the letter of the law but going against its spirit. In this case, illicit can be understood as something hidden or disguised.

It is generally accepted that the narrow definition is inadequate for describing tax-motivated IFFs. It fails to take into account several practices designed to reduce tax liability which go against the interests of society and ultimately harm the majority of the citizens, even if they cannot be proved to be illegal. In this *Report*, the key criterion used is whether such tax-motivated IFFs are justified from an economic point of view. If a given international financial flow is part of a "tax-optimization" scheme without any concrete related economic activity, it could be considered "illicit". To take a concrete example, several TNCs have taken advantage of a contentious loophole in Irish corporate law[15] known as the "double Irish". This allows them to be registered in Ireland without being considered a tax resident, because, as far as the Irish authorities are concerned, the company is a tax resident in Bermuda, which has a zero rate of corporate tax. Yet in practice, most of the real economic activities are not undertaken in Ireland or in Bermuda. Such aggressive tax planning arrangements also need to be considered when analysing the factors that may reduce fiscal space.

Empirical estimates show that tax-motivated IFFs account for the bulk of all the IFFs.[16] Among the three broad types of motivations – crime, corruption and tax abuse – that drive people and entities to turn to IFFs and tax havens, only about a third of total IFFs represent criminal money, linked primarily to drugs, racketeering and terrorism. It is noteworthy

that money from corruption is estimated to amount to just 3 per cent. The third component, which accounts for the remaining two thirds of the total, refers to cross-border tax-related transactions, about half of which consists of transfer pricing through corporations (Baker, 2005).

2. Cross-border tax dodging mechanisms

International tax dodging takes many forms, all of which aim at reducing tax liabilities. Such practices are arrayed along a spectrum of varying degrees of legality (Herson, 2014). One such practice is illegal *tax evasion*, which refers to a taxpayer's attempts to escape a tax liability under a country's law. It typically involves concealing from the fiscal authorities the income and assets which are liable for taxes or, in the case of fraud, falsifying paperwork. This implies a criminal activity or at least a failure to make a required disclosure.[17] Many tax evasion practices may occur only at the national level, but as the aim of this chapter is to analyse what structures in the global economy can favour such behaviours, purely national practices are not addressed here.

Another form of tax dodging is referred to as *tax avoidance*, including aggressive tax planning, whereby individuals or companies exploit loopholes in legislation to pay lower taxes. These practices may be within the law, but they can be perceived as crossing ethical boundaries. Tax avoidance is often understood as referring to practices designed to gain a tax advantage by contravening the intention, but not the letter, of the legislation (Herson, 2014). In practice, the difference between tax avoidance and tax evasion is frequently blurred. For instance, tax payments can be avoided by using mispricing techniques in intra-firm transactions or recording artificially high payments for intra-firm debt. The legality of these manoeuvres is open to question. Much of it depends on how domestic laws are drafted to avoid the existence of loopholes. Moreover, some strategies that have been argued as constituting "avoidance" have been judged as "evasion" when challenged and scrutinized in courts. This is even more relevant when tax schemes involve

> Empirical estimates show that tax-motivated IFFs account for the bulk of all the IFFs.

several jurisdictions. Since international taxation is extremely complex, tax payers embarking on such tax optimization strategies often are not sure whether these strategies are fully legal (Palan et al., 2010). It is for this reason that this *Report* refers to tax-motivated IFFs whenever the international structuring of transactions or asset portfolios has little or no economic substance, and their express purpose is to reduce tax liabilities.

For the purpose of tax avoidance, firms usually create one or more subsidiaries, affiliates or shell companies in one or several tax havens. This allows their real economic beneficiaries to relocate, at least on paper, a certain proportion of their activities to low-tax and/or secrecy jurisdictions to minimize their tax liabilities. Such relocation techniques often offer secrecy of ownership, no filing requirements, protection from creditors, low incorporation costs, and other subterfuges that facilitate sham operations.[18]

Many tax avoidance schemes exist worldwide. Evidence suggests that in developing countries trade and transfer mispricing is the main vehicle for tax avoidance, evasion and tax-related capital flight through tax havens (Palan et al., 2010).[19] Transfer pricing refers to the mechanism by which cross-border, intra-firm transactions are priced. It is often used in the global transactions of TNCs in the form of transfer of property or services among affiliates of the same TNC. The OECD has estimated that about one third of world trade takes place between such "related parties" (Lanz and Miroudot, 2011).[20] However, if the intra-company price does not reflect the true value, profits might effectively be shifted to low-tax or no-tax jurisdictions, while losses and deductions are shifted to high-tax jurisdictions. These practices clearly result in an overall erosion of the tax base and, *ceteris paribus*, in lower revenues.

> International cooperation across countries on tax matters remains limited.

It is generally accepted that pricing reflects the true value of transactions, including under Article 9 of the United Nations Model Double Taxation Convention between Developed and Developing Countries, when it occurs "at arm's length" (UN-DESA, 2011). This principle implies that the transfer price corresponds to the price that would be paid in a market where each participant is acting independently in its own interest. In practice,

however, it is often difficult to assess whether the reported price corresponds to an arm's length valuation. Many intra-firm transactions relate to specialized goods not traded in any market, or to fees for the use of intangibles whose value is inherently difficult to establish (e.g. royalties for brands). This makes such pricing susceptible to tax abuses. The practice of shifting profits for the minimization of customs duties or taxes through the manipulation of transfer prices is called transfer mispricing.

One purpose of transfer pricing regulations is to clearly determine how a firm's profits are distributed between two jurisdictions in order to avoid double taxation (i.e. when the cross-border activities of a company operating in several countries could be taxed by more than one tax authority). However, because of the separate entity principle in tax treaties, which restricts adoption of a unitary approach to corporate groups and requires the application of the so-called arm's length principle, international tax rules have provided a perverse incentive to tax "planning" or avoidance by using intermediary entities in secrecy jurisdictions. Hence, in practice the proliferation of bilateral tax treaties has often resulted in a double non-taxation.

Transfer mispricing and other practices aimed at tax avoidance can be challenged by tax authorities. Yet the process can be difficult, as those actions result from increased globalization in production processes, international competition amongst countries to attract capital and the aggressive exploitation of grey areas in tax laws. The latter is particularly common among TNCs that operate across several jurisdictions and hire specialized professionals and consultants specifically to handle tax planning. Moreover since international cooperation across countries on tax matters remains limited, for example in the area of transparency and exchange of information, it is difficult for an individual tax administration to control transfer mispricing and other tax avoidance practices. This is particularly true in low-income countries whose governments have fewer resources to fight tax-related capital flight and tax base erosion than corporations that plan their tax matters aggressively. In addition, the administrations in tax havens do not have a strong interest in cooperating with their counterparts in countries that may have legitimate claims, since they obtain some benefits from the situation.

Current international rules provide considerable scope for "base erosion and profit shifting" (BEPS). This refers to tax planning strategies, which enable companies to exploit gaps and mismatches in tax rules to make profits "disappear" for tax purposes. They do this by shifting their profits away from jurisdictions where the activities are taking place to jurisdictions where taxes are low, so that they pay little or no overall corporate tax (OECD, 2013a and b).

The overall effect of BEPS is a tendency to associate more profits with legal constructs and intangible rights and obligations, and to legally shift intra-group risk, which reduces the share of profits associated with substantive operations (OECD, 2013c). These tendencies become more pronounced over time as economic activities are increasingly based on information technology and intangibles. The overall effect of these corporate tax planning strategies is to erode the corporate tax base of many countries in a manner that is not intended by domestic policy. This reflects the fact that BEPS takes advantage of a combination of features of tax systems which have been put in place by home and host countries (OECD, 2013c). It implies that while international or bilateral cooperation to effectively combat BEPS behaviours is preferable, countries can also act individually to fight some of these practices.

> There is wide agreement that the public revenue losses due to tax abuses are huge.

3. Magnitude and impact of international tax abuses on mobilization of public revenue

The scale of IFFs, the amount of assets that foreigners hold in tax havens and the magnitude of the related public revenue losses are difficult to estimate. By their very nature, these activities are characterized by a lack of transparency, and estimates of the amount of such assets do not always consider exactly the same items or use the same methodologies and/or assumptions. Nevertheless, some recent and well-documented studies offer a hint of the magnitudes involved.

Regarding global offshore financial wealth, it has been estimated that it amounted to $5.9 trillion in 2008, suggesting that approximately 8 per cent of the global net financial wealth of households (bank deposits, equities, bonds and insurance contracts, net of debts) was held in tax havens, three quarters of which went unrecorded. Developing-country residents hold around 30 per cent of all offshore wealth, of which one third is owned by residents of oil-exporting countries (Zucman, 2013). These are probably underestimations; other estimates suggest a range of $21−$32 trillion in 2010, with roughly one third (between $7.3 and $9.3 trillion) originating in developing countries (Henry, 2012).[21] However, none of these studies takes into account non-financial wealth (such as real estate, yachts, racehorses and goldbricks) that can also be "owned" by offshore shell structures. This roughly corresponds to 10−15 per cent of all the estimated global financial and non-financial wealth.[22]

The loss of public revenue resulting from asset holdings in tax havens motivated by tax evasion is enormous. Henry (2012) estimates that if the unreported $21−$32 trillion had earned a modest rate of return of just 3 per cent, and if the income from the returns had been taxed at 30 per cent, this would have generated income tax revenues of $189−$288 billion per year. For developing countries, a similar calculation yields a tax gap of $66−$84 billion per year, which is about two thirds of total official development assistance (ODA). These are, by construction, conservative estimates, especially because they do not take into account the loss of tax revenue on the income generated by this capital before it was transferred to tax havens. Moreover, this figure would be considerably higher if additional taxes on this capital, such as taxes on inheritance, capital gains and wealth, were to be included.

With respect to the magnitude of IFFs, estimates are also very large. Nominal commercial illicit outflows from developing countries amounted to $946.7 billion in 2011, up 13.7 per cent from 2010. And they are estimated to have amounted to about 4 per cent of GDP over the past decade (Kar and

LeBlanc, 2013). In Africa, for instance, conservatively estimated cumulative illicit financial outflows totalled $437 billion over the period 2000–2008 (Kar and Cartwright-Smith, 2010). Similarly, Boyce and Ndikumana (2012) have estimated that illicit financial outflows from a group of 33 sub-Saharan African countries amounted to $814 billion (in constant 2010 dollars) from 1970 to 2010.

Estimating the revenue losses associated with IFFs, Christian Aid (2008) suggests that developing countries lose an annual $160 billion in revenues from corporation taxes due to transfer mispricing and falsified invoicing in international trade. Even though these practices represent only a subset of illegal activities resulting in public revenue losses, they amounted to more than one-and-a-half times the combined aid budgets of the entire developed world in 2007. FitzGerald (2012) looks at the gap between the tax revenue that could be legally collected and the actual revenue that results from tax misconduct associated with undeclared expatriated profits and overseas assets; estimates of public revenue loss for developing countries were $200–$250 billion annually in the mid-2000s. This figure is likely to have increased in subsequent years because of growth in the world economy and further financial integration. An earlier estimate by Cobham (2005) puts the revenue loss in developing countries at $385 billion annually. This includes tax losses due to domestic "shadow economic activity", together with the non-payment of taxes on income from assets held in OFCs and from profits earned by the corporate sector that were shifted to lower tax jurisdictions. TJN (2011) uses estimates from Schneider et al. (2010) on the size of the shadow economy (including, but not limited to, OFCs). It finds that tax evasion costs countries around the world more than $3.1 trillion annually. Of this total, Africa accounts for about $79 billion, Asia for $666 billion, Europe for $1.5 trillion, North America for $453 billion, Oceania for $46 billion and South America for $376 billion.

Some of these estimates are criticized on methodological grounds.[23] However, mostly, their magnitude is in line with that of national tax authorities or other official sources.[24] Notwithstanding the inherent limitations of such assessments, there is wide agreement that the public revenue losses due to tax abuses are huge. This calls for improving tax scrutiny, but also for preventing tax-related capital flight or complex tax schemes through tax havens

and shell companies whose sole function is to reduce tax liabilities without creating any economic value.

4. Recent attempts to tackle international tax leakages

The fallout from the global financial crisis of 2008-2009 crisis prompted intensified efforts, at both national and international levels, to target tax abuse and the secrecy jurisdictions that facilitate these practices. Tax leakages have always been a serious issue for developing countries, but in a context of fiscal austerity and spending cuts in developed economies, this has also become increasingly recognized by their governments and public opinion as an issue that needs to be tackled. Some of the main recent developments with cross-border effects are outlined below.

(a) Global Forum on Transparency and Exchange of Information for Tax Purposes

The Global Forum has been the main multilateral framework within which work on transparency and exchange of information for tax purposes and other related domains has been carried out since 2000.[25] The OECD, which initiated this process, later opened this platform to non-OECD countries. In September 2009, it was restructured in response to a call by the G20 to strengthen exchange of information so as to protect the tax bases of governments from non-compliance with their tax laws.[26] The work of the Forum involves three main initiatives as described below.

(i) Country classification and peer review process

The Global Forum has started to report on individual countries, based on internationally agreed tax standards. According to its classification, countries are divided into three groups: jurisdictions that have substantially implemented the internationally agreed tax standard (also referred as the "white list"); jurisdictions that have committed to the internationally agreed tax standard, but have not yet substantially implemented it ("grey list"); and jurisdictions that have not committed to the internationally agreed tax standard ("black list"). In April 2009, the third category was nothing but an empty shell, and since then most of the jurisdictions have moved from the second to the first category. This was not difficult: in order to be removed from the black list, it was sufficient to provide the OECD with the solemn assurance that it intended to abide by international agreements in the future. Acceptance into the white list requires a jurisdiction to have signed only 12 or more agreements that meet the standard. Thus, several grey list jurisdictions signed bilateral tax agreements among themselves to reach this threshold. Thus, the apparent disappearance of tax havens (according to this new OECD standard) was, above all, the result of skilful diplomacy. According to some critics "even the most notorious offshore financial centres have managed to quickly purge themselves of all suspicions of aiding and abetting tax evaders."[27] Johannesen and Zucman (2014) show that these new treaties have affected only a small proportion of offshore deposits, mainly through their relocation between tax havens, but have not resulted in significant repatriations of funds. The least compliant havens appear to have attracted deposits while the most compliant have lost some, leaving roughly unchanged the total amount of offshore-managed wealth. Meanwhile, the Global Forum's peer review process started in 2010, and in November 2013 it adopted ratings on the level of compliance with the internationally agreed standard for exchange of information. However, it has been criticized for its bias towards standards that align with the interests of OECD member States and for giving notorious tax havens a full seat at the table from the very beginning, which may explain why the agreed standards are weak (Meinzer, 2012).

(ii) Declaration on Automatic Exchange of Information in Tax Matters

At their meeting in the Russian Federation in September 2013, the G20 leaders issued the Declaration on Automatic Exchange of Information in Tax Matters (AEoI). This was endorsed in May 2014 by all 34 OECD member countries, as well as by Argentina, Brazil, China, Colombia, Costa Rica, India, Indonesia, Latvia, Lithuania, Malaysia, Saudi Arabia, Singapore and South Africa. Through this Declaration, these countries have thus committed to implementing a new single global standard on AEoI.[28] The standard mostly incorporates elements of both EU initiatives and the United States Foreign Account Tax Compliance Act (FATCA). These served to catalyse moves towards the automatic exchange of information in a multilateral context.

However, the lack of inclusion of developing countries in the design phase of the new system and the premature inclusion of countries known to be tax havens risk weakening the new system.[29] The poorer countries that are not yet in a position to provide reciprocal information will gain little from it, while some developed countries have suggested that developing countries be excluded because they cannot be trusted to keep information on their own taxpayers confidential.[30] One solution could be to establish a fixed transition period of some years during which developing and transition economies could receive data without reciprocity. This would allow them to ascertain the value of the data, adapt their own systems to make good use of it, and invest in the capacity to reciprocate (Cobham, 2014).

(iii) Initiatives on base erosion and profit shifting

In July 2013, at the request of G20 Finance Ministers, the OECD launched an Action Plan on Base Erosion and Profit Shifting (BEPS) to draw up new global tax rules to counter BEPS. This contains 15 actions to address a range of issues relating to tax transparency, accountability, information exchange and other potential changes to international taxation. The action plan also insists on the need for international agreement and cooperation so that countries will not have to act unilaterally. There are six key areas where there is urgent need for action (OECD, 2013c):

- International mismatches in entity and instrument characterization, which includes hybrid mismatch arrangements and arbitrage;

- Application of treaty concepts to profits derived from the delivery of digital goods and services;

- Tax treatment of related party debt-financing, captive insurance and other inter-group financial transactions;

- Transfer pricing, in particular in relation to the shifting of risks and intangibles, the artificial splitting of ownership of assets between legal entities within a group, and transactions between such entities that would rarely take place between independents;

- The effectiveness of anti-avoidance measures, in particular the general anti-abuse rule, controlled foreign company regimes, thin capitalization rules and rules to prevent abuse of tax treaties; and

- The existence of harmful preferential regimes.

Another topic that appears throughout the action plan concerns tax-related disclosures by companies to the tax authorities on a country-by-country basis. Using a common template, TNCs will be required to provide all relevant authorities with necessary information on their global allocation of income, economic activity and taxes paid. Although a majority of business leaders now support country-by-country reporting (CbCR), the publication of this data is being fiercely opposed by some business representatives and some national governments.[31]

(b)   Other G20 and related initiatives

In addition to the initiatives discussed above in the context of the Global Forum, in November 2008 G20 leaders declared their intention to promote information sharing with respect to all kinds of abuses and fraudulent activities (G20, 2008). At their London Summit, in April 2009, they announced that the era of bank secrecy was over. They called on all jurisdictions "to adhere to the international standards in the prudential, tax, and AML/CFT [anti-money laundering/combating the financing of terrorism] areas", with the aim of protecting their public finances and curbing tax abuses. Since then, several initiatives that could help tackle tax abuses have been launched by different actors, over and above those of the OECD. In particular, the Financial Stability Board has worked on the establishment of a global legal entity identifier system that will attribute a reference code in order to uniquely identify a legally distinct entity that engages in a financial transaction. This would help track financial flows, even in secrecy jurisdictions.

(c)   United Nations Committee of Experts on International Cooperation in Tax Matters

The work of the United Nations Committee of Experts on International Cooperation in Tax Matters (a subsidiary body of the Economic and Social Council) offers a useful framework for addressing international tax challenges. In particular, it aims at enhancing technical capacity in developing countries to handle complex matters in taxation. The Committee has recently provided two main contributions to influence international tax practices. One is the 2011 revision of the *United Nations Model Double Taxation Convention between Developed and Developing Countries* (UN-DESA, 2011). This addresses possible abuses with respect to capital gains, the importance of exchange of information and assistance in the collection of taxes. The other is the *United Nations Practical Manual on Transfer Pricing for Developing Countries* (United Nations, 2013a). This offers practical guidance to policymakers and administrators on the application of the arm's length standard among both developing and developed countries. Regarding the OECD and G20 BEPS project, in October 2013 the Committee established a specific subcommittee for monitoring developments on BEPS-related issues and communicating with officials in developing countries.

(d)   Other regional, bilateral and national initiatives with spillover effects

Regional cooperation between tax authorities via regional platforms, such as the Inter-American Centre of Tax Administrations and the African Tax Administration Forum (ATAF), has helped strengthen mutual assistance and capacity-building. In particular, the recently created ATAF has worked towards increasing the level of voluntary tax compliance whilst combating tax evasion and avoidance. Compared with these regional initiatives, regional cooperation among Asia-Pacific tax authorities in establishing frameworks and practices has been modest, so far (Araki, 2014).

In parallel to the progress made in the Global Forum on AEoI, numerous bilateral tax treaties (BTTs) and tax information exchange agreements (TIEAs) have been signed recently. However, many developing countries do not benefit from them. Indeed, only 8 per cent of BTTs, and 5 per cent of TIEAs,[32] have been signed with LDCs since 2008. Furthermore, some OECD tax havens have used the negotiations with developing countries for inclusion of information exchange clauses as a leverage to push for significant concessions from the partners to the agreements.[33]

In the *United States*, in the context of the post-crisis scandals related to foreign banks aiding tax evasion, FATCA has sought to recoup federal tax revenues by making it more difficult for taxpayers to conceal assets held in offshore accounts and shell corporations. In particular, FATCA requires all United States nationals, including those living abroad, to report their financial accounts held outside the country. It also requires foreign financial institutions to report on their United States clients to the Internal Revenue Service. However, this measure will only affect interest on directly held, non-business bank deposits of individuals. Wealthy individuals who use corporations and limited liability companies (LLCs) registered in Delaware, for instance, would not be affected.[34]

In December 2012, the European Commission presented an action plan for more effectively dealing with tax evasion and avoidance in the *EU*. The action plan specifies a comprehensive set of measures, to help member States protect their tax bases and recapture billions of euros legitimately due to them. The plan highlights the need to promote automatic information exchange as an international standard, and to end "double non-taxation" by companies and individuals. This includes, for instance, the Revised Savings Taxation Directive adopted in March 2014. EU governments are expected to implement the amended rules and adopt an EU-wide anti-abuse law – a safeguard against abusive tax practices – by the end of 2014.

In the *United Kingdom* in November 2012, the House of Commons Public Accounts Committee held hearings on the behaviour of three top United States TNCs that have used cross-border royalty payments, transfer pricing and siting of regional headquarters to lower their corporation tax payments. Members of parliament accused these TNCs of manipulating their accounts to minimize the corporate tax they paid in the United Kingdom, despite their significant commercial presence in that country. The consequent public outcry led one of the companies to announce voluntary payments of £20 million to HM Revenue and Customs within two years. This was after it emerged that the company had paid just £8.6 million in corporation taxes in 14 years of trading in the United Kingdom and none between 2009 and 2011.[35]

As a unilateral attempt to fight trade mispricing in commodities, *Brazil* introduced a simplified comparable uncontrolled price method in 2012 (Ernst & Young, 2013; Pereira Valadão, 2013). This aims to provide a reference price for commodities that Brazilian exporters and importers should use to avoid trade mispricing in their valuation of international trade. In particular, the Law (no. 12715/2012) authorizes the Brazilian tax authorities to determine what should be considered as commodities, and which commodity exchange should be recognized for applying the newly introduced methods. The law allows for price adjustments such as market premium and transportations costs, and, where there are no internationally recognized spot or futures quotations, the price of imported and exported goods could be compared with the prices obtained from independent data sources provided by internationally recognized research institutions.

D. Improving public revenue mobilization from the extractive industries

1. Fiscal regimes and tax incentives in the extractive industries

(a) Tax incentives: Risk of a race to the bottom

The generation of public revenues from the extractive industries and their use for financing development are central to the strategies of many developing countries. In resource-rich countries, these industries have been the main source of foreign currency and fiscal revenues. With the rise of commodity prices over the past decade, the magnitude of natural-resource rents and, consequently, their potential for supporting investment and growth have increased significantly. This has led to renewed interest in the issue of distribution of those rents among the owners of the resources and the companies that are assigned exploitation rights.[36]

As extractive industries are typically large scale and highly capital intensive, firms that invest in this sector tend to be very large. They normally possess the necessary financial resources and exploitation technology that most governments in developing countries lack. They are generally private TNCs, mostly based in developed countries, though an increasing number of State-owned enterprises, including from developing countries, are also operating in this sector. Investors have to negotiate the terms of their investment and subsequent operations with the governments of the countries owning the natural resources, which have sovereignty over these resources.[37]

Extractive industries present some special features that influence each party's position in such negotiations. Since the natural resources exploited by these industries are non-renewable, as a source of revenue they will be exhausted sooner or later. Hence, from the point of view of producing countries, capturing a significant proportion of the rents generated from their exploitation is crucial for financing diversification of the domestic economy to enable it to generate new sources of income, foreign exchange earnings and public revenues. In this context, the "fiscal linkage" is of particular importance since other linkages of the extractive industries with the domestic economy (e.g. employment and demand for domestically produced inputs) tend to be weak, except during the initial period when the production facilities and associated infrastructure are being built. Moreover, since most of the firms in the sector are TNCs, a large share of their revenues is likely to be repatriated rather than reinvested in the country where the natural resources are being exploited.

From the point of view of the TNCs, activities in this capital-intensive sector typically involve high sunk costs, investments have a long gestation period, and the prices for their products are volatile. Thus the profitability of their investment is extremely uncertain. Moreover, once an investment has taken place, it cannot be moved to another location. This is why they try to obtain special fiscal treatment and favour a stable tax regime.

Therefore, governments need to establish a fiscal framework for the extractive industries that responds to two major – and potentially conflicting – objectives: first, the fiscal conditions should be appropriate to attract investment; and second, they should ensure that the State receives an appropriate share of the rents for financing its development goals. Reconciliation of these two objectives results essentially from the respective bargaining power of governments and TNCs. Such bargaining power has changed significantly – in different directions – in the past few decades, based on developments in commodity markets.

With the commodity price hikes of the 1970s and the perceived risk of supply shortages, the bargaining power shifted in favour of the producing countries which owned the scarce resources. This led to a wave of nationalizations of the oil and mining sectors in many developing countries. However, following the debt crisis of the 1980s, and with commodity prices declining in the 1990s, the balance of power changed again in favour of TNCs. These firms owned the technologies and the financial resources that many developing producing countries lacked for profitably exploiting their resources at a time of low prices. Under these circumstances, governments in many developing countries sought to attract FDI to the extractive industries either by privatization of their State-owned enterprises, especially those on the mining sector, or by opening the sector to foreign companies while maintaining some State participation. In both cases, they used a variety of tax incentives for TNCs, many of which are still applied today.

> The "fiscal linkage" is of particular importance since other linkages of the extractive industries with the domestic economy tend to be weak.

These incentives can take the form of reduced tax rates (royalties or corporate tax rates) or tax holidays, accelerated depreciation periods, or capital cost allowances that allow them to recover capital costs during the first years of production or carry forward losses. Similarly, firms may have the possibility to consolidate revenues and losses of different investment projects if the government does not impose a ring-fencing regulation. Other incentives include lower corporate taxes for reinvested earnings, tax-free remittance of profits to home countries and exemptions on fuel and import duties. In addition, TNCs may be exempted from capital gains taxes. This particular tax incentive is set to become increasingly relevant in an evolving environment where small and high-risk-taking junior companies engaged in exploration activities tend to sell their rights to larger companies that extract the resources. There can also be stabilization clauses that fix fiscal conditions for long periods of time, or even for the entire life of an extractive industry project.

It is important to recognize that the granting of tax privileges in one country tends to have an impact on other countries. Foreign companies take their investment decisions in an international context, comparing the profitability of similar investments in different locations. Thus, a neighbouring country or a country in another region that is endowed with the same or similar natural resources may feel the pressure to offer similar or even better incentives to compete as a destination for FDI. This not only undermines the effectiveness of fiscal incentives, but also runs the risk of leading to a race to the bottom, where all countries reduce their taxes to harmfully low levels, with no winners but the foreign private firms, most notably the TNCs.

Privatization and liberalization of fiscal regimes in the extractive industries took place in many countries under the auspices of the Bretton Woods institutions in the context of structural adjustment programmes. In its Strategy for African Mining in 1992, the World Bank presented its private-FDI-led approach to the mining sector in African countries.[38] Similarly, in 1996 the World Bank formulated a mining strategy for Latin America and the Caribbean, although the principles underlying this strategy had been applied long before. The idea was that, thanks to increasing FDI, government revenues would automatically accrue from the rising production.

By the turn of the century, the mining sector in developing countries was largely dominated by TNCs, mostly from developed countries, that engaged in large-scale production.[39] By contrast, in the oil and gas sector, State-owned enterprises have continued to play a prominent role. This is probably because they managed to remain profitable even when oil and gas prices were low, and because the technology requirements for exploiting existing fields were lower than those in the mining sector.

Tax incentives have been widely questioned on the grounds that their costs in terms of foregone public revenues may often outweigh the benefits for the domestic economy. In particular, following the recovery of commodity prices since 2003, it is increasingly recognized that the public revenue gains often have not been commensurate with the increasing profitability of activities in this sector.[40] Civil society organizations have been playing a prominent role in raising awareness about what is seen by many as unfair fiscal regimes in many developing countries.[41] The World Bank (2010: 9) has also acknowledged that "Mining fiscal regimes developed in the past (often under Bank guidance) were not adequate to capture much of the large increase in rents generated by these price increases". For example, a study of four countries in East Africa (Kenya, Rwanda, Uganda and the United Republic of Tanzania) by Tax Justice Network-Africa and ActionAid International (2012) shows that tax incentives are resulting in large losses of government revenue of up to $2.8 billion annually, depriving those countries of critical resources for development and poverty reduction. The IMF has also emphasized the need for developing countries that are becoming new producers of natural resources to pay greater attention to the design of their fiscal regime in order to tap into this potential source of revenue (IMF, 2012).

Several international institutions and civil society organizations have warned about the lack of economic effectiveness of tax incentives to attract FDI (IMF et al., 2011; Tax Justice Network-Africa and ActionAid International, 2012). Similarly, the United Nations (2010: 2) concludes that "investment incentives are generally unnecessary for the mining sector because mining activities are location based and governments should collect the rents from such resources". This is equally applicable to oil and gas extraction.

Indeed, there are indications that, in many cases, tax privileges for foreign companies in the extractive industries have far exceeded reasonable limits, and that such privileges may often be unnecessary. For instance, the African Development Bank (AfDB) et al. (2010: 109) recognize that "most natural resources can be taxed, within the bounds of reason, without scaring away investors". Moreover, various surveys among investors have confirmed that tax motivations rank low among the factors influencing a decision on where to invest; in other words, in many cases investment would most likely take place anyway, even with lower or no special tax incentives (Keen and Mansour, 2009; Vale Columbia Center on Sustainable Investment, 2013).

> Tax incentives have been widely questioned on the grounds that their costs in terms of foregone public revenues may often outweigh the benefits for the domestic economy.

Since the early 2000s investment in natural resource exploitation, particularly FDI, has surged (UNCTAD, 2007),[12] particularly in Africa, Latin America, West Asia and the transition economies. However, there is no clear evidence that this was due to tax incentives (World Bank, 2012a: 132). Rather, it is more likely to have been motivated by the expectation of new profit opportunities resulting from increasing demand from emerging market economies, particularly China, and the commodity price boom since 2003. But there have been growing concerns that neither the higher commodity prices nor the increase in FDI have significantly improved development prospects in many producing countries.

TNCs in the extractive industries saw their profits soar during the price boom: between 2002 and 2012 revenues of the world's largest mining companies increased fivefold and net profits more than tenfold (Stevens et al., 2013). Meanwhile, government revenues from natural resources lagged far behind. Many commodity-dependent countries failed to achieve marked improvements in terms of income distribution, poverty reduction or human development.[43] By the second half of the 2000s, it had become evident that the incentives to attract FDI had been overly generous, especially in the context of the changed commodity markets environment. Therefore, it was considered necessary to revise taxation policies related to the extractive industries in order to protect the interests of the host countries. As in the 1970s, strong demand and higher prices again increased the bargaining power of producing countries, which provided additional political impetus for such revisions.

Host governments have also seen their bargaining position strengthened by the emergence of new major players in the extractive industries. While TNCs from developed countries continue to dominate the scene in commodity-producing developing countries, FDI from emerging countries is growing very rapidly. This gives producing countries a greater choice of investors. Therefore, contracts with these traditional TNCs may be negotiated more favourably for the host country.

(b) Forms of State participation in the extractive industries

There are different ways for the State to capture a share of the rents of the extractive industries. These range from royalties and various forms of taxation, to contractual arrangements such as production-sharing and services contracts, as well as full participation in production, either through public ownership or through joint ventures between State-owned enterprises and private firms. Methods of raising public revenue can be based on production or on profits. Production-based methods, in the form of per unit or "ad valorem" royalties, are more advantageous for the government as it receives them from the moment the project begins operation, even if the companies do not register profits in their accounts. For this reason, governments tend to prefer them. They are also relatively easy to administer, an advantage which is of particular importance in developing countries where tax administrations often find it difficult to correctly assess taxable revenues. Private companies, on the other hand, prefer taxation based on profits, mainly through corporate income taxes, as they start paying taxes only when they record profits. Special taxation in the extractive industries based on profits may also include resource rent taxes and taxes on windfall profits, although these are less common. Another advantage of profit-based taxes for TNCs, but a major disadvantage for producing countries, is that profits are more difficult to monitor which makes it easier for companies to adopt tax evasion and avoidance techniques (see section C).

Governments can also impose export taxes on the extractive industries, as another form of production-based taxation. They may offer the advantage of being easier to collect, while also helping to control the volumes, prices and qualities of the commodity exported at the customs point. For instance, a company may try to avoid taxation by underestimating the grade of the mineral ores or of possible by-products contained in the exported concentrate, and this could be controlled by the customs authorities in producing countries.[44] Such taxes could also be used as an instrument of industrial policy if the tax rate is lower for processed products than for the raw materials. Another way to increase public revenues in producing countries is by taxing capital gains in the extractive industries, which are increasing in importance, as mentioned above. Additionally, environmental taxes can be applied to internalize the external costs of extractive activity.

Overall, there is no universal recipe for an optimal taxation regime for this sector. In practice, governments tend to use a combination of instruments. The final outcome depends largely on the specific geological, economic, institutional and political circumstances of each country. As a result, there is no absolute benchmark or reference point based on which particular fiscal regime for the extractive industries could be judged as "fair" or "unfair". In practice, a wide range of taxation levels are applied in different countries.[45]

Producing countries should not only be able to negotiate a taxation system that effectively expands their fiscal space; they must also be able to enforce it, avoiding massive losses due to aggressive tax planning and accounting practices of TNCs, such as transfer mispricing and thin capitalization. This is particularly important, since the natural resources sector is usually the main source of illicit financial flows in resource-rich countries (AfDB and GFI, 2013).

Transfer mispricing practices appear to be quite common in the extractive industries. TNCs can manipulate profit reporting by inflating costs and undervaluing prices in their intra-firm operations. In this way they can shift profits from the tax jurisdiction of the natural-resource-producing country to a lower tax jurisdiction.[46] Tax losses from these kinds of practices may be huge. The United Nations Economic Commission for Africa (UNECA, 2013) has found that illicit financial flows from Africa in the form of trade mispricing are highly concentrated in a few sectors, notably in the extractive industries.

> Producing countries should not only be able to negotiate a taxation system that effectively expands their fiscal space...

> ... they must also be able to enforce it, avoiding massive losses due to aggressive tax planning and accounting practices of TNCs.

During the period 2000–2009, more than half (56 per cent) of those flows from Africa were from oil, precious metals and minerals, ores, iron and steel, and copper. And a report of the Africa Progress Panel (APP) titled "Equity in Extractives" prepared under the leadership of former Secretary-General of the United Nations, Kofi Annan, emphasized that Africa loses $38 billion annually due to trade mispricing (APP, 2013).

The abuse of transfer pricing is facilitated by the way in which TNCs design their corporate structures. In an attempt to unravel the labyrinthine corporate structures created by the biggest companies in this sector, PWYP (2011) found that the 10 most powerful corporations in the extractive industries owned 6,038 separate companies. Similarly, an investigation into extractive industries projects financed by the World Bank's International Financial Corporation (IFC) found that 57 per cent of the companies analysed channel their investments in developing countries through intermediate holding companies located in tax havens (Dan Watch, 2011). It may be difficult to explain why TNCs in the extractive industries have their headquarters or subsidiaries in low-tax jurisdictions if not to avoid paying taxes in the producing countries.[47]

Another damaging practice for producing countries, similar to transfer pricing, is that of thin capitalization. According to the United Nations (2013a) *Practical Manual on Transfer Pricing*, a company is said to be "thinly capitalized" when it has a high proportion of debt in relation to its equity capital. Excessive debt funding of a subsidiary company in a producing country is a disguised way of transferring profits to headquarters. This can lead to an unacceptable erosion of the revenue base of the producing country, such as when the interests paid are inflated so as to show higher costs, and consequently, lower profits.[48]

In addition to ensuring appropriate fiscal regimes and negotiation of contracts as well as adequate collection of taxes in the extractive industries, a final important aspect in the taxation chain is that of jurisdiction for the settlement of disputes between foreign investors and the government. In principle, according to the voluntary *OECD Guidelines for Multinational Enterprises*, foreign investors should abide by national laws. However, under bilateral investment agreements, investors can submit tax disputes to international arbitration.[49] TNCs can also file cases at international arbitration centres when governments review their tax regimes or renegotiate contracts on the ground of breaches of stability clauses (on this issue, see also chapter VI).

2. Distribution of rents in the extractive industries

An empirical assessment of the size of a State's participation in the rents from its natural resources remains a difficult task. Natural resource rents are defined as the difference between the sales value and the cost of production of the commodity concerned. Costs of production normally refer not only to operating costs but also to amortization and depreciation, as well as other costs such as interests from loans; and in the most comprehensive definition, normal profits are also considered a component of production costs. Calculation of the value of production is straightforward, because data on production by country and on international commodity prices are readily available. However, there is very little information on the cost of production. An additional complication is the availability of specific data on government revenues from natural resources, since few countries report them as a separate item.[50]

With these considerations, this subsection updates previous UNCTAD work in this area (*TDR 2005*, chap. III, section F and annex; and *TDR 2010*, chap. V, section D.5) in order to throw more light on the recent evolution of the share of government revenues in the rents of the extractive industries.[51] The results, by product and country, are shown in table 7.1. It was possible to perform calculations mainly for countries where a particular mineral or oil accounts for a major proportion of their natural resources production. For example, in the case of gold, the cost of production in African countries could be calculated by referring to the average production costs reported by major TNCs that provided these data in their annual reports. As governments do not report their natural resource revenues disaggregated by product, the data on revenues cover those from gold and other metals. Gold revenues account for most of government revenues from the extractive industries in these countries, and even though they lead to an overestimation of government's share in

Table 7.1

SHARE OF GOVERNMENT REVENUES IN RENTS FROM THE EXTRACTIVE INDUSTRIES, SELECTED COMMODITIES AND COUNTRIES, 2004–2012

(Per cent)

	2004	2005	2006	2007	2008	2009	2010	2011	2012	Cumulative share
Oil										
Angola	63.2	56.8	75.9	81.4	79.6	81.4	88.1	91.9	95.1	83.3
Colombia	32.7	28.7	34.1	44.3	39.0	52.4	34.0	37.0	55.1	41.1
Ecuador	71.8	67.4	69.5	68.8	65.8	66.6	72.9	93.1	93.5	76.3
Venezuela (Bolivarian Republic of)	58.4	54.9	70.1	72.1	52.0	56.4	63.5	70.3	70.9	64.1
Copper										
Chile	50.9	53.5	51.0	54.0	60.1	44.7	51.3	50.1	55.5	51.9
10 major private firms	*20.7*	*27.7*	*28.8*	*35.7*	*36.8*	*24.0*	*29.8*	*38.3*	*40.4*	*32.0*
CODELCO	*99.7*	*84.3*	*88.9*	*90.7*	*101.1*	*79.3*	*91.3*	*66.3*	*89.5*	*86.9*
Peru	23.5	37.5	30.9	24.5	31.0	34.0	32.2	33.7	47.0	32.7
Zambia	0.8	2.0	3.4	8.9	21.6	167.4	19.2	30.5	..	17.5
Gold										
Ghana	20.1	61.9	27.6	29.8	23.9	18.6	21.0	31.1	32.8	27.7
Mali	21.4	18.0	29.6	43.3	38.5	39.6	35.8	20.3	..	33.6
Peru	23.7	24.6	26.4	25.7	28.1	28.3	29.2	28.1	29.9	27.7
United Republic of Tanzania	17.3	37.5	12.8	12.6	17.4	13.2	12.2	13.9	28.5	17.9

Source: UNCTAD secretariat calculations, based on annual reports of producing companies; *UNCTADstat*; IMF, *Country Reports*, various issues; IMF, *International Financial Statistics* database; World Bureau of Metal Statistics, *World Metal Statistics Yearbook 2014*; BP, *Statistical Review of World Energy 2014*; EITI Country Reports, various issues; and national sources.

the rents, the data are considered to be valid as an approximation for this exercise.[52]

These estimations show that there is wide variation in the size of governments' shares of the rents, as expected. The main reason for the differences is the degree of ownership of the natural resource by the State. In those countries where the State participates in production through State-owned companies, such as Sonangol in Angola, PDVSA in the Bolivarian Republic of Venezuela, Petroecuador in Ecuador for oil, and CODELCO in Chile for copper, the governments' shares of the rents are relatively high.[53]

By contrast, in those countries and activities where private companies are the only or dominant actors, the share of government revenues in the rents is much lower. This is mainly the case for countries producing minerals, such as Zambia, where the State captured an extremely low share of the rents from copper up to the end of the last decade. This could be

attributed largely to the generous terms of the agreements that were reached between the Government and TNCs. For example, even though the royalty rate was 3 per cent in the general mining regime, in reality TNCs paid only 0.6 per cent as a result of specific development agreements. In the case of Ghana, where the range for royalties had been generally established at between 3 and 6 per cent, most companies paid at the lower level of the band. The share of the State in rents from gold production in the United Republic of Tanzania has also been very low. Similarly, the share of the State in the rents from mining production in Peru, which is controlled by the private sector, is relatively low.

In Latin America, the comparison of the distribution of copper rents in Chile and Peru provides interesting insights. In both these countries, when only private firms are taken into consideration, the government appropriates about one third of the rents. When considering the State-owned enterprise,

CODELCO, in Chile the public share is over 50 per cent. While CODELCO accounted for about 36 per cent of total copper production in the last decade, it contributed as much as 60 per cent of total government revenues from this activity. This difference is due to the fact that CODELCO transferred to the government more than 85 per cent of the rents generated.

In general, up to the turn of the decade, the amount of government revenues from mining was quite low, except in the case of Chile when CODELCO is included. While the share of the government in the rent has fluctuated over the period considered, particularly in African countries,[54] the cumulated flows show that the government captures between 17 per cent and 33 per cent of the rents. According to Daniel et al. (2013: 22) "Fiscal regimes around the world offer governments, on average, about half of the rents generated by mining, and two-thirds or more from petroleum—perhaps because petroleum usually generates more rent. Actual collections may be lower if there are loopholes or inefficiencies in collection. Fiscal policies that raise less than these benchmark averages may be cause for concern".

The increases in the share of the government in the rents that have occurred in the past few years may be partly related to recent changes in regulatory regimes for the mining sector, which aimed at raising the State's share (see below). It may also be due to the fact that companies that had benefited from accelerated depreciation and loss-carry-forward incentives had to start paying corporate income taxes when the period for these incentives expired.

Until recently, royalties were the main component of government revenues in the extractive industries. However, it appears that the trend is changing, probably due to the increasing importance of corporate taxes that TNCs are now being obliged to pay. In Latin America, the principal source of government revenues from mining is a tax on profits reported by the mining companies, while royalties account for only a small share (ECLAC, 2014b). This may not be the case yet for many African countries, where royalties still account for the major share of government revenues from the mining sector (Gajigo et al., 2012b). One reason for this difference may be that production in African countries started later, and therefore most TNCs operating there are still enjoying the benefits of accelerated depreciation. It may also be that the capacities of African countries to control

and prevent harmful tax management practices are more limited than those of Latin American countries.

3. Recent initiatives related to taxation in the extractive industries

(a) Changes in the regulatory environment for the extractive industries

With rapidly rising commodity prices, the perception grew that the distribution of rents between the State and foreign private corporations tended to be skewed in favour of the latter, thus depriving host-country governments of an appropriate share in the rising value of their natural resources. This has led, since the mid-2000s, to an increasing trend towards reviewing the fiscal conditions under which the extractive industries operate. In many natural-resource producing countries, governments have taken different measures to correct the situation. As illustrated with the selected examples presented in table 7.2, these may take various forms, including revision of contracts that may lead to their renegotiation or cancellation, increases in tax or royalty rates or the introduction of new taxes, and changes in State ownership of the extractive projects.

Although the main objective of these changes was generally to improve the distribution of the rent, on some occasions revisions in the regulatory environment may also aim at expanding the production or the local transformation of primary commodities. The government may apply the principle of "use it or lose it" if there is insufficient investment in, or development of, a particular concession or project. For example, in April 2012 the Government of Argentina assumed majority ownership of Repsol YPF, the largest oil-producing company in the country, by taking over the Spanish TNC, Repsol's 51 per cent stake in that company. The Government claimed that insufficient investment by the latter had led to a steep decline in oil and gas production and had turned Argentina into a net importer of hydrocarbons, from having been a net exporter. In less than two years, the State-controlled company reversed the decline in investment and production.[55] Taxes may also be introduced or raised for industrial policy purposes. For instance, in January 2014 Indonesia imposed an export tax, along with a ban on mineral ore exports, in order to induce mining companies to process the raw materials domestically.

In a number of countries, governments' attempts to introduce changes to their fiscal regimes for extractive industries have been foiled by various pressures. In Zambia, for instance, a 25 per cent windfall tax was introduced in 2008, but it was repealed in 2009 following a fall in copper prices after the global financial crisis. TNCs' warnings about the possibility of investment reductions and mine closures, and their threats to take legal action also played a role. Likewise, the Government of Ghana's plan to introduce a 10 per cent tax on windfall revenues in its 2012 budget was dropped following threats by mining companies to lay off workers.[56] However, in general, TNCs do not follow through on their threats to leave a country after it introduces regulatory changes. For instance, in Ecuador in 2010 most companies accepted the Government's request to renegotiate their contracts with the Government. Similarly, after the changes in public ownership in the natural gas sector in Bolivia in 2005-2006, TNCs stayed on in the country under the new conditions; and foreign TNCs are continuing to sign contracts with Argentina's YPF for exploration and exploitation of large shale oil and shale gas reserves in the country.

It is not only developing countries that have introduced, or attempted to introduce, changes to their fiscal regimes relating to the extractive industries; a number of governments in developed countries have also been reviewing their shares in the distribution of the rents from these industries. As shown in table 7.2, in the United Kingdom, the supplementary tax on oil production was increased in 2011, and in Australia, against heavy opposition from the booming mining sector and after a long (and ongoing) debate, the Government introduced a mineral resource rent tax in 2012 of 22.5 per cent".[57]

Revisions of the regulatory environment for the extractive industries are ongoing processes throughout the world. In a number of countries, discussions among different stakeholders continue to take place with a view to reforming tax and ownership regimes. These include Brazil, the Democratic Republic of the Congo, India, Mali, Mozambique, the Philippines and South Africa but also the United States.[58] In South Africa, there has been extensive debate on the issue of nationalization of the mining sector. This resulted in a report on State intervention in the mineral sector in 2012 (known as the SIMS report),[59] which ruled out nationalization, but considered ways for a fairer redistribution of mining profits, including through a resource rent tax of 50 per cent and the creation of a State mineral company to develop strategic minerals.

(b) Transparency-related initiatives

Increased transparency about the activities of both governments and TNCs is a key component for ensuring appropriate public revenue collection from the extractive industries. The main initiative concerning transparency in this context is the Extractive Industries Transparency Initiative (EITI) launched in 2003.[60] A multi-stakeholder initiative, EITI involves governments, companies, investors, civil society organizations and other partner organizations, who work together to improve openness and accountable management of revenues from natural resources. Countries implementing the EITI Standard are expected to ensure full disclosure of taxes and other payments made by oil, gas and mining companies to governments. These payments are disclosed in annual EITI Reports. By July 2014, there were 29 EITI-compliant countries (i.e. countries that were meeting all the requirements of the EITI Standard), all of which were developing and transition economies, except Norway, and 16 candidate countries (i.e. countries which were implementing EITI but not yet meeting all the requirements). In addition, 35 countries had produced EITI reports.[61]

The EITI marks significant progress towards increasing transparency in the extractive industries. Nevertheless, it has some major weaknesses. First, it is voluntary, and is therefore non-binding on both governments and private corporations. As a result, it has limited effect, since a considerable proportion of global production by the extractive industries remains outside its standards. Second, the EITI reconciliation exercise is unidirectional in that it only allows checking whether the revenues reported by

> Increased transparency about the activities of both governments and TNCs is a key component for ensuring appropriate public revenue collection from the extractive industries.

Table 7.2

EXAMPLES OF REVISIONS IN THE REGULATORY AND FISCAL REGIMES FOR THE EXTRACTIVE INDUSTRIES

Measure	Country	Details of change	Year
Contracts/ licences revisions or renegotiations	Democratic Republic of the Congo	An expert committee reviewing 61 mining deals concluded that they were all bad deals, and recommended cancellation of 22 and renegotiation of 39.	2009
	Dominican Republic	Renegotiation of contract with Barrick Gold Pueblo Viejo Mine.	2013
	Ecuador	Law compelling private oil companies to renegotiate their service contracts in order to replace the taxation arrangement in production-sharing agreements with a flat rate per barrel of oil.	2010
	Guinea	Review of validity of existing contracts.	Ongoing
	Liberia	Review of concession agreements signed between 2003 and 2006 (36 out of a total of 105 contracts were recommended for outright cancellation and 14 for renegotiation).	2006
	United Republic of Tanzania	Review of mining development agreements and the fiscal regime for the mineral sector, leading to renegotiations on a case-by-case basis.	2006
	Zambia	Ending of tax stability clauses in development agreements.	2008
Changes in royalty rates	Chile	Increase from 5 to 9 per cent.	2010
	Ghana	Increase from a range of 3–6 per cent (which in practice was normally 3 per cent) to 5 per cent.	2010
	Peru	Companies that do not have stabilization clauses or agreements with the Government must pay royalties of 1–12 per cent on operating profits (before the new law, rates ranged from 1 to 3 per cent on net sales), as well as a special tax ranging from 2 to 8.4 per cent of operating profits. Companies that have stabilization clauses must pay a special mining lien of between 4 and 13.12 per cent of operating profits.	2011
	United Republic of Tanzania	Royalty rate for copper, gold, silver and platinum group minerals increased from 3 per cent to 4 per cent, while that for other minerals, including gemstones and diamonds, remained at 5 per cent.	2010
	Zambia	Increase from 0.6 to 3 per cent.	2008
	Zambia	Increase from 3 to 6 per cent.	2012
Changes in corporate tax rates	Ghana	Increase from 25 to 35 per cent.	2012
	United Kingdom	Increase in supplementary tax rate from 20 to 32 per cent in the hydrocarbons sector.	2011
	Zambia	Increase in company income tax from 25 to 30 per cent.	2008
Introduction of new taxes	Australia	Resource super profits tax (RSPT) with a headline tax rate of 40 per cent, applicable to all mining projects (but replaced soon after approval).	2010
	Australia	Mineral resource rent tax, replacing RSPT, with a reduced headline tax rate of 30 per cent (effectively 22.5 per cent), applicable to coal and iron ore.	2010

Table 7.2 (concluded)

EXAMPLES OF REVISIONS IN THE REGULATORY AND FISCAL REGIMES FOR THE EXTRACTIVE INDUSTRIES

Measure	Country	Details of change	Year
	Chile	Mining royalty of 5 per cent.	2006
	Mongolia	Windfall tax of 68 per cent on profits from copper and gold.	2006
	South Africa	Royalty rate that varies with mine profitability.	2008
	Zambia	Windfall tax of 25 per cent.	2008 (but revoked in 2009)
	Zambia	Variable income tax rate, in addition to fixed rate of 30 per cent; it applies when assessable income is higher than 8 per cent of gross sales, with a maximum rate of 15 per cent.	2009
Increasing the State's equity participation	Algeria	Participation rate of national oil company Sonatrach is fixed at a minimum of 51 per cent.	2006
	Argentina	State takes a 51 per cent majority stake in hydrocarbons company YPF.	2012
	Bolivia (Plurinational State of)	Increased participation of the State in the hydrocarbons sector from 18 to 82 per cent of production value.	2005/2006
	Bolivia (Plurinational State of)	Law of mining rights increases State's expropriation powers targeting mines deemed unproductive, inactive or idle.	2013
	Guinea	Expropriation of half of Simandou iron ore deposit from Rio Tinto, claiming slow development of the deposit by the company.	2008
	Guinea	Mining code that grants the State a 15 per cent stake in all projects, as well as an option to buy up to 35 per cent equity.	2011
	Kazakhstan	Kazmunaigas (KMG), a State energy company, doubled its share in the Kashagan consortium to 16.6 per cent.	2008
	Namibia	State mining company, Epangelo, is established.	2008
	Papua New Guinea	Government takes full ownership of the Ok Tedi copper and gold mine.	2013
	United Republic of Tanzania	Increased government participation but percentage not stated in mining act.	2010
Other	Ghana	Tax depreciation reduced, introduction of ring-fencing.	2012
	United Republic of Tanzania	Income tax ring-fencing by mine licence area.	2010
	Zambia	Capital depreciation allowance reduced to 25 per cent.	2008 (but back in 2009)
	Zambia	Ring-fencing of non-contiguous mines.	2009

Source: UNCTAD secretariat compilation, based on Kingsley, 2014; Stevens et al., 2013; Medina Herasme, 2014; UNCTAD, 2012; Eigen, 2013; Sachs et al., 2012; Tarimo, 2013; Ralbovsky and Caywood, 2013; Muganyizi, 2012; ZIPAR, 2013; USGS, 2006; National Treasury of South Africa, 2008; Park and Benayad, 2013; EY Resource Nationalism Updates (various); Gray Molina, 2013; Hawala, 2013; and RioTinto Mongolia, available at: http://www.riotintomongolia.com/ENG/oyutolgoi/881.asp.

governments correspond to the payments reported by the companies, but there is no judgement about the appropriateness of TNCs' tax burden. Thus, the EITI focus is limited to preventing corruption in producing countries. Third, there is room for improvement in simplifying the presentation of the reports, which may be difficult for many stakeholders to understand. The quality, timeliness and consistency of the data could also be improved. Finally, there is no clear course of action when mismatches are found in data disclosure.

Since the global financial crisis, there has been growing interest in improving transparency in the extractive industries. In the context of reforms of the financial system, G8 and G20 countries have been supportive of country-by-country reporting on those industries. This trend has led to various developed countries passing new regulations concerning public disclosure of financial payments by private corporations. The United States took the lead, stimulating a wave of changes in other developed countries. New regulations for increased transparency in the extractive industries emerged from Section 1504 of the 2010 Dodd-Frank Wall Street Reform and Consumer Protection Act (known for short as the Dodd-Frank Act). On 22 August 2012, the Securities and Exchange Commission (SEC) adopted rules mandated by the Act requiring companies in the extractive industries to disclose certain payments made to the Government of the United States or to foreign governments. The activities covered by commercial development of oil, natural gas and minerals include exploration, extraction, processing and export, or the acquisition of a licence for such activities; trading is not included.[62] The disclosure provision applies to any company listed on a stock exchange in the United States. This includes 90 per cent of all major internationally operating oil and gas companies, and 8 of the 10 major mining companies globally. Payments by subsidiaries are also included (RWI, 2011). However, following a lawsuit filed by the American Petroleum Institute against this SEC rule, a United States Court ruled in favour of the Institute. As a result, the SEC has to reissue another rule before Section 1504 of Dodd-Frank Act can be implemented, which it has publicly pledged to do by March 2015. A large number of investors, government officials and civil society organizations have called on the SEC to reissue strong disclosure rules, by country and by project (PWYP, 2014). Similarly, on 26 June 2013, the European Parliament and the EU Council passed new laws requiring oil, gas, mining and logging companies to disclose payments made to governments annually on a country-by-country and project-by-project basis. The new disclosure rules are included in the EU Accounting Directive and the revised EU Transparency Directive. They apply to all companies, parent and subsidiaries, that are active in the extractive industry or in the logging of primary forests, and that are either listed on an EU-regulated stock market or are large extractive and forestry companies.[63] Activities include exploration, prospection, discovery, development and extraction. Once again, trading activities are excluded from these regulations.[64]

In addition, a number of developing countries have decided to publish all their contracts with companies in the extractive industries. These include Azerbaijan, the Plurinational State of Bolivia, Ecuador, Guinea, Liberia, Niger, Peru and Timor-Leste (Berne Declaration, 2012). Furthermore, the Vale Columbia Center on Sustainable Investment, the World Bank Institute and Revenue Watch Institute, in collaboration with a wide array of partners from civil society organizations, have developed a searchable database of publicly available oil, gas and mining contracts all over the world.[65]

(c) Other relevant initiatives in the extractive industries

Probably the most remarkable initiative that has been recently adopted at the regional level is the African Mining Vision (AMV), approved by the African Union Summit of Heads of State and Government in February 2009.[66] Its main goal is to create "a transparent, equitable and optimal exploitation of mineral resources to underpin broad-based sustainable growth and socio-economic development". According to the African Union (2009: 14), "African states with weak governance generally fail to impose resources tax regimes that ensure an equitable share of the rents, particularly windfall rents, due either to a lack of state capacity or the subversion of that capacity to produce overly investor friendly outcomes". The Vision underlines that revenues from the exploitation of minerals and responsible taxation that allows host countries to better capture windfall gains are central to the process of structural transformation. It recommends self-adjusting resource tax regimes that can respond to changing economic circumstances.

Focusing on the importance of the developmental state, the AMV calls for enhancing the capacity of governments to negotiate contracts with a view to securing better deals, and for improving their ability to audit, review and renegotiate existing mining agreements. It warns against stabilization clauses, as well as bilateral and international investment agreements that may have negative impacts on policy space. Enhancing tax administration capacities to prevent damaging illicit financial flows, including transfer mispricing, is also part of the strategy advocated by the AMV. Further, it favours a collaborative approach among different stakeholders in the sector, with a focus on regional cooperation and a pooling of resources for capacity development and the financing of such reforms. The Vision is translated into an Action Plan which is implemented through the African Minerals Development Centre created in December 2013. The main value of the Vision as an element of a development strategy is its cooperative ownership by African countries, which can help to improve policy space for development at the national and regional levels.

> The main value of the African Mining Vision as an element of a development strategy is its cooperative ownership by African countries.

Another relevant initiative at the regional level in Africa is the African Legal Support Facility created by the AfDB. It aims to assist African countries in the negotiation of contracts and complex transactions related to the extractive industries (Ngalani, 2013). There have also been attempts at the subregional level to harmonize mineral policies and regulatory regimes in the mining sector. One of the objectives of such initiatives is to prevent competition among countries in offering tax incentives that could lead to a race to the bottom. The Southern African Development Community (SADC) started the harmonization process in 2004, and appears to have made progress towards harmonization in a number of areas, including discouraging competitive behaviour among the member countries (Mtegha and Oshokoya, 2011). Similarly, the Economic Commission of West African States (ECOWAS) issued a Directive on the Harmonization of Guiding Principles and Policies in the Mining Sector in 2009. This included the implementation of a common mining code.

In other developing regions, there have been fewer efforts with regard to regional cooperation and harmonization of tax issues in the extractive industries. Nevertheless, in 2013 the Union of South American Nations (UNASUR) promoted a common strategy for the profitable use of natural resources, which could lead to increased cooperation in these matters. Also, in the Declaration of the First Ministerial Conference of Latin American States affected by Transnational Interests that took place in Ecuador in April 2013, it was agreed to establish a regional framework for coordinating actions to tackle the growing number of international dispute cases being filed against governments by TNCs, including those in the extractive industries. This included the creation of a regional arbitration centre (Khor, 2013).

In a context of high commodity prices, industrialized countries have directed their attention to strategies to secure access to these commodities. One example in this regard is the 2008 European Union Raw Materials Initiative (EU RMI),[67] which aims to promote undistorted access to raw materials on world markets. With an emphasis on trade and investment conditions, the resource diplomacy envisaged in the EU RMI would lead to pressure on developing countries to liberalize their raw materials markets, including their tax regulations. This has raised concerns about its effects on development policies as it may affect policy space in developing countries (Curtis, 2010; Fair Politics, 2011; Küblböck, 2013). In the spirit of a global partnership for development, it is of the utmost importance that the EU RMI does not undermine recent strong attempts by many developing countries to ensure that income generated in their mining and oil sectors effectively contributes to sustainable and inclusive growth and development.

E. Summary and conclusions

Fiscal space is consubstantial with policy space. Even if governments have the possibility to conduct their development policies within the multilateral, regional or bilateral frameworks, they will still need to finance the investment and other spending required by those policies. Therefore, strengthening government revenues is essential. Fiscal space has a quantitative dimension, roughly approximated by the share of government revenues in GDP and its capacity to expand public spending according to various macroeconomic goals and constraints. It also has a qualitative dimension, related to the desired structure of government revenues and spending, and the ability to reorient them as needed. Both dimensions are dynamic in nature, as they must adapt to the development process. Historical experience and the comparison between high- and low-income countries show a positive relationship between the share of governments' revenues and spending in GDP, on the one hand, and the level of development on the other. This relationship is neither linear nor mechanical, as different countries (or the same country at different times) make diverse choices with respect to the role of government in delivering social services and in assuming the tasks of a developmental State. Such choices frequently lead to larger or smaller levels of government revenues and expenditures in countries with similar levels of per capita GDP.

Fiscal space is both a cause and an effect of economic growth and structural change. Higher average income and the expansion of the modern sectors of the economy vis-à-vis the informal ones broaden the tax base and strengthen revenue collection capacity. This, in turn, allows for higher growth-enhancing public spending, both on the supply side (e.g. investment in infrastructure, research and education) and the demand side (e.g. social transfers). Reciprocally, the lack of fiscal space and the constraints on expanding it in many low-income countries are among the most serious obstacles to escaping the underdevelopment trap.

This general need for maintaining or expanding fiscal space faces particular challenges in the increasingly globalized economy. On the one hand, there is the possibility to increase fiscal space, at least temporarily, through foreign financing. In this context, ODA may be of vital importance for LDCs, and foreign credit may enlarge fiscal space if it is used for expanding production capacities, which in turn would generate more fiscal revenues. However, excessive reliance on foreign sources has in many cases led to overindebtedness and chronic deficits in the fiscal and external balances, limiting fiscal space in the long run. In addition, those deficits create the need for more foreign financing, which is subject to conditions that may significantly hamper overall policy space. Therefore, fiscal space should rely basically on domestic revenue mobilization if it is to sustain a national development strategy.

On the other hand, globalization has affected the ability of countries to generate domestic government revenues and to choose their taxation structure. Lowering trade tariffs has significantly reduced revenues from border taxes, while the increased mobility of capital and its intensive use of fiscal havens have greatly altered the conditions for taxing income and wealth. The globalized economy has favoured tax competition among countries, pushing them into a

> Globalization has affected the ability of countries to generate domestic government revenues and to choose their taxation structure.

"race to the bottom" in offering incentives to foreign investors in the form of lower taxes. Corporate tax rates have declined in developed and developing countries alike, and many of them have also offered subsidies or tax exemptions to attract or retain foreign investment. In addition, finance-led globalization has led to a proliferation of offshore financial centres, tax havens and secrecy locations that provide potential taxpayers, including internationalized firms and wealthy individuals, with various means for tax avoidance or evasion. This not only means a very significant loss of public resources, it also tends to make taxation systems more regressive if countries increase VAT and other indirect taxes in an attempt to offset declining revenues from direct taxes.

The main vehicle for corporate tax avoidance or evasion and capital flight from developing countries is the misuse of transfer pricing (i.e. the valuation of intrafirm cross-border transactions by international company groups). If the intracompany or intragroup price does not reflect the price that would be paid in a market where each participant acts independently in its own interest, profits within a company group can be effectively shifted to low-tax or no-tax jurisdictions, while losses and deductions are shifted to high-tax jurisdictions. Such operations explain the large number of companies registered in tax havens and offshore centres, and the significant proportion of financial and trade transactions that nominally transit through them.

> There are risks that the debate on international taxation issues will not fully take into account the needs and views of most developing and transition economies.

The negative consequences of secrecy jurisdictions, transfer pricing, profit shifting and all the other practices leading to an erosion of the tax base go well beyond their impact in terms of public revenue losses; they also affect the fairness of the tax system, undermine taxpayers' confidence in its integrity and distort trade and investment patterns as well as human and physical capital allocations.

The international tax architecture has failed so far to properly adapt to this reality. The opacity surrounding tax havens may partly explain the difficulties faced by policymakers in curbing tax evasion practices, but there are also significant political and economic obstacles. Offshore financial centres and the secrecy jurisdictions that host them are fully integrated into the global financial system, and large shares of trade and capital movements (including FDI) are channelled through them. Moreover, the most important providers of financial secrecy are some of the world's biggest and wealthiest countries, or specific areas within those countries. Thus, changing this system requires not only knowledge of the technicalities involved, but also strong political will and determination.

Recently, there have been a number of developments aimed at improving transparency and exchange of information on tax issues: in particular, since 2009 the OECD has hosted a restructured Global Forum on these specific issues, and has launched an Action Plan on Base Erosion and Profit Shifting; the G20 leaders declared their intention to promote information sharing with respect to all kinds of abuses and fraudulent activities; several national tax authorities or parliaments have also increased the monitoring of tax abuses by rich individuals and TNCs; and numerous bilateral tax treaties and tax information exchange agreements have been signed.

Although these initiatives are all steps in the right direction, their implementation has sometimes been slow, as has enforcement of the agreements reached. This is especially the case for transfer pricing abuses, which are particularly harmful for developing countries, as they result in the loss of not only public revenues, but also foreign exchange. Because these initiatives are mostly led by the developed economies – some of which themselves harbour secrecy jurisdictions and powerful TNCs – there are risks that the debate will not fully take into account the needs and views of most developing and transition economies. It will therefore be important to give a more prominent role to institutions like the United Nations Committee of Experts on International Cooperation in Tax Matters, and consider the adoption of an international convention against tax avoidance and evasion. A multilateral approach is essential because, if only some jurisdictions agree to prevent illicit flows and tax leakages, those practices will simply shift to other, non-cooperative locations.

A multilateral framework would also facilitate the adoption of measures for radically addressing tax avoidance by TNCs, such as rules of unitary taxation of such corporations, making the firms pay taxes in the countries where they actually conduct their activities and generate their profits (United Nations, 2014). This would require the implementation of country-by-country reporting employing an international standard supported by the International Accounting Standards Board or a similar body,[68] and ensuring that these data are placed in the public domain for all stakeholders to access. In addition, even without the establishment of a fully unitary taxation system, much could be improved by replacing the separate entity concept with a unitary approach (Picciotto, 2013).

Although the very nature of the problem calls for a multilateral approach, governments can also apply measures at the national level, such as including a general anti-avoidance rule in legislation to increase the probability that "aggressive" tax schemes end up being declared illegal once challenged in courts (European Commission, 2012). Governments can also more effectively address transfer mis-pricing in their international trade by using reference prices for a number of traded goods. This would be of particular relevance for commodity exports, which are relatively homogeneous goods, and usually account for a large share of the exports of commodity-producing countries.

Fiscal space and governance issues should be a prominent part of the post-2015 development agenda.

In many developing countries, increasing the generation of public revenues from natural resources – especially the extractive industries – is essential for the financing of development. Indeed, government revenues are often the main contribution of these activities to development, as they otherwise tend to generate enclave economies. Capturing a fair share of resource rents from a country's natural resources and deciding how they will be used for development is its government's responsibility, which cannot be transferred to the private companies exploiting the resources. Corporate social responsibility has a role to play here, but it should not be considered a primary means for TNCs in the extractive industries to contribute to the societies or communities in which they operate. The task of providing social services and infrastructure should be the government's responsibility. The principal contribution of TNCs to the producing country should be through taxation. Yet, while the rise of commodity prices in the last decade led to a tenfold increase in the profits of the world's largest mining companies, the gains for public revenues more often than not lagged well behind the growth of natural resource rents. This was mainly because taxation regimes in developing countries, which had been established at a time of low prices, and often on the recommendation of the Bretton Woods institutions, placed too much emphasis on attracting FDI through tax incentives.

Against this background, many governments – both from developed and developing countries – have begun to revise their policies with regard to the extractive industries. This has included renegotiation or cancellation of existing contracts, increases in tax or royalty rates, introduction of new taxes and changes in the degree of State ownership of extractive projects. Successful renegotiations have been facilitated by the stronger bargaining power of host governments resulting from the appearance of new major players in the extractive industry, such as companies from emerging economies.

A comprehensive policy aimed at improving revenues from natural resources needs to incorporate several elements. First, governments should retain sovereign capacity to review the tax regimes and ownership structures whenever deemed necessary for the economic and development interests of the country. A minimum level of taxation could also be negotiated at the regional or international levels to avoid a race to the bottom on this matter. Second, they should have the means to enforce the rules and obtain the due revenues by controlling transfer pricing manoeuvres and underreporting of export volumes. Third, they should be allowed to do so without the threat of legal retribution through the existing investment dispute mechanisms, for the reasons noted in chapter VI.

Most of the needed measures can be taken at the national level, but multilateral cooperation is still of the utmost importance. Transparency initiatives such as the Extractive Industries Transparency Initiative (EITI) should be made mandatory and extended: they should not focus only on governments, but also on producing firms and commodity trading companies. There is also a need to increase the focus on monitoring, auditing and accountability, as well as strengthen enforcement of the fiscal conditions and regulations under which extractive industries operate; for instance, frequently, the volume produced and exported is reported by the operating TNC with little or no effective control by host States. Institutional development and capacity-building are crucial, in particular to improve the capacity to monitor production costs, import and export prices, volumes, qualities and time of delivery of the natural resources extracted as well as to help in data collection and processing. Given its expertise in the area of commodities, transport, customs and trade, UNCTAD could provide support in this domain.

Regional cooperation initiatives for capacity-building can be very useful. The international donor community has an important role to play in supporting such initiatives. ODA and other international support could be significantly expanded in the area of improving developing countries' tax systems and contract negotiating capacities, as well as curtailing tax-motivated IFFs.

Much can be done also to curtail transfer mispricing. At present, recommended protocols for controlling this practice suggest comparing the prices fixed by TNCs with those of a similar operation made by non-related agents (a "compared uncontrolled price"), which would indicate the fair market (arm's length) price. In practice, finding such a "free market" comparable transaction may be complex (or virtually impossible), and requires strong administrative capabilities and costly procedures (United Nations, 2013a). A more workable alternative, already used by some developing countries, is to generate a clear benchmark of publicly quoted commodity prices which would be of mandatory use in commodity transactions, in particular those that take place between related parties (OECD, 2014). Extensive data processing will be necessary, not only to identify the right international prices, but also to adapt them to the specific conditions of the transactions. Such initiative could be facilitated by the creation of a public international database of reliable comparable prices, which would enable tax authorities in developing countries with limited resources to be better equipped to deal with potential abuses in this area.

Given their relevance for many developing countries and transition economies, fiscal space and governance issues should be a prominent part of the post-2015 development agenda. International cooperation in tax matters should be enhanced in a coherent manner in order to support national development objectives. Avoiding the resource drain caused by illicit financial flows would help provide the necessary resources to finance the attainment of development goals. ∎

Notes

1   In chart 7.2, East, South and South-East Asia includes: Afghanistan, China, Hong Kong (China), Taiwan Province of China, India, Indonesia, the Islamic Republic of Iran, the Republic of Korea, Lao People's Democratic Republic, Malaysia, Nepal, Pakistan, the Philippines, Singapore, Sri Lanka, Thailand and Viet Nam; Latin America includes: Argentina, the Plurinational State of Bolivia, Brazil, Chile, Colombia, Costa Rica, Cuba, the Dominican Republic, Ecuador, El Salvador, Guatemala, Haiti, Honduras, Mexico, Nicaragua, Panama, Paraguay, Peru, Uruguay and the Bolivarian Republic of Venezuela; Africa does not include: Botswana, Burkina Faso, Equatorial Guinea, Lesotho, Liberia, Madagascar, Mauritania, Mayotte, Saint Helena, Seychelles, Somalia, Western Sahara and Zimbabwe; West Asia does not include the Occupied Palestinian territory; Croatia is included in the transition economies; and developed economies includes: Australia, Canada, EU member countries (excl. Croatia), Iceland, Israel, Japan, New Zealand and the United States.

2   For example, Uruguay initiated a system where low-income households making purchases with credit cards could be paid a VAT refund through the electronic banking system.

3   Sources include KPMG International, *Corporate and Indirect Tax Survey 2012 and 2014*; http://www.kpmg.com/GLOBAL/EN/SERVICES/TAX/TAX-TOOLS-AND-RESOURCES/Pages/corporate-tax-rates-table.aspx and OECD tax database; available at: http://www.oecd.org/tax/tax-policy/tax-database.htm#C_CorporateCaptial.

4   Between 2002 and 2012, the average applied tariff imposed by developing countries in East Asia fell from around 8 per cent to 4 per cent, and in Latin America from 6 per cent to 4 per cent. In regions with a large number of LDCs (e.g. sub-Saharan Africa), the average applied tariff fell by a lesser extent, from 8 per cent to 7 per cent (UNCTAD, 2014).

5   Financial sector legislation has been one of the key priorities of the EU, and Europe's financial sector spends more than 120 million euros annually and employs over 1,700 lobbyists devoted to influencing EU institutions, according to new research by the Corporate Europe Observatory and the Austrian Federal Chamber of Labour and Trade Union Federation (Corporate Europe Observatory et al., 2014). This amounts to more than two financial industry lobbyists for every European Parliament member and 60-plus lobbyists for each Minister of the Council of the EU, in addition to the lobbyists from other sectors of the economy. By comparison, there were only 150 civil society organizations reported to be lobbying legislators covering all issues, not just finance. The financial sector outspends its civil society counterparts by a ratio of at least 30 to 1.

6   Americans for Tax Fairness and Public Campaign (2014) reports that 1,359 lobbyists supporting the package made more than 12,378 visits or contacts to members of Congress and their staff between January 2011 and September 2013. This represents a minimum of 93 contacts per week, on a single issue alone. There are more than 2.5 lobbyists for every member of Congress, and more than 21 for every member of the two tax-writing committees in Congress: the House Ways and Means Committee and the Senate Finance Committee.

7   See *The Economist*, "Onshore financial centres – Not a palm tree in sight", 16 February 2013.

8   These criteria are: (i) No or only nominal taxes are imposed on the relevant income; (ii) A "ring-fencing" regime effectively protects the sponsoring country from the harmful effects of its own regime on its domestic economy; (iii) Lack of transparency in the operation of tax laws makes it harder for the home country to take defensive measures; and (iv) Lack of effective exchange of tax information relating to taxpayers benefiting from the operation with foreign tax authorities.

9   See *BBC News*, "Sanctions threat to 'tax havens'", 26 June 2000; available at: http://news.bbc.co.uk/2/hi/business/806236.stm.

10   Full details of the FSI methodology are available at: http://www.financialsecrecyindex.com.

11   For further discussions on the myths linked to tax havens and other related issues, see, for example, Palan et al., 2010; and Shaxson, 2011.

12   For countries that are identified as tax havens by at least two different studies, see Palan et al., 2010, table 1.4.

13   *The Economist*, "Onshore financial centres – Not a palm tree in sight", 16 February 2013.

14   For more details, see: http://www.financialsecrecyindex.com/.

15   For further details about the Irish inversion, see *Financial Times*, "Tax avoidance: The Irish inversion", 29 April 2014.

16   Not all the IFFs are tax-motivated in a narrow sense. For instance, the main motivation for IFFs may be for evading exchange controls or for money laundering. Yet, even if they are not specifically tax-motivated, they do have fiscal consequences, and thus reduce fiscal space.

17   Herson (2014) notes that if the taxpayer falsifies paperwork, for example by knowingly making false statements in a tax return or engaging in false invoicing, this constitutes tax fraud. Tax evasion usually involves a wider range of practices, such as forgetting to declare some elements that must be taken into account in a taxpayer's tax returns. The distinction is important, because tax evasion, unlike tax fraud, is not (or has not been) treated as a criminal offence in every country. For this reason, some countries where this is, or has been, the case have systematically refused to provide judicial and administrative assistance to foreign countries in relation to tax offences that are not liable to prosecution in their country. A notable example is Switzerland, which, until recently, did not provide any administrative assistance in cases of tax evasion, except to a few countries with a double taxation agreement that conforms to the OECD standard.

18   The creation of trusts, foundations and Liechtenstein Anstalts (an anonymous company with a single secret shareholder) in secrecy jurisdictions provides the same kind of facilities to individuals (for further details, see, for example, Palan et al., 2010).

19   When such practices take place between unrelated, or apparently unrelated, parties they are referred to as "re-invoicing". When they take the form of cross-border intra-group transactions, they are referred to as "transfer mispricing".

20   Other studies suggest this figure is a rather conservative estimate. For instance, an article in the *OECD*

Observer noted that "more than 60 per cent of world trade takes place within multinational enterprises" (See: http://www.oecdobserver.org/news/archivestory.php/aid/670/Transfer_pricing:_Keeping_it_at_arms_length.html%22%20/l%20%22sthash.RvTzq9X0.dpuf.

21 Other estimates of global offshore financial wealth suggest $6.7 trillion in 2008 (Boston Consulting Group, 2009), $8.5 trillion in 2002 (Merrill Lynch and Cap Gemini Ernst & Young, 2002), $11.5 trillion in 2005 (TJN, 2005) and $12 trillion in 2007 (Frank, 2007).

22 Credit Suisse (2011) estimated total global wealth at $231 trillion in mid-2011, including financial assets and non-financial assets at market value.

23 For details, see, for instance, Fuest and Riedel, 2009; GIZ, 2010; and Henry, 2012.

24 Most of the official estimates were for developed economies. In the United Kingdom, for instance, total tax evasion and avoidance cost the Exchequer about £9 billion in both 2010/11 and 2011/12 (HM Revenue & Customs, 2012 and 2013). In the United States, the total "net tax gap", which refers to the amount of tax liability that will never be paid to the United States Internal Revenue Service (IRS), amounted to $290 billion in 2001 and $385 billion in 2006 (IRS, 2012). Finally, according to a report of the European Parliament (2013), an estimated one trillion euros of potential tax revenue for the EU is lost annually from tax fraud, tax evasion, tax avoidance and aggressive tax planning.

25 The Global Forum's main achievements have been the development of standards of transparency and exchange of information through the 2002 Model Agreement on Exchange of Information on Tax Matters, and the issuance of a paper setting out the standards for the maintenance of accounting records, titled, Enabling Effective Exchange of Information: Availability and Reliability Standard developed by the Joint Ad Hoc Group on Accounts in 2005. For a critical assessment of the Global Forum's work, see Meinzer, 2012.

26 More information of The Global Forum on Transparency and Exchange of Information for Tax Purposes is available at: http://www.oecd.org/tax/transparency/global_forum_background%20brief.pdf and http://www.oecd.org/tax/transparency/Frequently%20asked%20questions.pdf.

27 See Spiegel International Online, "The world's shortest blacklist: Why the fight against tax havens is a sham", 11 April 2009; available at: http://www.spiegel.de/international/world/the-world-s-shortest-blacklist-why-the-fight-against-tax-havens-is-a-sham-a-618780.html.

28 For more information, see: http://www.oecd.org/tax/transparency/automaticexchangeofinformation.htm.

29 See Thomson Reuters Foundation, "Developing countries not ready to join tax evasion crackdown – OECD", 26 May 2014.

30 See *Financial Times,* "Poorest nations will gain nothing from tax pledge", 9 May 2014.

31 *Reuters*, "CEOs back country-by-country tax reporting – survey", 23 April 2014.

32 UNCTAD secretariat calculations following the methodology of Misereor (2010) and based on the Tax Research Platform of the International Bureau of Fiscal Documentation (http://www.ibfd.org) and the OECD database on TIEAs, available at: http://www.oecd.org/ctp/exchange-of-tax-information/taxinformationexchangeagreementstieas.htm.

33 In the case of Switzerland, for instance, the developing countries concerned must, among other things, declare their readiness to lower withholding taxes on the earnings of Swiss companies abroad (Alliance Sud, 2014).

34 See, for instance, Sheppard, 2013.

35 *BBC News Business*, "Starbucks, Google and Amazon grilled over tax avoidance", 12 November 2012, and "Starbucks agrees to pay more corporation tax", 6 December 2012.

36 Rent is defined in this *Report* as the difference between the value of production (at international prices) and its cost, including normal profits.

37 The United Nations General Assembly Resolution 1803 (XVII) of 14 December 1962 established: "The right of peoples and nations to permanent sovereignty over their natural wealth and resources must be exercised in the interest of their national development and of the well-being of the people of the State concerned... The exploration, development and disposition of such resources, as well as the import of the foreign capital required for these purposes, should be in conformity with the rules and conditions which the peoples and nations freely consider to be necessary or desirable with regard to the authorization, restriction or prohibition of such activities... The profits derived must be shared in the proportions freely agreed upon, in each case, between the investors and the recipient State, due care being taken to ensure that there is no impairment, for any reason, of that State's sovereignty over its natural wealth and resources."

38 For a recent in-depth discussion on the role of the World Bank in mining reforms in Africa, see Jacobs, 2013; and Besada and Martin, 2013. See also UNCTAD, 2005.

39 One notable exception is Chile, where the public company, CODELCO, has continued to play an important role in copper production, although private firms now produce about two thirds of Chilean copper.

40 Increasing interest in the issue of taxation in the extractive industries is evidenced by the enormous

number of seminars and discussions on this issue that have been taking place at national, regional and international levels in recent years. Similarly, there has been a substantial increase in the body of research on this topic since the second half of the 2000s. In the United Nations, apart from the analyses on the distribution of rents from the extractive industries in *TDRs 2005* and *2010,* UNCTAD (2005 and 2007) have looked at issues relating to FDI in the extractive industries. At the regional level, the Economic Commission for Latin America and the Caribbean (ECLAC), for instance, has produced several studies on this issue. In addition, the United Nations Committee of Experts on International Cooperation on Tax Matters convened an Expert Group Meeting on Extractive Industries Taxation in May 2013 (see United Nations, 2013b and c). At the operational level, it is mainly the United Nations Development Programme (UNDP) that provides advice relating to this subject, mostly on a country-by-country case basis (see for instance, UNDP-Cambodia, 2008). The international financial institutions have also published relevant studies, including the IMF (2012) Daniel et al. (2010) for the IMF, Otto el al. (2006) for the World Bank, and the World Bank (2012a). Some examples of research on this topic by academia, civil society organizations and the private sector include PWYP (2013), the University of Calgary (2012), the German Development Institute (DIE, 2011), the Raw Materials Group (2013a) and the International Council on Mining and Metals (ICMM, 2009).

41 Indeed, much of the most useful research and case study analyses on issues related to fiscal regimes for the extractive industries and their consequences for developing countries during the first decade of this century have been produced by civil society organizations.

42 The analyses of UNCTAD's *World Investment Report* of subsequent years continued to confirm the importance of natural resources for FDI in Africa and Latin America.

43 For example, the World Bank (2012b) has shown that in Africa the decline in poverty rates in resource-rich countries has generally lagged behind that of counties that are not rich in natural resources.

44 This is also an advantage in the case of exports of more refined products, as it may be easier to check them for quality than it is to check ores.

45 For comparisons of taxation in the extractive industries in different countries, see, for example, Raw Materials Group, 2013b; Gajigo et al., 2012a; Conrad, 2012; and IHS-CERA, 2011. Global consulting companies, such as Deloitte, Ernst and Young, KPMG and PricewaterhouseCoopers (PWC) also produce regular reports providing information on taxation in the extractive industries around the world. Although this information is very illustrative,

it is likely intended as advice to corporations on how to optimize their tax payments.

46 Price manipulation can also occur in operations of commodity trading companies located in international trading hubs. A recent study has found that the average prices for commodity exports from developing countries to Switzerland, where several of these companies are located, are lower than those to other jurisdictions, while (re-)export prices for those commodities from Switzerland are higher than those from other countries, which may be due to a tax rate differential (Cobham et al., 2014).

47 An example of transfer mispricing in the extractive industries is the case of Mopani Copper Mines (MPM) in Zambia. MPM was the subsidiary company of Glencore International AG and First Quantum Mineral. In 2010 two auditing companies hired by the Zambian Government, found that MPM-Glencore had succeeded in substantially reducing accounting profits and therefore its tax payments over the period 2003–2008. The anomalies found included an unexplained increase in operating costs in 2007 of over $380 million, a declaration of very low cobalt production volumes compared with other companies of similar size in the region, and the manipulation of copper sale prices in favour of Glencore. In April 2011, five NGOs filed a complaint with the OECD against these corporations based on the findings of the audit report (Sherpa et al., 2011). However Glencore contested the allegations, questioning the information and methodology used in the report. Other examples of trade mispricing in Africa can be found in countries like Ghana, Malawi and the United Republic of Tanzania. In Australia, by July 2013 the tax Office was running 26 investigations into suspected profit shifting, 15 of which were in the energy and resources sector (see PWP, Out of Africa, tax tricks emerge, 6 July 2013 at: http://www.publishwhatyoupay.org/resources/out-africa-tax-tricks-emerge). In South Africa, Bracking and Sharife (2014) found discrepancies indicative of possible transfer pricing manipulation of rough diamond values.

48 For example, in Chile, as noted by Riesco (2005: 15), "Compañía Minera Disputada de Las Condes, a mine owned by Exxon, ostensibly operated at a loss for 23 years. Therefore, it did not pay any taxes at all and, on the contrary, accumulated $575 million in tax credits. Nevertheless, in 2002 Exxon (by then Exxon Mobil) sold this "money-losing" operation for $1.3 billion ... Exxon exported the mining operation's substantial profits, mostly disguised as interest payments to Exxon Financials, a subsidiary in Bermuda."

49 This is what happened recently in Mali, when the Government claimed a due payment of taxes from the gold producing company, Randgold Resources

(see EIU, 2013; and Randgold Resources's *Annual Report 2012*).

50 The IMF is currently attempting to improve this situation. It has developed a draft standard template for countries to use for the collection of data on government revenues from natural resources, which is available at its website: http://www.imf.org/external/np/sec/pr/2014/pr1454.htm .

51 The World Bank, in its *World Development Indicators* database, has provided estimations of the rents from natural resources for a wide range of countries, covering a long period of time. They are available at the Changing Wealth of Nations Dataset, at: http://data.worldbank.org/data-catalog/wealth-of-nations. These data are being increasingly used worldwide in analyses on this subject. However, the methodology of calculation remains unclear, and a comparison with previous UNCTAD estimates shows significant differences. Therefore, as UNCTAD remains cautious about World Bank data on the natural resource rents, it was decided to continue to use its own estimations.

52 The contribution of the extractive industries to government revenues is often measured in terms of the effective tax rate, or what is called government take. By whatever measure, it is important to clarify if the contribution is assessed against sales revenues or against the rents from the natural resources, as is the case here.

53 In the case of Colombia, although there is also a State-controlled enterprise (Ecopetrol) which produces about two thirds of total oil, the share of the rent captured by the government is comparatively low. This is due to the high proportion of profits retained by the company.

54 Table 7.1 shows remarkably high levels of the share of the governments in the rents for 2005 in Ghana and the United Republic of Tanzania and for 2009 in Zambia. This has not resulted, however, from significant changes in public revenues, but rather from temporary reductions in the magnitude of the rents. In the cases of Ghana and the United Republic of Tanzania, gold production costs increased much more than prices. In Zambia, the reason for the decline in the rent was the collapse in copper prices that followed the global financial crisis.

55 See, for instance *El País*, "La petrolera argentina YPF aumenta la producción y las reservas en 2013" (Oil company YPF increases production and reserves in 2013), 9 March 2014.

56 See *Reuters*, "Ghana puts plans for mining windfall tax on hold", 24 January 2014.

57 The Henry Tax Review (after Ken Henry, who was then the Secretary of the Treasury of Australia) recommended a uniform resource rent tax of 40 per cent to guarantee an appropriate return on non-renewable resources. The Government then proposed a resource super profits tax (RSPT) of 40 per cent for any profit above a given threshold, which would be applied to all minerals. There was strong opposition to this decision from the sector. The RSPT was later replaced by a mineral resource rent tax (MRRT) which took effect in July 2012 at a reduced effective rate of 22.5 per cent, and only for iron and coal projects. However, the controversy continued, and on 24 October 2013 the Government announced that it would seek to repeal the MRRT law with effect from 1 July 2014. Legislation to repeal the mining tax was rejected by the Australian Senate in March 2014. The Henry Tax Review can be accessed at: http://taxreview.treasury.gov.au/Content/Content.aspx?doc=html/home.htm.

58 See, for instance, GMP (2013) and recent EY Resouce Nationalism updates.

59 The SIMS report was commissioned by the African National Congress to inform the debate. Another relevant contribution in this context was the study of the Southern African Institute of Mining and Metallurgy on the rise of resource nationalism (see SAIMM, 2012).

60 The creation of the EITI had been announced earlier, in September 2002, by the Prime Minister of the United Kingdom at the World Summit on Sustainable Development in Johannesburg.

61 Source: EITI website at: http://eiti.org/countries (accessed 16 July 2014).

62 For more information, see SEC Adopts Rules Requiring Payment Disclosures by Resource Extraction Issuers; available at: http://www.sec.gov/News/PressRelease/Detail/PressRelease/1365171484028.

63 According to PWYP Australia (2013), regulations of the United States and the EU together will cover about 65 per cent of the value of the global extractives market, and over 3,000 companies, including most of the major international mining and oil and gas companies, as well as Chinese, Russian, Brazilian and other State-owned enterprises.

64 For detailed information, see PWYP Fact Sheet – EU rules for disclosure of payments to governments by oil, gas and mining (extractive industry) and logging companies, July 2013; available at: http://www.pwyp.ca/images/documents/Working_Group/EU_Fact_Sheet.pdf.

65 The database is available at www.resourcecontracts.org.

66 The AMV process was initiated through a Task Force involving different organizations at the multilateral and regional levels, including UNCTAD. For more information on the Vision, see: http://africaminingvision.org/.

67 The EU RMI is included in the Communication presented in November 2008 by the European Commission to the European Parliament and the Council under the heading, *The Raw Materials Initiative – Meeting Our Critical Needs for Growth*

and Jobs in Europe. It was further developed in 2011 in the European Commission Communication titled, "Tackling the Challenges in Commodity Markets and on Raw Materials".

68 In its present form, the International Accounting Standards Board (IASB) may not be the suitable body for this task, as it is not a public international body accountable to national or multilateral bodies.

The IASB is in fact a private organization financed by the Big Four accountancy firms, major banks and global multinationals. It is headquartered in the City of London and registered in Delaware (See IFRS, *Annual Report 2013*; available at: http://www.ifrs.org/The-organisation/Governance-and-accountability/Annual-reports/Documents/IFRS-Foundation-Annual-Report-2013.pdf).

References

Adelman I (2000). The role of government in economic development. In: Tarp F, ed. *Foreign Aid and Development: Lessons Learnt and Directions for the Future.* London, Routledge: 48–79.

AfDB and GFI (2013). Illicit financial flows and the problem of net resource transfers from Africa: 1980–2009. Tunis and Washington, DC, African Development Bank and Global Financial Integrity.

AfDB, OECD and UNECA (2010). *African Economic Outlook 2010.* Addis Ababa, Paris and Tunis.

African Union (2009). African Mining Vision, February. Addis Ababa; available at: http://pages.au.int/sites/default/files/Africa%20Mining%20Vision%20english_1.pdf.

Alliance Sud (2014). Financial centre policy riddled with contradictions. Bern; available at: http://www.alliancesud.ch/en/policy/tax_justice/financial-centre-policy-riddled-with-contradictions.

Americans for Tax Fairness and Public Campaign (2014). Corporate lobbying on tax extenders and the "GE loophole"; available at: http://www.americansfortaxfairness.org/report-on-lobbying-on-tax-extenders/.

APP (2013). Africa Progress Report 2013: Equity in Extractives. Stewarding Africa's Natural Resources for All. Geneva, Africa Progress Panel.

Araki S (2014). Enhancing cooperation among tax administrators in Asia-Pacific. *International Tax Review*; available at: http://www.internationaltaxreview.com/Article/3302780/Enhancing-cooperation-among-tax-administrators-in-Asia-Pacific.html.

Baker RW (2005). *Capitalism's Achilles Heel: Dirty Money and How to Renew the Free-Market System.* Hoboken, NJ, John Wiley & Sons.

Berne Declaration (2012). *Commodities – Switzerland's most dangerous business.* Lausanne and Zurich.

Besada H and Martin P (2013). Mining codes in Africa: Emergence of a "fourth" generation? The North-South Institute Research Report, Ottawa.

Besley T and Persson T (2013). Taxation and development. In: Auerbach A, Chetty R, Feldstein M and Saez E, eds. *Handbook of Public Economics* (5). Amsterdam, Elsevier: 51–110.

Boston Consulting Group (2009). *Global Wealth 2009: Delivering on the Client Promise.* Boston, MA; available at: http://www.bcg.com.cn/en/files/publications/reports_pdf/BCG_Global_Wealth_Sep_2009_tcm42-28793x1x.pdf.

Boyce JK and Ndikumana L (2012). Capital flight from sub-Saharan African countries: Updated estimates, 1970–2010. Amherst, MA, Political Economy Research Institute. University of Massachusetts; available at: http://www.peri.umass.edu/fileadmin/pdf/ADP/SSAfrica_capitalflight_Oct23_2012.pdf.

Bracking S and Sharife K (2014). Rough and polished. A case study of the diamond pricing and valuation system. Working Paper Series No. 4, Leverhulme Centre for the Study of Value, Manchester.

Christian Aid (2008). Death and taxes: The true toll of tax dodging. London; available at: http://www.christianaid.org.uk/images/deathandtaxes.pdf.

Clark T and Dilnot A (2002). Long-term trends in British taxation and spending. Briefing note no. 25, Institute for Fiscal Studies, London.

Cobham A (2005). Tax evasion, tax avoidance and development finance. Queen Elizabeth House Working Paper No. 129, University of Oxford, Oxford.

Cobham A (2014). Joining the club: The United States signs up for reciprocal tax cooperation. The Center for Global Development blog, 16 May; available at: http://www.cgdev.org/blog/joining-club-united-states-signs-reciprocal-tax-cooperation.

Cobham A, Janský P and Prats A (2014). Estimating illicit flows of capital via trade mispricing: A forensic analysis of data on Switzerland. Working Paper 350, Center for Global Development, Washington, DC.

Conrad RF (2012). Zambia's mineral fiscal regime. Working Paper 12/0653, International Growth Centre, London School of Economics and Political Science, London.

Corporate Europe Observatory, Austrian Federal Chamber of Labour and Trade Union Federation (2014). The firepower of the financial lobby: A survey of the size of the financial lobby at the EU level; available at: http://corporateeurope.org/sites/default/files/attachments/financial_lobby_report.pdf.

Credit Suisse (2011). *Global Wealth Report 2011*. Research Institute; available at: https://publications.credit-suisse.com/tasks/render/file/index.cfm?fileid=88E41853-83E8-EB92-9D5895A42B9499B1.

Curtis M (2010). The new resource grab: How EU trade policy on raw materials is undermining development. Traidcraft Exchange, Oxfam Germany, World Economy, Ecology & Development (WEED), Association Internationale de Techniciens, Experts et Chercheurs (AITEC), and Comhlamh – Development Workers in Global Solidarity Ireland.

Daniel P, Gupta S, Mattina T and Segura-Ubiergo A (2013). Extracting resource revenue. *Finance & Development*, 50(3): 19–22.

Daniel P, Keen M and McPherson C, eds. (2010). *The Taxation of Petroleum and Minerals: Principles, Problems and Practice*. New York, NY, Routledge and IMF.

DanWatch (2011). Escaping poverty - or taxes? A DanWatch investigation of tax planning opportunities in IFC-supported extractives projects in developing countries; available at: http://www.danwatch.dk/sites/default/files/documentation_files/danwatchifcnov2011.pdf.

Di John J (2010). Taxation, resource mobilization and state performance. Working paper no 84: Development as state-making. Crisis states working papers series no 2, LSE Development Studies Institute, London.

DIE (2011). Taxation of non-renewable natural resources: What are the key issues? Briefing Paper 5/2011, German Development Institute, Bonn.

ECLAC (2014a). *Fiscal Panorama of Latin America and the Caribbean: Tax reform and Renewal of the Fiscal Covenant*. Santiago, Chile.

ECLAC (2014b). *Compacts for Equality: Towards a Sustainable Future*. Santiago, Chile.

Eigen P (2013). A prosperous Africa benefits everybody. *The Journal of World Energy Law & Business Advance Access*, 7(1): 4–7.

EIU (2013). Mali. Country Report 4th Quarter 2013. Economist Intelligence Unit.

ESCAP (2013). *Economic and Social Survey of Asia and the Pacific: Forward Looking Macroeconomic Policies for Inclusive and Sustainable Development*. Bangkok.

Ernst & Young (2013). Brazil amends transfer pricing rules: New rules for deductibility of intercompany interest and new normative instruction. *EY Global Tax Alert*, 9 January; available at: http://taxinsights.ey.com/archive/archive-pdfs/2013G-CM3127-TP-Brazil-amends-TP-deductibility-rules.pdf.

European Commission (2012). Commission recommendation of 6 December 2012 on aggressive tax planning, *Official Journal of the European Union*; available at: http://ec.europa.eu/taxation_customs/resources/documents/taxation/tax_fraud_evasion/c_2012_8806_en.pdf.

European Parliament (2013). *Report on Fight against Tax Fraud, Tax Evasion and Tax Havens*. Brussels; available at: http://www.europarl.europa.eu/sides/getDoc.do?pubRef=-//EP//NONSGML+REPORT+A7-2013-0162+0+DOC+PDF+V0//EN.

Fair Politics (2011). The Raw Materials Initiative The new scramble for Africa?; available at: http://www.fairpolitics.eu/doc/fair_politics_eu/raw_materials_initiative/The%20RMI%20case%20updated.pdf.

FitzGerald V (2012). International tax cooperation and innovative development finance. Background paper prepared for UN-DESA's *World Economic and Social Survey 2012*; available at: http://www.un.org/en/development/desa/policy/wess/wess_bg_papers/bp_wess2012_fitzgerald.pdf.

Frank R (2007). *Richistan: A Journey Through the American Wealth Boom and the Lives of the New Rich*. London, Piatikus.

Fuest C and Riedel N (2009). Tax evasion, tax avoidance and tax expenditures in developing countries: A review of the literature. Oxford, Oxford University Centre for Business Taxation; available at: http://r4d.dfid.gov.uk/Output/181295/.

Gajigo O, Mutambatsere E and Ndiaye G (2012a). Fairer mining concessions in Africa: How can this be achieved? *Africa Economic Brief*, 3(3), African Development Bank, Tunis.

Gajigo O, Mutambatsere E and Ndiaye G (2012b). Royalty rates in African mining revisited: Evidence from gold mining. *Africa Economic Brief*, 3(6), African Development Bank, Tunis.

GIZ (2010). Addressing tax evasion and tax avoidance in developing countries. Eschborn, Deutsche Gesellschaft für Internationale Zusammenarbeit (GIZ) GmbH; available at: http://www.taxcompact.net/documents/2011-09-09_GTZ_Addressing-tax-evasion-and-avoidance.pdf.

GMP (2013). Taxation trends in the mining industry. Toronto, GMP Securities.

Gray Molina G (2013). Global governance exit: A Bolivian case study. Working Paper 2013/84, The Global Economic Governance Programme, University of Oxford, Oxford.

G20 (2008). Declaration on the Summit of Financial Markets and the World Economy. Special Leaders Summit on the Financial Situation in Washington,

DC, 14−15 November; available at: http://www.g20.utoronto.ca/2008/2008declaration1115.html.

Hawala E (2013). Role of Epangelo in the Namibian Mining Sector. Namibia Chamber of Mines. Presentation at Mining Expo; available at: http://www.chamberofmines.org.na/uploads/media/1.3.The_role_of_epangelo_in_the_Namibian_Mining_Industry.pdf.

Henry JS (2012). The price of offshore revisited. London, Tax Justice Network, 22 July; available at: http://taxjustice.blogspot.ch/2012/07/the-price-of-off-shore-revisited-and.html.

Herson M (2014). Tax-motivated illicit financial flows: A guide for development practitioners. U4 Issue No. 2, U4 Anti-Corruption Resource Centre at the Chr. Michelsen Institute Bergen; available at: http://www.u4.no/publications/tax-motivated-illicit-financial-flows-a-guide-for-development-practitioners/.

HM Revenue & Customs (2012). *Measuring Tax Gaps, 2012 Edition: Tax Gap Estimates for 2010–11*. London.

HM Revenue & Customs (2013). *Measuring Tax Gaps, 2013 Edition: Tax Gap Estimates for 2011–12*. London.

ICMM (2009). Minerals taxation regimes. A review of issues and challenges in their design and application. London, International Council on Mining and Metals.

IHS-CERA (2011). Comparative assessment of the federal oil and gas fiscal system. Herndon, VA, for the United States Department of the Interior.

IMF (2003). *World Economic Outlook*. Washington, DC, September.

IMF (2012). Fiscal regimes for extractive industries: Design and implementation. Washington, DC.

IMF, OECD, United Nations and World Bank (2011). *Supporting the Development of More Effective Tax Systems*. Report to the G-20 Development Working Group; available at: http://www.oecd.org/ctp/48993634.pdf.

IRS (2012). IRS releases new tax gap estimates; compliance rates remain statistically unchanged from previous Study, 6 January; available at: http://www.irs.gov/uac/IRS-Releases-New-Tax-Gap-Estimates;-Compliance-Rates-Remain-Statistically-Unchanged-From-Previous-Study.

Jacobs J (2013). An overview of revenue flows from the mining sector: Impacts, debates and policy recommendations. In: Campbell B, ed. *Modes of Governance and Revenue Flows in African Mining*. Hampshire, Palgrave MacMillan: 16–46.

Johannesen N and Zucman G (2014). The end of bank secrecy? An evaluation of the G20 tax haven crackdown. *American Economic Journal: Economic Policy*, 6(1): 65−91.

Kar D and Cartwright-Smith D (2010). Illicit financial flows from Africa: Hidden resource for development. Washington, DC, United States, Global Financial Integrity; available at: http://www.gfintegrity.org/report/briefing-paper-illicit-flows-from-africa/.

Kar D and LeBlanc B (2013). Illicit financial flows from developing countries: 2002–2011. Washington, DC,

United States, Global Financial Integrity; available at: http://iff.gfintegrity.org/iff2013/Illicit_Financial_Flows_from_Developing_Countries_2002_2011_HighRes.pdf.

Keen M and Mansour M (2009). Revenue mobilization in sub-Saharan Africa: Challenges from globalization, IMF Working Paper no. 157, Washington, DC.

Keen M and Simone A (2004). Is tax competition harming developing countries more than developed? Special supplement, *Tax Notes International*, 1317−1325.

Khor M (2013). Dealing with transnational corporations. *Third World Resurgence* No. 273, Third World Network, Penang.

Kingsley I (2014). No longer a curse? African leaders take action that could transform the mining sector. *Africa Renewal*, 28(1): 24–25.

KPMG (2012). Corporate and Indirect Tax Rate Survey 2012; available at: http://www.kpmg.com/FR/fr/IssuesAndInsights/ArticlesPublications/Documents/Corporate-and-indirect-Tax-Survey-2012.pdf.

KPMG (2014). Corporate and Indirect Tax Rate Survey 2014; available at: http://www.kpmg.com/Global/en/IssuesAndInsights/ArticlesPublications/Documents/corporate-indirect-tax-rate-survey-2014.pdf.

Küblböck K (2013). The EU Raw Materials Initiative and effects upon resource-based development: Lessons from Africa. Policy Note 08/2013, Österreichische Forschungsstiftung für Internationale Entwicklung, Vienna.

Lanz R and Miroudot S (2011). Intra-firm trade: Patterns, determinants and policy implications. OECD Trade Policy Paper No. 114, Paris; available at: http://dx.doi.org/10.1787/5kg9p39lrwnn-en.

Maddison A (2001). *The world economy: A millennial perspective*. Paris, OECD.

Medina Herasme A (2014). Mining tax regime as development tool. Presentation at the UNCTAD Multi-Year Expert Meeting on Commodities and Development, Geneva, 9–10 April.

Meinzer M (2012). The creeping futility of the global forum's peer reviews, Tax Justice Briefing, London; available at: www.taxjustice.net/cms/upload/GlobalForum2012-TJN-Briefing.pdf.

Merrill Lynch and Cap Gemini Ernst & Young (2002). *World Wealth Report 2002*. Merrill Lynch and Cap Gemini Ernst & Young.

Misereor (2010). Double tax treaties and tax information exchange agreements: What advantages for developing countries. Aachen; available at: http://www.taxjustice.net/cms/upload/pdf/DTTs_100126_TIEAs-Developing-Countries.pdf.

Mtegha HD and Oshokoya O (2011). Mining fiscal environment in the SADC: Status after harmonization attempts. *The Journal of Southern African Institute of Mining and Metallurgy*, 111(7): 455−458.

Muganyizi TK (2012). Mining sector taxation in Tanzania. Research report 1, International Centre for Tax and

Development, Institute for Development Studies, Brighton.

Murphy R (2008). Tax havens creating turmoil: Evidence submitted to the Treasury Committee of the House of Commons by the Tax Justice Network UK. Chesham, Tax Justice Network International Secretariat; available at: http://www.un-ngls.org/cfr/upload/1234518529_80.47.24.143_CreatingTurmoil.pdf.

National Treasury of South Africa (2008). Explanatory memorandum for the Mineral and Petroleum Royalty Bill; available at: http://www.treasury.gov.za/public%20comments/EM%20Royalty%20Bill%202008%20-%2020%20Aug%202008.pdf.

Ngalani CD (2013). Negotiation of fair contracts: For a sustainable development of extractive industries in Africa. *Great Insights*, 2(2): 23−24, European Centre for Development Policy Management. Maastricht.

Ocampo JA (2007). Market, social cohesion and democracy. In: Ocampo JA, Jomo KS, and Khan S, eds. *Policy Matters: Economic and Social Policies to Sustain Equitable Development*. London and New York, Orient Longman and Zed Books: 1–31.

OECD (1998). *Harmful Tax Competition: An Emerging Global Issue*. Paris.

OECD (2012). Dealing effectively with the challenges of transfer pricing. Paris; available at: http://dx.doi.org/10.1787/9789264169463-en.

OECD (2013a). Action Plan on Base Erosion and Profit Shifting. Paris; available at: http://dx.doi.org/10.1787/9789264202719-en.

OECD (2013b). BEPS - Frequently asked questions. Paris; available at: http://www.oecd.org/ctp/beps-frequentlyaskedquestions.htm.

OECD (2013c). Addressing base erosion and profit shifting, Paris; available at: http://dx.doi.org/10.1787/9789264192744-en.

OECD (2014). Transfer Prices Comparability Data and Developing Countries; available at: http://www.oecd.org/ctp/transfer-pricing/transfer-pricing-comparability-data-developing-countries.pdf.

Ortiz I and Cummins M (2013). The age of austerity: A review of public expenditures and adjustment measures in 181 countries. Working Paper No. 24, Initiative for Policy Dialogue and South Centre, New York, NY and Geneva.

Otto J, Andrews C, Cawood F, Doggett M, Guj P, Stermole F, Stermole J, Tilton J (2006). *Mining Royalties: A Global Study of Their Impact on Investors, Government, and Civil Society*. Washington, DC, World Bank.

Palan R, Murphy R and Chavagneux C (2010). *Tax Havens: How Globalization Really Works*. Ithaca, NY, Cornell University Press.

Park YS and Benayad S (2013). Hydrocarbons Law and Bidding Opportunities in Algeria *Journal KSMER*, 50(5): 750–759.

Pereira Valadão MA (2013). Transfer Pricing in Brazil. Presentation to the Panel discussion on Transfer Pricing Challenges for Developing Countries at the ECOSOC meeting on International Cooperation in Tax Matters, New York, 29 May; available at: http://www.un.org/esa/ffd/tax/2013ITCM/Valadao_TPChallenges_29may13.pdf.

Picciotto S (2013). Is the International Tax System Fit for Purpose, Especially for Developing Countries? ICTD Working Paper 13, Institute of Development Studies; available at: http://www.ictd.ac/sites/default/files/ICTD%20WP13_0.pdf.

PWYP (2011). Piping Profits; available at: http://www.publishwhatyoupay.org/sites/publishwhatyoupay.org/files/FINAL%20pp%20norway.pdf.

PWYP (2013). The case for windfall taxes – A guide to optimal resource taxation; available at: http://www.publishwhatyoupay.no/sites/all/files/Download%20-%20English_4.pdf.

PWYP (2014). SEC announces plan to implement landmark oil, gas and mining transparency law; available at: http://www.publishwhatyoupay.org/resources/sec-announces-plan-implement-landmark-oil-gas-and-mining-transparency-law.

PWYP Australia (2013). Australia: An unlevel playing field. Extractive Industry transparency on the ASX 200. Publish What You Pay; available at: http://publishwhatyoupay.org/sites/publishwhatyoupay.org/files/ASX.pdf.

Ralbovsky S and Caywood H (2013). Presentation at the PwC's 16th Americas School of Mines, Mining tax policy, Los Cabos, Mexico, 21−24 May; available at: http://www.pwc.com/gx/en/mining/school-of-mines/2012/pwc-hallie-caywood-school-of-mines-presentation.pdf.

Raw Materials Group (2013a). *Taxation, Royalties and Other Fiscal Measures Applied to the Non-Ferrous Metals Industry*. Report to the International Study Groups on Copper, Nickel, Lead and Zinc.

Raw Materials Group (2013b). The Rosia Montana Mine in Romania. Comparative Analysis of Mining Royalties, Taxation and State ownership in Selected Countries (For Gold and Base Metals); available at: http://rmgc.ro/Content/uploads/reports/report-raw-materials-group.pdf.

Richter BK, Samphantharak K and Timmons JF (2009). Lobbying and taxes. *American Journal of Political Science*, 53(4): 893−909.

Riesco M (2005). Pay your taxes! Corporate social responsibility and the mining industry in Chile. In: UNRISD, *The "Pay Your Taxes" Debate: Perspectives on Corporate Taxation and Social Responsibility in the Chilean Mining Industry*. Geneva: 14–54.

Rodrik D (2014). A Class on its Own; available at: http://www.project-syndicate.org/print/dani-rodrik-explains-why-the-super-rich-are-mistaken-to-believe-that-they-can-dispense-with-government.

RWI (2011). Dodd-Frank. The facts about disclosure requirements. New York, NY, Revenue Watch Institute.

Sachs LE, Toledano P, Mandelbaum J and Otto J (2012). Impacts of fiscal reforms on country attractiveness: Learning from the facts. In: Sauvant K, ed. *Yearbook on International Investment Law & Policy 2011–2012*. Oxford, Oxford University Press: 345–386.

SAIMM (2012). The rise of resource nationalism: A resurgence of State control in an era of free markets or the legitimate search for a new equilibrium. Cape Town, Southern African Institute of Mining and Metallurgy.

Schneider F, Buehn A and Montenegro CE (2010). Shadow economies all over the world: New estimates for 162 countries from 1999 to 2007. World Bank Policy Research Working Paper No. 5356, Washington, DC.

Shaxson N (2011). *Treasure Islands: Uncovering the Damage of Offshore Banking and Tax Havens*. New York, NY, Palgrave Macmillan.

Sheppard LA (2013). Will U.S. Hypocrisy on Information Sharing Continue? Tax Analysts; available at: http://www.taxanalysts.com/www/features.nsf/Articles/0C26B2CFD92F1FBE85257AFC004E8B38?OpenDocument.

Sherpa, Berne Declaration, Centre for Trade Policy and Development, L'Entraide missionnaire and Mining Alerte (2011). Specific instance regarding Glencore International AG and First Quantum Minerals Ltd. and their alleged violations of the OECD Guidelines for Multinational Enterprises via the activities of Mopani Copper Mines Plc. in Zambia; available at: http://www.google.ch/url?sa=t&rct=j&q=&esrc=s&source=web&cd=1&ved=0CB4QFjAA&url=http%3A%2F%2Foecdwatch.org%2Fcases%2FCase_208%2F925%2Fat_download%2Ffile&ei=VbjfU5u-A9SS7AaU5YDoAQ&usg=AFQjCNFd9QWOMYpLYKuRAqB0wP_kU7x20A&bvm=bv.72197243,d.ZGU&cad=rja.

Stevens P, Kooroshy J, Lahn G and Lee B (2013). *Conflict and coexistence in the extractive industries*. London, Chatham House.

Tarimo D (2013). Mining – Tax Landscape – Africa. PWC; available at: http://www.pwc.com/en_TZ/tz/pdf/mining-tax-landscape-africa.pdf.

Tax Justice Network (2005). The price of offshore. Briefing Paper, Buckinghamshire; available at: http://www.taxjustice.net/cms/upload/pdf/Briefing_Paper_-_The_Price_of_Offshore_14_MAR_2005.pdf.

Tax Justice Network (2011). The cost of tax abuse: A briefing paper on the cost of tax evasion worldwide. Buckinghamshire; available at: http://www.tackletaxhavens.com/Cost_of_Tax_Abuse_TJN%20Research_23rd_Nov_2011.pdf.

Tax Justice Network (2012). Tax us if you can, 2nd edition. Buckinghamshire; available at: http://www.taxjustice.net/cms/upload/pdf/TUIYC_2012_FINAL.pdf.

Tax Justice Network (2013). Financial Secrecy Index – 2013, Results. Buckinghamshire; available at: http://www.financialsecrecyindex.com/introduction/fsi-2013-results.

Tax Justice Network-Africa & ActionAid International (2012). Tax competition in East Africa: A race to the bottom? Nairobi and Johannesburg

UNCTAD (2005) *Economic Development in Africa Report 2005: Rethinking the Role of Foreign Direct Investment*. United Nations publication, New York and Geneva.

UNCTAD (2007). *World Investment Report 2007: Transnational Corporations, Extractive Industries and Development*. United Nations publication, New York and Geneva.

UNCTAD (2009). *The Least Developed Countries Report 2009: The State and Development Governance*. United Nations publication, New York and Geneva.

UNCTAD (2012). *World Investment Report 2012: Towards a New Generation of Investment Policies*. United Nations publication, New York and Geneva.

UNCTAD (2013). *World Investment Report 2013 – Global Value Chains: Investment and trade for Development*. United Nations publication, New York and Geneva.

UNCTAD (2014). The role of trade in financing for sustainable development. Intergovernmental Committee of Experts on Sustainable Development Financing. United Nations publications, Geneva.

UNCTAD (*TDR 1996*). *Trade and Development Report, 1996*. United Nations publication, sales no. E.96.II.D.6, New York and Geneva.

UNCTAD (*TDR 1997*). *Trade and Development Report, 1997. Globalization, Distribution and Growth*. United Nations publication, sales no. E.97.II.D.8, New York and Geneva.

UNCTAD (*TDR 2003*). *Trade and Development Report, 2003. Capital accumulation, growth and structural change*. United Nations publication, sales no. E.03.II.D.7, New York and Geneva.

UNCTAD (*TDR 2005*). *Trade and Development Report, 2005. New Features of Global Interdependence*. United Nations publication, sales no. E.05.II.D.13, New York and Geneva.

UNCTAD (*TDR 2008*). *Trade and Development Report, 2008. Commodity Prices, Capital Flows and the Financing of Investment*. United Nations publication, sales no. E.08.II.D.21, New York and Geneva.

UNCTAD (*TDR 2009*). *Trade and Development Report, 2009. Responding to the Global Crisis: Climate Change Mitigation and Development*. United Nations publication, sales no. E.09.II.D.16, New York and Geneva.

UNCTAD (*TDR 2010*). *Trade and Development Report, 2010. Employment, Globalization and Development*. United Nations publication, sales no. E.10.II.D.3, New York and Geneva.

UNCTAD (*TDR 2011*). *Trade and Development Report, 2011. Post-crisis Policy Challenges in the World Economy*. United Nations publication, sales no. E.11.II.D.3, New York and Geneva.

UNCTAD (*TDR 2012*). *Trade and Development Report, 2012. Policies for Inclusive and Balanced Growth*.

United Nations publication, sales no. E.12.II.D.6, New York and Geneva.

UNCTAD (*TDR 2013*). *Trade and Development Report, 2013.* Adjusting to the Changing Dynamics of the World Economy. United Nations publication, sales no. E.13.II.D.3, New York and Geneva.

UN-DESA (2011). *United Nations Model Double Taxation Convention between Developed and Developing Countries (2011 update).* New York, United Nations; available at: http://www.un.org/esa/ffd/documents/UN_Model_2011_Update.pdf.

UN-DESA (2013). *Report on the World Social Situation: Inequality Matters.* United Nations Department for Economic and Social Affairs, United Nations publications, New York.

UNDP-Cambodia (2008). The global petroleum context: Opportunities and challenges facing developing countries. Discussion Paper No. 6, United Nations Development Programme, New York.

UNECA (2013). *The State of Governance in Africa: The Dimension of Illicit Financial Flows as a Governance Challenge.* E/ECA/CGPP/3/2, Addis Ababa.

United Nations (2010). Secretariat note on agenda item 3(o) of the provisional agenda: Tax competition in corporate tax: Use of tax incentives in attracting foreign direct investment. E/C.18/2010/CRP.13, United Nations, New York.

United Nations (2013a*). United Nations Practical Manual on Transfer Pricing for Developing Countries.* ST/ESA/347, New York, United Nations.

United Nations (2013b). Issues concerning the taxation of the extractive industries for consideration of the Committee. Note by the Secretariat of the United Nations. Committee of Experts on International Cooperation in Tax Matters. E/C.18/2013/CRP.13, New York.

United Nations (2013c). Secretariat Report on the Expert Group Meeting on Extractive Industries Taxation. United Nations Committee of Experts on International Cooperation in Tax Matters. E/C.18/2013/CRP.19, New York.

United Nations (2014). Committee for Development Policy. Global Governance and Global Rules for Development in the Post-2015 Era. E.14.II.A.1, United Nations, New York.

University of Calgary (2012). Capturing economic rents from resources through royalties and taxes. SPP Research Papers, 5(30), School of Public Policy, Calgary.

USGS (2006). Mongolia. In: *2006 Minerals Yearbook.* United States Geological Survey.

Vale Columbia Center on Sustainable Investment (2013). Background paper for the Eighth Columbia International Investment Conference on Investment Incentives – The Good, the Bad and the Ugly: Assessing the costs, benefits and options for policy reform, Columbia University, New York, NY. 13–14 November.

Weeks J (2014). Interaction between fiscal space and economic growth; policies for middle- and low-income countries. Background paper for UNCTAD's *Trade and Development Report 2014*, unpublished.

World Bank (1992). Strategy for African Mining. World Bank technical paper no. 181. Washington, DC.

World Bank (1996). A mining strategy for Latin America and the Caribbean. World Bank technical paper no. 345. Washington, DC.

World Bank (2010). The World Bank's evolutionary approach to mining sector reform. Extractive Industries for Development Series No. 19, Washington, DC.

World Bank (2012a). *Rents to riches? The political economy of natural resource-led development.* Washington, DC.

World Bank (2012b). *Africa Pulse,* 6. Washington DC.

ZIPAR (2013). Mining tax in Zambia. Policy brief, Zambia Institute of Policy Analysis and Research; available at: http://www.zipar.org.zm/documents/mining%20tax%20brief.pdf.

Zucman G (2013). The missing wealth of nations: Are Europe and the U.S. net debtors or net creditors? *Quarterly Journal of Economics*, 128(3): 1321–1364.

**UNITED NATIONS CONFERENCE
ON TRADE AND DEVELOPMENT**

Palais des Nations
CH-1211 GENEVA 10
Switzerland
(http://unctad.org)

Selected UNCTAD Publications

Trade and Development Report, 2013   United Nations publication, sales no. E.13.II.D.3
Adjusting to the changing dynamics of the world economy   ISBN 978-92-1-112867-3

    Chapter   I   Current Trends and Challenges in the World Economy
               Annex: Alternative Scenarios for the World Economy
    Chapter   II   Towards More Balanced Growth: A Greater Role for Domestic Demand in
               Development Strategies
               Annex: Shifting Growth Strategies: Main Implications and Challenges
    Chapter III   Financing the Real Economy

Trade and Development Report, 2012   United Nations publication, sales no. E.12.II.D.6
Policies for Inclusive and Balanced Growth   ISBN 978-92-1-112846-8

    Chapter   I   Current Trends and Challenges in the World Economy
    Chapter   II   Income Inequality: The Main Issues
    Chapter III   Evolution of Income Inequality: Different Time Perspectives and Dimensions
    Chapter IV   Changes in Globalization and Technology and their Impacts on National Income Inequality
    Chapter   V   The Role of Fiscal Policy in Income Distribution
    Chapter VI   The Economics and Politics of Inequality Reconsidered

Trade and Development Report, 2011   United Nations publication, sales no. E.11.II.D.3
Post-crisis policy challenges in the world economy   ISBN 978-92-1-112822-2

    Chapter   I   Current Trends and Issues in the World Economy
    Chapter   II   Fiscal Aspects of the Financial Crisis and Its Impact on Public Debt
    Chapter III   Fiscal Space, Debt Sustainability and Economic Growth
    Chapter IV   Financial Re-Regulation and Restructuring
    Chapter   V   Financialized Commodity Markets: Recent Developments and Policy Issues
               Annex: Reform of Commodity Derivatives Market Regulations
    Chapter VI   The Global Monetary Order and the International Trading System

Trade and Development Report, 2010   United Nations publication, sales no. E.10.II.D.3
Employment, globalization and development   ISBN 978-92-1-112807-9

Trade and Development Report, 2009   United Nations publication, sales no. E.09.II.D.16
Responding to the global crisis   ISBN 978-92-1-112776-8
Climate change mitigation and development

Trade and Development Report, 2008   United Nations publication, sales no. E.08.II.D.21
Commodity prices, capital flows and the financing of investment   ISBN 978-92-1-112752-2

Trade and Development Report, 2007   United Nations publication, sales no. E.07.II.D.11
Regional cooperation for development   ISBN 978-92-1-112721-8

Trade and Development Report, 2006   United Nations publication, sales no. E.06.II.D.6
Global partnership and national policies for development   ISBN 92-1-112698-3

* * * * * *

Trade and Development Report, 1981–2011   United Nations publication, sales no. E.12.II.D.5
Three Decades of Thinking Development   ISBN 978-92-1-112845-1

* * * * * *

The Financial and Economic Crisis of 2008-2009
and Developing Countries
Edited by Sebastian Dullien, Detlef J. Kotte,
Alejandro Márquez and Jan Priewe

United Nations publication, sales no. E.11.II.D.11
ISBN 978-92-1-112818-5

Introduction

The Crisis – Transmission, Impact and Special Features

Jan Priewe
What Went Wrong? Alternative Interpretations of the Global Financial Crisis

Daniela Magalhães Prates and Marcos Antonio Macedo Cintra
The Emerging-market Economies in the Face of the Global Financial Crisis

Jörg Mayer
The Financialization of Commodity Markets and Commodity Price Volatility

Sebastian Dullien
Risk Factors in International Financial Crises: Early Lessons from the 2008-2009 Turmoil

The Crisis – Country and Regional Studies

Laike Yang and Cornelius Huizenga
China's Economy in the Global Economic Crisis: Impact and Policy Responses

Abhijit Sen Gupta
Sustaining Growth in a Period of Global Downturn: The Case of India

André Nassif
Brazil and India in the Global Economic Crisis: Immediate Impacts and Economic Policy Responses

Patrick N. Osakwe
Africa and the Global Financial and Economic Crisis: Impacts, Responses and Opportunities

Looking Forward – Policy Agenda

Alejandro Márquez
The Report of the Stiglitz Commission: A Summary and Comment

Ricardo Ffrench-Davis
Reforming Macroeconomic Policies in Emerging Economies: From Procyclical to Countercyclical Approaches

Jürgen Zattler
A Possible New Role for Special Drawing Rights In and Beyond the Global Monetary System

Detlef J. Kotte
The Financial and Economic Crisis and Global Economic Governance

* * * * * *

The Global Economic Crisis:
Systemic Failures and Multilateral Remedies
Report by the UNCTAD Secretariat Task Force
on Systemic Issues and Economic Cooperation

United Nations publication, sales no. E.09.II.D.4
ISBN 978-92-1-112765-2

Chapter   I   A crisis foretold

Chapter   II   Financial regulation: fighting today's crisis today

Chapter   III   Managing the financialization of commodity futures trading

Chapter   IV   Exchange rate regimes and monetary cooperation

Chapter   V   Towards a coherent effort to overcome the systemic crisis

* * * * * *

These publications may be obtained from bookstores and distributors throughout the world. Consult your bookstore or the United Publications Sales and Marketing Office, 300 E 42nd Street, 9th Floor, IN-919J New York, NY 10017, United States. tel.: +1 212 963 8302, fax: +1 212 963 3489, e-mail: publications@un.org, https://unp.un.org.

Regional Monetary Cooperation and Growth-enhancing Policies: The new challenges for Latin America and the Caribbean

United Nations publication, UNCTAD/GDS/2010/1

Chapter I   What Went Wrong? An Analysis of Growth and Macroeconomic Prices in Latin America

Chapter II   Regional Monetary Cooperation for Growth-enhancing Policies

Chapter III   Regional Payment Systems and the SUCRE Initiative

Chapter IV   Policy Conclusions

* * * * * *

Price Formation in Financialized Commodity Markets: The role of information

United Nations publication, UNCTAD/GDS/2011/1

1. Motivation of this Study

2. Price Formation in Commodity Markets

3. Recent Evolution of Prices and Fundamentals

4. Financialization of Commodity Price Formation

5. Field Survey

6. Policy Considerations and Recommendations

7. Conclusions

* * * * * *

These publications are available on the website at: http://unctad.org. Copies may be obtained from the Publications Assistant, Macroeconomic and Development Policies Branch, Division on Globalization and Development Strategies, United Nations Conference on Trade and Development (UNCTAD), Palais des Nations, CH-1211 Geneva 10, Switzerland; e-mail: gdsinfo@unctad.org.

UNCTAD Discussion Papers

No. 216	April 2014	Andrew CORNFORD	Macroprudential regulation: Potential implications for rules for cross-border banking
No. 215	March 2014	Stephany GRIFFITH-JONES	A BRICS development bank: A dream coming true?
No. 214	Dec. 2013	Jörg MAYER	Towards more balanced growth strategies in developing countries: Issues related to market size, trade balances and purchasing power
No. 213	Nov. 2013	Shigehisa KASAHARA	The Asian developmental State and the Flying Geese paradigm
No. 212	Nov. 2013	Vladimir FILIMONOV, David BICCHETTI, Nicolas MAYSTRE and Didier SORNETTE	Quantification of the high level of endogeneity and of structural regime shifts in commodity markets
No. 211	Oct. 2013	André NASSIF, Carmem FEIJÓ and Eliane ARAÚJO	Structural change and economic development: Is Brazil catching up or falling behind?
No. 210	Dec. 2012	Giovanni Andrea CORNIA and Bruno MARTORANO	Development policies and income inequality in selected developing regions, 1980–2010
No. 209	Nov. 2012	Alessandro MISSALE and Emanuele BACCHIOCCHI	Multilateral indexed loans and debt sustainability
No. 208	Oct. 2012	David BICCHETTI and Nicolas MAYSTRE	The synchronized and long-lasting structural change on commodity markets: Evidence from high frequency data
No. 207	July 2012	Amelia U. SANTOS-PAULINO	Trade, income distribution and poverty in developing countries: A survey
No. 206	Dec. 2011	André NASSIF, Carmem FEIJÓ and Eliane ARAÚJO	The long-term "optimal" real exchange rate and the currency overvaluation trend in open emerging economies: The case of Brazil
No. 205	Dec. 2011	Ulrich HOFFMANN	Some reflections on climate change, green growth illusions and development space
No. 204	Oct. 2011	Peter BOFINGER	The scope for foreign exchange market interventions
No. 203	Sep. 2011	Javier LINDENBOIM, Damián KENNEDY and Juan M. GRAÑA	Share of labour compensation and aggregate demand discussions towards a growth strategy
No. 202	June 2011	Pilar FAJARNES	An overview of major sources of data and analyses relating to physical fundamentals in international commodity markets
No. 201	Feb. 2011	Ulrich HOFFMANN	Assuring food security in developing countries under the challenges of climate change: Key trade and development issues of a fundamental transformation of agriculture
No. 200	Sep. 2010	Jörg MAYER	Global rebalancing: Effects on trade flows and employment
No. 199	June 2010	Ugo PANIZZA, Federico STURZENEGGER and Jeromin ZETTELMEYER	International government debt

* * * * * *

UNCTAD Discussion Papers are available on the website at: http://unctad.org. Copies of *UNCTAD Discussion Papers* may be obtained from the Publications Assistant, Macroeconomic and Development Policies Branch, Division on Globalization and Development Strategies, United Nations Conference on Trade and Development (UNCTAD), Palais des Nations, CH-1211 Geneva 10, Switzerland; e-mail: gdsinfo@unctad.org.

QUESTIONNAIRE

Trade and Development Report, 2014

In order to improve the quality and relevance of the Trade and Development Report, the UNCTAD secretariat would greatly appreciate your views on this publication. Please complete the following questionnaire and return it to:

Readership Survey
Division on Globalization and Development Strategies
UNCTAD
Palais des Nations, Room E.10009
CH-1211 Geneva 10, Switzerland
E-mail: tdr@unctad.org

Thank you very much for your kind cooperation.

1. What is your assessment of this publication?   *Excellent*   *Good*   *Adequate*   *Poor*

   Overall
   Relevance of issues   ☐   ☐   ☐   ☐
   Analytical quality   ☐   ☐   ☐   ☐
   Policy conclusions   ☐   ☐   ☐   ☐
   Presentation   ☐   ☐   ☐   ☐
   ☐   ☐   ☐   ☐

2. What do you consider the strong points of this publication?

   _____
   _____
   _____

3. What do you consider the weak points of this publication?

   _____
   _____
   _____

4. For what main purposes do you use this publication?

   Analysis and research   Education and training
   Policy formulation and management   ☐   Other (*specify*) _____   ☐
                                         ☐

5. Which of the following best describes your area of work?

   Government   Public enterprise
   Non-governmental organization   ☐   Academic or research   ☐
   International organization   ☐   Media   ☐
   Private enterprise institution   ☐   Other (*specify*) _____   ☐
                                  ☐

6. Name and address of respondent (*optional*):

   _____
   _____
   _____

7. Do you have any further comments?

   _____
   _____
   _____